*Les beaux arts sont au nombre de cinq, a savoir:
la peinture, la sculpture, la poésie, la musique et l'architecture,
laquelle a pour branche principale la pâtisserie.'*

*The fine arts are five in number:
painting, music, poetry, sculpture and architecture,
whereof the principle branch is pâtisserie.'*

Marie-Antoine Carême 1783 – 1833

Pâtisserie

William & Suzue Curley

Photography by Jose Lasheras

jacqui
small

First published in 2014 by
Jacqui Small LLP
an imprint of
Aurum Press Ltd,
The Old Brewery, 6 Blundell Street
London, N7 9BH
United Kingdom
www.QuartoKnows.com

In memory of my Mother.
You will always be part of me...

Publisher Jacqui Small
Managing Editor Lydia Halliday
Project Editor Abi Waters
Designer & Art Director Robin Rout
Photographer Jose Lasheras
Additional Photography Tino Tedaldi
Production Maeve Healy

British Library
Cataloguing-in-Publication Data
A catalogue record for this book
is available from the British Library.

ISBN 978-1-909342-21-7

2021

10 9 8 7 6 5 4

Printed and bound in China.

...and our adorable
daughter Amy Rose.

Contents

Foreword by Pierre Hermé

William Curley is a highly talented pâtissier, with a unique understanding and mastery of the basics of traditional pâtisserie; he introduces new flavours, inspired by both British and Japanese cultures, thanks to his wife Suzue. He fully embodies the spirit of modern pâtisserie through his savoir-faire and creativity.

William's passion for pâtisserie is an essential quality in our culinary craft, which can be seen in both his creations and his flavours and sensations.

His creative work on chocolate can in fact be found in his pâtisserie because, unlike others, his quintessentially personal touch features in his creations, as for instance in the Venezuelan Cadeaux or the Earl Grey & Coconut Entremet.

This book is essentially about great pâtisserie classics, such as the Gâteau Basque, the Tarte Alsacienne, the Chausson aux Pommes or the Bakewell Tart, but also includes more personal creations with a unique twist, like the Pineapple Tarte Tatin, the Matcha Mont Blanc or the Green Tea and Azuki Bean Dome.

I feel extremely honoured to be writing a foreword for this book. I encourage William to continue on his excellent career path echoing the values of the association Relais Desserts, of which he is a member. The association brings together the international elite of French Haute Pâtisserie and its purpose is to promote it throughout the four corners of the world. William Curley is fully committed to this.

William Curley est un immense pâtissier, avec une grande maîtrise des bases de pâtisserie classiques qu'il met en œuvre de façon remarquable, il introduit des goûts nouveaux, différents, originaux emprunts de culture anglaise et de culture japonaise, grace à sa femme Suzue. Il incarne pleinement la pâtisserie moderne de par son savoir-faire et sa créativité.

Sa générosité, qualité essentielle dans nos métiers dits « de bouche », est perceptible dans ses créations, autant que dans son travail sur les sensations et le goût.

Le travail de création qu'il fait sur le chocolat se retrouve dans ses créations pâtissières. Particulièrement intéressant car différent de ce que l'on peut trouver ailleurs, un style très personnel transparait dans ses créations, comme le Venezuelan Cadeaux, Entremet de Thé Earl Grey et Noix de Coco.

Cet ouvrage traite des grands classiques de la pâtisserie tels que le Gâteau Basque, la Tarte Alsacienne, le Chausson aux Pommes ou la Bakewell Tart et présente également des créations plus personnelles comme la Pineapple Tarte Tatin, le Matcha Mont Blanc ou le Green Tea et Azuki Bean Dome.

Particulièrement honoré d'écrire la préface de ce livre, encourageant ainsi William Curley à continuer dans la voie d'excellence qu'il a tracée, faisant écho aux valeurs de l'association Relais Desserts dont il fait partie. Cette association rassemble l'élite mondiale de la Haute Pâtisserie française afin de la faire rayonner aux quatre coins du globe, William Curley y contribue pleinement.

Pierre Hermé

A Passion for Pâtisserie

Pâtisserie is what brought Suzue and I together; it is what drove us to open our first shop in 2004 and it brings joy and happiness to our lives and, we hope, to our customers. Pâtisserie has come a long way since the Roman Empire initially spread early primitive pastry throughout its regions, and now it stretches far and wide with many countries developing their own style. Today, we both still take great pleasure in visiting well-respected pâtissiers-chocolatiers, whether on a day trip to Paris, a weekend in Strasbourg or a family visit to Japan to see and taste and be inspired. As pâtissiers and chocolatiers, we feel that we have a duty to pass on the skills of our craft to the next generation and we take great pride in being able to provide the inspiration to do so.

It was our love for pâtisserie and what we had experienced in Paris and around the world that drove us to open a boutique that shares our passion with our customers today – together we have been able to fulfil this ambition. We chose to open boutiques in areas where we felt we could reach as many customers as possible; customers who would appreciate what we were striving to achieve and who would frequent our boutiques on a regular basis. We feel that our boutiques have become part of the local community, creating a sense of 'togetherness' and harmony with our customers.

Our main focus is, of course, to arouse and surprise the taste buds. A pleasure that we hope we can, in some way, bring to everyone, through the recipes in this book.

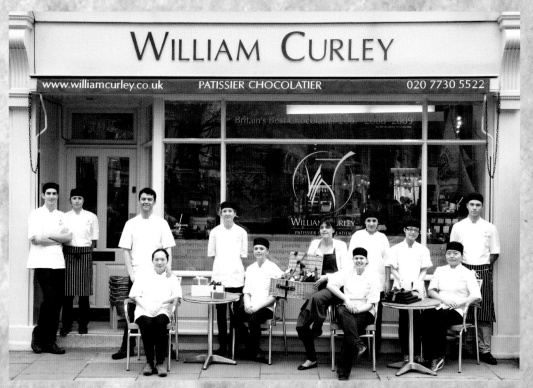

I have always had a sweet tooth (I don't consider that a bad thing) and I used to love helping my grandmother bake every Sunday. Her Millionaire's Shortbread was the most amazing treat! With no formal qualifications, I left school and started at a catering college at the age of 15. My father was a docker and when I told him I was going to be a pâtissier, he laughed – he thought I was joking. I have never asked him why he found it funny. Maybe he thought it wasn't a tough enough trade for his 'laddie'. It's quite ironic, because the cooking industry at the top end is one of the toughest jobs going, with long unsociable hours and hard work. He began to realize this when I used to call late at night to get the football updates and he would wonder why I was whispering. I had sneaked downstairs to the basement phone at La Tante Claire to make a sneaky phone call! Now he understands and really admires my dedication to the industry and the craft.

It may come as something of a surprise to many that a Scotsman becomes a Pâtissier-Chocolatier. Most would probably find it a little strange to pick up a pâtisserie book by a Scottish chef who makes French pâtisserie with a Japanese influence. But in fact, as you will see, this is not so very strange after all. Ironically, Scotland and France have been inextricably linked from as far back as the 11th century. France had a notably strong influence in Scottish cuisine, brought about mainly as a result of the Auld Alliance, a political bond between the kingdoms of Scotland and France. The Scots word *auld*, meaning 'old', had become partly an affectionate term for this periodic alliance between the two countries before the Treaty of Edinburgh in 1560 – which united Scotland and England – permeating French influence through all areas of Scottish culture, including the cuisine. This influence was seen mainly during the Late Middle Ages and Early Modern Era, especially during the reign of Mary, Queen of Scots. Mary, on returning to Scotland, brought with her a whole entourage of French staff and it is they who are considered responsible for revolutionizing Scottish cooking. Even today you may come across Scottish recipes of undoubtedly French origin that have been adapted and modified by the Scots as their own.

I have a particular passion when it comes to the history and evolution of pâtisserie. A turning point in my research and discovery about the subject was after I moved to London and bought two original early edition books by Gaston Lenôtre. These books fascinated me and opened a door in my mind, to a whole new world of pâtisserie, where pastry intertwined with science, craftsmanship and precision. Reading these books was rather like solving a puzzle of how dishes transformed into what I was then creating in the restaurants I worked in. I discovered that books left a legacy from, and for, chefs and pâtissiers. Learning from the likes of Carême, Lacam and Escoffier, learning about what they achieved and how they shaped the desserts and pâtisserie of today is, in my view, essential reading for any pâtissier or chef. These legends certainly paved the way for my future in pâtisserie.

It wasn't until I arrived at Gleneagles at the age of 17 that I realized what a pastry kitchen was all about. I was an eager apprentice working under Ian Ironside. On my first day, I discovered a huge kitchen and within this a pâtisserie kitchen with many different sections. The smells and the sights are what got me first: enormous ovens blasting away in the corner, the rich caramelized scent of cinder toffee bubbling away in another corner, trays of mille-feuille in preparation, Saint-Honoré with its light fluffy clouds of Chiboust cream and flaky pastry. There was the Tourier, the backbone to the profession, preparing all kinds of doughs and pastry. Then there was the Glacier creating the most wonderful ice creams, sorbets and iced desserts. There were sections for Afternoon Teas, plated desserts and buffets. There was the Chocolatier, creating truffles, caramels and bonbons and there was the Boulangier, who would work tirelessly throughout the night so that all the breads and viennoiserie were prepared for the forthcoming day. The whole world of pâtisserie was opening up to me and I could never have imagined then the wonderful journey this profession would take me on. I quickly realized how much I loved working in kitchens; I loved the camaraderie amongst my fellow chefs and the discipline required to meet the deadlines of service. I loved the rush of adrenaline fuelling me on to reach my goals.

I left Gleneagles in the early nineties to train with some of the most respected chefs at some of the world's best Michelin-starred restaurants in the country, and on the Continent: Pierre Koffmann at La Tante Claire, Raymond Blanc at Le Manoir aux Quat'Saisons, Marco Pierre White at The Restaurant and Marc Meneau at L'Espérance. They all helped me develop and gave me a foundation in my craft that could not be bettered. I had spent many an evening in Paris and Lyon gazing into shop windows daydreaming and it wasn't until I started as Chef Pâtissier at The Savoy that my culinary journey came full circle, and I realized my dream was achievable.

I was in love with the pâtisserie shops, chocolatiers and boulangeries of France and longed to have my own shop in London. I had a dream of creating a pâtisserie-chocolaterie boutique, but something was missing. I needed someone with the knowledge and the ability to ground me and make my dream a reality. Suzue joined my team at The Savoy while I was Chef Pâtissier and she took charge of the Afternoon Teas. We immediately had a connection and it was wonderful to meet someone who shared the same interests and true passion for the craft as I did. She had a fantastic understanding of our craft and a delicate Japanese flair to her work that changed my perception of pâtisserie as I knew it. Suzue opened up a whole new view of pâtisserie for me that I didn't realize existed until I visited Japan, with its classic French pâtisserie and distinct Japanese style that was precise as much as it was refreshing. Suzue has influenced me in many ways, in particular in my use of ingredients, and for that I am ever grateful.

I was born in Osaka in Japan and from a very young age, I was involved in the catering industry, being the daughter of a local restaurateur. A favourite pastime of mine was preparing the traditional sweet rice cakes served in my father's restaurant and rolling the rice balls in kinako powder. Cuisine was a way of life for me. When friends visited they would always comment on the enticing aromas that surrounded us, but to me it was normal, just part of daily life. We were always fully stocked with the finest ingredients; family and relatives would send us the very best peaches, grapes, sharon fruits, as soon as they were in season. We would always get the winter crops first – my auntie would send them straight away. Today, in our business, we are always looking for the best quality ingredients – vibrant raspberries, flavoursome cherries, ripe, plump strawberries, as fresh as possible for our products. So for me, food was always the most natural environment for me to work in.

Right from an early age, my dream was to own a Salon de Thé in Japan that sold exquisite pâtisserie. During the eighties, there was a massive boom in pâtisserie in Japan, influenced by the French. Inspirational pâtissiers such as Hidemi Sugino led the way during this movement and even today William and I are always stunned by the number of high-quality pâtisserie shops in Japan. Like many other Japanese chefs, I knew I needed to come to Europe to train. I left Japan with that goal in mind, my intention at the time being to return to Japan at a later stage.

I actually started my journey in general cuisine as, despite my future aim, I wanted to explore other areas of cooking to firmly establish where my passion lay. After having specialized in basic pâtisserie at Le Cordon Bleu in Paris, I realized it was indeed pâtisserie that I wanted to focus on. For me, pâtisserie was a precise art, an art form that involved an element of elegance, but also demanded perfection. I guess my Japanese background was useful in this regard, as in Japan, precision is essential. There is also, of course, the other appealing factor that a pâtisserie kitchen is far calmer, less hot and frantic and more organized than a general cuisine kitchen, and this suited me well too. Having made my decision, I spent time honing my skills in French pastry under the expert guidance of top French chef Laurent Duchêne. I then came to London in 1996 and continued my training at Le Cordon Bleu in London, and finally finished my training at Claridge's, before starting a new job at The Savoy. There, I was given my first opportunity to put my previous training into practice – I was put in charge of the prestigious Afternoon Teas, a huge responsibility and a huge honour, one which I was delighted to accept!

It was here that I met William. Being part of his team, we worked closely together, and soon discovered that we actually had a lot in common, despite our different cultures and backgrounds. We quickly found that we complemented one another with our ideas and worked well with each other; something that has continued to this day.

For William, chocolate and pastry seemed like a logical path, a path that I was more than happy to join him on, for I shared his vision – it was both our ambitions to own our own business selling the finest chocolate and pâtisserie in the country. Fast forward a few years and here we find ourselves, our ambitions having become a reality. It's been quite a journey... I never did make it back to Japan!

The Evolution of Pâtisserie

Today people often have no idea of the extraordinary journey taken by the food sitting in front of them waiting to be eaten.

One of the most interesting and colourful journeys in food is that of baking and pâtisserie. Even the simplest of pâtisserie has a story behind it; one that has often become distorted and eroded over time. These stories involve many people from various times in history, from royalty to the anonymous pâtissier, and often evolved by invasions, alliances and marriages. A study of such culinary creations requires the explorer to embark on a journey through centuries and across continents in an attempt to retrace the countless secrets of baking and pâtisserie that overlap important moments in history.

The Beginning

The first evidence of baking occurs with the Neolithic man creating primitive flat breads. Baking continued through the Ancient Mediterranean; the Romans, Greeks and Phoenicans all produced filo style pastries in their culinary traditions. There is also strong evidence that the ancient Egyptians produced pastry-like confections; they had professional bakers who had the skills to do so, and they also had ingredients such as flour, oil and honey.

Baking flourished in the Roman Empire. Around 300 BC, the pastry cook became an occupation for Romans (known as a *pastillarium*). It became a respected profession because pastries were considered decadent, and the Romans loved festivity and celebration. Pastries were often cooked for large banquets and pastry cooks inventing new creations were very highly prized. A baker's guild was established in 168 BC in Rome and by around 1 AD there were more than 300 pastry cooks in the city. As a result of their vast and expanding empire, the Romans discovered an endless variety of condiments and ingredients to be used in their cooking and spread many of their culinary techniques throughout the European empire, especially their early techniques of making pastry.

During the Middle Ages in Northern Europe, pastry began to be made with shortening and butter instead of oil, creating a crisper, richer pastry. Pastry and baking also became heavily influenced by the addition of almonds and honey, brought to Europe from Africa during the Moors invasion of 711 AD. As a result, almond-based products became popular in Europe during the Middle Ages and bakers in France formed guilds to protect and further their craft. In the 15th century, pastry chefs took pastry-making away from the bakers, and from this point on the profession of pastry-making developed rapidly, with chefs creating many new kinds of pastry products.

The discovery of the Americas in 1492 sparked a revolution in pastry-making with the introduction of sugar, and latterly cocoa, brought back from the new world. These new ingredients continued to make pâtisserie more sophisticated, and by the 17th and 18th centuries, many of the foundation recipes like Pâte Feuilletée and Pâte Sucrée were being made.

The 1830s saw the beginning of the Golden era for pâtisserie, sparked by Marie-Antonin Carême (see below). He was the catalyst in changing and evolving pâtisserie (and gastronomy) to what it is today. After the French Revolution, which ended in 1799, pâtissiers who had been servants in the houses of nobility started independent businesses and emulated the creations from the kitchens of the aristocrats and the wealthy so that the general public were able to buy and enjoy fine pâtisserie. Many highly influential French pâtissiers such as Chiboust, the Julien Brothers and Jules Gouffe began flexing their culinary muscles and really came to the fore; they left a lasting legacy and inspire pâtissiers to this day with notable creations seen in many a pâtisserie window, including the Saint-Honoré, the Savarin and the Éclair to name a few. Through studying each of these legendary dishes, it becomes apparent that pâtisserie is in essence an art form, something created through imagination, passion and skill, blending older models and adapting them to create art of the modern day.

Legendary Inspiration

Over the centuries, several pâtissiers of notable importance came to the fore and their influence over the pâtisserie world is still evident today.

Marie-Antonin Carême (1783–1833), born in Paris, was the first notable culinary genius and the father of *haute cuisine*, revered by many as the 'King of Chefs' and the 'Chef of Kings'; he is often regarded as the first 'celebrity chef'.

Abandoned by his parents in 1794, after the impact of the French Revolution, he found work as a kitchen boy at a Parisian chophouse in exchange for food and board. In 1798 he was taken on as an apprentice in the kitchens of Sylvain Bailly, a renowned pâtissier with a shop near the Palais-Royal. Bailly recognized and nutured the talent and ambition of the young and enthusiastic Carême, who gained fame in Paris for his *pièces montées*, elaborate constructions used as centrepieces which Bailly then displayed in his pâtisserie window. Carême made these confections, which were sometimes several feet high, entirely out of foodstuffs such as sugar, marzipan and pastry. He modelled them on temples, pyramids and ancient ruins, taking ideas from architectural history books that he studied at the nearby Bibliothèque National. (He notoriously said that The Fine Arts are five in number: painting, music, poetry, sculpture and architecture, whereof the principle branch is pâtisserie.)

Right Collecting cookery books from the masters is a passion of mine. These are a few of my favourites.

In the winter of 1803, he opened his own shop, the Pâtisserie de la rue de la Paix, largely funded by freelance work he had been doing for members of Parisian high society, most notably French diplomat Charles Maurice de Talleyrand-Périgord and Napoleon. It was while working on his creations in the private kitchens of Parisian society that he extended his culinary skills to cuisine. In 1804, Napoleon (who was famously indifferent to food, but he understood the importance of social relations in world diplomacy) gave Talleyrand money to purchase Château de Valençay, a large estate outside Paris. The château was intended to act as a diplomatic gathering place. When Talleyrand moved there, he took Carême with him. Carême was set a test by Talleyrand – to create a whole year's worth of menus, without repetition, using only seasonal products. Carême passed the test and completed his training in Talleyrand's kitchens.

Carême also spent time in London serving as Chef de Cuisine to the Prince Regent, later George IV, before returning to Paris where he did a stint as chef to banker James Mayer Rothschild.

Carême wrote several encyclopaedic works on pâtisserie and cookery including *Le Pâtissier Royal Parisien* (Paris 1815), *Le Pâtissier Pittoresque* (Paris 1828) and *Le Cuisinier Parisien* (Paris 1828.) In his ailing latter years, he devoted himself exclusively to writing, when he was reputed to have said 'when we no longer have good cooking in the world, we will have no literature, nor high and sharp intelligence, nor friendly gathering, nor social harmony'. Carême wanted to shine and be more than just an artisan. He redefined the very nature of pâtisserie; it wasn't just a pastry, but actually encompasses elegance, craft and spectacle.

He died in his Paris house on the Rue Neuve Saint Roche at the age of 48, perhaps due to the many years inhaling the toxic fumes of the charcoal on which he cooked. He is remembered as the founder of our craft and *haute cuisine* and is interred in the Cimetière de Montmartre in Paris.

Charles Elmé Francatelli (1805–1876), an Anglo-Italian cook, was born in London and was educated in France, where he studied the art of cookery under the legendary Carême. Revered for his blending of the best of Italian and French cuisine, Francatelli was regarded as a leading chef in Victorian London and spent most of his career in Britain directing the kitchens of several aristocrats and nobleman, subsequently becoming chef at Crockford's Club. He left there to become chef to Queen Victoria, undoubtedly a highlight in his career. He was the author of many culinary books, his most famous being *The Royal English and Foreign Confectionery Book* (1862). Often quoted, he once remarked that 'he could feed every day a thousand families on the food that was wasted in London'.

Jules Gouffé (1807–1877) gathered a wealth of knowledge on French gastronomy throughout his career that he recorded in *Le Livre de Cuisine* (1867) and *Le Livre de Pâtisserie* (1873).

The son of two pâtissiers who owned a pâtisserie shop, Gouffé began his training there, under his father's guidance, later continuing his training under the expert guidance of Marie-Antonin Carême, who scouted out the young protégé himself. In passing one day, Carême noticed Gouffé's *pièce montée* in the window of his father's shop. Carême enquired as to who had created such a splendid piece. When Gouffé's father proudly replied that it was his son, who was only 16, Carême was so impressed he immediately took him on as an apprentice. The pâtisserie books Gouffé later wrote became famous, with many being translated into English by his brother. His signature *pièce montée* is the Croquembouche de Meringue and his legacy lives on today.

Urbain Dubois (1818–1901) After his apprenticeship in the Rothschild family, he worked successfully in three major Paris institutions: The Café Tartoni, The Café Anglais and the Rocher de Cancale. He was famous for the artistic decoration of his desserts. One of his trademarks was the addition of sugar and marzipan decorations to his desserts.

The Julien Brothers (circa 1821–1887) were three brothers who opened a Parisian bakery named Julien Frères. They are credited for creating products like the Savarin named in honour of Brillat-Savarin (1755–1826), originally a French Lawyer and politician who gained recognition as a gastronome from his book *Physiologie du Gout* (the Physiology of Taste). The brothers are also credited with the discovery of the Genoise sponge which one brother, Auguste, observed while visiting a pastry shop in Bordeaux.

Chiboust owned a pâtisserie shop on Rue St Honoré in Paris, and in 1846 he created the aptly named Gâteau St Honoré, which is in homage not only to the street his shop was on but also to the patron saint of bakers, Saint Honoré. He gives his name to Chiboust cream, a pastry cream lightened with meringue, which he created.

Pierre Lacam (1836–1902) was responsible for the creation of 'petits fours'. He also spent a large part of his career writing about the art of pâtisserie and devoted his life to the promotion of pâtisserie in his work and in his writings. He published his first book, *Le Pâtissier-Glacier*, in 1865 and his second book *Le Mémorial Historique et Géographique de la Pâtisserie* in 1890.

Auguste Escoffier (1846–1935) was a highly acclaimed French chef restaurateur and culinary writer in his own right. Famous for updating and popularizing traditional French cooking methods and modernizing French cuisine, he achieved this great feat through the writing and publication of *Le Guide Culinaire* (1903), which is still used as a major reference work by many chefs and pâtissiers today. Escoffier's tips, techniques, recipes, notes on methods and advice on kitchen management are still very influential and have been adopted by many chefs across France and the world. One of his most celebrated creations is the Peach Melba (see pages 308–309).

Cyriaque Gavillon allegedly created the famous Opéra cake at the pâtisserie Dalloyau in 1955. He wanted to create a new cake shape with visible layers. He also wanted to be able to get a sense of the whole pâtisserie's taste in just one bite. It was named 'Opéra' by Gavillon's spouse, Andrée, as a tribute to an opera prima ballerina.

Gaston Lenôtre (1920–2009) was known by the French as the 'Gentleman Pâtissier' and was the most celebrated pastry chef since Marie-Antonin Carême. Lenôtre is widely credited with rejuvenating the world of pâtisserie in the 1960s. He had a good eye and a scientific temperament, and by introducing lighter ingredients and bright new fruit flavours, he transformed what had become rather stodgy into something more suitable for the modern palate. Among his most popular inventions were his *Succès*, almond-flavoured meringue with almond praline and nougatine, and his *Feuille d'Automne*, an almond and vanilla-perfumed meringue layered with dark chocolate mousse. He also began the craze for prettily coloured, fruit-flavoured macarons. Lenôtre had made himself into a brand; he was changing the perception of the modern pâtissier.

Born in 1920 on a small farm in Normandy, Lenôtre developed a passion for baking early; both his parents had worked as cooks in Paris, but after his father's illness forced them to return to Normandy, he struggled to find an apprenticeship in a restaurant kitchen. His gifts were eventually recognized and in 1947, he opened his first bakery in the small town of Bernay. Success there allowed him to buy a small bakery in the 16th arrondissement of Paris in 1957, with his first wife, Colette, who would prove to be a formidable business partner. His uncompromising approach to quality and ingredients, together with some interesting technical innovations, helped win over Parisians. In 1964, he branched out into savoury cooking and outside catering, rapidly developing an international chain of chic pâtisserie and catering outlets.

In 1971, Lenôtre opened a school in the town of Plaisir, west of Paris, training professional pâtissiers. It was a rigorous course and Lenôtre-trained chef-pâtissiers are now the backbone of the industry in France. David Bouley, a New York-based chef who attended the school, recalled four intense days devoted solely to egg whites: 'He was a master at building production. He was the first one to use gelatine in his buttercreams, and to make such extensive use of the freezer.' Like Carême, Lenôtre insisted that pastry was the best training for chefs, teaching precision and perfectionism. With 3,000 students passing through his school every year, Lenôtre trained chefs who have preserved and transformed the industry in France and all over the world.

For his 80th birthday in 2000, a veritable army of trainee chefs celebrated by constructing a 37-foot high cake at the Trocadero gardens, where its height could be compared to the nearby Eiffel Tower. Lenôtre died in 2009 at the age of 88, whereupon President Sarkozy felt moved to comment: 'He succeeded with his talent and his creativity, his rigour, and his high standards, in raising pâtisserie to the rank of an art.'

As the famous Paul Bocuse once said, 'A Lenôtre signature on a pâtisserie is akin to Christain Dior on a dress.'

The British Connection

Dating back to 1815, Marie-Antonin Carême was employed by the then Prince Regent at his ornate pavilion in Brighton. Although he stayed only two years before moving on, he and the Prince had set a trend. Banquets were now a mark of wealth and excess and the only chef that would do was a French one. The extent of his influence can be seen in the pages of a book called *London at Table* (1851) by Chapman and Hall Publishers – probably Britain's first ever restaurant guide.

The arrival in 1890 at London's newly opened The Savoy Hotel of Auguste Escoffier, in partnership with César Ritz, the greatest hotelier of his generation, underlined the dominance of the French in Britain's kitchens.

Afternoon tea is one of the most recognizable British traditions. It is believed that it originated from Anna the 7th Duchess of Bedford's habit of serving dinner between 8 and 9p.m. which left the Duchess hungry by late afternoon. To stave off the hunger, she would order tea, bread and butter and cakes to be served in her room. Later on she began to invite friends to join her at her home and the light tea was such a success the habit caught on. During the Edwardian period, the 'At Home' faded as the desire to travel increased. Tea began being served in the new tea lounges of the recently opened luxury hotels like the Ritz, Claridges and The Savoy, and high-end stores such as Fortnum & Mason and Harrods.

Afternoon tea in the 20th century evolved from serving baked cakes to serving miniature versions of pâtisserie, hugely inspired by the pâtisserie shops of Paris.

In 1959 a young French chef arrived from the British Embassy in Paris to cook for the renowned Cazalet family in Kent. Four years later his brother arrived in London to work for the Rothschilds. Their names were Albert and Michel Roux and, in 1967 they opened Le Gavroche and then in 1972, the Waterside Inn. These two iconic restaurants have trained many of the top chefs and pâtissiers in Britain today.

The Rise of the East

Although Japan has no cultural heritage with French pâtisserie, it has become increasingly popular since the 1970s. Chefs came from Europe to work in the 5-star hotels and equally Japanese chefs travelled to Europe, and France in particular, to work under the famous chefs and pâtissiers in the great restaurants, hotels and boutiques. Of course, many of them took the route of cuisine, but many others chose the world of pâtisserie, working with pâtissiers like Lucien Peltier,

Gaston Lenôtre and Jean Millet. Japanese pâtissiers like Hidemi Sugino, Yukihiko Kawaguchi and Katsuhiko Kawata took the French culture of pâtisserie shops back to Japan. The Japanese people have adopted the culture and it is well engrained in modern society, with many department stores having pâtisserie counters in the food halls, along with pâtissiers opening their own shops in many towns and cities throughout Japan.

Ovens & Innovation

In the early 15th century, bakers and pâtissiers in France used ovens that were partly built outside the main bakery or pâtisseries. The first written historical record of a professional oven refers to one in 1490, in Alsace, France. This oven was made entirely of brick and tile, including the flue. During this period the ovens were fuelled by wood, which were stoked and left to burn until the interior was hot enough. Long utensils were used to prepare the ovens, rakes to remove the ashes and long flat wooden shovels to lift the baked goods in and out.

Culinary historians credit the Greeks for developing bread baking into an art as front-loaded bread ovens were developed in ancient Greece. The Greeks created a wide variety of doughs, loaf shapes and styles of serving bread with other foods. Baking developed as a trade and profession as bread was increasingly prepared outside the family home by specially trained workers to be sold to the public.

According to Pierre Lacam, the first coal-fuelled oven was installed in the Boulevard Sebastopol boulangerie in Paris in 1858, paving the way for coal to replace wood in most of France's pastry ovens by 1860. Later in the 18th century, stone or brick ovens were replaced by cast iron but still fuelled by coal, and no thermostatic control. James Sharpe invented the first successful gas oven in the late 1820s, but it was not until a century or so later electric ovens began to compete with the gas ovens. In the 1920s, the thermostat was invented, helping to regulate and control heat within the gas or electric ovens.

Ovens are a fundamental part of pastry creation, but do need to be treated with respect. Temperatures will vary from oven to oven and many recipe books give different temperatures for static and fan ovens. Know your oven – if you know yours needs to be 10 degrees less, then adjust the temperature. The French have a wonderful term, *au pif* (by the nose), that is used to describe cooking or baking in that fashion. If a recipe says bake for 15 minutes and you feel it looks ready in 12 don't be afraid to take it out. I have never found two ovens that bake the same. Make judgement calls on your instinct and cook 'by the nose'.

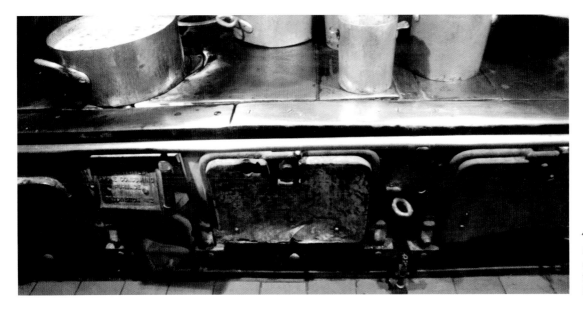

'The Last of Escoffier's Ovens' as featured on the wall of our Richmond shop.

Sugar Innovation

Sugar was first discovered and extracted from sugar cane thousands of years ago. Around 2,000 years ago, the first manufacturing processes turned cane sugar into sugar loaves. The spread of cultivation in the medieval era in the Islamic world led to the upscaling of manufacture and production methods. During the 16th century, cultivation of cane sugar in the West Indies and the Americas began. In the 19th and 20th centuries came the development of sugar from beet. It was the changes in production methods creating increased production that changed sugar from a 'fine spice' to the cheaper commodity it became in the 19th and 20th centuries.

Everything in Moderation...

It is my belief that fresh and natural is best; this is reflected throughout the book and within my boutiques. When making products, I like to use fresh herbs and fruit purées to create the most natural flavour and we use high-quality butter and cream. In society, we are encouraged to frown upon our consumption of salt, sugar and fats, but these should not be totally removed from our diet. To quote the Roux brothers, '... used in moderation, sugar and salt are essential to a balanced diet and our physical well-being.' So enjoy a Sunday afternoon with family and pâtisserie and do not feel guilty; enjoying eating good food is one of life's pleasures.

Relais Desserts International

As an apprentice pâtissier at Gleneagles Hotel, the first book I ever bought was *The Roux Brothers on Pâtisserie*. I was already immersed in a world of pâtisserie, chocolate and desserts, but the Roux Brothers' book gave me a greater understanding and insight into my chosen craft. A few pages in, it read: 'The Seminar for the Maîtres Pâtissiers of France' – I was excited to find out more! I discovered that Relais Desserts International was a professional association created in 1981. It brings together some of the biggest names in the pastry world, all united by one common aim: to promote Haute Pâtisserie – the equivalent of the Michelin Star Association for restaurants. Each year master pâtissiers from around the world gather for a three-day gastronomic event full of culinary demonstrations. Amongst them are some of the most famous pâtissiers from France, other parts of Europe, Japan and the USA.

The association puts strong emphasis on training the next generation of pâtissiers and chocolatiers and believes that encouraging young people to work with their hands and take up such a skilled craft is very important to our society. To this end, the association gives opportunities to apprentices who are keen to get to the top of their profession.

When we opened our Richmond shop in 2004, it was an ambition of mine to become part of Relais Desserts. I was overjoyed to become a member in September 2012, thanks to the support of my mentors Pierre Hermé and Alain Roux; and of course the tireless efforts of Suzue and our team in creating exceptional products that are always finished with expert precision and to the height of perfection. To be recognized by the association is a huge honour and each member is counted as part of the elite of the pastry world.

The Master of Culinary Arts

Inaugurated in 1987, 'The Master of Culinary Arts' (MCA) is held every four years and is seen to be the ultimate accolade awarded in recognition of outstanding craftsmanship in our industry in the UK. Based on the traditions of the 'Meilleur Ouvrier de France' (MOF) the MCA was and still is intended to instil the same respect and recognition of craft that exists in France; respectively the very best in culinary skills. To be considered one of the country's finest craftsmen is an honour and something I can truly say I have dreamed of for a long time.

After completing the semi-final earlier in the year the final was held at Westminster college on the 28 September 2013. Over 25 years of experience could not have prepared me enough for the months of practice, late nights, the advice from dedicated mentors, team and family. It was time to condense all of this into 10 precise hours, which included all aspects of our craft – this was to be no easy task. As they announced my name to collect the award, I realized my work as a pâtissier-chocolatier had received the ultimate recognition and I had been honoured with the title Master of Culinary Arts 2013.

William's Relais Desserts presentation:
Chocolate sculpture and Apricot & Wasabi entremets.

The Basics

For me, good-quality ingredients are fundamental; always buy the best you can afford or find. Search around, whether it be in a local shop, at a farmers' market or online, or you can also track down specialist food shops for those hard-to-find ingredients – Japanese food stores can be good for ingredients such as yuzu, sudachi and matcha (green tea) powder. The following pages list the main ingredients you will come across in this book and give advice on choosing the best-quality ingredients, as well as a bit of background on what they are. For a list of suppliers, please refer to the back of the book *(page 344)*.

I have been fortunate enough to cook in kitchens with a wonderful array of equipment. Good-quality equipment does not come cheap but it is worth it in the long run. I advise using stainless steel bowls and silicone moulds but it is not always essential. I have also had the misfortune of working in kitchens with limited space, wonky ovens and little equipment – the secret is being able to adapt. I would always advise shopping around and looking online for the best price. I would recommend a few basic items that are essential throughout this book – digital scales, stainless steel bowls, whisks, spatulas and a step palette knife – please see the detailed equipment section in the pages that follow. Also included in this section are just a few notes to bear in mind before getting started. They are not recipes but ways of working that will help you along the way.

Chocolate

Chocolate in its raw form is known as cocoa and originates from South America, growing in Venezuela, Ecuador, Mexico and the Caribbean. These native countries continue to grow cocoa today and are noted for producing some of the best cocoa in the world.

The cocoa tree lives in the lower canopy of the rainforest with mother trees protecting their fragility from extensive wind and rain. Cocoa grows best at 10–20° latitude either side of the equator, which is how cocoa migrated across the globe. The trees flourish in a very humid atmosphere at about 20–35°C (68–95°F) in South America, the Caribbean, Central America, along the west coast of Africa and parts of Asia.

There are three varieties of the cocoa tree:

Criollo The Criollo pod produces a small amount of cocoa beans of superior quality, delicate in flavour yet also complex. The Criollo only represents 2–3% of the world's cocoa market and is native to Central America, but is now also grown in the Caribbean.

Forestero The Forestero is the most common of the cocoa trees, making up approximately 85% of the world's cacao population. This is due to its hardy nature and ability to produce large yields of beans. It was initially native to the Amazon; it now makes up all of Africa's cocoa crops.

Trinitario The Trinitario is a hybrid of the Criollo and Forestero cocoa varieties, making up approximately 12% of the world's cacao population. It originates from Trinidad after an introduction of Forestero to the local Criollo crop.

Components of Cocoa

Cocoa pods are cut from the trees by hand with machetes or long-handled tools.

Cocoa beans are carefully removed from the cocoa pods once they have been cut open.

Cocoa nibs are what remain once the husks and shells of the cocoa beans are removed.

Cocoa mass is the name for the paste that is produced when the nibs are crushed.

Cocoa butter is removed from the cocoa mass by being pressed or drained.

Cocoa powder is the residue left behind when the cocoa butter is removed.

Couverture chocolate is a high-quality chocolate, used by professionals for dipping, coating and moulding. We recommend using couverture for all our recipes. The high amount of cocoa butter that it contains makes it easier to work with. Couverture chocolate is the most important ingredient in our business and in our opinion the brand Amedei *(see page 344)* really does lead the way. All of our recipes in our shops and this book are developed to work the best characteristics of Amedei chocolate.

Bean to Bar – Processing of Chocolate

Ripe cocoa pods are harvested by cutting the pod from the tree or knocking it off with a stick. The pod is then sliced in half and the beans and the surrounding pulp are scooped out. They are then placed into large wooden crates, usually lined with banana leaves and left to ferment for 4–6 days. The sweet pulp aids the fermentation process that develops the flavour of the cocoa.

The beans are then spread out onto large trays and allowed to dry naturally in the sun; sun drying also adds flavour to the cocoa – the process generally takes around 1–2 weeks. The dried beans are then graded and packed into hessian sacks and shipped to a chocolate manufacturer. When the beans arrive they are lightly roasted to develop the flavour. The beans are then put through a machine where they are crushed and the husks removed. The cocoa nibs are then graded.

The nibs are ground by passing them through a series of rollers to make the cocoa mass. The cocoa mass together with extra cocoa butter, sugar and vanilla (and potentially soya lecithin), are placed in a mixer that pulverizes and kneads together the chocolate, which at this stage will be gritty on your palate. To make it taste completely smooth and silky, the mixture now has to be conched (which will also take away any remaining bitterness). 'Conch' comes from the Spanish word *concha*, which means 'shells', and the original vessel was shaped like a conch shell. At Amedei, granite rollers grind the chocolate to a velvety texture. The characteristic taste, smell and texture of chocolate are developed at this stage. It takes up to 12 hours for commercial chocolate; however, for premium chocolate it takes much longer (about 40–75 hours). Amedei's ideal conching time is 72 hours for example.

Overview of Chocolate used in Pâtisserie

Dark chocolate gives a richness and intensity to any chocolate recipe. We mostly use dark chocolate in our recipes – there are so many wonderful characteristics as the natural flavours are much more prominent. We would recommend using a dark chocolate with at least 60% cocoa solids. (US dark chocolate is referred to as 'bittersweet'.) We have given this information in brackets in every recipe to be clear. Store in a cool dry place ideally 16–18°C (60–64°F).

Milk chocolate has the addition of milk powder. Look for one with at least 30% cocoa solids. I like a milk chocolate with caramel or malty notes. Store in a cool dry place at ideally 16–18°C (60–64°F).

White chocolate works well with acidic fruits like passion fruit or raspberry. You have to be careful when selecting white chocolate and make sure that it is only made with cocoa butter and no additional fats. Store in a cool dry place ideally 16–18°C (60–64°F).

Cocoa powder is made by pressing the cocoa butter out of the unsweetened cocoa mass. Natural cocoa powder has a red colour and can be quite acidic. Dutch-processed powder has been alkalized, has a milder flavour and darker, red colour. I would generally recommend the latter variety, but always buy unsweetened cocoa powder with nothing artificial added. Once opened, store in a sealed airtight container in a cool dry place.

Cocoa nibs are produced once the cocoa beans have been roasted and shelled and add a deep crunchy flavour. Once opened, keep cool and dry in a sealed airtight container.

COUVERTURE CHOCOLATE

COCOA BUTTER

COCOA POWDER

COCOA MASS

COCOA NIBS

COCOA BEANS

COCOA POD

Eggs

Eggs are the heroes of the pastry world and an essential part of pâtisserie – without them our world would be totally different. All of my recipes are based on large eggs and for consistency, I always weigh the eggs (whites and yolks separately) to be sure of the measurement – generally 1 egg yolk is about 20g (¾oz), 1 egg white is about 30g (1oz) and a whole egg is about 50g (1¾oz). I always store my eggs in the fridge at 3–5°C (37–41°F), as they remain fresher than when stored at room temperature. Bring out from the fridge 2 hours before using for sponges, meringue and aerated goods.

Egg whites freeze extremely well and their proteins also break down slightly during the freezing process meaning they whisk better than fresh whites. Always freeze them in small batches, so you don't encounter waste and when required, thaw in the fridge overnight. Alternatively, they can be stored in the fridge for 2–3 days. Egg whites contain mostly water and protein with a small amount of minerals. The proteins in the egg white are extremely important to the functionality of the egg whites. Compared to egg yolk, the egg white has very little flavour or colour. As the egg ages, the egg white thins and loses its ability to aerate and make stable meringues.

Egg yolks don't freeze as well as egg whites. They can be stored in the fridge in a sealed container for 2–3 days. Egg yolks are made up of about half water and half yolk solids. As eggs age, they pick up additional moisture from the egg whites. They have a protective membrane encasing the yolk which weakens with age and makes it more difficult to separate the yolk from the white. The yolk solids consist of proteins, fats and lecithin (emulsifier), small amounts of mineral ash and yellow-orange carotenoids.

Egg shells serve as a hard protective covering, although the egg shell is porous so any strong odour in your fridge, from garlic for example, will penetrate and can alter the flavour of the egg.

Yeast

I always use fresh yeast; it is readily available by asking at the bakery section of supermarkets, or at your local baker.

Dairy

Butter Always use good-quality butter and never substitute for margarine as this will have a huge bearing on the quality of your final dish. Most of the recipes use unsalted butter unless stated where I use speciality sea salted butter. With some recipes using butter you may need to think ahead, some require softened butter so I would recommend getting it out of the fridge before to come to room temperature. Store in the fridge at 3–5°C (37–41°F).

Sea salted butter I specially order in sea salted butter from Brittany in France. It differs in flavour and appearance from salted butter – the salt crystals are large and when the butter is cut into, you can see them throughout. You can now find this butter in the supermarkets, usually as their own premium brand. Store in the fridge at 3–5°C (37–41°F).

Cream In the United Kingdom cream is legally defined determined on its percentage of fat content.

Double cream is made of 48% fat and single cream is 18% fat. Whipping cream is made up of 35% milk fat and can be whipped well and is lighter than double cream. This is why it is a favourite in making pâtisserie, as it produces the most beautiful mousses. It is the cream we most commonly use in our recipes. Store cream in the fridge at 3–5°C (37–41°F); fresh is best so buy what you need and use as soon as possible.

Fromage frais (also known as **fromage blanc**) is a dairy product, originating from the North of France and the South of Belgium. The name means 'fresh cheese' in French (fromage blanc translates as 'white cheese'). Fromage frais is a creamy soft cheese made with whole or skimmed milk and cream. It has the consistency of cream cheese, but with fewer calories and less cholesterol. Make sure that you buy an unsweetened fromage frais as some varieties in the supermarket add sugar.

Milk Always use full fat milk. There is no point in substituting with a low-fat alternative. Trust us on this one. Store in the fridge at 3–5°C (37–41°F).

FRESH YEAST

Sugars

Sugar comes in many natural forms such as honey and maple syrup as well as the familiar refined granulated product, the most common sugar. It is processed from beet or sugar cane through a process of filtration, crystallization, washing and centrifugation, where the impurities are separated from the sugar. Below are the main types of sugar you will encounter throughout this book. It is recommended to use the sugar that is stated in the recipe. Store all types of sugar in a cool and dry place in sealed airtight containers.

Demerara sugar A light brown sugar with large crystals, it is dry and free-flowing unlike the moist muscovado sugar. Like muscovado, it is made from cane sugar, although it only retains around 2% of the molasses content.

Muscovado sugar From raw cane sugar, the muscovado sugar is soft and moist and consists of fine crystals coated in molasses – the colour and flavour of the sugar will vary with the molasses content. A light muscovado sugar has approximately 6% molasses and can be used to make many cakes as it creams really well. Dark muscovado sugar is stronger with an approximate 18% molasses content but works really well in heightening flavours in cakes and biscuits.

Caster (superfine) sugar The most common form of sugar used in cake making. It is especially good for whisked sponges, creamed mixtures and meringues because of its small and regular sized grains which dissolve more quickly in liquids and also allow the incorporation of smaller air cells into cake batters and creamed pastes.

Granulated sugar This is a little coarser than caster (superfine) sugar. If used in a creamed mixture it may result in a slightly gritty texture and speckled appearance, which will also reduce the volume of the cake. I generally use it for syrups.

Icing (powdered) sugar Can also be called 'confectioners' sugar', this is refined white sugar pulverized into a very fine powder.

Neige Décor An icing sugar combined with cornflour (cornstarch) so that it does not dissolve in humid conditions.

Isomalt is a very versatile, crystalline substance with many different applications. It is derived from sucrose and its clear colour clarity and the fact that it is less hygroscopic than sugar make it ideal for decorative sugar work.

Invert sugar Sugar is a molecule of glucose and fructose bonded together referred to as sucrose. During the process of inverting sugar, the sugar is mixed with water to create a solution and with the addition of an enzyme or heat and acid it will break the bond of the sucrose molecule, releasing the glucose and fructose to create a liquid non-crystallized product.

Glucose is another type of invert sugar, generally used for the prevention of re-crystallization of sugar, especially when making caramels and boiled sugar for pulling.

Honey is a natural invert sugar because enzymes in the honeybee invert the sucrose (sugar) found in the flower nectar to fructose and glucose. Good-quality honey will have natural characteristics of the flowers and the environment that the honeybee pollinates.

Fondant is made from sugar and water cooked to the soft-ball stage, cooled slightly and then beaten into an opaque mass of creamy consistency. This can be made from scratch but takes time and skill to prepare. It is also readily available pre-made.

DEMERARA

MUSCOVADO

CASTER

GRANULATED

ICING

NEIGE DÉCOR

Salt & Flour

Salt There are two main places of salt production, from the sea and from underground salt mines. Salt comes in rock or crystal form, granulated table salt and flake salt. Recipes in this book will define which salt to use. All types of salt should be stored in a cool, dry place in an airtight container.

Soft flour Virtually all the recipes you will find here involving flour require soft flour; we use a French T55 flour. If you find this a challenge to get hold of, I would suggest sticking to a good-quality plain (all-purpose) flour.

Strong flour A few recipes require strong flour; we use a T45 French flour. You can also use strong white bread flour.

Store all flours once opened in a cool, dry place in a sealed airtight container.

Flour is made from milling wheat grains. The grain is made up of endosperm, bran and germ. The endosperm makes up over 80% of the grain (the whitest part). It is milled for white flours which are used in pâtisserie making. The endosperm is made up of tightly packed starch granules embedded in chunks of protein. Two important proteins present in the endosperm are the gluten-forming proteins, glutenin and gliadin. When the wheat flour is mixed with water, glutenin and gliadin form a network of gluten, which is important for the structure of fermented goods like brioche, to retain the gas created by the yeast and also when the steam is created in baking.

For pâtisserie we mainly use two types of white flour which are classified by being soft or strong – strong white flour (bread flour) is high in protein and forms the strong gluten network required for the elasticity needed in a fermented dough. Soft flours (plain/all-purpose) are low in protein, typically forming weak gluten that tears easily, which produces a more tender product, which is desirable when we are making pastry, biscuits and baked cakes. Flour has a natural moisture content of around 14%. Any excess moisture can attract mould so always ensure you store flour in a cool dry place.

Baking powder is a leavening agent mainly used in the baked cake section which reacts with water to create gas and create rise in products. Do not use old baking powder if it has been open a long time as its activity will have decreased.

ROCK SALT

CRYSTAL SALT

BAKING POWDER

SOFT FLOUR

STRONG FLOUR

Fruit

Keep to the seasons with fruits. They will be at their best when in season and remember, use your senses. Fruit should look luscious and rich in colour and should be ripe and smell sweet and fragrant. Be careful when choosing berries: always check the base of the punnet to check for unripe or squashed items hidden below the better looking ones. Store fruit in the fridge to keep it fresher, some softer fruits like bananas should be stored cool and dry. You can freeze the best quality fruit when it is in season; summer fruits such as raspberries and blackberries freeze well as do stone fruits such as peaches, apricots and plums. Once frozen, they can be used later in the year for making compotes or jams. Before freezing you can also make them into purées which you can bring out and use later in the year for mousses. Frozen whole fruits never look as good as fresh ones once defrosted as they will soften. You should always use fresh ripe fruits for decoration.

Vegetables Certain vegetables lend themselves well to pâtisserie due to their sweetness. Beetroot and carrot are commonly used but tomato and sweet potato have also been used in pâtisserie and desserts.

Dried and candied fruits are frequently used in pâtisserie and can be purchased in supermarkets or food markets. Look for softer dried fruits as they are more flavoursome.

Frozen fruit purées Select flavours are now available in some supermarkets, although if you cannot source them it is easy enough to make your own from frozen fruits. Store in the freezer 16–18°C (60–64°F).

Feuillantine wafers are dried crêpes, wonderful for texture in pâtisserie. You can buy them online from professional suppliers.

Marzipan The higher the quality of marzipan, the higher the proportion of almonds to sugar – a rough guide to a good quality is 65% almonds to 35% sugar. However, this proportion will vary depending on the manufacturer. Once opened, wrap in cling film (plastic wrap) to stop it drying out and store in an airtight container.

Praline paste is widely used by pâtissiers. Making your own praline will produce the best flavoured praline paste but it is possible to buy it ready-made. Store in a cool, dry place in an airtight container.

Nuts

Always buy nuts fresh as they do not improve with age and can go rancid. Keep in a cool, dry place in an airtight container. You can also store them in the freezer in an airtight container to keep them fresh.

Almonds The fruit of the almond tree is called a drupe. Almonds are sold shelled or unshelled.

Blanched almonds are shelled almonds that have been treated with hot water to soften the seed coat. I prefer to use almonds from Avola in Southern Sicily. They have a high oil content and a delicate perfume.

Ground almonds and **Ground hazelnuts** are made with finely ground blanched almonds or hazelnuts.

Flaked almonds and **Baton almonds** are made with blanched almonds that have been sliced.

Hazelnuts are the seed of the hazel tree native to Italy where it thrives. The shell is removed and the nut is edible and used raw or roasted, or ground into a paste. I prefer to use Piedmont hazelnuts as they are smooth and creamy in flavour, have a sweet note and no bitterness or acidity.

Pistachios come from the pistachio tree originally from Central Asia and the Middle East. I like to use Sicilian Bronte known as the 'green gold' pistachio. They are produced in a rugged land at the base of Etna volcano on the Italian island of Sicily.

Walnuts The two most common major species of walnuts that are grown for their seeds (nut) are the Persian or English walnut and the Black Walnut. The commercially produced walnut varieties are nearly all hybrids of the English walnut.

Peanuts are available in many forms; buy unsalted and unroasted peanuts.

Desiccated coconut The various parts of the coconut have a number of culinary uses. The white, fleshy part of the seed, the coconut meat, is used fresh or dried in cooking. The desiccated coconut is made by the white flesh being shredded into the desired size, then dried.

Tea & Coffee

Houji cha A Japanese green tea that is distinguished from others because it is roasted in a porcelain pot over charcoal; most Japanese teas are usually steamed. The tea is fired at a high temperature, altering the leaf colour tints from green to reddish-brown. The process was first performed in Kyoto, Japan in the 1920s and its popularity persists today. The roasting replaces the vegetative tones of standard green tea with a toasty, slightly caramel-like flavour. The roasting process used to make Houji cha also lowers the amount of caffeine in the tea.

Fukamushi green tea is from Shizuoka, Japan. Green tea goes through minimal oxidization during processing. This green tea is from the first and second flush of leaves in direct sunlight. It is steamed for longer than most green teas. Suzue has chosen this particular green tea for serving in our boutiques and making pâtisserie as it has a slightly sweeter note than some other varieties of green tea.

Earl Grey tea is a black (oxidized) tea infused with the fragrance of bergamot oil. Each blend can have its own distinctive characteristics; our house blend Earl Grey has rose petals within the tea adding a floral note.

Jasmine tea is made with either green or white tea – here we use a white jasmine needle. The tea is blended with jasmine flowers and stored overnight. During the night, jasmine flowers open, bloom and release their fragrance into the tea. It takes over 4 hours for the tea to absorb the fragrance and flavour of the jasmine blossoms. This scenting process may be repeated as many as 6–7 times. The tea absorbs moisture from the fresh jasmine flowers so it must be dried again to prevent spoilage.

Sakura tea in Japan it is brewed for celebrations like weddings and engagements, although the tea is limited because of the short season of the blossoms in Japan. Depending upon the blend, the tea can be made with the blossom or the dried leaves of the tree. Some Sakura tea also has the addition of green tea in the blend.

Coffee Good-quality coffee undergoes many of the same processes as cocoa. The seeds of the plant are removed from the flesh, they are fermented and then dried and roasted. The two main coffee trees are the Arabicas and the Robusta. The Arabica produce the better beans and make up around 70% of the world's harvest. There are three main coffee growing regions: Africa/Arabia, Indonesia and Central/South America. In the broadest possible terms, African coffee tends to have a bright, fruity or citrus-like acidity, Indonesian tends to have a lot of body, with some earthiness or spiciness, and not very much acidity, and Central/South American tends to have a bright, clean acidity and a medium body. I use coffee from Square Mile in London, the coffee is roasted fresh here in London.

HOUJICHA

GREEN TEA

EARL GREY

JASMINE TEA

SAKURA TEA

COFFEE BEANS

Vanilla Pods (beans)

You can buy vanilla extract, but I prefer to use the real thing. It can be expensive to buy the best quality vanilla, however the difference in flavour is huge. I tend to buy Tahitian vanilla with its delicate flavour or Madagascan with its fruitier notes. (Bourbon and Mexican are also good). Store it in an airtight container in the fridge to keep it moist and fresh.

VANILLA PODS

Gelatine

All of our recipes that include gelatine are based on silver leaf gelatine, which is available in good food stores and supermarkets. I always weigh it as the weight changes in different brands. Once opened, store in an airtight container.

Fresh Herbs

Grow your own where possible and if not buy from a local supplier or market, where they will have a more intense flavour and character. Avoid supermarket herbs as they are grown quickly and lack flavour. Store them in the fridge. Fresh is best so I advise on buying them on the day you need them and store in the fridge wrapped in damp kitchen paper.

MINT

THYME

ROSEMARY

BASIL

Alcohol

You do not need to buy the most expensive brands, but it should be drinkable and something you would enjoy yourself. As you will see, dark rum, kirsch and Grand Marnier feature heavily throughout the book so it is good to keep these in your storecupboard.

Spices

To get the best flavour, you can buy them whole and grate them or crush in a pestle and mortar as you need them. Once they have been ground they lose their distinct flavour and aromatic notes, so buy in small quantities and freeze in an airtight container.

STAR ANISE

CLOVES

WHOLE BLACK PEPPERCORNS

FRESH GINGER

WHOLE NUTMEG

CINNAMON

SZECHUAN PEPPER

CARDAMOM PODS

FRESH CHILLI

OLIVE OIL

JAPANESE BLACK VINEGAR

BALSAMIC VINEGAR

SUDACHI

YUZU

WASABI POWDER

FRESH WASABI

EDAMAME

AZUKI BEAN PASTE

BLACK BEANS

SHISO

KINAKO POWDER

MATCHA POWDER

AZUKI BEANS

Oils & Vinegars

Olive oil All production begins by transforming the olive fruit into olive paste. This paste is then malaxed (slowly churned or mixed) to allow the microscopic oil droplets to concentrate. This virgin oil is extracted by means of pressure (traditional method) or centrifugation (modern method). After extraction, the remnant solid substance, called pomace, still contains a small quantity of oil. Other grades of olive oil use chemicals to extract the remaining oil from the pomace. I prefer to use extra-virgin or virgin olive oil which is only from virgin extraction.

Balsamic vinegar Only two consortia produce true traditional balsamic vinegar, Modena and neighbouring Reggio Emilia. True balsamic vinegar is made from a reduction of pressed Trebbiano and Lambrusco grapes. The resulting thick syrup, called *mosto cotto* in Italian, is subsequently aged for a minimum of 12 years in casks made of different woods like chestnut, acacia, cherry, oak, mulberry and ash. True balsamic vinegar is rich, glossy, deep brown in colour and has a complex flavour that balances the natural sweet and sour elements of the cooked grape juice with hints of wood from the casks.

Japanese black vinegar is a vinegar made from fermented rice or rice wine. Black vinegar is made from black glutinous rice (also called 'sweet rice'). Rice vinegars are very mild and sweet compared to distilled and more acidic Western vinegars which, for that reason, are not appropriate substitutes for rice vinegars.

Japanese Ingredients

We have a strong Japanese influence running through our products due to Suzue's heritage and many visits to Japan. As such you will find some of our pâtisserie makes use of traditional Japanese ingredients. Listed here are the main ones that you will come across in this book, they are all available in Japanese stores or can be sourced online; certain supermarkets now stock some of these products as well.

Wasabi This can be purchased in powder form or fresh and we find that the latter has a subtle and more balancing flavour. Fresh wasabi should be bought as fresh as possible so the intensity of the flavour does not diminish. Powdered wasabi can be stored in a sealed airtight container.

Yuzu This is a Japanese citrus fruit that we use a lot, it is more fragrant and aromatic than oranges or lemons. It can be difficult to buy fresh but you can buy it as dry or frozen pre-prepared zest.

Sudachi is a Japanese citrus fruit similar to a lime, but with a more intense flavour.

Sake is a Japanese distilled alcoholic beverage made from fermented rice. Store in a cool, dry place.

Shochu is a Japanese distilled beverage, which is typically distilled from barley, sweet potatoes or rice. Store in a cool, dry place.

Plum wine or **umeshu** is a Japanese alcoholic drink made from steeping green plums in shochu. Store in a cool, dry place.

Azuki beans are small red, black or white beans. They are prepared by boiling and blanching until tender. If they are sweetened they are cooked in a sugar syrup and then kept whole or mashed into **azuki bean paste**.

Black beans are soy beans prepared in the same way as the azuki beans.

Matcha powder is very finely ground green tea leaves. There are many grades and I would suggest spending time to find a favourite. Storing, cool and dry, in a sealed container is good but a freezer is preferable to keep its flavour fresh.

Kinako powder Also known as soy bean flour, it is made by finely grinding roasted soy beans into a powder. Store in a sealed airtight container.

Houji cha is a roasted green tea powder, which gives a nuttier flavour to pâtisserie. Store in an airtight container.

Edamame is the preparation of immature soy beans in the pod, cooked either by boiling or steaming. Available fresh or frozen from Japanese stores.

Shiso is an Asian culinary herb from the mint family, although it has different flavour notes from mint. Just like mint, there are different varieties of shiso, each with a unique scent and flavour. Shiso is available in both green and purple, and the leaves have either smooth or curled edges. It has a slightly anise flavour combined with citrus and cinnamon overtones.

Selecting Equipment

Baking Essentials

Wire cooling rack A standard wire cooling rack is useful for cooling cakes and sponges and is also used for glazing and spraying entremets.

Rolling pin While technology has improved much equipment available, I still prefer an old-fashioned French-style rolling pin, which is simply a spindle of wood.

Baking beans These ceramic or metal small beads or beans are used for blind baking, weighing down the pastry to keep the shape of the tart while it cooks.

Pastry cutters are excellent for pastry work. It's best to get a straight-edged set and a fluted-edge set in a selection of sizes. I would recommend either stainless steel or exoglass/plastic. These were invented by the executive chef of the King of Prussia in 1740. The first pastry cutter that the chef used was made from the metal band of an old spur from his master's boots.

Baking trays (sheets) I prefer rimless baking trays (sheets) and avoid flimsy trays that will buckle while baking. The recommended size is 30 x 40cm (12 x 20 inches), but if you cannot find it, use as close to this size as possible.

Pastry docker This is a roller with protruding points, used to make a number of small holes in pastry doughs.

Tart rings These are stainless steel rings, which are used to support pastry in the making and cooking of tarts. They are easily available at most good cook shops or online catering suppliers. Originally tart rings were made out of copper, although in 1840 a French pâtissier called Trottier invented the steel flan rings that are still used today.

Kugelhopf mould Available in non-stick coated moulds, as shown in the picture, but the traditional mould, made from varnished earthenware, is also available.

Loaf tins (pans) Available in a variety of shapes and sizes, they are either tin or non-stick and should be lined before baking. Traditional loaf tins are easily available in good cook shops; the long thin cake tin is a speciality shape originating from Japan (see page 328).

Canelle moulds Traditionally these are copper moulds, although they are also now available in non-stick baking mat varieties.

Savarin, Dariole (Baba) and Madeleine moulds These are available in traditional tin moulds, non-stick baking tins (pans) and now also in non-stick baking mats.

Tart cases Available in a variety of shapes and sizes in tin moulds but also in non-stick as pictured here. Round traditional tarts are easily available in good cook shops and other shapes are available from online catering suppliers. A few of the different varieties are pomponette, which has a rounded shape with a flat bottom, square and the round traditional tart.

Brioche à tête mould This is a fluted round, flared tin (pan). It is the most common shape associated with brioche and is available in tin or non-stick. Available from online catering suppliers.

Bar Guides These are excellent for creating layers in Petit Gateaux and Entremets. They give an even and sharp appearance.

Note: tin moulds will need to be lined with butter and flour before using (see page 30).

Pans & Bowls

Saucepans It's always worth investing in decent saucepans. Cheap pots and pans will warp with the heat and can sometimes end up leaking, losing their handles and generally falling into disrepair quite early on in their lives. They can also develop hotspots, causing your food to cook unevenly and stick to the bottom.

Porringer pot This is great for tempering chocolate, retaining heat and decorating and dipping chocolates. It also prevents steam from escaping and getting into your chocolate, which can make it thicker. This is an inexpensive way to start tempering.

Mixing bowls In the kitchen we have stacks of these in all different sizes, as often creating a dish requires the use of many bowls of varying sizes. It is important to make sure that mixing bowls are washed in hot to water to eliminate traces of grease, which can have disastrous consequences to mixes such as meringues and sponges.

Trivet A trivet should be used whenever a hot pan or baking tray is placed onto the side; it allows an airflow to cool the pan and also protects the surface from the heat. Trivets come in many modern shapes and forms: wooden, metal and also silicone.

Deep metal tray Ideal for pouring products like crème pâtissière into, to cool quickly.

WIRE COOLING RACK / BAKING SHEET / ROLLING PIN / PASTRY DOCKER / KUGELHOPF MOULD / PASTRY CUTTERS / TARTLET MOULD / LOAF TINS (PANS) / BAKING BEANS / CANNELLE MOULDS / SAVARIN MOULD / TART RINGS / POMPONETTE MOULDS / BRIOCHE À TÊTE MOULD

PORRINGER POT / DEEP METAL TRAY / SAUCEPANS / MIXING BOWLS / TRIVET

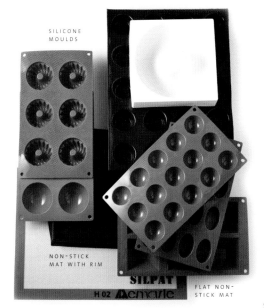

SILICONE MOULDS

NON-STICK MAT WITH RIM

SILPAT
H 02 Demarle

FLAT NON-STICK MAT

Non-stick Baking Mats

Silicone baking mats and moulds are one of the most evolutionary technological advances in modern pâtisserie. Not only can you bake cakes, they can also be used to build entremets and petits gâteaux, available in a limitless array of shapes and sizes. The pâtisserie cabinet of today can be eye-catching in shapes as well as colours.

Flat non-stick baking mats I generally use silicone mats, which are flexible sheets of a non-stick material that can withstand extreme temperatures and are reusable. You can buy them in cook shops or online. Siliconized baking paper also works well.

Non-stick baking mats with rims These are similar to the non-stick baking mats but they have a rim and are great for making sheet sponges.

Silicone moulds Silicone moulds come in a huge array of shapes and sizes and can be used for making petits gâteaux or baked cakes.

SERRATED KNIFE

CHOPPING KNIFE

OFFICE KNIFE

SANTOKU KNIFE

PETIT KNIFE

CAKE-SLICING KNIFE

LARGE STEP PALETTE KNIVES

SMALL STEP PALETTE KNIVES

MEDIUM STEP PALETTE KNIVES

MEDIUM FLAT PALETTE KNIFE

PASTRY WHEELS

Knives

I would strongly advise using knives made from stainless steel. If you look after them they will last you a lifetime. You will need to buy a good-quality steel to sharpen them. Never put them through the dishwasher as it will damage your blades. I like to use Japanese knives as they are lightweight and made of layered forged steel, keeping them sharper for longer. I cannot stress enough the importance of a sharp knife, they are the tools of the trade.

I recommend the following knives as a good base set for pâtisserie-making: a small office knife, chef's chopping knife and a serrated pastry knife.

Pastry wheels are adjustable 5-wheel strip cutters mounted on an expandable frame that are used for cutting dough into strips, marking out sizes and cutting chocolate sheets.

Palette Knives

A palette knife is essential for anyone making pâtisserie. I recommend having a selection of sizes. Large step palette knives are good for spreading sponges and smaller palette knives are great for delicate work.

Hand Equipment

Pastry scrapers I find these a must in a professional kitchen. They are not an expensive investment. Plastic versions are great for getting all the dough cleanly out of a mixing bowl and scraping work surfaces clean. I use the metal version when working with chocolate as it is sturdier.

Spatula This is a very important tool in the kitchen; we use these for anything from folding sabayon into a mousse and mixing cremeux. Go for the heatproof silicone version, ideally with a slight curve on the blade.

Spatula thermometer These are a wonderful invention; the silicone spatula has an integral digital thermometer that displays a precise temperature as you heat and you are able to stir the ingredients at the same time, preventing sticking and burning on the base of the pan.

High-heat plastic spoon In the professional kitchen these have replaced wooden spoons. They are good for making caramel and stirring fondant.

Ladle A small- to medium-sized ladle is important throughout the book; it is useful for handling liquids.

Wide-handled flat-based palette knife These are good for lifting pâtisserie onto serving dishes.

Whisks Go for good-quality whisks that can withstand a good beating. I prefer stainless steel whisks. Balloon whisks are excellent for whipping cream or egg whites if you do not have a whisking machine. I would recommend a straight whisk with a long handle for whisking in pans. Originally whisk were made from heather, and later from cytisus wood, commonly known as broom. During the mid-1600s it was changed to boxwood and not until 1860 was the metallic whisk invented.

WIDE PALETTE KNIFE

PASTRY SCRAPERS

SPATULAS

SPATULA THERMOMETER

HIGH-HEAT PLASTIC SPOON

LADLE

WHISKS

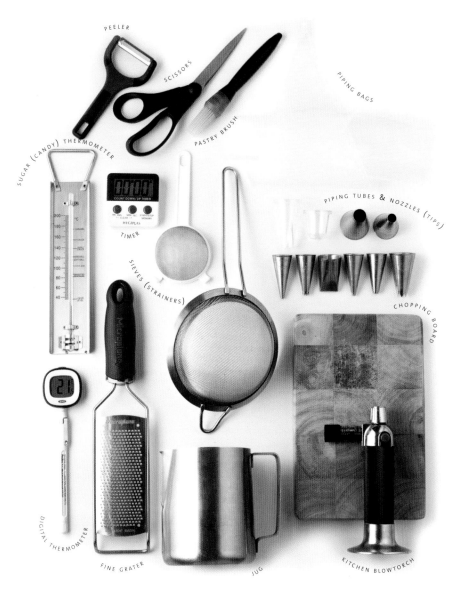

PEELER

SCISSORS

PIPING BAGS

PASTRY BRUSH

SUGAR (CANDY) THERMOMETER

PIPING TUBES & NOZZLES (TIPS)

TIMER

SIEVES (STRAINERS)

CHOPPING BOARD

DIGITAL THERMOMETER

FINE GRATER

JUG

KITCHEN BLOWTORCH

Small Essentials

Digital thermometer An essential piece of equipment for checking the temperature of custards and also for tempering chocolate.

Fine grater This is a fine sharp grater, used for grating the zest of citrus fruits, spices like nutmeg and fresh spices like ginger.

Jug Essential throughout the book, especially when glazing entremets and petits gâteaux.

Chopping board A durable board made from either wood or plastic. There are also chopping boards available made of glass, steel or marble, but these tend to damage and blunt knives due to their hardness. It is advisable to place a small damp cloth underneath your chopping board to prevent it from slipping.

Kitchen or crème brûlée torch (blowtorch) You can pick up small butane-filled sized crème brûlée torches in most cookware stores. They are ideal for lightly caramelizing the tops of your crème brûlée and essential for de-moulding entremets from stainless steel rings.

Sugar (candy) thermometer Essential for checking the temperatures of caramels and other candies, jellies and preserved fruits. These can read a much higher temperature than can be read on most digital thermometers.

Timer Many ovens have these built in, but you should ideally buy a digital timer, as time is everything in a baking kitchen. You will not regret it.

Sieve (strainer) A stainless steel fine mesh sieve (strainer) is best for pouring creams and custards through. Keep a separate sieve for sieving dry ingredients, such as flour and cocoa powder. A small sieve is excellent for dusting for decoration in the macaron section *(see pages 294–303)*.

Piping (pastry) bags Most reuseable piping bags are made of reinforced cotton and can be purchased from good cookery stores. Although not as eco-friendly, most people now buy disposable plastic ones, which again can be purchased in supermarkets and cookery stores. The piping bag was invented in 1847 by a Frenchman called Aubriot, and it was originally made out of cloth.

Piping tubes & nozzles (tips) The nozzle was invented in the middle of the 19th century by French pâtissier, Trottier. They can come in either plastic or stainless steel. Piping nozzles (tips) should always be washed immediately after use. The main two tubes used throughout the book are either a plain nozzle or star nozzles of different sizes. Some specific recipes may require specialist tubes, such as St Honore tube, which is shaped with a V cut out; Mont Blanc piping tube, which has 7 or 8 very small holes on one tube; and Buche piping tube, which is flat on one side and has lots of small v's cut out on the other (and was originally used for decorating traditional Yule logs).

Pastry brush Ideal for glazing, buttering your moulds and for soaking cakes and sponges. I stopped using soft bristle brushes and now use silicone ones, as there is no risk of a stray hair on a dish.

Peeler A good-quality, durable peeler is very useful.

Scissors A good-quality pair of scissors is always useful in the kitchen but always ensure you keep them sharp.

Scales

Probably the most important piece of equipment in my kitchen, you will not get very far without it. I would recommend a digital set (a reasonably priced set should do the trick), ideally going up in 1g increments to get the fine detail required.

Entremet Frames & Rings

Ideally go for stainless steel frames that are strong and won't bend. Entremets rings are easily available from good cookery stores. The more interesting shapes can be found from catering websites.

Gâteau trois frères mould This shape of mould was created by the Julien Brothers *(see page 12)* in the 19th century. They named it after themselves – the 'Trois frères' (three brothers).

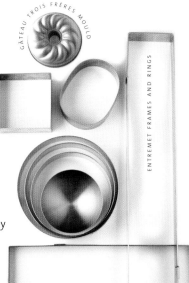

GÂTEAU TROIS FRÈRES MOULD

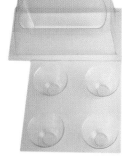

ENTREMET FRAMES AND RINGS

PLASTIC MOULDS

Plastic Moulds

PCB creation *(see page 344)* are renowned for making a wide variety of thin plastic moulds in different shapes and sizes. Although they are not as durable as stainless steel moulds they are reasonably priced and a great way to get started.

Specialist Equipment

Caramelizer This is used for caramelizing sugar on top of pâtisserie and originally was an iron that would have been placed into the fire. Technological advances created this electric version.

Matcha tea whisk (chasen) A bamboo whisk with fine bristles to whisk and dilute the Matcha powder.

Matcha Tea spoon (chashaku) (also called tea scoop) A bamboo spoon to measure the powdered tea into the tea bowl. Not the same size as a Western teaspoon.

Chausson cutter A specialist pastry cutter in an oval shape specifically for the Chausson au Pommes *(see page 166)*.

Japanese vegetable turner This piece of equipment makes light work of vegetables and fruit, creating evenly sliced strings (spaghetti) and paper-thin slices. It has four blades for different effects; in the book we have used the thin shoestring garnish blade *(see page 312)*.

Other Equipment

Food processor I use a food processor, for making things like the praline paste *(see page 116)* and for puréeing fruits *(see page 110)* by hand. It also has slicing and grating attachments. It is advisable to get a good-quality one.

Hand-held electric blender Hand blenders are ideal and essential when making ganache and cremeux throughout the book to enhance a good emulsification.

Free-standing mixing machine A good mixing machine is essential for anyone who loves baking and making pâtisserie; it is a worthwhile investment. Make sure that it has the three main attachments – dough hook, beater and a whisk – each of these is essential throughout the book.

Fryer These are relatively inexpensive nowadays but essential if you are making anything fried as it is a safe and consistent way of cooking. The oil should be as fresh as possible and should be cleaned out and fresh oil replaced at regular intervals.

Dehydrator Available from good cook shops and online. It can be used to dry out fruit and vegetables, we also use it for fruit tuiles *(see page 121)*. It dries with a low heat over a longer period of time, and can achieve lower temperatures that conventional ovens cannot.

Ice cream machine In our business we use a Pacojet to churn our ice cream – it uses a revolutionary method of freezing the custard in a canister and churning once frozen, rather than churning the ice cream as you freeze. A small blade turns at vast spins per second, thus creating the lightest, smoothest ice cream. However, we don't all have a huge amount of money to spend, and thankfully there are several inexpensive machines on the market, so shop around to find a good price.

CARAMELIZER

MATCHA TEA SPOON

CHAUSSON CUTTER

MATCHA TEA WHISK

JAPANESE VEGETABLE TURNER

Here are just a few notes to bear in mind before getting started.
They are not recipes but ways of working that will help you along the way.

Home Kitchen vs. Industrial Kitchen

As with my previous book, *Couture Chocolate*, this book is designed as an inspiration as well as a recipe book. It has taken over 25 years for me to gain these skills and the knowledge presented in this book. It offers a wide range of recipes and dishes to try at home. As you develop your techniques, your confidence will grow.

Our book contains recipes we use in our kitchens. They have been adapted the best way we can to be accessible and possible to re-create in your own homes. While we have done our utmost to make these recipes as home-kitchen-friendly as we can, you must remember that there are some fundamental differences between how you will make a product and how we will make it here in our professional kitchen.

You will notice in the photographs in this book that we often use pieces of equipment that you may not have in the home kitchen. Feel free to use alternative items, but do be aware that results may differ slightly due to the changes made.

A freezer is a vital tool in any pâtisserie kitchen, most things can be frozen. When freezing any product it is key to wrap it well – it will preserve flavour and freshness and also keep the moisture from the freezer affecting its finished look. Throughout the Petits Gâteaux and Entremets chapters *(see pages 212–255 and 256–293)* a freezer is used for building neat layers within the finished product, freezing components to place them into the final stage of the building. When making biscuits and cakes, some can be frozen and taken out and baked at a later date – they will not be affected by the freezing process and you can always have treats to hand if a friend drops by. Some recipes, especially those in the dough section, do not work well being made in small quantities. Raw pastry dough can be frozen, syrups and compotes can be stored in airtight containers in the fridge and macarons can be frozen after being baked. It is important that any mousses are made as close to the assembly of the final pâtisserie as possible to avoid them setting prematurely.

Be Prepared

- Always read through the whole recipe before starting so that you can be aware of what is involved in each step.
- Make sure you have all your utensils and ingredients ready before you begin. It sounds obvious, but check the recipe for everything you need.
- It is also advisable to weigh all your ingredients out beforehand so you don't get confused halfway through if you are missing something.
- Prepare what you can in advance, especially when making some of the more layered pâtisserie.
- For advice on oven temperatures also *see page 14* for more information. Be aware that these are approximations only so use initiative and knowledge of your own oven.

Sieving (straining)

Working Clean

I have always believed that to be a good chef, you have to have the right attitude and the right approach to your work. The very foundation of this lies in the way you work; organization is key. Being organized, working methodically and cleanly is not necessarily something that can be taught, more, it is engrained in your character... something that is part of who you are. A chef has to have the desire to work in this fashion. I am a firm believer that chefs with this philosophy work better and more effectively and efficiently; things run better and more smoothly. Overall this creates a more harmonious work environment – my kitchen runs on this belief.

Weighing

A good set of digital scales and precision when weighing is essential – always follow what the recipe states. Pâtisserie is a precise chemistry in the kitchen and for this reason, precision matters more in baking than in savoury cooking. For example, when making a baked cake, too much baking powder will react vigorously and the quantity of other ingredients will be out of balance so will not be able to stabilize the reaction.

Resting Pastry

When preparing pastry it is important to let the pastry rest for at least 30 minutes in the fridge. Resting the dough allows the gluten that may have formed to relax, by relaxing the dough after it has been made and rolled. It allows the gluten strands that may have been developed to adjust to the new length or shape. If the pastry is not rested, it will shrink and change shape upon baking.

Sifting

Sifting dry ingredients is particularly important, especially when making pâtisserie. The act of sifting breaks up any lumps that may have formed if the ingredients have been sitting for some time. When using baking powder it is advisable to sift with the dry ingredients twice, this will evenly disperse it throughout the dry ingredients.

Eggs

Eggs provide many functions throughout pâtisserie, the three main being that eggs provide structure, can be aerated and can also be used as an emulsifier.

Structure builders Coagulated egg proteins in both egg whites and egg yolks are important structure builders in baked goods. Eggs are as important as flour in the structure of cakes, in fact without eggs most cakes will collapse. Coagulated (cooked) egg proteins provide thickening and gelling forming structure in pastry cream, crème anglaise and many others. Whole eggs coagulate at around 70°C (158°F), although diluted with other ingredients, the temperature rises to 82–84°C (180–183°F). Egg yolks coagulate at 65–70°C (149–158°F) and egg whites 60–65°C (140–149°F), although again, if diluted with other ingredients the temperature of coagulation will rise. As eggs are heated the proteins gradually denature or unfold and these unfolded proteins move through the liquid and bond with each other. Properly bonded egg proteins form a strong yet often flexible network that traps water and other liquids. We need to be careful though as when the proteins are heated the tighter and more rigid the structure becomes, until they become over coagulated, shrinking and squeezing out liquids, which we call curdling. Being vigilant when cooking eggs is especially important when making something like crème anglaise.

However in some circumstances like making crème pâtissière and sponges the water that is released from the over coagulated proteins evaporates, or is absorbed by other ingredients. In sponges the water is released and gelatinizes the starches in the flour.

Aeration Egg yolks, egg whites, and whole eggs all have the ability to be aerated creating foams which consist of tiny bubbles of air surrounded by a liquid or solid film. Aerating eggs assists in the leavening process, the actual leavener is air. All parts of the egg have different foaming powers, this refers to how high they can be whipped. Egg whites have a high foaming power and can whip up to eight times their volume. Whole eggs and egg yolks do not foam as well as whites, whole eggs foaming more than egg yolks.

When making a meringue, egg whites are aerated (whipped) with sugar which greatly stabilizes the meringue. The sugar should be added slowly to provide time for the sugar crystals to dissolve and not weigh down the foam. As the eggs are whipped two things happen simultaneously: air bubbles are beaten into the liquid, and certain egg proteins denature or unfold. The proteins bond around the bubbles forming a network.

Aeration Whites

Soft peak When you turn the whisk upside down the peaks should just be starting to hold. The mix has a soft texture and the peak will fall back into the mixture after a second.

Stiff peak When the whisk is held upside down, the peaks should point straight up without collapsing. The mix is thick and heavy in texture.

One to watch: over whipping/under whipping Both over and under whipped egg whites are unstable. After the stiff peak stage, egg whites will start to become grainy and dull. This is caused as the proteins break down and separate. When over beaten, the whisked egg whites will eventually collapse back on themselves as they have nothing to support them. If the egg whites have been under whipped, proteins are not fully denatured forming a strong network; the whites will break down.

Soft peak

Stiff peak

Ribbon stage

Aeration Egg Yolks/Whole Eggs

Ribbon stage Egg yolks and whole eggs can also be aerated, although are never as light as with egg white. For a fully aerated egg yolk and whole egg mixture, it is also whisked with sugar and you are looking for the 'ribbon stage'. As you lift the whole egg from the mixture it will fall back on itself and a trail or 'ribbon' will be left across the surface. The ribbon will hold shape for a moment, and then sink back into the mix.

Under whipped

Emulsification

Egg yolks are effective natural emulsifiers; they keep water and fat from separating. This is especially important when eggs are added to creamed butter in cake mixes and dough. You must add in the eggs slowly and the yolk will bind the fat and water in the eggs together. A poorly emulsified cake batter will result in a cake that may not rise properly and a coarse crumb.

Egg Wash

Used for glazing baked goods, it turns shiny and golden when baked. There are many variations, I like to use a recipe of one egg, plus one egg yolk with a pinch of sugar and a pinch of salt.

Over whipped

Mixing Egg & Sugar

When sugar is added to egg yolks and not mixed, the egg yolks gel together and appear to cook. In fact it is the sugar that is pulling the moisture from the egg yolks and drying them. Always mix the egg yolks and sugar together until light in colour.

Using the Right Metal

Do not use aluminium bowls, beaters or saucepans. When working with egg mixtures, use stainless steel instead. The aluminium will discolour the egg mixture and make it a dull grey.

Top Tips

A collection of techniques you'll need to know.

Preparing, Filling & Using a Piping Bag

Using piping (pastry) bags and nozzles (tips) enables the chef to achieve a professional finish.

- Fold back the piping bag to form a cuff, if required place a piping nozzle into the bag and cut off the point of the bag to form an opening. *(1–3)*

- Press the bag into the nozzle to form a seal to prevent mixtures from pushing through while you are filling the bag. *(4)*

- Hold the prepared bag with one hand, or rest in a jug. Scoop in the piping mixture to no more than halfway. An overfilled piping (pastry) bag can be difficult to use. *(5–6)*

- Fold back the bag and twist to create pressure, pushing the mixture until it comes through the tip. *(7)*

- When holding a piping bag, have one hand maintain the pressure created in the twist, squeezing with your hand so that the mixture comes out. Your other hand should be at the tip, holding the piping nozzle and guiding the flow of the mixture being piped. *(8)*

Making a Paper Cornet

Paper cornets are useful for very fine piping, such as an intricate decoration or writing.

- Cut a sheet of silicone baking paper into triangles; make sure that you have one longer side and two smaller sides. *(1)* Position the paper in front of you with the middle corner pointing towards you and the long side of the triangle facing away from you.

- Curl one corner over to the centre to create a cornet. *(2)* Holding the cone with one hand, curl the other corner over the cornet so that it meets with your hand holding the cornet. *(3)* Hold the back of the cornet with both hands, then fold the excess parchment into the cornet to secure it. *(4)*

Lining Tins

To ensure that baked goods do not stick inside the baking moulds it is essential to line them first.

- Brush the inside of the baking mould with some softened butter, ensuring it is well covered including corners. *(1)*

- Dust with plain (all-purpose) flour and move it around the whole of the inside of the mould so that it sticks to the butter. *(2)*

- Tap out any excess flour, *(3)* then line with a sheet of silicone baking paper (this is optional and depends on the shape of the mould). *(4–5)*

Bain-marie (water-bath)

Throughout the book a bain-marie (water bath) is used to melt chocolate, warm eggs for meringue and sponges, etc. It is also a useful method while tempering chocolate if you do not have a porringer pot.

- Set a bowl over a saucepan of simmering water. It is important that the base of the bowl does not touch the water.

An ice bain-marie is used to cool mixtures down rapidly.

- Simply set a bowl in a tray of iced water.

Using Gelatine

When working with leaf gelatine it is essential to soak the leaves first in ice-cold water.

- Add each leaf or sheet to the water individually, then leave to soak for about 5 minutes until it is soft. It is important that you add the leaves separately to prevent them from sticking to each other as this can result in not all of the leaf softening. *(1)*

- Squeeze off the excess water and add as directed within the recipe. *(2)*

Using Vanilla

I use vanilla pods (beans) in many of my recipes. This is an easy way to split and scrape the seeds from inside the pod (bean).

- Hold the end of a fresh vanilla pod (bean) on a chopping board and run a sharp knife through the centre of the pod (bean) to cut it in half lengthways. *(1)*

- Lay the halves cut side up and scrape the edge of the knife down the length of the open pod (bean). *(2)*

- The vanilla seeds will collect on the knife and are ready to be added as instructed. The empty split pod (bean) is usually also added for extra flavour. *(3)*

Note: To make crystallized vanilla sticks – cut the leftover scraped pods (beans) into thin strips, then brush with a little syrup and roll in caster (superfine) sugar; leave to dry out for a couple of hours in a dehydrator or low oven. These are used as decorations for some of the dishes and can be stored in an airtight container.

Working with Fondant

Fondant can be heated directly in a saucepan but to help avoid over heating, warm it over a bain-marie (water bath) to slowly heat it. It should be heated to a little below blood temperature, 32–35°C (90–95°F).

You may also need to adjust the consistency a little by adding syrup to soften and make it a good workable consistency. The consistency should be fluid but thick enough to hold its shape for a moment when the mixture is poured into the rest of the fondant. To maintain a soft smooth consistency and attractive sheen, do not overheat the fondant – otherwise the fondant has a tendency to crystallize.

Bain-marie

Ice bain-marie

1

2

1

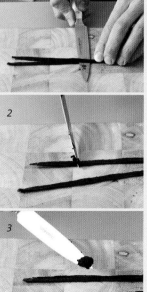

2

3

Heating slowly

Correct consistency

Whipping Cream

The best way to whip is to start with a dry cool bowl (you can pop a bowl in the fridge in advance to keep it cool until you need it). Once the cream is whipped, cling film (plastic wrap) the bowl and put it straight back in the fridge. Use within 1 hour or the cream will begin to fall back. Always make sure your cream is well chilled before using to reduce the chances of it splitting a mixture or mousse. Take care not to overwhip the cream or you risk it turning to butter. For small quantities I like to whisk the cream by hand as it gives more control over its stage. The ribbon stage consistency is ideal for folding into a base for mousses and creams.

Poaching Fruit

Poaching is used to soften fruit and bring out certain flavours, making it ideal for use in pâtisserie. The addition of spices or vanilla and cinnamon can also enhance flavour. It is important to keep the heat low and cook until the fruit is just cooked and softened.

- Prepare a **Light Syrup** *(see page 103)*. Peel and prepare the fruit, cut into halves, place in the syrup and cover with a cartouche (parchment paper disc). *(1)*

- Weigh it down with a wooden lid if required. *(2)* Cook over a gentle heat until the fruit has softened, then cool in the syrup.

Clarified Butter

Clarifying butter removes the milk solids and moisture from the butter, this prevents the milk solids from burning when butter is used for glazing fruits that are baked.

- Put cubes or slices of unsalted butter in a saucepan and melt gently over a low heat.

- Let the butter gently simmer until the white foam rises to the top of the melted butter. *(1)*

- When no more foam seems to be rising to the surface, take the butter off the heat and skim off as much of the foam as you can with a ladle. *(2)*

- Line a sieve (strainer) with a few layers of muslin (cheesecloth) and set over a bowl. Gently pour the butter through the lined sieve (strainer), which will remove any remaining white particles. *(3–4)*

Beurre Noisette

Beurre noisette is made when the milk solids within butter caramelize, creating a nut-like aroma and taste.

- Put cubes of unsalted butter in a saucepan over a medium heat. Let the butter melt, stirring frequently. *(1)*

- Once the butter has melted it will begin to foam a little then subside, continue to cook stirring frequently *(2)* until the milk solids start to turn a light brown. *(3)*

- Remove from the heat and pour into a tray, then leave to cool. *(4)*

Ribbon stage

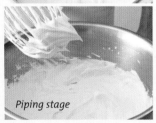

Piping stage

Working with Caramel

Caramel will show up in many of my recipes and I'm a big fan of combining it in different ways with different flavours. The process of caramelization consists of heating sugar slowly to around 170°C (338°F). As the sugar heats, it breaks down the molecules of the sugar forming the colour and aroma we know as caramel. Although it's not difficult to successfully caramelize sugar, if you've never done it before it can be daunting. If you follow these steps and look out for the warning signs then I'm sure you can make the perfect caramel. There are two methods of making caramel: a **wet caramel** and a **dry caramel**.

There are two key things to watch out for when making your caramel – **crystallization** and **burning**.
- Crystallization happens when sugar crystals form together into one big lumpy mass and can be avoided by ensuring your sugar is free of impurities and your pan is clean and dry.
- Sometimes you may find your cookware develops hot spots, so it's important to keep watch during this process to ensure your sugar is heated evenly and does not burn.
- Always use a heavy-based pan that's large enough to allow for expansion – this is especially important for recipes with cream.
- Make your caramel with refined or granulated sugar.

Wet caramel Put the sugar and water in a heavy-based pan and stir together. *(1)* Bring to the boil and brush the sides with water to remove sugar crystals. *(2)* Continue to boil and cook to an amber colour, about 170°C (338°F). *(3–4)* Remove from the heat and plunge the pan into a bowl of cold water. *(5)* Use immediately.

Note: *I use this caramel for dipping buns and sugar decorations.*

1

2

3

4

5

Dry caramel Heat a heavy-based pan. When it is hot, add one-third of the sugar *(1)* and heat slowly, until it forms a light caramel. Use a heatproof spatula or marise and begin to stir. *(2–3)* Add the remaining sugar *(4)* and continue to cook until you get an amber caramel. *(5)* This will take about 10 minutes, but there are lots of variables so you must be vigilant and keep watch while it is cooking. You will now need to add a liquid to break the caramel, such as cream or orange juice.

1

2

3

4

5

Note: *This method gives a more intense flavour and is great for caramels and sauces.*

Working with Chocolate

My first book, Couture Chocolate, *covers working with chocolate in great detail, but here are some important techniques and pointers to do with working with this versatile ingredient.*

Tempering Chocolate

The seeding method is a great way to temper chocolate; it requires no marble and it is very clean. You will need a porringer pot or double boiler – if you have neither of these you will need a classic bain-marie *(see page 31)*, a metal bowl placed over a pan of simmering water, and a thermometer.

> 300g (10½oz) dark (plain/bittersweet) chocolate (anything over 60% cocoa solids) *finely chopped (or use chocolate buttons)*

- Put two-thirds of the chopped chocolate into the porringer pot, double boiler or over a bain-marie (water bath). Do not boil the water as this may scald the chocolate. Stir regularly until all the chocolate has completely melted and has reached 45–50°C (113–122°F), ensuring the chocolate has melted evenly. *(1–2)*

- Gradually add the remaining chocolate – this is the seed. Stir vigorously and continue to stir until all of the chocolate has fully melted and the chocolate cools to 28–29°C (82–84°F) and thickens. Warm up to 31–32°C (87–89°F). The chocolate is now tempered and ready to use. If the temperature drops below this, simply warm it up over the bain-marie again. *(3–4)*

Tempering Tips

- When the chocolate reaches 31–32°C (88–90°F) this is known as the working temperature. The chocolate is tempered and ready to use. To test this manually, dip the end of the palette knife into the chocolate, then leave to set. If the chocolate is smooth and glossy when set *(see right)*, you have successfully tempered your chocolate.

- Be careful when using a bain-marie (water bath) that none of the water or steam gets into the chocolate. Chocolate is made up of cocoa solids, cocoa butter, sugar, vanilla and possibly milk powder. A small drop of water will moisten the ingredients and make the cocoa solids clump together and separate from the butter (in the same way that oil and water do not mix). You should never cover melting chocolate with a lid as the steam will condense and drop into the chocolate.

- Over heating separates the cocoa solids and the other dry ingredients from the cocoa butter; it will begin to burn if over heated, the result being a dry, discoloured paste. There is no retrieving burnt chocolate so be careful when tempering and melting.

- For milk chocolate, follow the same as above and melt to 45–50°C (113–122°F), cool to 26–27°C (79–81°F) and temper at 29–30°C (84–86°F). For white chocolate, follow the same as above and melt to 45°C (113°F), cool to 26–27°C (79–81°F) and temper at 29–30°C (84–86°F).

UNTEMPERED CHOCOLATE

TEMPERED CHOCOLATE

Spraying Chocolate

Finishing entremets with sprayed chocolate creates a wonderful velvety finish. Chocolate itself is too thick to spray so a solution is made with the addition of cocoa butter to thin it enough to feed through the spray gun.

For dark (bittersweet) spraying chocolate:
150g (5½oz) fine dark (bittersweet) chocolate
100g (3½oz) cocoa butter

For white spraying chocolate:
100g (3½oz) white chocolate
100g (3½oz) cocoa butter

- Demould the product required for spraying and place on a wire rack set over a metal tray. Return to the freezer until ready to spray.

- Melt the cocoa spraying solution, then leave to cool to 32–35°C (90–95°F). Place the spray gun in a warm area so it reaches 30°C (86°F) – on top of a warm oven is a good place.

- Prepare an area for spraying – I like to use a large plastic container that can easily be cleaned. Pass the mixture through a fine sieve (strainer) to remove any large particles and fill the spray gun with the spraying solution. Take the prepared products from the freezer and place into the prepared spraying area.

- Stand at a distance of around 1 metre (40 inches) away, turn on the spray gun and spray the product with a continuous motion, turning it around for full coverage. You may need to return the sprayed product to the freezer for 5 minutes, then repeat for a second coat.

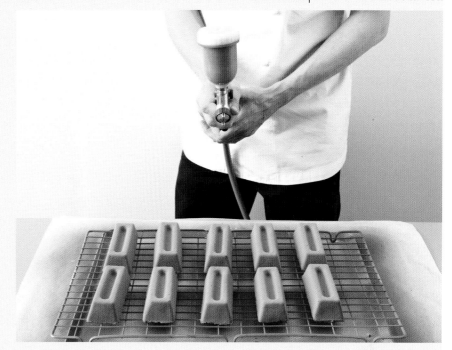

Glazing Entremets & Petits Gâteaux

Finishing entremets or petits gâteaux with a glaze creates a wonderfully shiny and glossy finish. Unlike spraying there is no specialized equipment involved.

- Place a wire cooling rack onto a tray with sides to catch any excess glaze.

- Demould the product required for glazing and place back into the freezer. *(1–2)*

- Prepare the glaze as instructed in the recipe and place into a jug for pouring. When the glaze is at the correct temperature, take the product from the freezer and place it on the wire rack.

- Gently pour the glaze over the product, paying close attention to corners and sides to make sure that it is evenly coated. For a smooth shiny finish, you should glaze slowly and in one fluid action. *(3–4)*

- Gently run a palette knife across the top of the entremet ensuring a thin coating. *(5)* Place in the fridge and leave to set. *(6)*

The Foundation

The recipes in the following chapter form the basis of what
we do and are the essentials for what we learn as pâtissiers.
When I was a young apprentice these were the first jobs
I was taught, forming the foundation of our craft.
From a classic Baba au Rhum to a stunning Entremet,
you will always need these recipes to get you through.

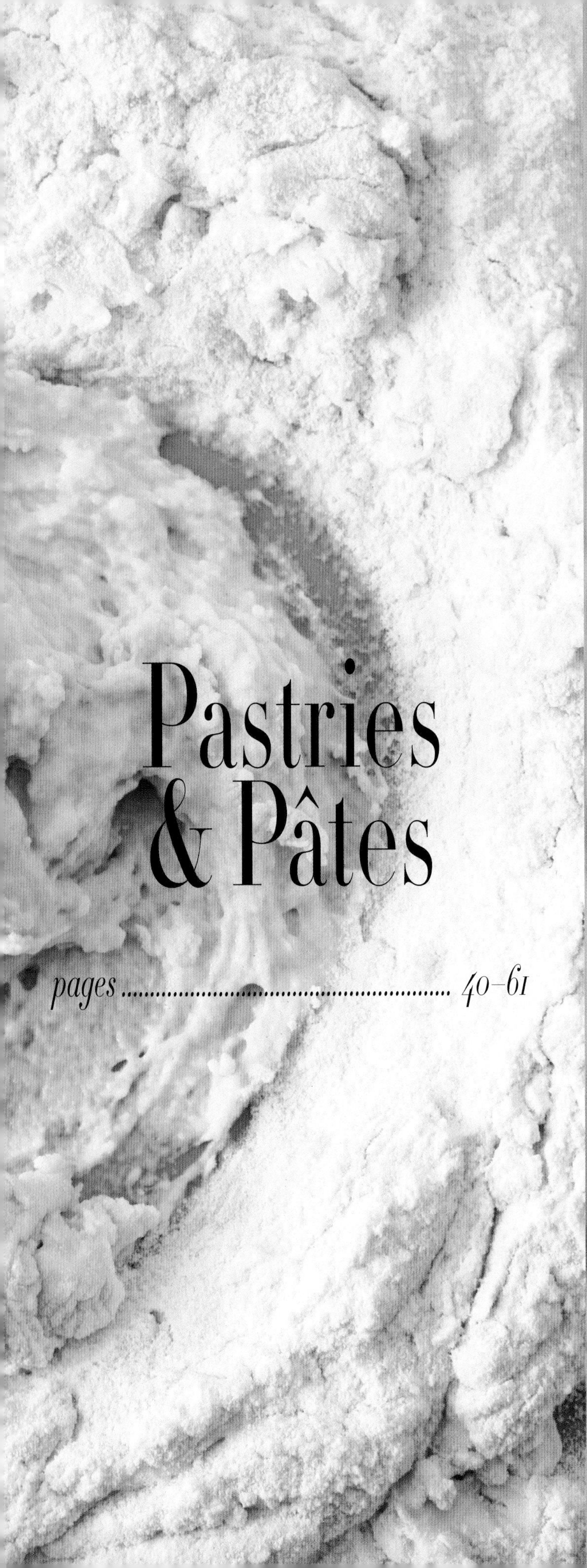

Pastries & Pâtes

Leavened Doughs

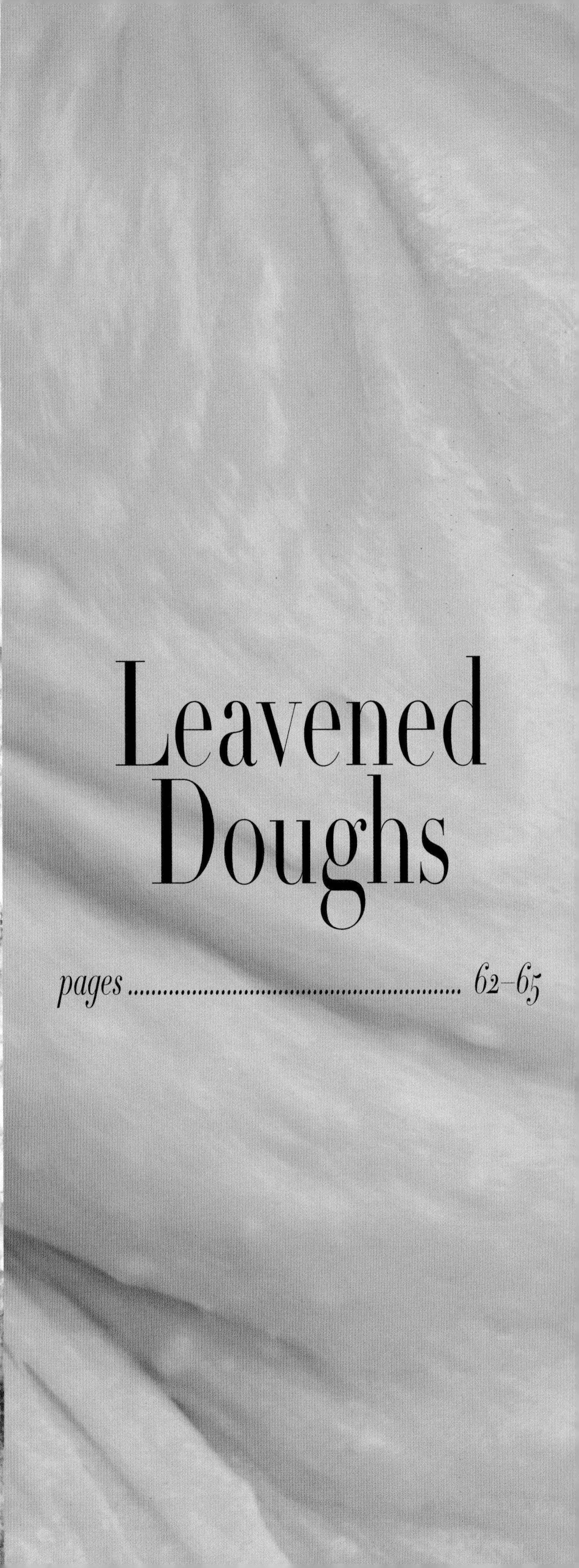

Sponges

Meringues & Dacquoise

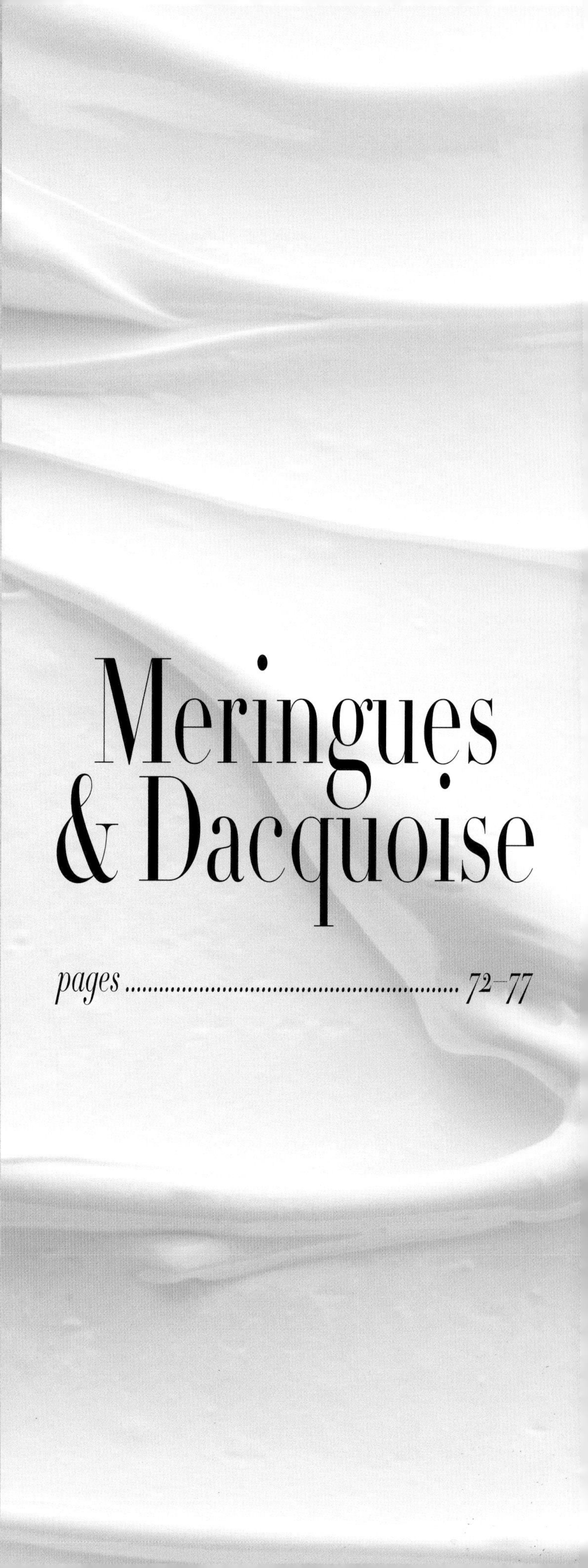

*There are two main methods for making a pastry dough:
the crumbing method and the creaming method.*

The Crumbing Method

All the dry ingredients (flour, salt and sugar) and butter are placed into a bowl and rubbed together until there are no lumps of butter – you should stop rubbing before the mixture becomes a paste. When the butter has no more lumps, the liquids (eggs and sometimes water) are added and mixed to a paste.

1

- Put the dry ingredients directly on the work surface, make a well in the centre and add the cubed butter. *(1)*

- Use your fingers to rub the flour and butter together until no lumps of butter remain. *(2–4)*

- Make a well in the centre again and add the wet ingredients. *(5–6)*

- Use your fingers to mix the wet and dry ingredients together to form a smooth, homogenous dough. *(7–9)*

- Shape the dough into a block, wrap it in cling film (plastic wrap) and put it in the fridge to rest for 2–3 hours. *(10–11)*

Note: *see pages 46–49 for specific pastry recipes.*

5

9

> ### Rubbing In
> Fat inhibits the formation of gluten strands – this is particularly the case in pastes and doughs. When fat is rubbed with flour it coats the particles of flour, which limits the flour's ability to absorb water and the ability for the gluten to form. This term is called shortening. Short pastry dough has a crumbly and soft, yet crisp texture.

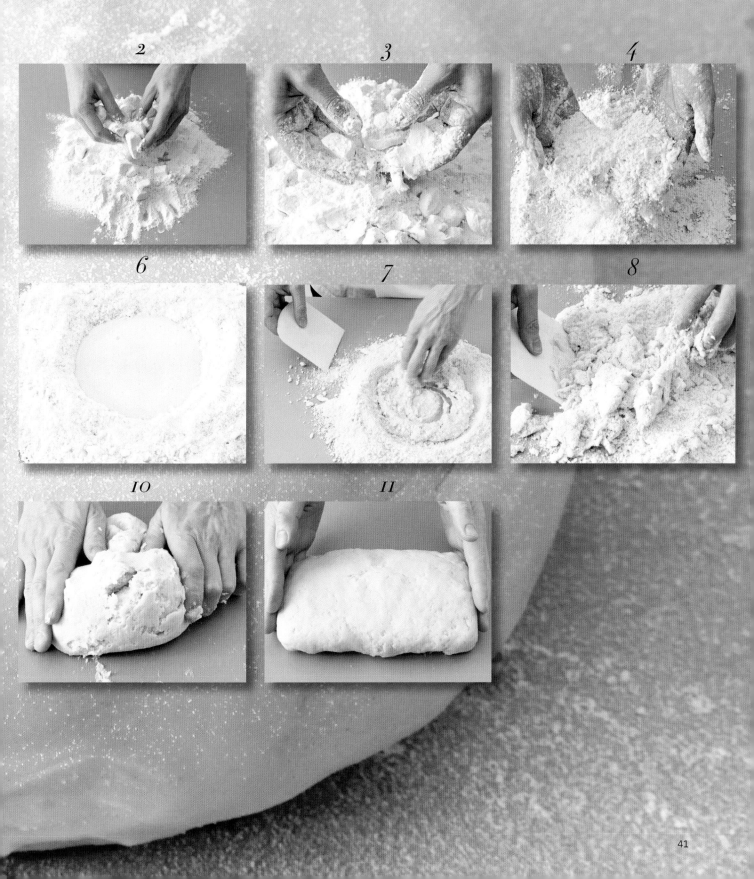

2

3

4

6

7

8

10

11

The Creaming Method

The butter and the sugar are placed into a mixing bowl and gently beaten until smooth, before the liquids (eggs, milk and sometimes water) are gradually added. The dry ingredients (flour, salt and sugar) are then added and mixed together to form a paste.

- Put the butter in a mixing bowl and beat until soft and smooth. *(1)*

- Add the icing (powdered) sugar and vanilla seeds (if required) and beat together until smooth. *(2–3)*

- Gradually incorporate the eggs, until they become fully mixed and emulsified. *(4–5)*

- Put the dry ingredients directly on the work surface. Make a well in the centre and use a spatula to spoon the butter mix into the middle of the flour. *(6)*

- Use your hands or a pastry scraper to gradually work the flour and butter mixture together. *(7–8)*

- Use your fingers to mix the wet and dry ingredients together to form a smooth, homogenous dough. *(9–10)*

- Make the dough into a block and wrap it in cling film (plastic wrap). Put it in the fridge to rest for 2–3 hours. *(11)*

Note: *see pages 46–49 for specific pastry recipes.*

1

5

9

2

3

4

6

7

8

10

11

Lining & Blind Baking

Lining Tins with Pastry

- Take the rested dough from the fridge and place on a lightly floured work surface. Cut into manageable pieces and work gently on the bench to soften and make it more pliable for rolling. *(1–2)*

- Make the dough into a ball again; it is now ready to begin rolling. *(3–4)*

- Roll the dough out to the desired thickness, lightly flouring the work surface and dough when required to make sure that it does not stick. *(5)*

- Cut the dough to the desired size for the tart, this should be about 3–5cm (1¼–2 inches) bigger than the tart ring or tin, depending on the size and depth of the tart. Gently place the rolled dough into the base of the tart ring or tin. *(6)*

- Gently push the dough into place, ensuring that it sits against the edge and is pushed into the bottom corners. *(7)*

- Place the lined ring or tin onto a baking tray (sheet) lined with a non-stick baking mat or silicone paper.

- Trim the edges gently by running the rolling pin over the top edge of the tin. *(8)*

- Use your fingers to ensure the pastry is pressed into the side of the tin and lightly pinch up the edges to form a little crest. *(9)*

- Prick the base of the pastry all over with a fork. *(10)* Place in the fridge to rest for at least 30 minutes.

Note: recipes for doughs are made with specific amounts of flour. When rolling out doughs for lining tarts, use only the minimum amount to prevent it from sticking to the bench.

1

6

Blind Baking

- First, you need to make a circle of silicone paper: fold a sheet in half, now fold it in half again across the other side. *(1–2)*

- Fold one corner to another; you should now have a triangle. *(3)*

- Now fold the triangle in half twice again; you should have a long, thin triangle. *(4)*

- Hold the triangle's point in the centre of the tart case and cut it to about 2.5cm (1 inch) larger than the tart. *(5–6)*

- Unfold and place the circle of silicone paper into the lined tart. *(7)*

- Ensure the paper fills the tart base and pushes up against the sides. *(8)*

- Generously top the paper circle with baking beans so that the tart base is completely covered. *(9)* Rest for at least 30 minutes.

- Transfer the tart to a preheated oven and bake until the edges are lightly golden. Remove the tart from the oven, carefully remove the beans from the tart case, then return the tart to the oven to continue cooking until the base of the tart is also lightly golden. *(10)*

1

6

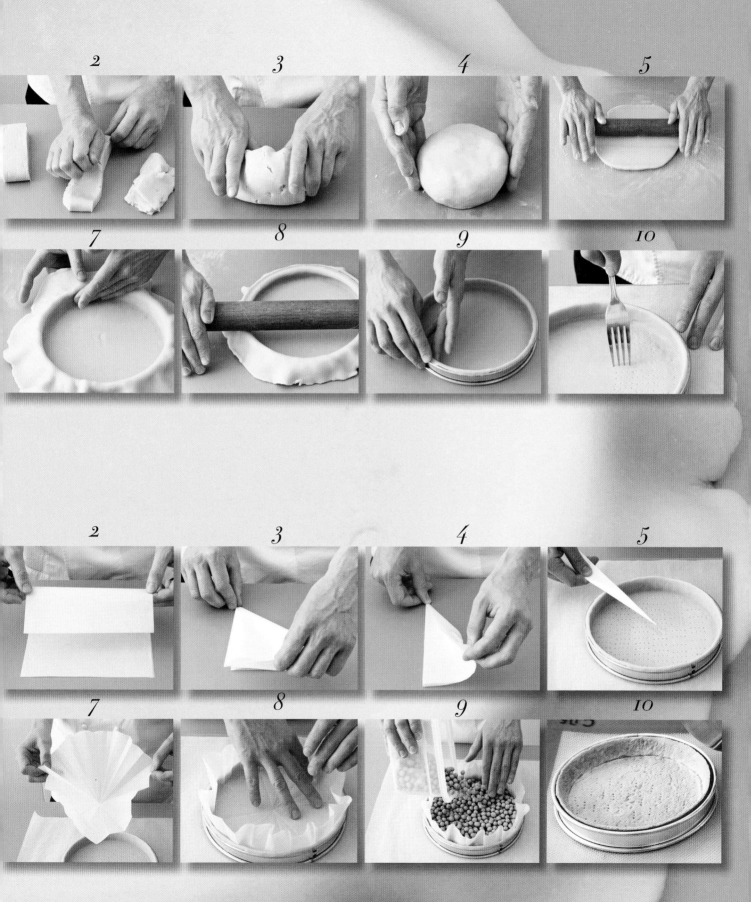

2   3   4   5

7   8   9   10

2   3   4   5

7   8   9   10

Pâte Brisée
Crumbing method

Literally translated *pâte brisée* means 'broken dough', which describes the flaky, layered texture of the finished pastry. The addition of the eggs creates a firmer and sturdier finished pastry. *Pâte Brisée* can be used for all manner of tarts. The key, like with all pastry, is the quality of the butter.

Makes 950g (2¼lb)

500g (1lb 2oz/3½ cups) plain
   (all-purpose) flour *sifted*
10g (¼oz) salt
20g (¾oz) caster (superfine) sugar
300g (10½oz/1⅓ cups)
   cold unsalted butter *cubed*
40g (1½oz) egg yolks *(about 2 eggs)*
80ml (3½fl oz/⅓ cup) water

- Put the dry ingredients directly on the work surface. Add the cubed butter and rub together until no lumps of butter remain.

- Make a well in the centre, add the wet ingredients and mix to form a smooth, homogenous mass.

- Shape the dough into a block and wrap it in cling film (plastic wrap). Put the dough in the fridge to rest for 2–3 hours.

This pastry can be kept refrigerated for 3 days and frozen for up to 1 month.

Used in
Tarte Alsacienne
(pages 142–143)
Fig & Hazelnut Tart
(pages 140–141)

Pâte Sablée
Crumbing method

Translated, *pâte sablée* means 'sandy dough' because of the crumbing method (also known as 'sanding' in French) that is used to make it. This is a delicate dough used for biscuits and sweet tarts. It is more enriched than the *Pâte Sucrée (see opposite)* and the texture is more crumbly and buttery.

Makes 1kg (2¼lb)

500g (1lb 2oz/3½ cups)
   plain (all-purpose) flour *sifted*
1g (a pinch) salt
200g (7oz/¾ cup) icing (powdered) sugar *sifted*
350g (12oz/1½ cups)
   cold unsalted butter *cubed*
30g (1¼oz) egg yolks *(about 1 egg)*
½ vanilla pod (bean) *split lengthways*

- Put the dry ingredients directly on the work surface. Add the cubed butter and the seeds scraped from the split vanilla pod (bean) and rub together until no lumps of butter remain.

- Make a well in the centre, add the egg yolks and mix to form a smooth, homogenous mass.

- Shape the dough into a block and wrap it in cling film (plastic wrap). Put the dough in the fridge to rest for 2–3 hours.

This pastry can be kept refrigerated for 3 days and frozen for up to 1 month.

Used in
Rhubarb & Ginger Sablé
(pages 160–161)

Pâte Sucrée
Creaming method

Literally translated, *pâte sucrée* means 'sugared dough'. It is similar to the *Pâte Brisée (see opposite)*, but with the addition of sugar and a higher proportion of eggs. This results in a more golden colour when baked as a result of the sugar caramelizing.

Makes 1kg (2¼lb)

250g (9oz/generous 1 cup)
   room temperature unsalted butter *cubed*
200g (7oz/¾ cup) icing
   (powdered) sugar *sifted*
100g (3½oz) whole eggs
   (about 2 eggs)
500g (1lb 2oz/3½ cups) plain
   (all-purpose) flour *sifted*
3g (½ tsp) salt

• Put the butter in a mixing bowl and beat until soft and smooth. Add the icing (powdered) sugar and beat together until smooth.

• Gradually incorporate the eggs, making sure the mixture becomes fully emulsified.

• Mix in the flour and salt and mix to a smooth, homogeneous mass.

• Turn the dough out onto the work surface, shape it into a block and wrap it in cling film (plastic wrap). Put the dough in the fridge to rest for 2–3 hours.

This pastry can be kept refrigerated for 3 days and frozen for up to 1 month.

Used in
Bakewell Tarts
(pages 144–145)

Tarte Bourdeloue
(pages 150–151)

Lemon Meringue Tarts
(pages 146–147)

Chocolate & Cherry Linzer Tarts *(pages 148–149)*

**Passion Fruit
& Pink Grapefruit Tart**
(pages 152–153)

Hazelnut & Almond Pastry
Creaming method

This recipe is a derivative of the *pâte sucrée*, with the ground nuts adding richness and flavour.

Makes 1.3kg (2lb 12oz)

375g (13oz/1⅔ cups) room temperature unsalted
   butter *cubed*
155g (5½oz) icing (powdered) sugar *sifted*
125g (4½oz) whole eggs *(about 2½ eggs)*
500g (1lb 2oz/3½ cups)
   plain (all-purpose) flour *sifted*
85g (3½oz/¾ cup) ground hazelnuts
85g (3½oz/¾ cup) ground almonds
2g (¼ tsp) salt

• Put the butter in a mixing bowl and beat until soft and smooth. Add the icing (powdered) sugar and beat together until smooth.

• Gradually incorporate the eggs, making sure the mixture becomes fully emulsified.

• Mix in the flour, ground nuts and salt and mix to a smooth, homogeneous mass.

• Turn the dough out onto the work surface, shape it into a block and wrap it in cling film (plastic wrap). Put the dough in the fridge to rest for 2–3 hours.

This pastry can be kept refrigerated for 3 days and frozen for up to 1 month.

Variation: *this can also be made into just an almond pastry by replacing the ground hazelnuts with the same amount of ground almonds.*

How much pastry?
About 1kg (2¼lb) dough will make 3–4 large tarts or 20–24 individual tarts. Wrap any leftover well and refrigerate or freeze for future use.

Used in
Yuzu & Praline Tarts
(pages 158–159)

Mirlitons d'Amiens
(pages 156–157)

Sable Breton

This pâte is enriched using egg yolks and flavoured with sea salt. It originates from the Brittany region in France, which is famous for its salt.

Makes 1.3kg (2lb 12oz)

500g (1lb 2oz/3½ cups) plain (all-purpose) flour *sifted*
16g (3 tsp/½ oz) baking powder
3g (½ tsp) sea salt
375g (13oz/1⅓ cups) room temperature unsalted butter *cubed*
150g (5½oz) egg yolks *(about 7½ eggs)*
325g (11oz/1⅓ cups) caster (superfine) sugar

- Sift together the flour, baking powder and salt.
- Put the butter in a mixing bowl and beat until soft and smooth. *(1)*
- Put the egg yolks and sugar in a separate mixing bowl and whisk until light in colour. *(2)*
- Add the softened butter to the eggs and sugar mixture and mix together until fully incorporated. *(3)*
- Fold in the sifted dry ingredients. *(4–5)*
- Mix together to form a dough. *(6–7)*
- Roll out the dough between two sheets of silicone baking paper and bars of the desired thickness, then put it in the fridge to rest for 2–3 hours. *(8)*

This pastry should be used the same day as it is made, or can be frozen for up to 1 month.

Used in
Strawberry & Pistachio Breton Tart
(pages 162–163)
Caramelized Pear, Blackcurrant & Chocolate Breton
(pages 164–165)

1

2

3

4

5

6

7

8

Feuilletage

Literally translated, the French term *pâte feuilletée* or *feuilletage* means 'leaved dough' and refers to its thin layers. This method of making a dough is known as laminating. The lamination is created by folding the dough and creating layers of dough and butter. The layers trap pockets of air in between them and when baked the moisture in the dough and the melting of the butter creates steam that forces the layers to rise, puffing up the pastry and creating a flaky and light texture.

There are several specialized terms referred to in the making of feuilletage:

- **Détrempe** – a simple dough composed of flour, salt, water and butter.
- **Beurrage** – a block of butter, sometimes with a little flour.
- **Paton** – the détrempe is folded around the beurrage to form the paton.
- **Tourage** – the paton is rolled and folded to form turns.

There are three types of **feuilletage**: **pâte feuilletée**, **feuilletage rapide** and **pâte feuilletée inverse**.

Used in
Chausson aux Pommes *(pages 166–167)*
Gâteau St Honoré *(pages 168–170)*

Pâte Feuilletée

This classic feuilletage is referred to as puff pastry in English and is the most frequently used method for feuilletage. It is suitable for most preparations, although time-consuming to prepare because of the resting time. The result is a crisp, buttery, layered pastry with an even rise.

Makes 1.2kg (2lb 10oz)

250g (9oz/1¾ cups) plain (all-purpose) flour *sifted*
250g (9oz/1¾ cups) strong flour *sifted*
10g (¼oz/2 tsp) salt
50g (1¾oz/½ stick) cold unsalted butter, *cubed*, plus
   450g (1lb/2 cups) unsalted butter *shaped into a square 15 x 15cm (6 x 6 inches)*
200ml (7fl oz/scant 1 cup) cold water

- Firstly make the détrempe: place the dry ingredients directly on the work surface. Add the 50g (1¾oz) cubed butter and rub it into the flour until no lumps of butter are left. *(1–2)*
- Make a well in the centre and add the water. *(3)*
- Use your fingers to mix together to form a smooth, homogenous mass. *(4)*
- Knead until the dough becomes smooth and elastic. *(5)*
- Shape the dough into a ball and cut a cross in the top about 2.5cm (1 inch) deep. *(6)*
- Wrap in cling film (plastic wrap) and put in the fridge to rest for 1 hour. *(7)*
- Take the détrempe out of the fridge and push out and roll each quarter until a cross is formed. *(8–9)*
- Place the 450g (1lb) rectangle of butter in the centre. *(10)*
- Fold each of the flaps over to encase the butter within the détrempe. *(11)*
- Begin to roll the paton and then make 2 turns *(see pages 52–53 for all turning instructions)*. Wrap the dough and rest in the fridge for at least 1 hour. *(12)*
- Take the paton out of the fridge, unwrap and make another 2 turns. Wrap the dough and rest in the fridge for at least 1 hour.
- Take the paton out of the fridge and make another 2 turns. Wrap the dough and rest in the fridge for at least 1 hour. You should now have completed 6 turns and the feuilletage classic is finished.

This pastry can be kept refrigerated for 2 days and frozen for up to 1 month.

Turning the puff pastry

When turning puff pastry we make 2 turns at once, then the puff pastry is rested for at least 1 hour before turning again.

- Starting from the paton, the feuilletage classic *(see pages 50–51)* and inverse *(see pages 54–55)* both have 6 turns in total and the rough puff pastry has 4 turns in total.

- Roll the paton to create a 60 x 30cm (24 x 12 inch) rectangle. *(1–3)*

- Brush off any excess flour with a pastry brush. *(4)*

- Fold one short side over so that the edge lies at two-thirds of the length of the rectangle. *(5)*

- Fold the other short side over this to make 3 layers. *(6)*

- This is the first turn. *(7)*

- Rotate the rectangle 90 degrees. *(8)*

- Roll out again. *(9)*

- Repeat the process of folding the paton (this is your second turn). *(10)*

- Use two fingertips to make 2 indentations in one corner so that you will know how many turns you have completed. *(11)*

- Wrap in cling film (plastic wrap) and put in the fridge to rest for 1 hour. Continue like this for as many turns as instructed.

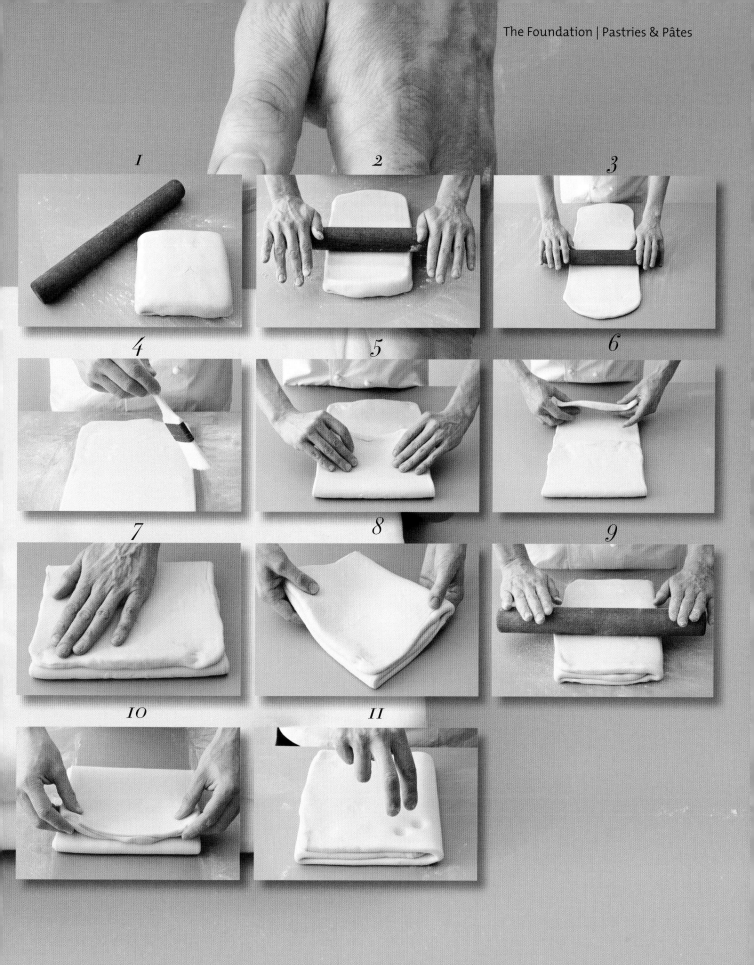

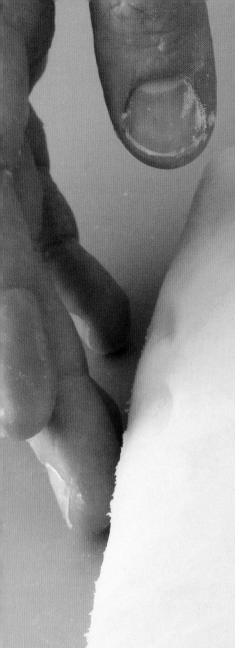

Feuilletage Inverse

As the name suggests, this puff pastry is made in the inverted or reverse method. The positions of the détrempe and the beurrage are reversed so that the beurrage is on the outside rather than encased. This pastry has a more delicate and tender flake than the pâte feuilletée. Feuilletage inverse has recently been popularized by Pierre Hermé.

Makes 1kg (2¼lb)

300g (10½oz/generous 2 cups) strong flour *sifted*
200g (7oz/scant 1½ cups) plain (all-purpose) flour *sifted*
400g (14oz/1¾ cups) cold unsalted butter *cubed*,
  plus 60g (2oz/½ stick) softened unsalted butter
10g (¼oz/2 tsp) salt
140ml (4½fl oz/1⅓ cups) water

- Firstly make the beurrage: put 50g (1¾oz/⅓ cup) of the strong flour, 50g (1¾oz/⅓ cup) of the plain (all-purpose) flour and the 400g (14oz/1¾ cups) cubed unsalted butter on a clean work surface and knead together until fully combined. Shape the beurrage into a square, wrap in cling film (plastic wrap) and put in the fridge to rest for at least 1 hour.

- For the détrempe, place the remaining flours and the salt on the work surface. Add the 60g (2oz) of softened butter and rub into the flour so that no lumps of butter are left. *(1)*

- Gradually add the water and mix together to form a smooth, homogenous mass. Knead until the dough becomes smooth and elastic, wrap in cling film (plastic wrap) and put in the fridge to rest for 1 hour. *(2)*

- Take the beurrage and the détrempe from the fridge and make sure they are a similar consistency. *(3)*

- Roll the beurrage into a large square big enough to encase the détrempe. *(4)*

- Place the détrempe on top; it should look like a square in a diamond. *(5)*

- Fold over the flaps so that the détrempe is encased by the beurrage and then seal by pinching the beurrage together. *(6)*

- Begin to roll the dough and then make 2 turns *(see page 52)*. Wrap the dough and rest in the fridge for at least 1 hour.

- Take the dough out of the fridge, unwrap and make another 2 turns. Wrap the dough and rest in the fridge for at least 1 hour. *(7)*

- Take the dough out of the fridge, unwrap and make another 2 turns. Wrap the dough and rest in the fridge for at least 1 hour. You should have completed 6 turns and the feuilletage inverse is finished.

This pastry can be kept refrigerated for 2 days and frozen for up to 1 month.

1

2

3

4

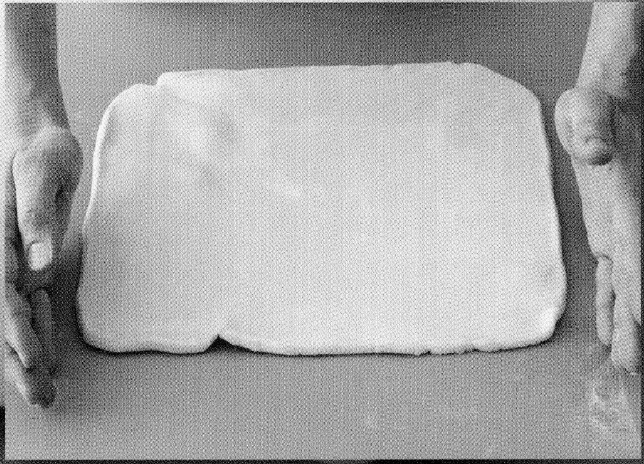

5

6

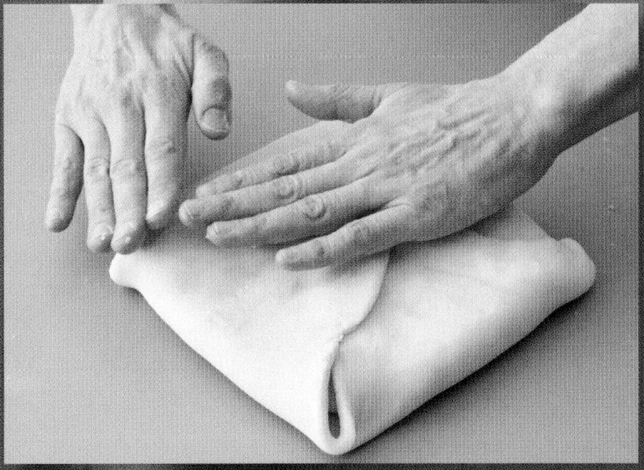

7

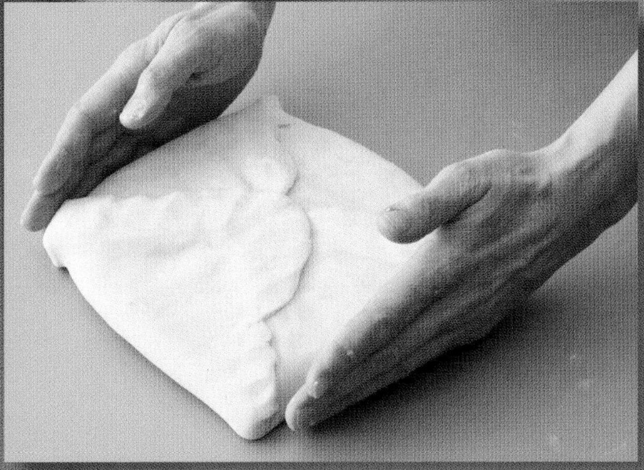

Used in
Chestnut Pithivier
(pages 171–173)
Gâteau Mille-feuille
(pages 174–175)

Feuilletage Rapide

This is a quick method for puff pastry and is often referred to as rough puff pastry. The butter is mixed through the détrempe in large pieces, then turned to create the layers. It does not rise as high or as evenly as the other methods.

Makes 1.2kg (2lb 10oz)

250g (9oz/1⅔ cups) plain (all-purpose) flour *sifted*
250g (9oz/1⅔ cups) strong flour *sifted*
10g (¼oz/2 tsp) salt
500g (1lb 2oz/2¼ cups) unsalted butter *cubed*
225ml (7½fl oz/1 cup) cold water

- Sift the flours and salt onto a clean work surface, make a well in the centre and add the cubed butter. Using your fingertips, work the ingredients together until the lumps of butter become smaller and the mixture becomes grainy. *(1–2)*

- Make a well in the centre and pour in the cold water, mixing until the dough starts to come together. *(3)*

- Form the dough into a mass that still contains flakes of butter – but do not knead. *(4)*

- Wrap the dough in cling film (plastic wrap) and rest in the fridge for at least 30 minutes.

- Take the paton out of the fridge, unwrap, begin to roll the dough and make 2 turns *(see page 52)* – then roll the dough to 50 x 25cm (20 x 10 inches). Wrap the dough and rest in the fridge for at least 1 hour.

- Take the paton out of the fridge and make another 2 turns. Wrap the dough and rest in the fridge for at least 1 hour. You should now have completed 4 turns and the feuilletage rapide is finished.

This pastry can be kept refrigerated for 2 days and frozen for up to 1 month.

Used in
Thin Mango Tart *(pages 180–181)*
Pineapple Tarte Tatin *(pages 182–184)*
Gâteau Conversation *(pages 176–177)*
Puits d'Amour *(pages 178–179)*

Pâte à Choux

Catherine de Medici's chef created the first version of choux pastry in around 1540. Originally it was known as *pâte à panterelli* after the chef. Later it became known as *pâte à popelini*, then *pâte à popelin*. Popelins were cakes made in the Middle Ages in the shape of woman's breasts. A pâtissier called Avice developed the paste during the 18th century and created choux buns. Marie-Antonin Carême went on to perfect the recipe in the 19th century and that is what we know today as pâte à choux.

Makes 800g (1lb 12oz)

125ml (4fl oz/½ cup) water
125ml (4fl oz/½ cup) milk
125g (4½oz/generous 1 stick) unsalted butter *cubed*
12g (¼oz) caster (superfine) sugar
162g (5½oz/generous 1 cup) plain (all-purpose) flour *sifted*
2g (¼ tsp/a pinch) salt
250g (9oz) whole eggs *(about 5 eggs) beaten*

- Heat the water, milk, butter and sugar in a saucepan. Bring up to the boil. *(1)*

- Take the pan off the heat and add the sifted flour and salt. *(2)*

- Use a spatula to stir until completely combined. *(3)*

- Return the pan to the hob, reduce the heat to low and continue stirring with a spatula until the dough leaves the sides of the pan. *(4)*

- Take off the heat, transfer the dough to a mixing bowl and leave to cool for 2–3 minutes, stirring occasionally.

- Gradually add the beaten eggs into the dough. *(5)*

- Beat with a spatula until the mixture is smooth. The consistency should be neither too soft nor too hard; it should drop off the spoon leaving a smooth 'V' shape. *(6)*

- The choux dough is now ready to be piped into shapes and should be used immediately.

Note: *when cooking choux pastry it is vital that you do not open the oven for 12–15 minutes after placing the choux into the oven. Choux pastry rises when the moisture in the dough heats and creates steam; if the oven is opened before the outside of the dough has time to cook, the steam comes out of the paste and the pastry collapses.*

4

5

6

Used in
Chocolate Eclairs
(pages 192–193)
Matcha Eclairs
(pages 191–193)
Choux à la Crème
(pages 188–190)
Gâteau St Honoré
(pages 168–170)

Pâte Filo

This is also known as *pâte pastis*, which I learnt while in the kitchens of Pierre Koffmann. There are several different types of pastis that differ from region to region. *Pastis Bourrit*, which originated from the Basque region of France, is a type of brioche that is sweetened and flavoured with lemon zest and rum and typically served hot and dredged in icing sugar. Pastis from Béarn, which I use in this book, is traditionally very thin rounds of pastry, which are brushed with oil and honey, placed on top of each other and cooked in a hot oven.

Makes 900g (1lb 14oz)

500g (1lb 2oz/3½ cups)
  very fine flour (type 00 pasta flour) *sifted*
2g (a pinch) salt
80g (3oz) egg yolks *(about 4 eggs)*
200ml (7fl oz/scant 1 cup) warm water *(about 37°C/99°F)*
120g (4oz) egg whites *(about 4 eggs)*
20g (¾oz) caster (superfine) sugar
15ml (½oz/1 tbsp) rapeseed oil *plus a little extra for coating*

- Mix the sifted flour and salt together in a mixing bowl.

- Whisk the egg yolks in a bowl until light in colour, then mix with the warm water. *(1)*

- Put the egg whites in a bowl with the sugar and mix to a light meringue. *(2)*

- Add the egg yolk mixture to the light meringue and mix until combined. *(3)*

- Make a well with the flour and salt and add the egg mixture, then work to form a dough. *(4–6)*

- Work the dough on the surface for 15–20 minutes until the dough becomes elastic. *(7–10)*

- Make a slight well in the dough and pour in the oil. Continue to work the dough until the oil is completely absorbed and will release from the working surface. *(11–13)*

- Split the finished dough into 2 pieces. Coat with a little extra oil, wrap in cling film (plastic wrap) and put in the fridge to rest for at least 2–3 hours. *(14–15)*

*This pastry can be kept refrigerated for 1 day
and frozen for up to 1 month.*

Used in
Croustade aux Pommes
(pages 185–187)

There are two main methods for making fermented doughs: the straight or direct method and the pre-ferment method.

For the **Brioche** *(see page 64)* and **Beignet Alsacienne** *(see pages 206–207)*, I use a straight dough method. This is the simplest way of making fermented doughs. The flour, salt, yeast and liquids are brought together in a mixing bowl and kneaded until smooth and elastic, then the soft butter is added gradually until incorporated and kneaded again until it is elastic.

For the **Pâte à Savarin** *(see opposite)*, I use a Polish pre-ferment method where the yeast, milk and some of the flour are mixed together and allowed to develop at room temperature. This particular method adds to the flavour and crumb characteristics of the baked dough.

Pâte à Savarin

A rich fermented dough, which is proved and baked. It is then soaked in sweet syrup flavoured traditionally with rum. It was created by the famous Julien brothers *(see page 12)* in 1834, when Auguste saw some pâtissiers soaking Genoese sponges. Inspired by this idea, he experimented with new recipes and different types of syrup. One of his brother's creations was the Savarin, initially made with wheat flour, sugar, eggs, diced orange peel, salt, yeast and milk and placed in a special ring mould sprinkled with nibbed almonds. The Savarin was then soaked with the syrup specially created by Auguste.

Makes 550g (1lb 4oz)

60ml (2¼fl oz/¼ cup) milk
20g (¾oz) fresh yeast
230g (8oz/1⅔ cups) plain (all-purpose) flour *sifted*
20g (¾oz) caster (superfine) sugar
1g (a pinch) salt
150g (5½oz) whole eggs *(about 3 eggs)*
100g (3½oz/scant 1 stick) softened unsalted butter *plus a little extra for greasing*

- Put the milk in a saucepan and heat gently to a temperature of around 30–34°C (86–93°F) – be careful not to overheat or you will kill the yeast. Add to the yeast and stir until it is dissolved. *(1)*

- Mix in 30g (1oz) of the sifted flour and leave in a warm place for about 20 minutes until doubled in size (this is the sponge ferment). *(2–4)*

- Put the remaining flour, sugar and salt in the bowl of an electric mixer and combine. Add the eggs and the sponge ferment and mix on a moderate speed with a dough hook until the dough comes away from the side of the bowl, about 10–12 minutes. Add the butter and continue to mix for 2–3 minutes until combined. *(5–8)*

- Pour the mixture into a large bowl and cover with cling film (plastic wrap). *(9)*

- Leave the mixture to prove in a warm area until it has doubled in size, about 45 minutes. Knock back the dough. *(10–12)*

Use immediately.

Used in
Savarin au Pêche
(pages 200–201)
Baba au Rhum
(pages 198–199)

Brioche

Brioche is a rich fermented dough that can be moulded into a variety of designs, each design having a different name. Known as Apostle or prophet cake in the 17th century, brioche originated from the Brie region, north of Paris, which is more famous for its cheese. The original brioche had Brie cheese added to it to give it flavour. At a later date the water was replaced with milk, eggs were added and finally butter introduced. At some point the Brie cheese was excluded from the recipe.

Makes 1.25kg (2lb 12oz)

15g (½oz) fresh yeast
70ml (2¾fl oz/⅓ cup) full-fat milk
500g (1lb 2oz/3½ cups) strong flour *sifted*
14g (½oz/1 tbsp) salt
30g (1¼oz/2 tbsp) caster (superfine) sugar
300g (10½oz) whole eggs *(about 6 eggs)*
350g (12oz/1½ cups) softened unsalted butter *cubed*

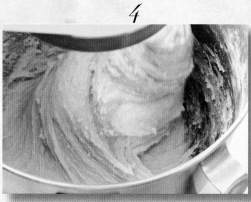

- Put the yeast in a small bowl and pour in the milk. Whisk together. *(1)*

- Sift together the flour, salt and sugar and put into the bowl of an electric mixer fitted with a dough hook. Add the eggs to the flour mixture with the yeast mixture and beat together. *(2–3)*

- Continue beating for 10–12 minutes until the mixture is elastic and comes away from the sides. *(4)*

- Add the softened butter to the dough in the machine bowl. *(5)*

- Continue to beat until the mixture comes away from the sides again. *(6–7)*

- Cover with cling film (plastic wrap) and leave the mixture to prove in a warm area for about 45 minutes. *(8–9)*

- Knock back, cover with cling film (plastic wrap), then place in the fridge for at least 1 hour. *(10–11)*

Use immediately.

2

3

5

6

8

9

II

Used in
Bostock
(pages 204–205)
Brioche Polonaise
(pages 202–203)

Sponges are made using three main methods: the sabayon method, the split-mix method or the meringue method.

The **Sabayon method** places the whole eggs with the sugar, which is gently warmed to blood temperature, whisked until the mixture is full in volume with a ribbon stage *(see page 29)*, before the dry ingredients are folded in.

Genoise
Sabayon method

Genoise is a sponge cake named after the city of Genoa. It was created by an Italian pâtissier working in Bordeaux. He was observed by August Julien, who took the recipe back to his pâtisserie that he worked at in Paris and named it after the Genoise pâtissier who created it. The air is incorporated in the sponge through warming and whisking of the eggs to create a light foam mixture to which the flour is then folded through.

Makes two 30 x 40cm (12 x 16 inch) baking trays (sheets)

300g (10½oz) whole eggs *(about 6 eggs)*
300g (10½oz/1½ cups) caster (superfine) sugar
300g (10½oz/generous 2 cups)
  plain (all-purpose) flour *sifted*
125g (4½oz/generous ½ cup) unsalted butter *melted*

- Preheat the oven to 190°C (375°F/Gas 5) and line two 30 x 40cm (12 x 16 inch) baking trays (sheets) with silicone paper (you could also use a non-stick baking mat of the same size).

- Put the eggs and sugar in a clean, sterilized bowl. Whisk over a bain-marie *(see page 31)* to 37°C (99°F). *(1)*

- Remove the bowl from the pan of water and continue to whisk to the ribbon stage *(see page 29)*. *(2)*

- Carefully begin to fold the flour through the whisked sabayon mixture using a spatula. *(3)*

- When the flour is three-quarters folded through, take 2 large scoops of the mixture and add it to the melted butter. *(4)*

- Add the butter mixture to the base sabayon mixture and continue to fold through. Mix until the mixture is incorporated and smooth. *(5)*

- Pour into the prepared baking trays (sheets) or non-stick baking mat and spread out evenly with a step palette knife. *(6)*

- Bake in the preheated oven for about 15 minutes until golden brown and the sponge springs back when pressed gently. *(7)*

Ideally use immediately, or freeze for up to 1 month.

1

2

3

4

5

6

7

Flavour Variations
Chocolate Genoise

Makes two 30 x 40cm (12 x 16 inch)
  baking trays (sheets)

300g (10½oz) whole eggs *(about 6 eggs)*
300g (10½oz/1½ cups) caster
  (superfine) sugar
230g (8oz/1⅔ cups) plain (all-purpose)
  flour *sifted*
60g (2oz/4 tbsp) cocoa powder *sifted*
75g (2¾oz/⅓ cup) unsalted butter *melted*

• Make the sponge following the Genoise
  method opposite, with the cocoa powder
  being added with the flour.

Use immediately or freeze for up to 1 month.

Alhambra Chocolate Sponge

Makes two 30 x 40cm (12 x 16 inch)
  baking trays (sheets)

200g (7oz) whole eggs *(about 4 eggs)*
50g (1¾oz) egg yolks *(about 2–3 eggs)*
80g (3oz/⅓ cup) caster (superfine) sugar
25g (1oz/1¾ tbsp) plain (all-purpose)
  flour *sifted*
25g (1oz/1¾ tbsp) cornflour
  (cornstarch) *sifted*
30g (1¼oz/2 tbsp) cocoa powder *sifted*
100g (3½oz/1 scant stick) unsalted butter

• Make the sponge following the Genoise
  method opposite, with the egg yolks being
  added with the whole eggs and sugar
  and the cornflour (cornstarch) and cocoa
  powder being added with the flour.

Use immediately or freeze for up to 1 month.

Used in
Fraisier *(pages 268–269)*
Yuzu & Praline Tarts
(pages 158–159)
Lemon Meringue Tarts
(pages 146–147)
Nectarine & Cassis Entremet
(pages 258–259)

Used in
Apricot & Pistachio Delice
(pages 225–227)

The **Split-mix method** is where a batter is made with eggs and generally ground nuts, then aerated by beating separately. Egg whites are whisked to a full meringue, then the meringue is folded into the batter.

Pain de Gène
Split-mix method

Pain de Gène or Genoa cake is named after the Italian port town of Genoa. In 1800 the town lay siege to a French marshal and the people of the city were starving, their only food being rice and almonds. During the siege they consumed more than 50 tonnes of almonds. Pain de Gène was created in a French pâtisserie during this time. It is made with eggs, sugar, flour and almonds. The creator, head pâtissier Fauvel, named it after the Italian port in remembrance of the besieged people. It is traditionally baked in a tin.

Makes two 30 x 40cm (12 x 16 inch) baking trays (sheets)

75g (2¾oz) whole eggs
60g (2oz) egg yolks *(about 3 eggs)*
110g (4oz/1 cup) ground almonds
110g (4oz/¾ cup) icing (powdered) sugar
75g (2¾ oz/¾ stick) unsalted butter
60g (2oz/scant ½ cup) plain (all-purpose) flour *sifted*
90g (3oz) egg whites *(about 3 eggs)*
50g (1¾oz/¼ cup) caster (superfine) sugar

- Preheat the oven to 190°C (375°F/Gas 5) and line two 30 x 40cm (12 x 16 inch) baking trays (sheets) with silicone paper (you could also use a non-stick baking mat of the same size).

- Put the whole eggs and egg yolks, ground almonds and icing (powdered) sugar together in a mixing bowl and beat together for 10–12 minutes until the mixture is light and aerated. *(1)*

- Melt the butter (ensuring it is not to warm). Fold the flour into the egg mixture and mix. *(2)*

- Put the egg whites and caster (superfine) sugar in a clean, sterilized bowl and whisk to a firm meringue *(see page 29)*. Alternatively, whisk in an electric mixer fitted with a whisk attachment or by hand. *(3)*

- When the flour is folded through, take 2 large scoops of the mixture and add it to the melted butter. Be careful not to overmix *(4)*

- Add the butter mixture back into the base mixture and continue to fold through. Mix until the mixture is incorporated and smooth. *(5)*

- Fold the meringue into the base mixture and mix until combined. *(6)*

- Spread onto the prepared baking trays (sheets). *(7)*

- Bake in the preheated oven for 12–15 minutes until golden brown and the sponge springs back when pressed gently. *(8)*

Ideally use immediately or freeze for up to 1 month.

5

6

7

8

Biscuit Joconde
Split-mix method

Named after the famous painting of the Mona Lisa, which is called *La Joconde* in French. It is a sponge cake made with whole eggs, egg whites and almonds, baked in thin layers and is used in linings of charlottes and in the famous Classic Opéra.

Makes two 30 x 40cm (12 x 16 inch) baking trays (sheets)

125g (4½oz/scant 1 cup) icing (powdered) sugar *sifted*
125g (4½oz/generous 1 cup) ground almonds
40g (1½oz/⅓ cup) plain (all-purpose) flour *sifted*
160g (5¾oz) whole eggs *(about 3–4 eggs)*
30g (1oz/2 tbsp) unsalted butter *melted*
100g (3½oz) egg whites *(about 3–4 eggs)*
30g (1oz/2 tbsp) caster (superfine) sugar

- Preheat the oven to 200°C (400°F/Gas 6) and line two 30 x 40cm (12 x 16 inch) baking trays (sheets) with silicone paper (you could also use a non-stick baking mat of the same size).

- Put the icing (powdered) sugar, ground almonds and flour in a mixing bowl.

- Add the whole eggs and beat together for about 10–12 minutes until the mixture is light and aerated.

- Melt the butter (ensuring it is not to warm). Slowly add it to the mixture, beating well until the butter is fully incorporated.

- Put the egg whites and caster (superfine) sugar in the clean, sterilized bowl of an electric mixer fitted with a whisk attachment and whisk to a firm meringue *(see page 29)*. Alternatively, use an electric hand-held whisk.

- Fold the meringue into the egg mixture and then spread onto the prepared baking trays (sheets). Bake in the preheated oven for about 12–15 minutes until golden brown and the sponge springs back when pressed gently.

Ideally use immediately or freeze for up to 1 month.

Used in
Green Tea & Azuki Bean Dome *(pages 233–235)*
Redcurrant & Fromage Frais Entremets
(pages 262–264)
Rice Pudding, Rhubarb & Elderflower Verrine
(pages 314–315)

Used in
Fraise de Bois & Sudachi Teardrop *(pages 214–217)*
Classic Opéra *(pages 248–249)*

The **Meringue method** is where egg whites and sugar are whisked together until they form a full meringue, then the dry ingredients are folded through.

Biscuit à la Cuillère
Meringue method

Although variations of the recipe date back to the 1500s, the recipe as we know it today was created in France at the end of the 1700s. French statesman Charles Maurice de Talleyrand suggested to Marie-Antonin Carême that the shape of his biscuits needed to be changed as he was unable to dip them into his glass of Madeira wine. This left Carême puzzled as it was before the invention of a piping bag. With a flash of inspiration he placed the mixture inside a large funnel and pushed it through onto a baking tray (sheet) in the shape of fingers.

Makes two 30 x 40cm (12 x 16 inch) baking trays (sheets)

120g (4¼oz) egg yolks *(about 6 eggs)* beaten
190g (6¼oz/scant 1 cup) caster (superfine) sugar
180g (6oz) egg whites *(about 6 eggs)*
190g (6¼oz/1⅓ cups) plain (all-purpose) flour *sifted*
icing (powdered) sugar *for dusting*

- Preheat the oven to 190°C (375°F/Gas 5) and line two 30 x 40cm (12 x 16 inch) baking trays (sheets) with silicone paper (you could also use a non-stick baking mat of the same size). Put the egg yolks and half the sugar in a bowl and whisk until it reaches the ribbon stage *(see page 29)*. *(1)*

- Whisk the egg whites in a clean mixing bowl, gradually adding the remaining sugar and increasing the speed. Whisk to a soft peak meringue *(see page 29)*. *(2)*

- Transfer the egg yolk mixture to a clean mixing bowl and fold in the meringue. *(3)* Fold in the sifted flour. *(4–5)*

- Spoon the mixture into a piping (pastry) bag fitted with a 10mm (½ inch) plain nozzle (tip). Pipe the mixture in diagonal lines across the baking trays (sheets). *(6)*

- Lightly dust with icing (powdered) sugar. *(7)* Bake in the preheated oven for 12–15 minutes until golden brown and the sponge springs back when pressed gently. *(8)*

Ideally use immediately or freeze for up to 1 month.

Used in
Nectarine & Cassis Entremet
(pages 258–259)

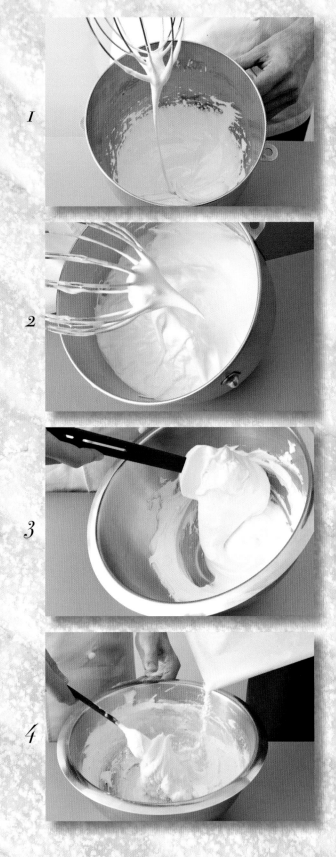

1

2

3

4

5

6

7

8

Biscuit Macaron
Makes two 30 x 40cm (12 x 16 inch) baking trays (sheets)

190g (6½oz) egg whites *(about 6 eggs)*
150g (5½oz/¾ cup) caster (superfine) sugar
40g (1½oz/2½ tbsp) plain (all-purpose) flour *sifted*
115g (4oz/1 cup) icing (powdered) sugar *sifted*
115g (4 oz/1 cup) ground almonds

- Preheat the oven to 190°C (375°F/Gas 5). Make the sponge by whisking the egg whites and caster (superfine) sugar to a soft peak meringue, then folding through the dry ingredients. Continue as opposite, but spread the mixture into two baking trays (sheets) and bake for 15–18 minutes. *Ideally use immediately or freeze for up to 1 month.*

Pistachio Biscuit Macaron
Makes two 30 x 40cm (12 x 16 inch) baking trays (sheets)

190g (6½oz) egg whites *(about 6 eggs)*
150g (5½oz/¾ cup) caster (superfine) sugar
75g (2¾oz) Pistachio Paste *(see page 116)*
40g (1½oz/2½ tbsp) plain (all-purpose) flour *sifted*
115g (4oz/1 cup) icing (powdered) sugar *sifted*
115g (4oz/1 cup) ground almonds

- Preheat the oven to 190°C (375°F/Gas 5). Make the sponge as opposite but mix the Pistachio Paste with the flour, icing sugar and almonds before adding. Spread the mixture into two baking trays (sheets) and bake for 12–15 minutes. *Ideally use immediately or freeze for up to 1 month.*

Flourless Chocolate Sponge
Makes two 30 x 40cm (12 x 16 inch) baking trays (sheets)

130g (4½oz) egg yolks *(about 6 eggs)* beaten
180g (6oz/scant 1 cup) caster (superfine) sugar
200g (7oz) egg whites *(about 4 eggs)*
60g (2oz/4 tbsp) cocoa powder *sifted*

- Make the sponge as opposite. Split in two and spread into the trays (sheets). Bake for 12–15 minutes. *Ideally use immediately or freeze for up to 1 month.*

Used in
Raspberry Casket
(pages 244–247)

Meringue is a mixture of whisked egg white and sugar.

The first type of meringue was created in the early 18th century by a Swiss pâtissier called Gasparini in his pâtisserie in a small Saxon town called Mehrinyghen. The creation was named after the town and eventually the name was shortened to meringue. At this time the meringue was spooned as individual shapes onto a baking tray (sheet) and then cooked. It was not until a later date after the invention of the piping bag that meringue could be made into more elaborate shapes.

Dacquoise is a French meringue that has been enriched with ground hazelnuts and almonds. Originating from the town of Dax in southwest France, it is traditionally eaten as layers of dacquoise sandwiched with buttercream or whipped cream.

This section contains the three different types of meringues and their methods: **French**, **Italian** and **Swiss**. It also contains a **dacquoise** recipe where the meringue is used as the base of the recipe and other ingredients are folded in.

Italian Meringue

This meringue was created in the early 19th century. It was originally called 'Italian cream' and used mainly as a filling or coating for gâteaux and tortes. It is made with a boiled sugar syrup that is added to the egg whites, then whisked until cold.

180g (6oz) egg whites *(about 6 eggs)*
300g (10½oz/1½ cups) caster (superfine) sugar
25g (1oz/2 tbsp) liquid glucose
85ml (3fl oz/⅓ cup) water

- Whisk the egg whites in the clean bowl of an electric mixer fitted with the whisk attachment. Alternatively, use an electric hand-held whisk or whisk by hand. *(1)*

- Combine the sugar, glucose and water in a saucepan over a medium heat and boil to a temperature of 121°C (250°F). *(2)*

- Gently pour the boiling syrup very slowly into the meringue – have the machine on a slow speed while this is in process. *(3)*

- When all the syrup is incorporated, return the machine to full speed and whisk to a stiff meringue and until the mixture is cold in temperature. *(4)*

Use immediately.

Used in
Brioche Polonaise
(see pages 202–203)

French Meringue

This was the first method of meringue to be discovered in the early 18th century and used by Marie Antoinette. She was said to have made the meringue herself at the Chateau of Versailles in 1790. The egg whites are whisked and the sugar is gradually added in stages.

150g (5½oz) egg whites *(about 5 eggs)*
200g (7oz/1 cup) caster (superfine) sugar
100g (3½oz/scant ¾ cup)
  icing (powdered) sugar *sifted*

- Place the egg whites in the clean mixing bowl of an electric mixer fitted with a whisk attachment. Alternatively, use an electric hand-held whisk or whisk by hand. Whisk until it begins to foam.

- Add half the caster (superfine) sugar and continue to whisk to form soft peaks *(see page 29)*. *(1)*

- Continue to whisk again and add the remaining caster (superfine) sugar. Whisk to form a stiff meringue *(see page 29)*. *(2)*

- Fold in the icing (powdered) sugar. *(3–5)*

Use immediately.

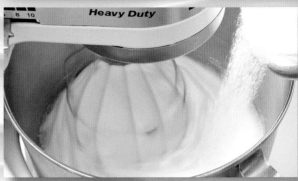

1

2

3

4

5

Used in
Pavlova
(pages 284–285)
Matcha Mont Blanc
(pages 250–252)

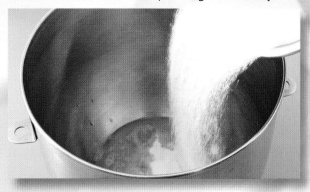

Swiss Meringue

This is the last variety of meringue to be created in the middle of the 19th century. It is made by whisking egg whites and sugar together over hot water in a bain-marie *(see page 31)*. This method is also the base meringue for our macarons.

150g (5½oz) egg whites *(about 5 eggs)*
300g (10½oz/1½ cups) caster (superfine) sugar

- Combine the egg whites and sugar in a mixing bowl until light and fluffy. *(1)*

- Place the bowl over the bain-marie and whisk together. *(2)*

- Continue to whisk until the mixture reaches 45–50°C (113–122°F) on a thermometer. *(3)*

- Remove the bowl from the heat and continue to whisk in an electric mixer fitted with the whisk attachment until the meringue is cool. *(4–5)*

Use immediately.

Used in
Lemon Meringue Tarts *(pages 146–147)*

Hazelnut & Almond Dacquoise

Dacquoise has a lovely crisp but chewy texture, which I love using as the base layer for entremets and petits gâteaux.

Makes two 30 x 40cm (12 x 16 inch) baking trays (sheets)

112g (4oz/1 cup) ground hazelnuts
75g (2¾oz/⅔ cup) ground almonds
58g (2oz/½ stick) unsalted butter *melted*
300g (10½oz/1½ cups) caster (superfine) sugar
38g (1⅓oz/2½ tbsp) cornflour (cornstarch)
195g (7oz) egg whites *(about 6–7 eggs)*
icing (powdered) sugar *for dusting*

1

4

8

- Preheat the oven to 180°C (350°F/Gas 4). Spread the hazelnuts and almonds out on a baking tray (sheet) and roast for 8–10 minutes. Set aside to cool. *(1)*

- Melt the butter, making sure not to over heat. *(2)*

- Mix the roasted nuts, half the caster (superfine) sugar and the cornflour (cornstarch) together thoroughly and place on a sheet of silicone paper. *(3)*

- Whisk the egg whites and remaining caster (superfine) sugar in the clean bowl of an electric mixer fitted with a whisk attachment to a stiff meringue *(see page 29)*. Alternatively, use an electric hand-held whisk or whisk by hand. *(4)*

- When the meringue is three-quarters whisked, fold the dry ingredients into the meringue. *(5)*

- Add a spoonful of the meringue mix to the melted butter and fold together. *(6)*

- Pour the butter mix into the rest of the meringue. *(7)*

- Mix with the spatula until you have a smooth, homogeneous mixture. *(8)*

- Pipe or spread onto a non-stick baking mat or a baking tray (sheet) lined with silicone paper. *(9)*

- Liberally dust with icing (powdered) sugar. *(10)*

- Bake in the preheated oven for 18–20 minutes. *(11)*

Use immediately or wrap in cling film (plastic wrap) and store in the freezer for up to 1 month.

Used in
Chocolate & Chestnut Buche
(pages 278–279)

2 *3*

5 *6* *7*

9 *10* *11*

Flavour Variations

Almond or Hazelnut Dacquoise: make as above but use either all ground hazelnuts or all almonds.
Coconut Dacquoise: make as above but use the same weight of desiccated coconut instead of ground hazelnuts and almonds.

Creams

pages 80–91

Custards

pages 92–97

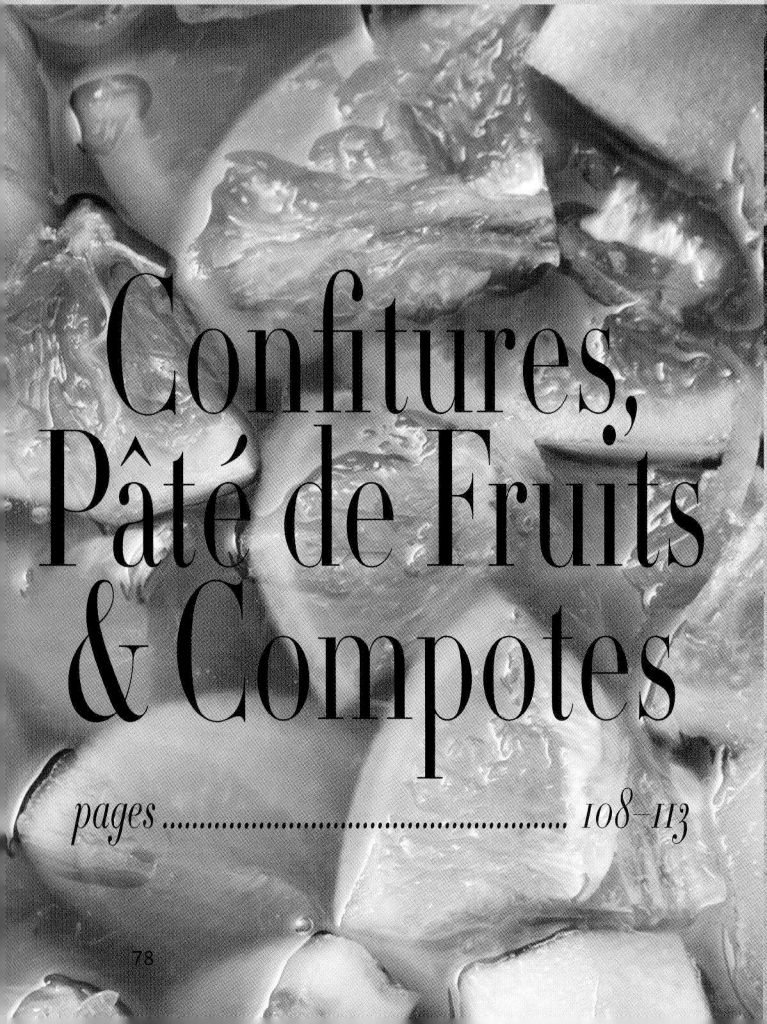

Confitures, Pâté de Fruits & Compotes

pages 108–113

Marinated Fruits

pages 114–115

78

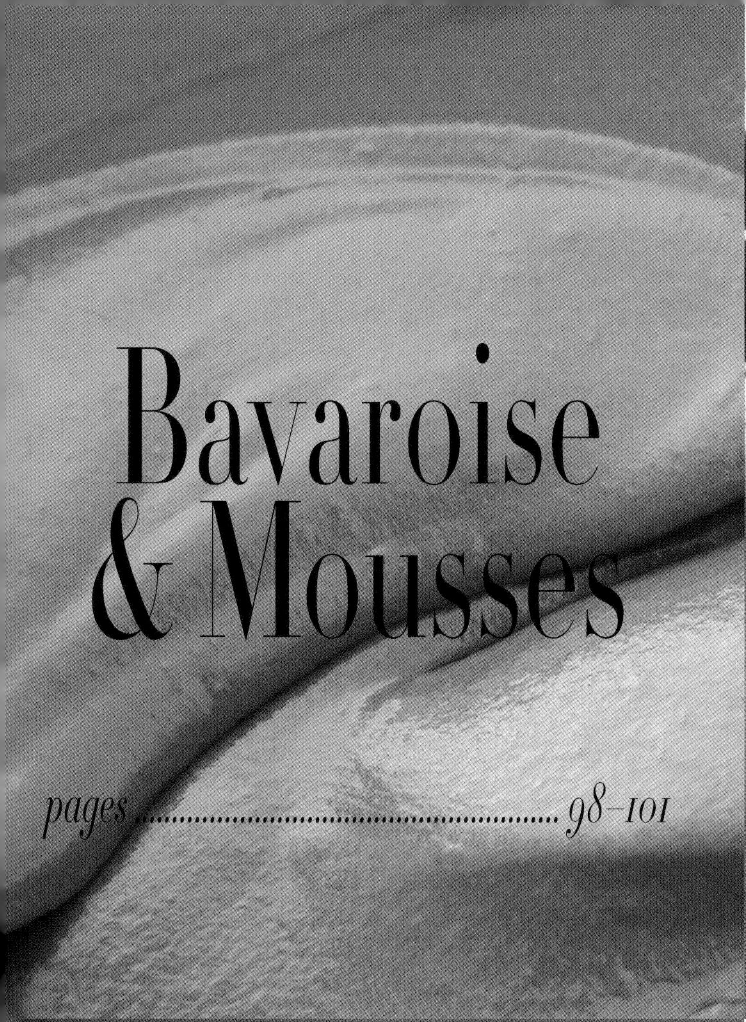

Bavaroise
& Mousses
pages 98–101

Syrups
& Glazes
pages 102–107

Praline &
Caramel
pages 116–119

Decorations
pages 120–135

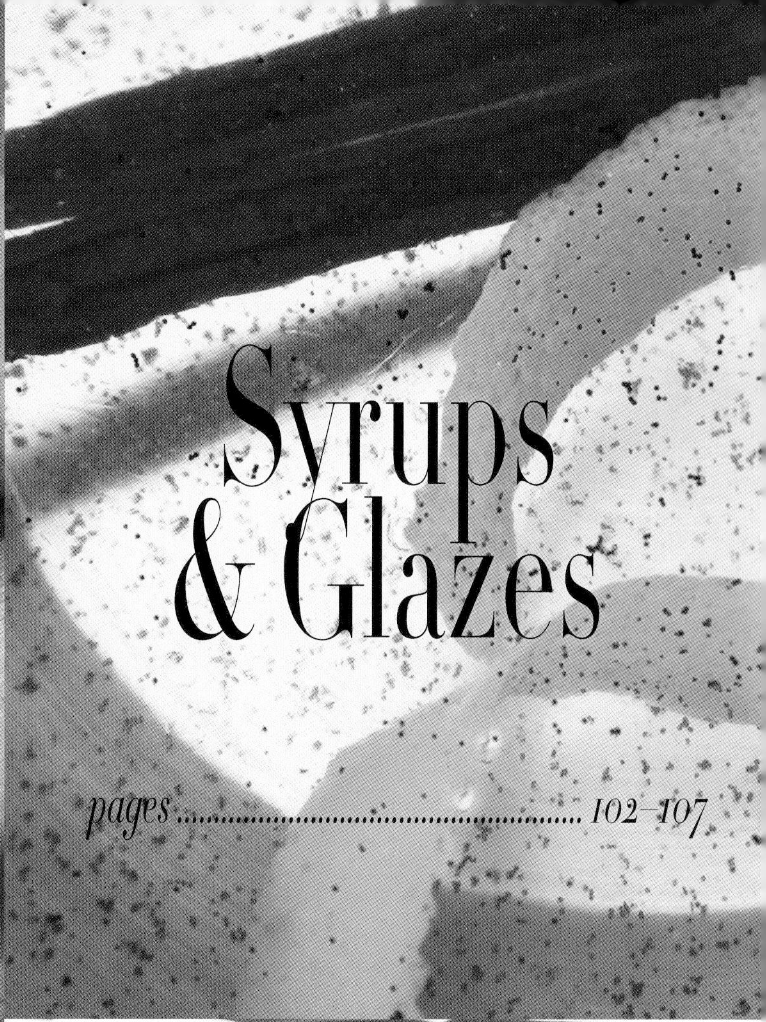

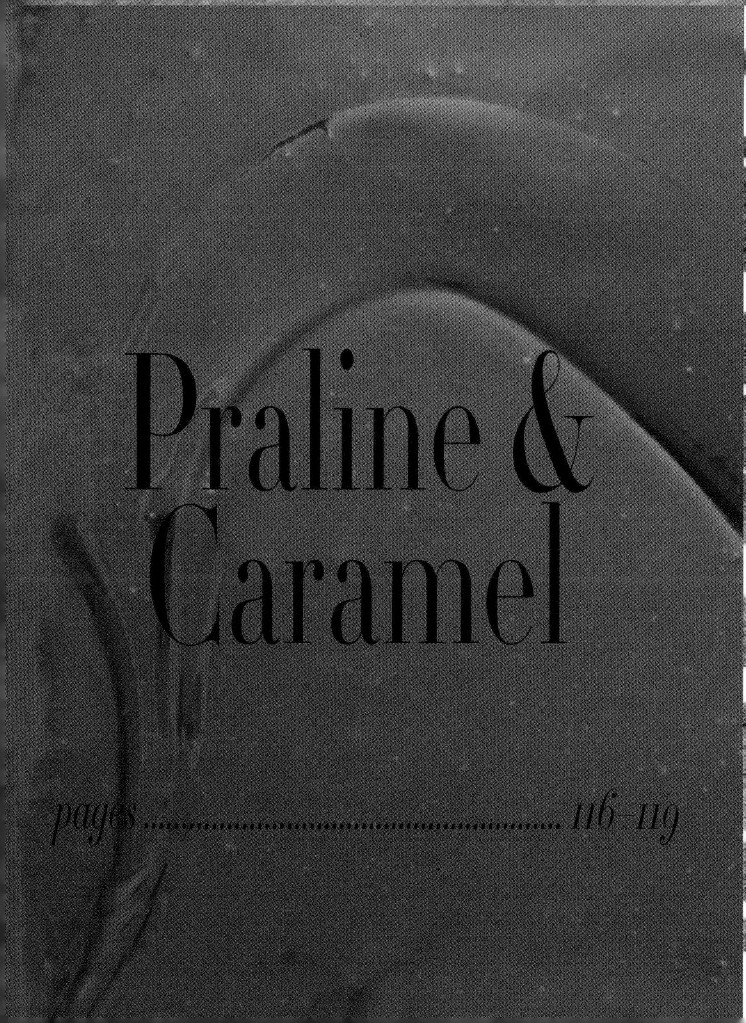

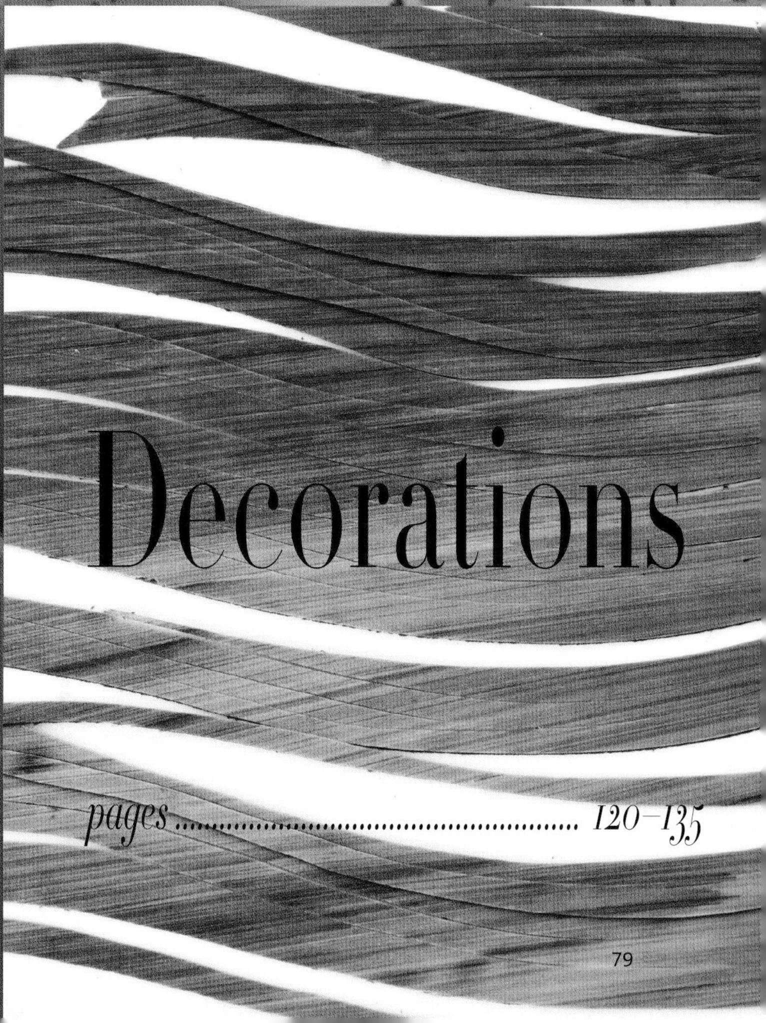

Crème Pâtissière

During the time of the great French pâtissier Marie-Antonin Carême *(see page 10)*, this cream was called *l'ancienne*, which means 'the old way', indicating that it originated from before that time period. As the recipe has evolved over time, the quantities of eggs and sugar used has been reduced. It is not only a crème in itself, it is also the base for other recipes, such as **Crème Mousseline** *(see page 84)*, **Crème Chiboust** *(see page 82)* and **Crème Diplomat** *(see page 83)*.

Makes 750g (1lb 10oz)

500ml (18fl oz/generous 2 cups) milk
1 vanilla pod (bean) *split lengthways*
120g (4oz) egg yolks *(about 6 eggs)*
100g (3½oz/½ cup) caster (superfine) sugar
50g (1¾oz/⅓ cup) plain (all-purpose) flour *sifted*

- Put the milk in a saucepan. Scrape the seeds from the split vanilla pod (bean) into the milk and drop in the split pod too. Bring to the boil. *(1)*

- In a mixing bowl, whisk together the egg yolks and sugar. Continue whisking until the mixture slightly thickens and turns light in colour, 2–3 minutes. Add the sifted flour and whisk again until smooth. *(2)*

- Pour half the infused milk into the mixing bowl and whisk again until there are no lumps. *(3)*

- Pass this mixture through a fine sieve (strainer), then return the mixture back to the remaining milk in the pan. *(4)*

- Continuously whisk the mixture until it comes to the boil. *(5)*

- Reduce the temperature to a simmer and continue to stir and cook for 5–6 minutes. *(6)*

- Take the pan off the heat and pour the crème pâtissière into a shallow dish or tray. *(7)*

- Cover with cling film (plastic wrap) and cool rapidly. *(8)*

Store, covered, in the fridge for up to 2 days.

Used in
Gâteau Mille-feuille *(pages 174–175)*
Brioche Polonaise *(pages 202–203)*
Fruit Tart *(page 336)*
Choux à la Crème *(pages 188–190)*
Gâteau Religieuse *(pages 194–195)*
Puits d'Amour *(pages 178–179)*

Creams

2

4

6

8

Flavour Variations

Crème Pâtissière Chocolat

500ml (18fl oz/generous 2 cups) milk
½ vanilla pod (bean) *split lengthways*
120g (4oz) egg yolks *(about 6 eggs)*
100g (3½oz/½ cup) caster (superfine) sugar
40g (1¼oz/¼ cup) plain (all-purpose) flour
40g (1¼oz/¼ cup) cocoa powder
50g (1¾oz) dark (bittersweet) chocolate
 (70% cocoa solids) *chopped*

Follow the recipe opposite, but add the cocoa powder with the flour in **step 2**. Also add the chopped chocolate at the end of **step 6**, mix until the chocolate has been fully incorporated before pouring into the dish or tray. *Store, covered, in the fridge for up to 2 days. Makes 825g (1lb 12oz).*

Crème Pâtissière Caramel

500ml (18fl oz/generous 2 cups) milk
½ vanilla pod (bean) *split lengthways*
120g (4oz) egg yolks *(about 6 eggs)*
275g (9¾oz/1⅓ cups) caster (superfine) sugar
70g (2¾oz/½ cup) plain (all-purpose) flour
50ml (2fl oz/¼ cup) water

Follow the recipe opposite but whisk 25g (1oz) of the sugar with the eggs in **step 2**. Make a dry caramel with the remaining caster sugar, cook to a deep amber and then deglaze with the water. Add the caramel to the crème pâtissière at the end of **step 5** and stir through. Return the crème pâtissière to the heat, bring to the boil, then simmer for 8–10 minutes. Pour into the dish or tray as instructed in **step 8**. *Store, covered, in the fridge for up to 2 days. Makes 900g (1lb 14oz).*

Used in
Gâteau Religieuse
(pages 194–195)
Chocolate Eclair
(pages 191–193)
Choux à la Creme
(pages 188–189)

Crème Chiboust

This crème was first created by pâtissier Chiboust (*see page 12*) while creating his legendary Gâteau St Honoré. It commemorates the street his shop was on, the rue St Honoré, the patron saint of bakers and lastly himself. This is a delicate cream and must be used immediately or the meringue will break down.

Makes 550g (1lb 4oz)

For the crème:
5g (⅛oz/1 tsp) leaf gelatine
250ml (8½fl oz/1 cup) milk
1 vanilla pod (bean) *split lengthways*
120g (4½oz) egg yolks (*about 6 eggs*)
50g (1¾oz/¼ cup) caster (superfine) sugar
25g (1oz) cornflour (cornstarch)

For the meringue:
150g (5½oz) egg whites (*about 5 eggs*)
50g (1¾oz/¼ cup) caster (superfine) sugar

- Use the egg whites and sugar to prepare a French Meringue (*see page 74*). Continue whisking on a medium speed while the crème is prepared.

- Soak the gelatine in a bowl of ice-cold water for a few minutes until soft. Squeeze the gelatine to remove any excess water (*see page 31*).

- To make the crème: use the milk, vanilla, egg yolks, sugar and cornflour (cornstarch) to prepare a Crème Pâtissière following the method on page 80. Once boiled, cook for 2–3 minutes, then add the pre-soaked gelatine and beat in well. *(1)* Pour into a mixing bowl and leave to cool in the fridge, stirring occasionally.

- Add a large spoonful of the meringue to the crème and whisk until mixed. *(2–3)*

- Spoon this into the remaining meringue and fold in until mixed. *(4)*

Use immediately.

Used in
Gâteau St Honoré
(pages 168–170)

Crème Diplomat

A lightened **Crème Pâtissière** *(see page 80)* with the addition of whipped cream, or alternatively a firmer **Crème Chantilly** *(see page 84)*.

Makes 500g (1lb 2oz)

2g (⅛oz) leaf gelatine
½ quantity of **Crème Pâtissière** *(see page 80)*
150ml (5fl oz/⅔ cup) double (heavy) cream

- Soak the gelatine in a bowl of ice-cold water for a few minutes until soft. Squeeze the gelatine to remove excess water *(see page 31)*.

- Prepare the Crème Pâtissière, remove from the heat and add the pre-soaked gelatine. *(1)*

- Pour into a mixing bowl and leave to cool, stirring occasionally. *(2)*

- Semi-whip the cream and fold into the cooled Crème Pâtissière. *(3–5)*

Put in the fridge for at least 30 minutes before use.

Flavour Variation

Ginger Diplomat: make an infusion with 20g (¾oz) freshly grated ginger and the milk from the main Crème Pâtissière recipe *(see page 80)*. Leave to infuse for 30 minutes. Strain and continue to prepare the Ginger Diplomat as above. *Use immediately.*

Used in
Nectarine & Sesame Gâteau
(pages 289–291)
Rhubarb & Ginger Sablé
(page 160–161)
Fraisier *(pages 268–269)*

Crème Mousseline

Mousseline is a Crème Pâtissière *(see page 80)* that is enriched with butter and beaten to make it light in texture.

Makes 550g (1lb 4oz)

½ quantity of **Crème Pâtissière** *(see page 80)*
200g (7oz/scant 1 cup) room temperature unsalted butter *cubed*

Used in

Strawberry & Pistachio Breton Tart *(pages 162–163)*

Raspberry & Pistachio Macaron *(pages 260–261)*

- Prepare the Crème Pâtissière, remove from the heat and pour into the bowl of an electric mixer.

- Beat on a low speed until it reaches room temperature, ensuring you scrape the sides of the bowl as it mixes. *(1)*

- Increase the speed, then gradually add the butter cube by cube, until it is fully combined. *(2–3)*

Use immediately.

Crème Chantilly

This is thought to have been created by a Frenchman called Vatel in 1660, who was the maître d'hotel within the Château de Chantilly for the prince of Condé. It is whipped cream with the addition of sugar and vanilla.

Makes 375g (13oz)

180ml (6fl oz/¾ cup) whipping (pouring) cream *(35% butter fat)*
180ml (6fl oz/¾ cup) double (heavy) cream *(48% butter fat)*
½ vanilla pod (bean) *split lengthways*
18g (½ oz) caster (superfine) sugar

Used in

Baba au Rhum *(pages 198–199)*

Marron Barquette *(page 336)*

Rhubarb & Ginger Sablé *(pages 160–161)*

Choux à la Crème *(pages 188–190)*

Trois Frères *(pages 273–275)*

- Whisk both creams, the vanilla seeds from the pod (bean) and the sugar together until soft peaks form. *(1–3)*

Use immediately.

Note: *ensure that all of your equipment is cool and immediately whip the cream. Use straight away or return to the fridge – this is to ensure that the cream does not separate.*

Chocolate Crème Chantilly

This is quick and easy to make, but needs to be used immediately as it will set rapidly.

Makes 375g (13oz)

195g (7oz) dark (bittersweet) chocolate *(65% cocoa solids) chopped*
175ml (6fl oz/¾ cup) whipping (pouring) cream

Used in

Choux à la Crème *(pages 188-190)*

Saint Marc *(pages 228–229)*

- Put the chopped chocolate in a bowl and melt over a bain-marie *(see page 31). (1)*

- Meanwhile, gently whip the cream until soft peaks form. Once melted, take the chocolate off the heat and fold in the whipped cream until you have a smooth, homogenous cream. *(2–3)*

Use immediately.

I *2* *3*

I *2* *3*

I *2* *3*

Crème au Beurre

This buttercream was created by a pâtissier called Quillet around the early 19th century and originally named after him as *crème à Quillet*, it later changed to simply *crème au beurre*. There are many recipes and methods to make buttercream but the original recipe by Quillet was made in the same way as this recipe, where a sugar syrup is streamed onto whisking egg yolks, then softened butter is beaten in when it is cooled.

Makes 385g (13½oz)

100g (3½oz/½ cup) caster (superfine) sugar
30ml (1fl oz/2 tbsp) water
60g (2oz) egg yolks *(about 3 eggs)*
225g (8oz/1 cup) unsalted butter *softened*

- Put the caster sugar and water in a saucepan, bring to the boil and heat to 121°C (250°F).

- Put the egg yolks in the bowl of an electric mixer and whisk. *(1)* Slowly pour the hot syrup into the sabayon and whisk until it is thick and cool. *(2)*

- Gradually add the softened butter while still whisking. *(3)* When all the butter has been incorporated, continue to beat until light and aerated. *(4–5)*

Use immediately.

Flavour Variations

Coffee Crème au Beurre: mix together 10ml (2 tsp) Simple Syrup *(see page 102)* and 10g (2 tsp) freeze-dried coffee granules and mix to dissolve. Prepare the crème au beurre as above, then mix in the coffee solution.
Chestnut Crème au Beurre: make as above, with the addition of 100g (3½oz) unsweetened chestnut purée, beaten until soft, added with the butter.

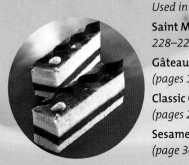

Used in
Saint Marc *(pages 228–229)*
Gâteau Religieuse *(pages 194–195)*
Classic Opéra *(pages 248–249)*
Sesame Macarons *(page 301)*

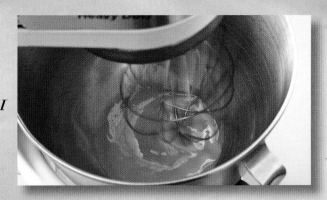

1

2

3

4

5

Italian Buttercream

Instead of egg yolks as in the previous recipe, this buttercream uses an Italian Meringue *(see page 73)* base to which the softened butter is beaten in, hence its name. I find this to be the most durable of all the buttercreams, but also the lightest.

Makes 385g (13½oz)

60g (2oz) egg whites
  (about 2 eggs)
100g (3½oz/½ cup)
  caster (superfine) sugar
30ml (1fl oz/2 tbsp) water
225g (8oz/1 cup)
  unsalted butter *softened*

- Whisk the egg whites in an electric mixer to a soft meringue. *(1)*

- Meanwhile, put the caster sugar and water in a saucepan, bring to the boil and heat to 121°C (250°F).

- Slowly pour the hot syrup into the meringue and whisk until thick and cool. *(2–3)*

- Gradually beat in the softened butter. *(4)*

- When all the butter has been incorporated, continue to beat until light and aerated. *(5)*

Use immediately.

Used in
Les Misérables
(pages 241–243)

1

2

3

4

5

Used in

Gâteau Conversation *(pages 176–177)*

Bakewell Tarts *(pages 144–145)*

Bostock *(page 204)*

Marron Barquette *(page 336)*

Chestnut Pithivier *(pages 171–173)*

Crème d'Amande

Almond cream was created in the early 1500s by a French pâtissier called Provenchère. The family patented the cream until the reign of Louis Philippe in 1830.

Makes 1kg (2¼lb)

250g (9oz/generous 1 cup) unsalted butter *softened*
250g (9oz/1¼ cups) caster (superfine) sugar
250g (9oz) whole eggs *(about 5 eggs) beaten*
250g (9oz/generous 2 cups) ground almonds
50g (1¾oz/⅓ cup) plain (all-purpose) flour *sifted*

- Put the butter and caster (superfine) sugar in a mixing bowl and beat until smooth. *(1–2)*

- Gradually beat in the eggs and mix until combined. *(3)*

- Fold in the ground almonds and the flour and mix until smooth. *(4–6)*

Use immediately.

Flavour Variation

Crème Noisette: use ground hazelnuts instead of the ground almonds.

6

Frangipane

This is an enriched Crème d'Amande with the addition of Crème Pâtissière and rum beaten in.

Makes 900g (2lb 3oz)

½ quantity of **Crème Pâtissière**
   (see page 80)
½ quantity of **Crème d'Amande** *(see left)*
40ml (1½fl oz/2½ tbsp) dark rum

- Beat the Crème Pâtissière in a mixing bowl until smooth. *(1)*
- Fold this into the prepared Crème d'Amande. *(2)*
- Stir through the rum. *(3–5)*

Use immediately.

Almond Cream & Frangipane

The first recipes for frangipane date back to the 1500s when Catherine de Medici, a young Italian noblewoman, married King Henry of France. To enable her to settle in her new country she brought her own chefs and servants over from Italy. Her personal chef, Popelini, introduced many Italian recipes to the French court; an influence that was to affect French cuisine. A favourite of the young queen was the classic Italian dish, polenta. Unable to obtain all the necessary ingredients in France he adjusted the recipe slightly. The new recipe contained brown sugar, wheat flour, guinea fowl eggs, salt, almonds, powdered roots, milk and butter. Catherine adored the new highly flavoured and scented cream, reminding her of a very fashionable French perfume of that time created by Italian noblemen Marquis Frangipani who lived in Paris. She christened the delicacy Frangipane cream in his honour.

The cream is a favourite in Parisian pâtisserie and has evolved over the years. Now with the addition of crème pâtissière and rum to add richness it has lasted the length of time and is as popular now as it ever was.

Used in
Tarte Bourdeloue
(pages 150–151)
Apricot Frangipane
(page 334)
Croustade aux Pommes
(pages 185–187)

1

2

3

4

5

Dark Chocolate Ganache

Ganache is an emulsion of couverture chocolate and cream. Other liquids can also be added, such as fruit purées. The key to a good ganache is the quality of the ingredients. We always use Amedei chocolate for the best results.

Makes 575g (1lb (5oz)

300ml (½ pint/1¼ cups)
  whipping (pouring) cream
250g (9oz) dark (bittersweet) chocolate .
  (65% cocoa solids) *finely chopped*
25g (1oz) unsalted butter *softened*

- Put the cream in a saucepan. Bring to the boil. *(1)*

- Put the chopped chocolate in a mixing bowl. Pour the boiled cream over the chocolate and mix until emulsified and a ganache consistency is formed. *(2–3)*

- Add in the softened butter and mix well until fully incorporated. *(4–5)*

- Leave to set at room temperature for about 2–3 hours.

Ideally use immediately. Once it starts to set, the ganache can be stored in the fridge for 2 days, but you will need to leave it to return to room temperature before using.

Flavour Variations

These variations on a basic chocolate ganache are used in many recipes, in particular with the contemporary and classic macaron recipes on pages 294–303. All of the variations below are made using the method for the Dark Chocolate Ganache opposite.

Milk Chocolate Ganache: use a mixture of 150g (5½oz) chopped milk chocolate (35% cocoa solids) and 135g (4¾oz) chopped dark (bittersweet) chocolate (65% cocoa solids).

Shiso Ganache: infuse 5g (1 tsp) shiso leaves with the cream as you boil it, then leave to infuse for 30 minutes. Strain the infused cream, return to the boil, then continue with the method.

Raspberry Ganache: use 250g (9oz) Raspberry Purée (see page 110) instead of the cream and increase the butter to 60g (2oz/½ stick).

Lemon Ganache: use a mixture of 125g (4½oz) chopped milk chocolate (35% cocoa solids) and 125g (4½oz) chopped dark (bittersweet) chocolate (65% cocoa solids). Pour 200ml (7fl oz/1 scant cup) boiled cream over the chopped chocolate. Add 100ml (3½fl oz) lemon juice and stir through. Lastly add 25g (1oz) butter and mix well.

Beurre de Sel Ganache: use 100g (3½oz) chopped Toscano 65% chocolate, 75ml (3fl oz/⅓ cup) whipping (pouring) cream and 75g (2¾oz) Sea Salt Caramel (see pages 118–119).

Pistachio Ganache: use 250g (9oz) chopped Toscano 65% chocolate and also add 30g (1¼ oz) Pistachio Paste (see page 116) with the butter at the end.

Matcha Ganache: use a mixture of 150g (5½oz) chopped milk chocolate (35% cocoa solids) and 135g (5oz) fine dark (bittersweet) chocolate (65% cocoa solids), but mix 8g (1½ tsp) matcha powder and 8g (1½ tsp) water to a paste and add to the cream before boiling.

Orange & Balsamic Ganache: infuse 3g (½ tsp) finely grated orange zest with the cream as you boil it, then leave to infuse for 30 minutes. Strain the infused cream, return to the boil, then continue with the method and also add 14g (½oz) balsamic vinegar with the butter at the end.

Passion Fruit & Mango Ganache: use 150g (5½oz) each of Passion Fruit Purée (see page 110) and Mango Purée (see page 110) instead of the cream.

Roasted Sweet Potato Ganache: use puréed sweet potato instead of the cream: preheat the oven to 180°C (350°F/Gas 4). Bake 300g (10½oz) purple sweet potato for 40 minutes until soft, then leave to cool slightly. Remove the flesh from the skin, place it in a blender, then blitz until you have a smooth paste. Pass through a sieve (strainer) into a pan and gently bring to the boil. Pour the boiled potato purée over the chopped chocolate and continue as opposite.

Spiced Ganache: make an infusion by adding 1 cinnamon stick and 1g (a pinch) ground nutmeg to the boiled cream. Leave to infuse for 30 minutes, then continue as opposite.

Infusing/flavouring

- If infusing/flavouring, put the cream in the saucepan and bring to the boil. Remove from heat, add the required ingredients (see flavour variations, right) and cover with cling film (plastic wrap). (6–7)

- Leave for 30 minutes to infuse, then reheat to boiling point. Strain and continue with the ganache recipe.

6

7

Used in
Macarons
(pages 294–303)

Crème Anglaise

The French call egg custard *crème anglaise*, which translated means 'English cream'. Custard is an English creation and the technique is essential when learning the basics. It can be used on its own, as an accompaniment to desserts, as the base for ice cream and is also part of the recipe for bavaroise, crémeux and certain chocolate mousses.

Makes 720ml (1¼ pints/3 cups)

400ml (14fl oz/1¾ cups) milk
100ml (3½fl oz/scant ½ cup) whipping (pouring) cream
1 vanilla pod (bean) *split lengthways*
120g (4½oz) egg yolks *(about 6 eggs)*
100g (3½oz/½ cup) caster (superfine) sugar

- Prepare an ice bain-marie *(see page 31). (1)*

- Put the milk and cream in a saucepan. Scrape the seeds from the split vanilla pod (bean) into the pan and drop in the split pod (bean) too. Bring to a simmer. *(2)*

- Meanwhile, beat together the egg yolks and caster (superfine) sugar until a ribbon is formed and the mixture is light in colour. *(3)*

- Pour one-third of the liquid – make sure it is not boiling – onto the egg yolks and sugar. *(4)*

- Whisk until the milk is fully incorporated. *(5)*

- Return the mixture to the pan of milk and place over a low heat. Stir continuously using a wooden spoon until the mixture thickens, coats the back of the spoon and reaches a temperature of 82–84°C (180–183°F). *(6)*

- Take the custard off the heat and pass through a fine sieve into a bowl in the ice bain-marie to cool rapidly. Place the vanilla back into the anglaise to continue infusing as it cools. *(7–8)*

Store in an airtight container in the fridge and use within 2 days.

Used in
Pistachio & Cherry Arctic Roll *(pages 292–293)*
Nectarine & Sesame Gâteau *(pages 289–291)*

Crème Brûlée

Translated into English, crème brûlée simply means 'burnt cream'. The recipe dates back to the 18th century when it became a well established dessert in the east coast of Scotland. The original recipe was probably created at an earlier date in France; it is well known that when Mary Queen of Scots returned to Scotland after growing up in France, Scottish cookery then became greatly influenced by France as French chefs were employed by wealthy households during that period. Crème brûlée is traditionally served in a dish topped with caramelized sugar. We like to use the custard part within layers in our pâtisserie. This recipe can also easily be served on its own in the traditional way.

1   *2*   *3*   *4*   *5*   *6*

Makes 720ml (25fl oz/3 cups)

- 500ml (18fl oz/generous 2 cups) whipping (pouring) cream
- 1 vanilla pod (bean) *split lengthways*
- 120g (4½oz) egg yolks *(about 6 eggs)*
- 100g (3½oz/½ cup) caster (superfine) sugar

- Put the cream in a saucepan. Scrape the seeds from the split vanilla pod (bean) into the pan and drop in the split pod (bean) too. Bring to the boil. *(1–2)*

- Take the pan off the heat, cover with cling film (plastic wrap) and leave to infuse for 30 minutes. *(3)*

- In a mixing bowl, whisk together the egg yolks and caster (superfine) sugar. Mix until light in colour. *(4)*

- Mix the infused cream into the egg yolk and sugar mixture, remove the vanilla pod (bean) and mix until the mixture is smooth. *(5)*

- Pass the custard through a fine sieve (strainer) before cooking as described in your chosen recipe. *(6)*

Store in an airtight container overnight to increase the flavour. Use within 2 days.

Used in
Cadeaux au Chocolat *(pages 253–255)*
Jasmine & Mandarin Pyramid *(pages 218–219)*

Flavour Variation

Jasmine Crème Brûlée: boil the cream and vanilla together in a saucepan as above. Add 6g (1 tsp) jasmine tea, take off the heat and cover with cling film (plastic wrap). Leave to infuse for 1 hour. Strain the infused cream and continue with the method as above.

Dark Chocolate Crémeux

This is similar to a ganache, but made with a Crème Anglaise. Its smooth silky texture is ideal for layers in entremets and piping in petits gateaux.

Makes 750g (1lb 10oz)

250g (9oz) dark (bittersweet) chocolate (66% cocoa solids) *finely chopped*
110ml (4fl oz/½ cup) milk
250ml (8½fl oz/scant 1 cup) whipping (pouring) cream
½ vanilla pod (bean) *split lengthways*
90g (3oz) egg yolks *(about 4–5 eggs)*
45g (1½oz/¼ cup) caster (superfine) sugar
25g (1oz) unsalted butter *cubed*

- Put the chocolate in a bowl. Put the milk and cream in a saucepan, add the vanilla pod (bean) and scraped seeds and bring to the boil. *(1)*

- Whisk the egg yolks and sugar together until light in colour. *(2)*

- Add half the boiling liquid to the egg mixture, whisk until smooth, then return to the pan. *(3)* Over a low heat, stir the mixture and cook until it coats the back of a spoon (around 82–84°C/180–183°F). *(4)*

- Take the pan off the heat and pass through a fine sieve (strainer) over the bowl of chocolate. Mix until smooth. *(5–6)* Gradually add the butter; mix until smooth. *(7–8)*

Use immediately if pouring into a mould, or leave to semi-set if piping.

Used in

Caramelized Pear, Blackcurrant & Chocolate Breton *(pages 164–165)*
Yuzu & Praline Tarts *(pages 158–159)*
Apricot & Wasabi Entremet *(page 286)*
Coffee & Walnut Dacquoise *(page 230)*

Lemon Curd

Lemon curd dates back to the early 1800s, traditionally served with toast, scones or as a filling for small tarts. We use curd as a layer within entremets for a different texture and it also adds a wonderful tangy flavour.

Makes 925g (2lb 3oz)

200ml (7fl oz/scant 1 cup) lemon juice
grated zest of 4 lemons
450g (1lb) whole eggs *(about 9 eggs)*
160g (5¾oz/¾ cup) caster (superfine) sugar
170g (6oz/¾ cup) unsalted butter *cubed*

- Put the lemon juice and zest in a saucepan and bring to the boil. *(1)*

- In a mixing bowl, whisk together the eggs and sugar until light in colour. *(2–4)*

- Add half the lemon juice to the egg mixture and whisk until fully incorporated. *(5)*

- Return this mixture to the saucepan and continue to cook the curd over a low heat for a further 5 minutes. *(6)*

- Take the pan off the heat and pass the mixture through a fine sieve (strainer) into a mixing bowl. *(7)*

- Mix in the butter, piece by piece, until fully incorporated. *(8)* Pour into a shallow dish or tray and cover with cling film (plastic wrap). *(9)*

Use immediately.

Flavour Variations

Orange Curd: put 400ml (14fl oz/generous 1½ cups) orange juice in a pan and bring to the boil, continue to cook on a low heat until the orange juice reduces by half. Continue with the lemon curd recipe as above.

Lime Curd: make as above, but use grated lime zest and juice instead of lemons.

Redcurrant Curd: make as above, but use 200ml (7fl oz) redcurrant purée instead of lemon juice.

Sudachi Curd: make as above, but use sudachi juice instead of lemon juice and the finely grated zest of 2 sudachis.

2

3

5

6

8

9

Used in

Citrus Slice *(pages 238–240)*

Lemon Meringue Tarts *(pages 146–147)*

Redcurrant & Fromage Frais Entremet
(pages 262–264)

Gâteau Religieuse *(pages 194–195)*

Classic Bavaroise

Originally bavaroise was not a dessert but a drink. It was created in the middle of the 18th century in Paris and named in honour of the Princess of Bavaria who favoured a sweet tea drink, that has eventually evolved into this crème.

Makes 1.1kg (2lb 5oz)

500ml (18fl oz/generous 2 cups) milk
1 vanilla pod (bean) *split lengthways*
80g (3oz) egg yolks *(about 4 eggs)*
80g (3oz/scant ½ cup) caster (superfine) sugar
12g (⅓ oz) leaf gelatine
450ml (15fl oz/2 cups) whipping (pouring) cream

- Put the milk in a saucepan. Scrape the seeds from the split vanilla pod (bean) into the pan and drop in the split pod (bean) too. Bring to the boil.

- In a mixing bowl, whisk together the egg yolks and sugar until they are well combined and light in colour.

- Pour half the boiled liquid onto the egg mixture and mix well. *(1)*

- Return the mixture back to the saucepan of milk and return to the heat. Stir with a wooden spoon. *(2)*

- Continue cooking the liquid until it thickens, coats the back of the wooden spoon and reaches a temperature of 82–84°C (180–183°F) on a thermometer. *(3)*

- Soak the gelatine in a bowl of ice-cold water for a few minutes until soft. Squeeze to remove any excess water *(see page 31)*. Add the soaked gelatine to the custard and strain through a fine sieve (strainer) into a bowl set in an ice bain-marie *(see page 31)*. *(4)*

- Whip the cream in a separate bowl to the ribbon stage *(see page 32)*. When the custard is cold, remove the bowl from the bain-marie. Be careful not to let it set. Fold the whipped cream into the cold custard. *(5–6)*

Use immediately.

Used in
Trois Frères
(pages 273–275)
Yuzu & Praline Tarts
(pages 158–159)

Flavour Variations

Yuzu Bavaroise: make as above, but boil 7g (⅛ oz) grated yuzu zest with the milk and vanilla, then leave to infuse for 20 minutes. Strain, return to the boil again, then continue as in the main recipe.

Rhubarb Bavaroise: make as above, but replace the milk with rhubarb purée *(see page 110)*.

Fruit Mousse

The word mousse dates back to the early 18th century and is a derivative of the old French word *mosse*, which dates back to 1226. Translated into English, mousse means the froth that appears on the surface of water when it is agitated. The word was later used to describe a dessert which is light and frothy in texture.

Makes 940g (2lb)

11g (¼ oz) leaf gelatine
500ml (18fl oz/generous 2 cups) whipping (pouring) cream
350g (12oz) **Fruit Purée** *(see page 110) made with apricots (or other fruits)*
80g (3oz/scant ½ cup) caster (superfine) sugar

- Soak the gelatine in a bowl of ice-cold water for a few minutes until soft *(see page 31)*. Whip the cream in a bowl to the ribbon stage *(see page 32)*.

- Put 150g (5½oz) of the apricot purée in a saucepan and add the sugar. Gently warm until the sugar has dissolved completely. *(1)*

- Squeeze the excess water from the soaked gelatine and add to the pan. Stir until the gelatine has dissolved. *(2)*

- Strain through a sieve (strainer) into a mixing bowl. *(3)* Add the remaining apricot purée. *(4)*

- Pour in the whipped cream and fold together until combined. *(5–6)*

Use immediately.

Note: *you can use any flavour of fruit purée to make fruit mousse as long as you use the same weight (350g/12oz); such as apple, nectarine, raspberry, etc.*

Used in

Apple & Edamame Verrine *(pages 312–313)*

Earl Grey & Coconut Entremet *(pages 265–267)*

Nectarine & Cassis Entremet *(pages 258–259)*

Apricot & Pistachio Delice *(pages 225–227)*

Fraises de Bois & Sudachi Teardrop *(pages 214–217)*

Raspberry & Rose Entremet *(pages 280–283)*

Note: *it is important that any mousses are made as close to the assembly of the final pâtisserie as possible to avoid them setting prematurely.*

Dark Chocolate Mousse

When selecting chocolate to make a chocolate mousse, it is good to look at the characteristics of the chocolate and marry this with the pâtisserie you are creating. We use two different methods to make our dark (bittersweet) chocolate mousse.

Sabayon method
This method will give a slightly lighter result.

Makes 900g (2lb 2oz)

300g (10½oz) dark (bittersweet) chocolate (66% cocoa solids) *finely chopped*
140g (5oz) egg yolks *(about 7 eggs)*
80g (3oz/⅓ cup) caster (superfine) sugar
40ml (1½fl oz/2½ tbsp) water
380ml (13fl oz/1½ cups) whipping (pouring) cream

- Melt the chocolate in a bain-marie *(see page 31)* until it reaches 45°C (113°F). *(1)*

- Whisk the egg yolks in an electric mixer fitted with the whisk attachment.

- Meanwhile, put the sugar and water in a saucepan and bring to the boil. Heat until it reaches 121°C (250°F), then slowly pour the sugar syrup over the egg yolks and continue to whisk to a full sabayon (until the mix reaches the ribbon stage, becoming thick and pale). Continue to whisk the mixture until it is cool.

- In a separate bowl, whip the cream until it reaches the ribbon stage, then fold the sabayon into the cream. *(2–3)* Carefully fold one-third of the mixture into the melted chocolate. *(4–5)* Fold in the remaining cream. *(6–8)*

Use immediately.

Used in
Apricot & Wasabi Entremet *(pages 286–288)*
Cadeaux au Chocolat *(pages 253–255)*
Jasmine & Mandarin Pyramid *(pages 218–219)*
Chocolate & Chestnut Buche *(page 278)*
Coffee & Walnut Dacquoise *(page 230)*
Jaffa Cake *(pages 276–277)*

Anglaise method
This method works better for smaller batches and I would recommend it for the beginner.

Makes 1.1kg (2lb 5oz)

550ml (19fl oz/scant 2½ cups) whipping (pouring) cream
150ml (¼ pint/⅔ cup) milk
60g (2oz) egg yolks *(about 3 eggs)*
30g (1oz/2 tbsp) caster (superfine) sugar
320g (11oz) dark (bittersweet) chocolate (66% cocoa solids)

- Put 150ml (¼ pint/⅔ cup) of the cream in a saucepan and add the milk. Bring to the boil.

- Meanwhile, whisk the egg yolks and sugar together in a large mixing bowl until the mix becomes light in colour, about 2–3 minutes. *(1)*

- When the milk has boiled, pour half of it onto the egg and sugar mixture and mix thoroughly. *(2)*

- Pour this mix back into the pan and cook over a low heat, stirring continuously, until the mixture is thick enough to coat the back of a spoon, about 82–84°C (180–183°F). *(3)*

- Take the pan off the heat and pass through a fine sieve (strainer) onto the chopped chocolate in a mixing bowl. *(4)*

- Using a spatula, mix until smooth and emulsified, then leave to cool. *(5)*

- Put the remaining cream in a mixing bowl and whip until soft peaks form. Alternatively, whisk in an electric mixer fitted with a whisk attachment.

- Carefully fold the whipped cream into the chocolate mixture. *(6–8)*

Use immediately.

Used in
Chocolate, Banana & Peanut Caramel Bar
(pages 222–224)

Simple Syrup

This is a basic recipe used throughout the pâtisserie kitchen for soaking sponges, cakes and poaching fruits.

Makes 400ml (14fl oz/1²⁄₃ cups)

225ml (8fl oz/scant 1 cup) water
190g (6¾oz/scant 1 cup)
  caster (superfine) sugar
1½ peels of lemon zest
½ vanilla pod (bean) *split lengthways*

- Put the water, sugar and lemon zest in a saucepan. Scrape the seeds from the split vanilla pod (bean) into the water and drop in the empty pod (bean) too. *(1)*

- Bring to the boil and cook for 2–3 minutes. *(2)*

- Take off the heat and leave to cool. *(3)*

Store in an airtight container in the fridge for up to 1 month.

Used in
Lemon Poppy Seed & Olive Oil Cake *(page 323)*
Green Tea & Azuki Bean Dome *(pages 233–235)*
Matcha Eclairs *(pages 191–193)*
Apricot & Wasabi Entremet *(pages 286–287)*
Fraise de Bois & Sudachi Teardrop *(pages 214–217)*
Nectarine & Sesame Gâteau *(pages 289–291)*
Pistachio & Cherry Arctic Roll *(pages 292–293)*

Light Syrup

Lighter syrups are less sweet than the Simple Syrup opposite and are used for soaking savarins and babas where a simple syrup can become too sweet.

Makes 800ml (24fl oz/3½ cups)

600ml (1 pint/2⅓ cups) water
300g (10½ oz/1½ cups) caster (superfine) sugar
1 vanilla pod (bean) *split lengthways*

- Put the water and sugar in a saucepan. Scrape the seeds from the split vanilla pod (bean) into the water and drop in the empty pod (bean) too.
- Bring to the boil and cook for 2–3 minutes. Take off the heat and leave to cool.

Store in an airtight container in the fridge for up to 1 month.

Flavour Variation

Alcohol syrup: make the **Simple Syrup** as opposite, then add 200ml (7fl oz/scant 1 cup) alcohol of your choice (such as Grand Marnier, rum or kirsch) once the syrup has cooled.

Used in
Brioche Polonaise *(see pages 202–203)*
Bostock *(see pages 204–205)*
Matcha Mont Blanc *(see pages 250–252)*
Nectarine & Cassis Entremet *(see pages 258–259)*
Redcurrant & Fromage Frais Entremet *(see pages 262–264)*
Yuzu & Praline Tarts *(see pages 158–159)*
Jasmine & Mandarin Pyramid *(see pages 218–219)*
Apricot & Pistachio Delice *(see pages 225–227)*
Chocolate & Chestnut Buche *(see pages 278–279)*
Chocolate & Jasmine Sphere *(see pages 236–237)*
Chocolate, Banana & Peanut Caramel Bar *(see pages 222–224)*
Fraisier *(see pages 268–269)*
Jaffa Cake *(see pages 276–277)*
Trois Frères *(see pages 273–275)*

Used in
Baba au Rhum *(pages 198–199)*
Rice Pudding, Rhubarb & Elderflower Verrine *(pages 314–315)*

Apricot Nappage

This is a traditional glaze used for a variety of pâtisserie and cakes.

Makes 850g (1lb 13oz)

200g (7oz) cox apples
  washed and roughly chopped
200g (7oz) fresh apricots
  stoned and roughly chopped
400g (14oz/2 cups) caster
  (superfine) sugar
100ml (3½fl oz/scant ½ cup) water
12g (¼oz) pectin
5g (1 tsp) lemon juice

- Put the apples and apricots in a pan with half the sugar and the water. *(1–2)*

- Cook over a low heat for about 15–20 minutes until the apples become soft. Remove from the heat, then leave to cool slightly. *(3)*

- Transfer to a food processor and blend until smooth. *(4–5)*

- Put the puréed fruit in a clean saucepan, return to the heat and bring to the boil. *(6)*

- Mix together the remaining sugar with the pectin in a bowl. Take the boiling purée off the heat, add the pectin and sugar, return to the heat and cook over a low heat for 5 minutes. *(7)*

- Add the lemon juice, bring back to the boil, then remove from the heat and leave to cool slightly. *(8)*

- Pass though a fine sieve (strainer) into an airtight container and leave to cool before transferring to the fridge. *(9–10)*

Store in an airtight container in the fridge and use within 1 week.

Used in

Light Fruit Nappage

This is a very light glaze generally used for glazing fruits used for decorations.

Makes 625g (1lb 4oz)

300ml (½ pint/1¼ cups) water
300g (10½oz) liquid glucose
40g (1½oz/scant ¼ cup) caster (superfine) sugar
18g (¾oz) pectin

- Place the water and glucose in a saucepan and bring to the boil.

- Mix together the sugar and pectin in a small bowl, whisk into the boiling mixture and cook for about 2–3 minutes. Transfer to an airtight container and leave to cool before transferring to the fridge.

Store in an airtight container in the fridge and use within 1 week.

Used in

Fig & Hazelnut Tart
(pages 140–141)

Fruit Glaze

This glaze is ideal for glazing the tops of entremets and petits gâteaux.

Makes 275g (9¾oz)

8g (¼oz) leaf gelatine
175g (6oz) nectarine purée
  (or other fruit purée)
100g (3½oz) **Simple Syrup**
  (see page 102)
½ vanilla pod (bean)
  split lengthways

- Soak the gelatine in a bowl of ice-cold water for a few minutes until soft. Squeeze to remove any excess water *(see page 31)*. Put the nectarine purée and Simple Syrup in a saucepan. *(1)*

- Scrape the seeds from the split vanilla pod (bean) into the pan and drop in the empty pod (bean) too. Bring to the boil. *(2)*

- Take off the heat, add the soaked gelatine *(3)* and strain into an airtight container. Cool. *(4)*

Store in an airtight container in the fridge and use within 1 week.

Flavour Variation

You can use different flavoured fruit purées to make this fruit glaze, such as raspberry, apricot, blackcurrant and also orange juice.

Used in

Fraisier *(pages 268–269)*
Nectarine & Cassis Entremet *(pages 258–259)*
Pineapple Tart Tatin *(pages 182–184)*
Redcurrant & Fromage Frais Entremet *(pages 262–264)*
Fraise de Bois & Sudachi Teardrop *(pages 214–217)*

Dark Chocolate Glaze

A wonderfully simple glaze, ideal for coating chocolate entremets and petits gâteaux.

Makes 750g (1lb 10oz)

18g (¾oz) leaf gelatine
235ml (8fl oz/1 cup) water
300g (10½oz/1½ cups) caster (superfine) sugar
100g (3½oz/1 cup) cocoa powder *sifted*
170ml (6fl oz/¾ cup) whipping (pouring) cream

- Soak the gelatine in a bowl of ice-cold water for a few minutes until soft. Squeeze to remove any excess water *(see page 31)*.

- Put the water and sugar in a saucepan, bring to the boil, then continue to simmer over a low heat for 2–3 minutes.

- Add the sifted cocoa powder and the cream. *(1)*

- Bring back to the boil and simmer for 4–5 minutes. *(2)*

- Take the pan off the heat, add the pre-soaked gelatine and stir until dissolved. *(3)*

- Strain, then leave to cool. *(4–5)*

Store in an airtight container in the fridge and use within 4 days.

Note: *see page 35 for glazing instructions.*

Milk Chocolate Glaze

This glaze is rich in flavour as it is made with real milk chocolate.

Makes 650g (1lb 7oz)

400g (14oz) milk chocolate (35% cocoa solids) *finely chopped*
260ml (9fl oz/1¼ cups) whipping (pouring) cream
40g (½oz) liquid glucose

- Put the chopped chocolate in a mixing bowl. Put the cream and liquid glucose in a saucepan and bring to the boil.

- Pour the boiled cream over the chocolate and mix well until emulsified. Transfer to a container and leave to cool.

Store in an airtight container in the fridge and use within 4 days.

Note: *see page 35 for glazing instructions.*

Used in
Jasmine & Madarin Pyramid *(pages 218–219)*
Apricot & Wasabi Entremet *(pages 286–287)*
Chocolate & Chestnut Buche *(pages 278–279)*
Coffee & Walnut Dacquoise *(pages 230–232)*

Used in
Earl Grey, & Coconut Entremet *(pages 265–267)*

White Chocolate Glaze

A versatile glaze that gives a glossy finish and can be adapted with the addition of different coloured ingredients.

Makes 850g (2lb)

15g (½oz) leaf gelatine
210ml (7¼fl oz/scant 1 cup) water
105g (3oz/½ cup) caster (superfine) sugar
210g (7¼oz) liquid glucose
140ml (4½fl oz/¾ cup) double (heavy) cream
210g (7¼oz) white chocolate *finely chopped*

- Soak the gelatine in a bowl of ice-cold water for a few minutes until soft. Squeeze to remove any excess water *(see page 31)*.
- Put the water, sugar and glucose in a saucepan, bring to the boil and heat to 103°C (218°F).
- Add the cream and soaked gelatine. Pour over the white chocolate in another bowl, then blitz with a hand-held electric blender.

Store in an airtight container in the fridge and use within 4 days.

Note: *see page 35 for glazing instructions.*

Flavour Variation

White Chocolate & Matcha Glaze: make as above, with 10g (2 tsp) matcha powder mixed with 1½ tbsp water added in.

Used in
Raspberry & Rose Entremet
(pages 280–283)

Dark Chocolate Ganache Glaze

This is a light chocolate ganache used as a glaze. It has a wonderful flavour as real chocolate is used as opposed to cocoa powder.

Makes 600g (1lb 6oz)

260ml (9fl oz/scant 1¼ cups) whipping (pouring) cream
50g (1¾oz/¼ cup) caster (superfine) sugar
40g (1½oz) liquid glucose
250g (9oz) dark (bittersweet) chocolate (66% cocoa solids) *chopped*

- Put the cream, sugar and liquid glucose in a saucepan and bring to the boil. *(1)*
- Gradually add the hot cream to the chopped chocolate, mixing continuously to form an emulsion. *(2–3)* Pour into an airtight container and leave to cool before transferring to the fridge.

Store in an airtight container in the fridge and use within 4 days.

Note: *see page 35 for glazing instructions.*

Used in
Classic Opéra
(pages 248–249)

1

2

3

Raspberry Confiture

Confiture is the French word for Jam. The name jam came into the English language in the 18th century; prior to that it was referred to as preserve or conserve. Methods of preserving fruit are ancient in history. In Roman times a scientist and historian wrote about a preparation of quinces that were candied in honey; this was the most likely ancestor of confiture. During the crusades the crusaders brought back Arabian recipes of preserving fruit. By the 14th century confiture was highly valued in France and it was during this century that the first recipes of confiture were published; although the main sweetener in these recipes was honey and not sugar.

Makes 2 x 200g (7oz) jars

150g (5½oz) **Fruit Purée** *(see page 110) made with raspberries*
150g (5½oz/1¼ cups) raspberries
120g (4oz/⅔ cup) caster (superfine) sugar
20g (¾oz) pectin
10ml (2 tsp) lemon juice

- Put the raspberry purée, raspberries and 75g (2¾oz/⅓ cup) of the sugar in a heavy-based saucepan and bring to the boil. *(1)*

- Mix the remaining sugar with the pectin in a small bowl. *(2)*

- Whisk the pectin mixture into the boiling raspberry liquid. *(3)*

- Continue to cook over a low heat, stirring continuously until the mixture reaches 104°C (219°F). Add the lemon juice and continue to cook for a further 2–3 minutes. *(4)*

- Test to see if the confiture has reached setting point. Spoon a small amount of confiture onto a cold plate or saucer, then put it in the fridge for 2 minutes. Gently press the edge of the confiture with a spoon. It is set if a skin has formed and the edges wrinkle. If it doesn't, continue to cook the confiture for another 2 minutes and then check again. *(5)*

- Pour the confiture into a sterilized jam jar and leave to cool before closing the lid. *(6)*

The confiture can be stored in the fridge for up to 1 month.

Used in

Beignet Alsacienne *(pages 206–207)*

Bakewell Tarts *(pages 144–145)*

Jammy Dodger *(page 332)*

Caramelized Pear, Blackcurrant & Chocolate Breton *(pages 164–165)*

Strawberry & Pistachio Breton Tart *(pages 162–163)*

Chocolate & Cherry Linzer Tarts *(pages 148–149)*

Gateux Conversation *(pages 176–177)*

Puits d'Amour *(pages 178–179)*

Macarons – whole section *(pages 294–303)*

Blackcurrant Pâte de Fruit

Pâte de fruit was created in the 17th century by a French pâtissier called Gilliers. During this period, gelatine was used instead of pectin and originally it was a mixture of fruit purée, brown sugar, gelatine and spices.

Makes one 28 x 22cm (11 x 8½ inch) non-stick baking mat

240g (8½oz) **Fruit Purée** *(see page 110) made with blackcurrants*
50g (1¾oz) blackcurrants
225g (8oz/generous 1 cup) caster (superfine) sugar
95g (3oz) liquid glucose
10g (¼oz) pectin
2.5g (½ tsp) lemon juice

- Put the blackcurrant purée, whole blackcurrants, 150g (5½oz/¾ cup) of the sugar and the liquid glucose in a saucepan and bring to the boil. *(1)*

- Mix the remaining sugar with the pectin in a small bowl. *(2)*

- Whisk the pectin mixture into the boiling blackcurrant purée. *(3)*

- Continue to cook over a low heat, stirring continuously, until the mixture reaches 104°C (219°F) on a sugar thermometer. *(4)*

- Mix in the lemon juice and continue to cook for 3–4 minutes. *(5)*

- Pour the blackcurrant mixture into a non-stick baking mat with raised sides and leave to set for 2–3 hours in a cool, dry place. *(6)*

Use as required – if you have extra leftover you can cut into squares, roll in sugar and use as petits fours.

Will keep for 2 weeks wrapped well in a cool, dry place.

Used in
Purple Sweet Potato Macaron
(page 301)

Stone Fruit Purée

This method is used for firm fruits to break them down and prevent discolouring.

Makes 550g (1lb 3oz)

50ml (2fl oz/scant ¼ cup) water
50g (1¾oz/¼ cup)
  caster (superfine) sugar
500g (1lb 2oz/3 cups) cherries *stoned*
  (or other fruits)
10ml (2 tsp) lemon juice

• Put the water, sugar and cherries in a saucepan, bring to the boil, then simmer over a low heat for 10 minutes. Take off the heat, add the lemon juice, then leave to cool. *(1–2)*

• Transfer to a food processor, blitz until smooth, then strain *(3–4)* into an airtight container. Leave to cool, then transfer to the fridge.

Store in an airtight container in the fridge for 2–3 days.

Used in
Chocolate & Cherry Linzer Tarts
(pages 148–149)
Pistachio & Cherry Arctic Roll
(pages 292–293)

Soft Fruit Purée

A quick and easy way to make purée. This method works best with soft fruits – such as strawberries, raspberries and rhubarb. Maximum flavour is retained as the fruit is not cooked.

Makes 600g (1lb 6oz)

500g (1lb 2oz/4½ cups) strawberries
50ml (2fl oz/scant ¼ cup) water
50g (1¾oz/¼ cup) caster
  (superfine) sugar
10ml (2 tsp) lemon juice

• Wash and hull the strawberries, place in a food processor and blitz to a purée. *(1–2)*

• Put the water and sugar in a saucepan and bring to the boil. Remove from the heat and leave to cool slightly.

• Pour the warm syrup and lemon juice into the strawberries and mix. *(3)* Pass the purée through a fine sieve (strainer) into an airtight container. *(4)* Leave to cool, then transfer to the fridge.

Store in an airtight container in the fridge until required for 2–3 days.

1

Fruit Compote

Compotes are an essential part of entremets and petits gâteaux and bring an intensity of flavour with the fresh fruit used.

Makes 200g (7oz)

15g (1 tbsp) caster (superfine) sugar
5g (1 tsp) pectin
100g (3½oz) **Fruit Purée** *(see page 110) made with redcurrants*
100g (3½oz) whole redcurrants *(or other fruit)*

• Mix together the sugar and pectin in a small bowl.

• Put the fruit purée and whole fruit in a saucepan and bring to the boil. Add the sugar and pectin and cook for 2–3 minutes. *(1–2)*

• Pour into a shallow tray. Leave to cool, then put in an airtight container and transfer to the fridge. *(3–4)*

Store in an airtight container in the fridge for up to 3–4 days.

2

Used in
Redcurrant & Fromage Frais Entremet *(pages 262–264)*
Fraisier *(pages 268–269)*
Nectarine & Cassis Entremet *(pages 258–259)*
Peach Melba *(pages 308–309)*
Lemon Tart *(page 336)*
Raspberry & Pistachio Macaron *(pages 260–261)*
Rice Pudding, Rhubarb & Elderflower Verrine *(pages 314–315)*
Rhubarb & Ginger Sablé *(pages 160–161)*
Choux à la Crème *(pages 188–190)*
Chocolate & Jasmine Sphere *(pages 236–237)*
Fraise de Bois & Sudachi Teardrop *(pages 214–216)*
Pistachio & Cherry Arctic Roll *(pages 292–293)*
Raspberry & Rose Entremet *(pages 280–283)*

3

4

Marmalade

The creator of marmalade is unknown, but I like to believe a little Scottish folklore. The story goes that a grocer, James Keillor, took advantage of a Spanish ship in Dundee harbour carrying a cargo of Seville oranges. He bought a large quantity, but found he was unable to sell them. Not wishing to waste the fruit, his wife used the oranges to make some preserve. They proved to be so popular that the Dundee public demanded more and the grocer from then on ensured a regular order for Seville oranges.

Makes 600g (1lb 6oz)

2 seville oranges *(weighing about 225g/8oz in total)*
½ a lemon
500ml (18fl oz/generous 2 cups) water
400g (14oz/2 cups) jam sugar
25g (1oz) dark soft brown sugar

- Remove the orange peel in long strips using a peeler, trim any white pith from the peel, finely slice and place in a muslin (cheesecloth) bag. *(1–2)*

- Roughly chop the oranges and lemon, put in a saucepan with the water, both sugars and the peel in the muslin (cheesecloth) bag. Simmer over a low heat, uncovered, for about 2 hours until the fruit is tender. Remove the muslin (cheesecloth) bag and set aside to drain. *(3–5)* Line a colander with layers of muslin (cheesecloth) and set over a bowl. Strain the contents of the pan through the muslin, then leave to drain for 30 minutes, then squeeze the remaining liquid by twisting the cloth. *(6–7)*

- Return the strained liquid and the peel from the muslin (cheesecloth) to a clean pan, bring to the boil and cook until it reaches 104°C (219°F), stirring continuously. *(8)* Test the marmalade is setting: spoon a small amount onto a cold plate and leave to cool. If it sets, take the marmalade off the heat and place in a sterilized jar; seal. If it does not set, try again after a few more minutes. *(9–10) Store in an airtight container in the fridge for up to 1 month.*

Flavour Variation

Yuzu Marmalade: make as above but use the same weight of yuzu instead of oranges.

Used in
Jaffa Cake *(pages 276–277)*
Matcha Macarons *(page 302)*

1

2

3

4

5

Confit Fruit

We use this as a decoration on the Jaffa Cake *(see pages 276–277)*. It could also be cut, dried and coated in chocolate.

Makes 750g (1lb 10oz)

3 Navel oranges *(or other fruit, see Variations) (about 750g/1lb 10oz)*
500ml (18fl oz/generous 2 cups) water
375g (13oz/scant 2 cups) caster (superfine) sugar
1 vanilla pod (bean) *split lengthways*

- Score around the outside of the oranges in quarters, then gently take off each quarter of the peel. *(1)*

- Bring a pan of water to the boil, then add the orange peel and blanch for 2 minutes. Drain the peel and discard the water. Refresh under cold water, then repeat the blanching process twice more. *(2)*

- Put the water and sugar in a saucepan with the split and scraped vanilla pod (bean) and bring to the boil. Add the drained orange peel to the syrup and bring back to the boil. Reduce to a low heat and continue to cook for 2 hours until the orange is soft and candied. *(3)*

- Pour into a shallow tray and leave to cool before transferring to the fridge. *(4)*

Store in an airtight container in the fridge for up to 1 month.

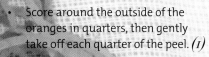

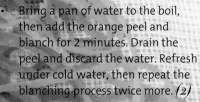

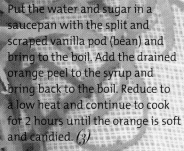

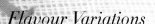

Flavour Variations

Other fruits suitable to be made into confit are grapefruit, lemon and yuzu. Just use the same weight of fruit.

To make crystallized confit fruit: leave the confit fruit to drain on a wire rack for 3–4 hours, cut into cubes, then roll in granulated (white) sugar.

Armagnac-marinated Prunes

I adore these marinated prunes, as does my friend Richard Bertinet in Bath, who quite often has one as a mid-morning snack! Great in pâtisserie and cakes, they can also be enjoyed with a bowl of vanilla ice cream.

Makes 2 x 200g (7oz) jars

425ml (15fl oz/generous 1¾ cups) water
90g (3oz/scant ½ cup) caster (superfine) sugar
5g (1 tsp) Earl Grey tea leaves
250g (9oz/2½ cups) prunes *(ideally prunes d'agen) pitted*
125ml (4fl oz/½ cup) Armagnac

- Put the water and sugar in a saucepan and bring to the boil. Put the tea leaves in an infuser bag. *(1)*

- Put the bag in the saucepan of syrup. Take the pan off the heat and leave to infuse for 2 minutes. *(2)*

- Add the prunes to the tea-infused syrup. Leave to marinate for 1 hour. *(3–4)*

- Remove the tea bag and add the Armagnac. *(5)*

- Spoon the prunes into 2 sterilized jars and pour over the marinating syrup. Cover the jars and leave to cool. Once completely cool, close the lids and leave to marinate overnight or preferably up to 1 month before use. *(6)*

Store in the fridge for up to 3 months.

Used in
Far Breton *(page 324)*
Classic Gâteau Basque *(pages 154–155)*

Rum-marinated Sultanas

These are simple to prepare, they also marinate quickly. They add a delicious dimension to dishes.

Makes 350g (12oz)

250g (9oz/1¼ cups) sultanas (golden raisins)
100ml (3½fl oz/scant ½ cup) dark rum

- Bring a saucepan of water to the boil and add the sultanas (golden raisins). *(1)*

- Simmer for 2–3 minutes, then strain. *(2–3)*

- Spoon the sultanas (golden raisins) into sterilized jars *(4)* and pour over the dark rum. *(5)*

- Seal and leave to marinate for at least 24 hours.

Store in the fridge for up to 3 months.

Used in
Kugelhopf *(pages 208–209)*
Cadeaux au Chocolat *(pages 253–255)*
Stollen *(pages 210–211)*

Praline Paste

Praline paste is a mixture of sugar and nuts cooked over a high heat until it caramelizes. After cooling, it is pounded between steel rollers until the desired smoothness is obtained. Praline was created in 1732 by a French head waiter called Clement Jaluzot employed by the Duc de Choiseul, Comte de Plessis-Pralin. The idea for the paste was sparked by one of Jaluzot's apprentices, who was eating almonds with pieces of caramel; he commented on the wonderful combination of the nuts and confectionery. Jaluzot named the new paste praline in honour of the Duke. The paste was first served in the shape of bonbons or sweets at a banquet held by the Duke.

Makes 2 x 200g (7oz) jars

150g (5½oz/generous 1 cup) hazelnuts
150g (5½oz/generous 1 cup) almonds
300g (10½oz/1½ cups) caster (superfine) sugar
10ml (2 tsp) hazelnut oil

- Preheat the oven to 200°C (400°F/Gas 6). Spread the nuts out on a baking tray (sheet) lined with a non-stick baking mat. *(1)*

- Roast in the preheated oven for 8–10 minutes until lightly golden and then transfer to a heavy-based saucepan. *(2)*

- Cook over a medium heat while gradually adding the sugar and stirring continuously. *(3–6)*

- Continue to cook and stir until the sugar turns an amber caramel, about 15–18 minutes. *(7)*

- Pour the caramelized nuts onto a baking tray (sheet) lined with a non-stick baking mat and leave to cool. *(8)*

- When the nuts have cooled, break up the praline and transfer it to a good food processor or blender. Add the hazelnut oil. *(9)*

- Blitz until you have a smooth paste. *(10–12)*

Store in an airtight container for up to 2 months.

Used in
Coffee & Walnut Dacquoise *(pages 230–232)*
Chocolate, Banana & Peanut Caramel Bar *(pages 222–224)*

Flavour Variations

Walnut Paste: make as above, but use 300g (10½oz) walnuts instead of hazelnuts and almonds.

Peanut Paste: make as above, but use 300g (10½oz) unsalted roasted peanuts instead of hazelnuts and almonds.

Pistachio Paste
Makes 115g (4oz)

100g (3½oz) pistachios
15ml (1 tbsp) pistachio oil
 (or other nut oil)

- Put the pistachios and oil in a food processor and blitz together until it becomes a smooth paste.

Caramelized Gianduja
Makes 650g (1lb 7oz)

150g (5½oz/generous 1 cup) almonds, *lightly roasted*
150g (5½oz/generous 1 cup) hazelnuts, *lightly roasted*
150g (5½oz/¾ cup) caster (superfine) sugar
50ml (2fl oz/scant ¼ cup) water
150g (5½oz) dark (bittersweet) chocolate
 (65% cocoa solids)
150g (5½oz) milk chocolate (35% cocoa solids)

- Put the almonds and hazelnuts in a saucepan. Put the sugar and water in another pan, bring to the boil and continue to cook to 118°C (244°F). Pour the syrup over the nuts and place over a medium heat and continue to cook, stirring, until the nuts have caramelized. Pour the nuts onto a non-stick baking mat and separate the nuts as they cool.

- Once cooled, place the chocolates in a mixing bowl and melt over a bain-marie *(see page 31)*. Put the nuts in a food processor and blitz to a smooth runny paste. Add the paste to the melted chocolates, then leave to cool.

Store in an airtight container in a cool room for up to 2 months.

Sea Salt Caramel

Salted caramel originates from Brittany, France, where fleur de sel is produced. The origin of the word 'caramel' can be traced to the Latin word *caramellis* (sugar cane). Caramel itself dates a long way back; the most primitive versions dating back to 1000 AD. This early caramel was made by the Arabs who called it *kurat al milh* or 'sweet ball of salt', due to its appearance. It was made by boiling sugar cane in water. The result was hard and crunchy, whereas today's caramel comes in many different consistencies.

Makes about 500g (1lb 2oz)

185ml (6½fl oz/generous ¾ cup) whipping (pouring) cream
1 vanilla pod (bean) *split lengthways*
365g (12½oz/generous 1¾ cups) caster (superfine) sugar
60g (2oz) liquid glucose
300g (10½oz/1⅓ cups) room temperature sea salt butter *cubed*

- Put the cream in a saucepan. Scrape the seeds from the split vanilla pod (bean) into the cream and drop in the empty pod (bean) too. Bring to the boil. Take off the heat and leave to infuse for 30 minutes. *(1–2)*

- Heat an empty heavy-based saucepan. When it is hot, add one-third of the sugar with the liquid glucose and heat slowly until it forms a light caramel and the sugar crystals have dissolved. *(3–4)*

- Add the remaining sugar and continue to cook until you get an amber caramel. This will take up to 10 minutes, but there are lots of variables so you must be vigilant and keep watch while it is cooking. *(5–7)*

- Gradually add the cream to the caramel (discarding the vanilla as you do). Mix well, then take off the heat. *(8)*

- Add the butter, cube by cube. *(9)*

- Pour onto a shallow tray and leave to cool. *(10)*

Store in an airtight container in a cool room for up to 1 month.

Flavour Variation

Japanese Muscovado Caramel: make the recipe as above but use half caster (superfine) sugar and half Japanese muscovado sugar.

Used in
Caramel Chantilly *(pages 220–221)*
Chocolate, Banana & Peanut Caramel Bar *(pages 222–224)*
Coffee & Walnut Dacquoise *(pages 230–232)*
Les Misérables *(pages 241–243)*
Chocolate Macaron *(page 298)*

Tuiles

These are simple to make and add a wonderful dimension to dishes with elegance and texture.

Lemon Tuile

Makes two 30 x 40cm (12 x 16 inch) baking trays (sheets)

3g (½ tsp) pectin
150g (5½oz/¾ cup) caster (superfine) sugar
50ml (2fl oz/scant ¼ cup) lemon juice
100g (3½oz/scant ½ cup) unsalted butter
50g (1¾oz) liquid glucose

- Preheat the oven to 180°C (350°F/Gas 4). Mix together the pectin and sugar in a small bowl. Put the lemon juice, butter and glucose in a saucepan and bring to the boil. Take off the heat and whisk in the pectin and sugar mixture. Return to the heat and bring back to the boil. Take off the heat and leave to cool slightly.

- Spread the mixture out thinly on a baking tray (sheet) lined with a non-stick baking mat. *(1–3)*

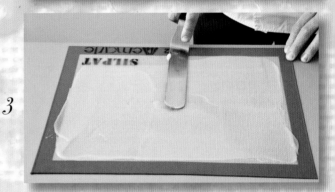

- Place another non-stick baking mat on top, then bake for 8–10 minutes. *(4–5)* Leave to cool, then carefully remove the non-stick baking mat.

Store in an airtight container and use within 2–3 days.

Used in
Apple & Edamame Verrine *(pages 312–313)*

Lemon & Basil Posset *(pages 310–311)*

Peach Melba *(pages 308–309)*

Rice Pudding, Rhubarb & Elderflower Verrine *(pages 314–315)*

Caramelized Pear, Blackcurrant & Chocolate Breton *(pages 164–165)*

Chocolate, Banana & Peanut Caramel Bar *(pages 222–224)*

1

2

3

4

5

Sesame Tuile

Makes two 30 x 40cm (12 x 16 inch) baking trays (sheets)

50g (1¾oz) isomalt
5g (⅛oz/1 tsp) white sesame seeds *roasted*
5g (⅛oz/1 tsp) black sesame seeds

- Preheat the oven to 200°C (400°F/Gas 6). Put the isomalt in a food processor or blender and blitz until fine. Sift the isomalt powder onto a baking tray (sheet) lined with a non-stick baking mat. Sprinkle the sesame seeds over the top, then place another non-stick baking mat on top. Bake for 5–6 minutes until the isomalt has melted. Leave to cool, then carefully remove the baking mat. *Store in an airtight container and use within 2–3 days.*

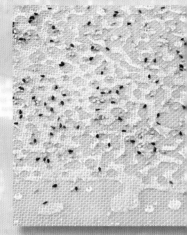

Chocolate Tuile

Makes two 30 x 40cm (12 x 16 inch) baking trays (sheets)

40g (1½oz) plain (all-purpose) flour
7g (1½ tsp) cocoa powder
150g (5½oz/¾ cup) caster (superfine) sugar
1g (a pinch) pectin
60ml (2¼fl oz/¼ cup) full-fat milk
50g (1¾oz/½ stick) unsalted butter

- Preheat the oven to 180°C (350°F/Gas 4). Sift the flour and cocoa powder together in a bowl. Mix 30g (1¼oz) of the sugar and the pectin together in another bowl. Put the milk, butter and the remaining sugar in a saucepan and bring to the boil. Add the pectin and sugar mixture and cook for 2 minutes, stirring continuously. Take off the heat and add the dry ingredients. Mix until smooth. Spread the mixture out thinly on a baking tray (sheet) lined with a non-stick baking mat. Place another non-stick baking mat on top, then bake for 8–10 minutes. Leave to cool, then carefully remove the baking mat. *Store in an airtight container and use within 2–3 days.*

Rhubarb Tuile

Makes one 30 x 40cm (12 x 16 inch) baking tray (sheet)

40g (1½oz) caster (superfine) sugar
10g (¼oz) pectin
120g (4½oz) **Fruit Purée** *(see page 110) made with rhubarb*

Note: *you can also use other fruit purées for this tuile.*

- Mix the sugar and pectin together in a small bowl. Put the rhubarb purée in a saucepan and bring to the boil. Take off the heat and whisk in the sugar and pectin. Return to the heat and bring back to the boil, stirring continuously. Cook for 1 minute, then take off the heat. Spread out thinly on a non-stick baking mat using a step palette knife. Place in a dehydrator at 60°C (140°F) for 4 hours. Alternatively, you can use an oven preheated to its lowest setting – this may take less time to dry. Leave to cool, then carefully remove the baking mat. *Store in an airtight container and use within 2–3 days.*

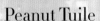

Peanut Tuile

Makes two 30 x 40cm (12 x 16 inch) baking trays (sheets)

100g (3½oz/½ cup) caster (superfine) sugar
1g (a pinch) pectin
40ml (1½fl oz/scant ¼ cup) milk
35g (1¼oz/2½ tbsp) butter
30g (1¼oz/2 tbsp) plain (all-purpose) flour *sifted*
25g (¾oz) peanuts *lightly roasted and roughly chopped*

Almond Tuile Variation: *replace the peanuts with lightly roasted flaked almonds.*

- Preheat the oven to 180°C (350°F/Gas 4). Put 20g (¾oz) of the sugar and the pectin in a small bowl and mix together. Put the milk, remaining sugar and butter in a small saucepan and bring to the boil. Take off the heat and whisk in the sugar and pectin. Return to the heat and bring back to the boil. Take off the heat and mix in the flour. Spread a thin layer on a baking tray (sheet) lined with a non-stick baking mat using a step palette knife. Spread the chopped peanuts over the top, then top with a sheet of silicone baking paper. Bake for 8–10 minutes until golden brown. Leave to cool, then carefully remove the baking mat. *Store in an airtight container and use within 2–3 days.*

Decorative Nuts

Crystallized and caramelized nuts add colour and a crunchy texture to our finished dishes.

Used in

Dundee Cake
(pages 318–319)

Thin Mango Tart *(pages 180–181)*

Chocolate & Cherry Linzer Tarts *(pages 148–149)*

Crystallized Pistachios

Makes 100g (3½oz)

100g (3½oz/¾ cup) pistachios
10ml (2 tsp) kirsch
30g (1¼oz/2 tbsp) caster (superfine) sugar

- Preheat the oven to 200°C (400°F/Gas 6). Mix the pistachios and kirsch together in a bowl *(1)*, add the sugar *(2)* and mix well.

- Spread the nuts out on a non-stick baking mat. *(3)* Bake in the preheated oven for 4–5 minutes, turning regularly, until crystallized. Separate the nuts and leave to cool. *Store in an airtight container and use within 2 weeks.*

Used in

Fig & Hazelnut Tart
(pages 140–141)

Crystallized Hazelnuts (or Almonds)

Makes 300g (10½oz)

250g (9oz/1¾ cups) hazelnuts (or almonds) *lightly roasted*
100g (3½oz/½ cup) caster (superfine) sugar
40ml (1½fl oz) water

- Put the hazelnuts in a saucepan and lightly warm on the stove. At the same time, put the sugar and water in another saucepan and cook to 118°C (244°F). Pour the cooked sugar onto the hazelnuts and mix well. *(1)* Place the pan onto the stove and, stirring continuously, cook over a medium heat until the sugar crystallizes. *(2)* Remove from the heat, spread and separate out the nuts on a non-stick baking mat and leave to cool. *(3) Store in an airtight container and use within 2 weeks.*

Used in

Green Tea & Azuki Bean Dome *(pages 233–235)*

Peach Melba
(pages 308–309)

Jaffa Cake
(pages 276–277)

Saint Marc *(pages 228–229)*

Caramelized Almond Batons

Makes 350g (12oz)

250g (9oz/2 cups) almond batons *lightly roasted*
40ml (1½fl oz) water
100g (3½oz/½ cup) caster (superfine) sugar
12g (½oz/1 tbsp) unsalted butter

- Put the almond batons in a saucepan and lightly warm on the stove. At the same time, put the water and sugar in another small saucepan and cook to 118°C (244°F). Pour this syrup over the almonds *(1)*, then set over a medium heat and cook until the almond batons crystallize and then gradually caramelize, stirring continuously. Take off the heat, then add the butter. *(2)* Spread and separate the nuts out on a baking tray (sheet) lined with a non-stick baking mat and leave to cool. *(3) Store in an airtight container and use within 2 weeks.*

These decorations have been used throughout the pâtisserie section, but please feel free to experiment and use different shapes and variations on the following suggestions to adorn your finished pâtisserie.

All the chocolate decorations require tempered chocolate (see page 34) to be successful. If the chocolate is not tempered it can result in the decorations not peeling away from the acetate or moulds, nor having a shiny finish. Once made the decorations need to be left for at least 2 hours in a cool, dry place to allow the chocolate to set properly before gently removing it from the acetate.

Note: *all chocolate decorations should be stored in an airtight container in a cool, dry place and used within 2 months.*

Flat Sheet Techniques

This technique is used for many of the different chocolate decorations. They are either cut with a set of pastry wheels, round cutters or a small knife and ruler.

Preparing a coloured base for spreading

- Gently melt 50g (1¾oz) cocoa butter in a bain-marie (*see page 31*) and mix in 5g (1 tsp) powdered colour for chocolate work. Heat to 45°C (113°F), then leave to cool to 32°C (90°F).

- Lightly stick a sheet of acetate to a plastic tray with a little oil to stop it slipping and rub over with cotton wool to remove any bubbles. Use a clean, dry sponge or a fine-haired paintbrush to cover the acetate in the coloured cocoa butter. (*1*) Use straight, fluid motions all in the same direction to create the desired effect. (*2*)

- If you wish the colour to be darker, let the first layer set and go over it again until you have the depth of colour you want. To enhance further you can brush a very thin layer of a different coloured luster dust on top.

- Follow the instructions below for spreading the chocolate.

Preparing & spreading chocolate – plain sheet

- Lightly stick a sheet of patterned or plain acetate to a plastic tray with a little oil, pattern facing up, and rub over with cotton wool to remove any bubbles.

- Thinly and evenly spread the tempered chocolate over the top. (*1*)

- Leave to semi-set, then cut or score the chocolate using a knife following the specific instructions for the desired decoration on pages 126–127. (*2*)

- Alternatively, cut or score the chocolate using pastry wheels for multiple squares or rectangles. (*3*)

- Place another sheet of acetate on top of the chocolate followed by a plastic tray to keep it flat while it sets. (*4*) Once the chocolate has fully set and you are ready to use, carefully peel the acetate away from the chocolate.

Advanced techniques

- You can buy pre-printed designs on acetate sheets (from PCB, *see page 344*), made with coloured cocoa butter.

- You can also buy textured plastic (from PCB, *see page 344*), which will imprint a different pattern on your flat sheet chocolate (*see page 126* Coffee & Walnut Dacquoise).

Flat Sheet Techniques *continued*

These specific cut shapes all use the techniques outlined on the previous page.

On the opposite page more advanced techniques use other tools and equipment to create more shapes.

Once mastered, the flat sheet technique offers endless opportunities for you to create your own unique decorations.

Small squares

- Cut with the pastry wheels 2cm (¾ inch) apart to create squares.

Used in
Yuzu & Praline Tarts
(pages 158–159)

Rectangles

- Score the chocolate with a small knife and ruler into 9 x 3cm (3½ x 1¼ inch) rectangles.

Used in
Apricot & Pistachio Delice
(pages 225–227)

Red rectangles

- Spread the acetate with the red-coloured cocoa butter *(see page 124)*, then the tempered chocolate and cut into 20 x 3cm (8 x 1¼ inch) rectangles.

Used in
Pistachio & Cherry Arctic Roll
(pages 292–293)

Large patterned squares

- Using textured plastic, score the chocolate into 7cm (2¾ inch) squares with a small knife and ruler.

Used in
Coffee & Walnut Dacquoise
(pages 230–232)

Red & white rectangles

- Spread the acetate with red cocoa butter, then the tempered white chocolate, then cut or score the chocolate into 4 x 2cm (1½ x ¾ inch) rectangles.

Used in
Redcurrant & Fromage Frais Entremet
(pages 262–264)

Saint Marc triangle

- Use a sheet of acetate 10 x 7cm (5 x 2¾ inches) in size. Randomly dust the acetate with silver powder on some cotton wool. *(1)* Thinly and evenly spread the tempered chocolate over the top with a step palette knife.

- When semi-set, take a knife and a ruler and score long triangles lengthways across the chocolate. *(2)*

- Place another sheet of acetate the same size on top. Quickly place between 2 sheets of corrugated plastic and gently push down. *(3)*

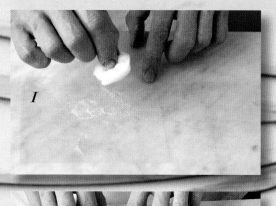

Used in **Saint Marc** *(pages 228–229)*

Slivers

- Spread the acetate with your desired colour of cocoa butter, then chocolate. Cut the semi-set chocolate into elongated 's' shapes across the length of the acetate.

Used in **Matcha Eclairs** *(pages 191–193)*

Apricot & wasabi palette

- Use an 8cm (3¼ inch) cutter to cut out discs, then use a 5cm (2 inch) cutter to cut discs inset to create a half moon effect. Then use a 12mm (⅝ inch and 7mm (¼ inch) piping nozzle to cut holes in the half moon shapes.

Used in **Apricot & Wasabi Entremet** *(pages 286–287)*

Red & white discs

- Spread the acetate with red cocoa butter, then tempered white chocolate, then cut the chocolate with a 3cm (1¼ inch) diameter cutter.

Used in **Raspberry & Rose Entremet** *(pages 280–283)*

Combing Techniques

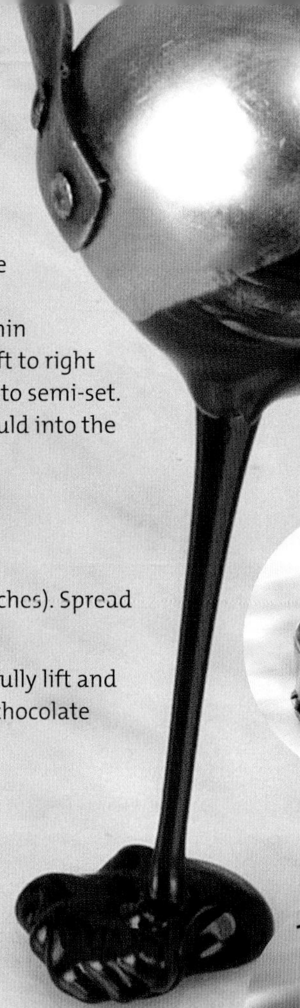

Basic technique

- Spoon a small amount of tempered chocolate onto an acetate strip, then use a small step palette knife to spread the chocolate into a thin layer. *(1)* Scrape with a comb scraper from left to right over the length of the acetate *(2)*, then leave to semi-set. Place another strip of acetate on top and mould into the desired shape.

Combed hoops

- Cut a strip of acetate to 4 x 22cm (1½ x 8¾ inches). Spread and comb the chocolate as above. *(1)*

- Once the combed chocolate is semi-set, carefully lift and wrap it around a metal rolling pin, with the chocolate against the tube. *(2)*

Used in
Jaffa Cake
(pages 276–277)

Combed wiggle

- Cut a rectangle of acetate 12 x 7cm (4½ x 2¾ inches) and when combing the chocolate, comb across the acetate in a wave. *(1)*

- Top with another sheet of acetate, then place a tray on top to set.

- Carefully remove the plastic and separate the strands once they are set. *(2)*

Used in
Les Misérables
(page 241–243)

Combed chocolate sticks

- Cut a sheet of acetate to 12 x 7cm (4½ x 2¾ inches) and spread and comb as above. *(1)*

- Leave the chocolate to set and place a sheet of acetate on top, followed by a plastic tray to keep it flat. Separate out the sticks once the chocolate is completely set. *(2)*

Used in
**Passion Fruit
& Pink
Grapefruit Tart**
(pages 152–153)

Combed wave

- Cut a sheet of acetate to 22 x 6cm (8½ x 2½ inches). Spread with white chocolate and comb as above. *(1)*

- Once it is semi-set, place a sheet of acetate the same size on top, then position it between 5cm (2 inch) rings to create elegant bends. *(2)*

- Carefully remove the plastic and separate the strands once they are set. Trim to your desired size.

Used in
Citrus Slice
(pages 238–240)

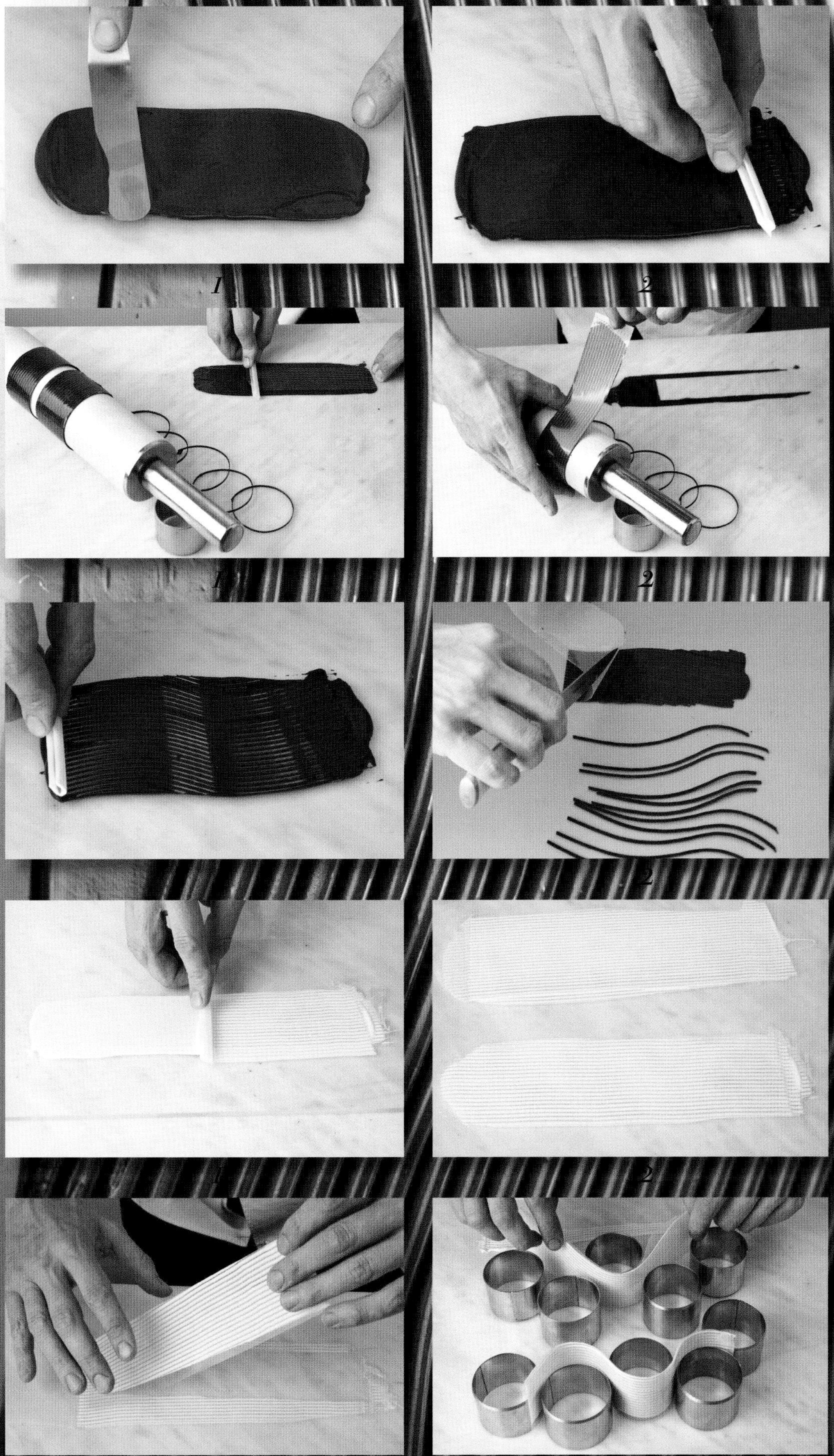

1

2

1

2

1

2

1

2

Piped Techniques

All of the following techniques require creating the decoration with chocolate from a paper piping cornet *(see page 30)*. Once the chocolate is tempered, fill the paper cornet half full, then cut the tip so you have a 0.5mm hole.

Curls

- Cut a rectangle of acetate 4 x 18cm (1½ x 3¼ inches). Pipe thin straight lines of chocolate along the acetate, then leave to semi-set. *(1)*

- Carefully lift the chocolate-coated acetate and curl it around to create a spiral. Place it on a curved tray to set. *(2)*

Joined hoops

- Cut out a rectangle of acetate to the required size. Pipe fine lines of chocolate across the length of the acetate, ensuring that you have a margin of 1cm (½ inch) on the left-hand side. Join the lines together with chocolate at the left-hand side. *(1)*

- Create a hoop with the acetate ensuring that the right-hand side of the acetate pushes into the join on the chocolate lines. Place into a 5cm (2 inch) ring mould to set. *(2)*

I

2

I

2
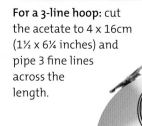

- **For a 3-line hoop:** cut the acetate to 4 x 16cm (1½ x 6¼ inches) and pipe 3 fine lines across the length.

Used in
Classic Opéra
(pages 248–249)

Used in
Green Tea & Azuki Bean Dome *(pages 233–235)*

Piped Copeaux

- Cut a 15 x 5cm (6 x 2 inch) strip from a sheet of acetate and position it horizontally in front of you. Starting 3cm (1¼ inches) up, pipe a line horizontally along the acetate strip. Pipe diagonally up to the 3cm (1¼ inch) line both ways, creating a net effect. *(1)* Carefully create a tube by rolling the bottom of the acetate into the piped line and continue to roll *(2–3)*. Secure with tape. When ready to use, use a knife to cut the tape and carefully unroll.

- **For a 7-line hoop:** cut the acetate to 8 x 16cm (3¼ x 6¼ inches) and pipe 7 fine lines across the length. *(3–4)*

Note: *you can pipe as many lines as you like to make different widths of hoops depending on your pâtisserie.*

Used in
Apricot & Pistachio Delice
(pages 225–227)

Used in
Pavlova
(pages 284–285)

Moulding Techniques

Chocolate semi-spheres

- Polish a plastic sphere mould. Using a ladle, fill the cavities up to the rim with tempered chocolate *(1)*, scraping off any excess.

- Tap the sides of the mould with the scraper to remove any air bubbles. *(2)*

- Turn the mould upside down over a large bowl and tap again to remove any further excess chocolate. *(3)*

- Scrape off any excess chocolate *(4)*, and place the mould upside down on a plastic tray lined with silicone baking paper. Leave to set for 2 hours in a cool, dry place or until the chocolate comes away from the mould.

- Twist the mould like an ice cube tray to loosen the spheres, then turn it upside down onto a clean surface. *(5)*

- To join the 2 halves together, follow the instructions on page 236 for the **Chocolate & Jasmine Sphere**.

Note: *when assembling it is always best practice to wear plastic gloves to prevent fingerprint marks on the chocolate.*

Copeaux

- Spread a thin layer of tempered chocolate onto a marble or granite slab using a step palette knife and leave to semi-set. *(1)*

- Using a metal scraper, push at an angle against the layer of chocolate to create thin cigar shapes (copeaux) *(2)* – a short sharp movement to the side will cause the copeaux to stay on the marble. Leave the copeaux to set on the surface for a few minutes, then remove with the metal scraper. *(3)*

Two-tone copeaux

- Spread a thin layer of tempered white chocolate onto a marble or granite slab using a step palette knife and leave to semi-set. Using a comb scraper, drag vertically down, creating stripes. *(1)*

- On top of the white chocolate stripes spread a thin layer of dark chocolate to fill the newly made gaps and leave to semi-set. *(2)*

- Using a metal scraper, push at an angle against the layer of chocolate to create thin cigar shapes (copeaux) *(3)* – a short sharp movement to the side will cause the two-tone copeaux to stay on the marble. Leave the two-tone copeaux to set on the surface for a few minutes, then remove with the metal scraper.

Note: *this background image is of Crystallized Vanilla Sticks (see page 31)*

2

3

Used in
**Chocolate &
Jasmine Sphere**
(pages 236–237)

2

3

Used in
**Matcha
Mont Blanc**
(pages 250–252)

2

3

Used in
**Marron
Barquette**
(page 336)

Moulding Techniques *continued*

Triangle flicks

- Cut out long thin triangles of your desired size from a sheet of acetate. Spread each triangle with a thin layer of tempered chocolate using a step palette knife. Leave to semi-set. *(1)*

- Carefully using the tip of a small knife, lift the triangle from the layer of chocolate. *(2)*

- Place it in a curved tray at an angle and leave to set. *(3)* Carefully peel off the acetate to use.

Triangle wiggle

- Cut a long thin triangle out of acetate 2 x 20cm (1 x 8 inches) long. Spread the triangle with a thin layer of chocolate and leave to semi-set. *(1)*

- Carefully using the tip of a small knife, lift the triangle from the layer of chocolate. *(2)*

- Place it in between 5cm (2 inch) rings to create elegant bends and leave to set. *(3)* Carefully peel off the acetate to use.

I

I

3

3

Used in
**Nectarine &
Cassis Entremet**
(pages 258–259)

Used in
**Earl Grey & Coconut
Entremet**
(pages 265–267)

134

Swiped flick

- Place a sheet of acetate on a plastic tray. Dip the tip of your index finger into a small bowl of tempered chocolate. Carefully swipe your finger on the acetate creating a delicate shape. Leave to set. Carefully peel the flick off the acetate to use.

Chocolate shavings

- Using a small knife, scrape the back of a tempered block of chocolate held at an angle to create chocolate shavings.

- Leave the shavings to stand for a few minutes to firm before moving.

Used in
**Cadeaux
au Chocolat**
(pages 253–255)

Used in
**Chocolate &
Chestnut Buche**
(pages 278–279)

Gold &
silver leaf

- We use gold and silver leaf to decorate many of our pâtisserie. Using the point of a sharp knife, carefully remove a piece of the gold/silver leaf and stick onto the surface of your dish.

Used in
**Jasmine &
Mandarin
Pyramid**
(pages 218–219)

The Pâtisserie

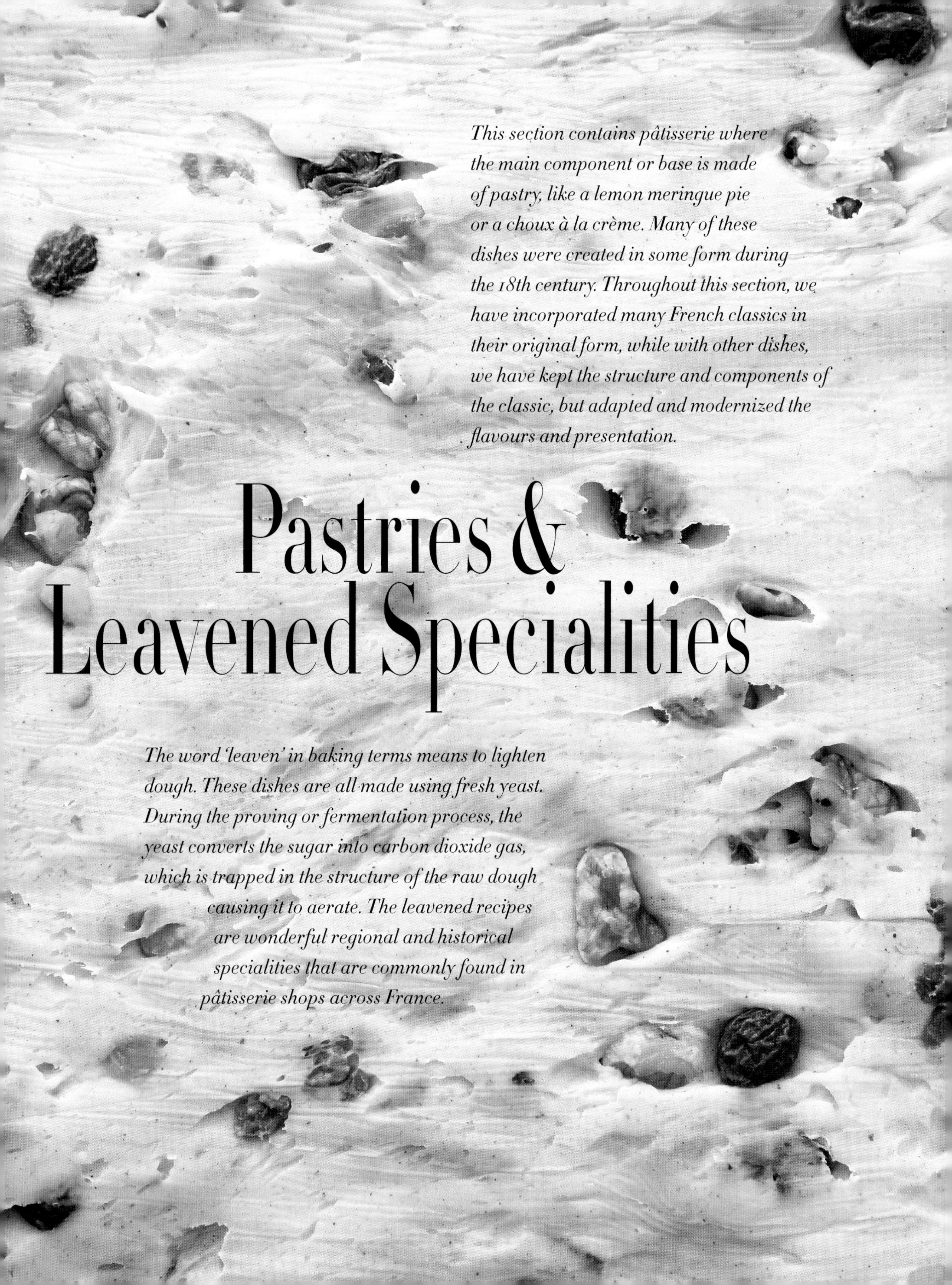

This section contains pâtisserie where the main component or base is made of pastry, like a lemon meringue pie or a choux à la crème. Many of these dishes were created in some form during the 18th century. Throughout this section, we have incorporated many French classics in their original form, while with other dishes, we have kept the structure and components of the classic, but adapted and modernized the flavours and presentation.

Pastries & Leavened Specialities

The word 'leaven' in baking terms means to lighten dough. These dishes are all made using fresh yeast. During the proving or fermentation process, the yeast converts the sugar into carbon dioxide gas, which is trapped in the structure of the raw dough causing it to aerate. The leavened recipes are wonderful regional and historical specialities that are commonly found in pâtisserie shops across France.

I love cooking with black Turkish figs; they are the sweetest variety and have the best flavour. They are only in season from late August through to October. Here figs complement the richness of the hazelnuts and the Scottish heather honey. Delicious served on its own or accompanied with Crème Anglaise (see pages 92–93).

Fig & Hazelnut Tart

*Makes 2 tarts
(each serves 6)*

1 quantity of **Pâte Brisée** *(see page 46)*
½ quantity of **Crystallized Hazelnuts** *(see pages 122–123)*
½ quantity of **Crème Noisette** *(see Variation, page 88)*
15 fresh figs *cut in half*
40g (1½oz) clear (runny) honey
100g (3½oz) **Clarified butter** *(see page 32) for brushing*
100g (3½oz) **Light Fruit Nappage** *(see page 105) to glaze*

You will also need:
two 14cm (5½ inch) tart rings
a 10mm (½ inch) plain piping nozzle (tip)

First, make the pastry & Crystallized Hazelnuts:

* Prepare the Pâte Brisée as instructed and chill for 2–3 hours. Prepare the Crystallized Hazelnuts, leave to cool, then store in an airtight container until needed.

* Take the pastry from the fridge and roll out to 3mm (⅛ inch) thick. Use the rolled out pastry to line the tarts *(see pages 44–45)*, then prick the bases well with a fork. Place the tarts in the fridge to rest for a further 30 minutes.

Meanwhile, preheat the oven to 180°C (350°F/Gas 4) & prepare the Crème Noisette.

* Spoon the Crème Noisette into a piping (pastry) bag fitted with an 10mm (½ inch) nozzle (tip) and pipe a ring into the base of each tart. *(1–2)*

To bake & finish:

* Place the figs on top of the crème. *(3–4)* Brush the figs with clear (runny) honey, then with the clarified butter. *(5)*

* Bake for 25–30 minutes until golden brown. Remove from the oven and leave to cool on a wire rack. Gently warm the nappage in a saucepan and use it to glaze the top of the tarts. Sprinkle with the Crystallized Hazelnuts to finish.

Best served the same day.

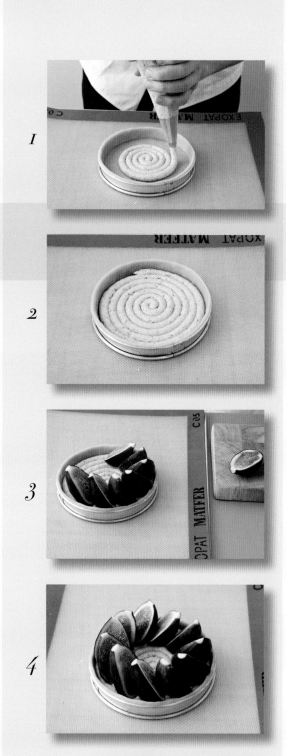

1

2

3

4

5

Tarte Alsacienne

Makes 2 tarts
(each serves 8)

Tartes aux pommes, or apple tarts, come in many different styles, and are eaten hot or cold. Different regions in France have their own speciality, with different ways of preparing and cooking. This version is the speciality of the Alsace region from the northwest of France.

1 quantity of
Pâte Brisée *(see page 46)*
1 **Crystallized Vanilla Stick**
(see page 31) to decorate

For the filling:
200g (7oz) whole eggs
  (about 4 eggs)
120g (4oz/⅔ cup)
  caster (superfine) sugar
2 vanilla pods (beans)
  split lengthways
240ml (8½fl oz/generous 1 cup)
  whipping (pouring) cream
240ml (8½fl oz/generous 1 cup)
  whole milk

For the caramelized apples:
8 apples
200g (7oz/1 cup)
  caster (superfine) sugar
60g (2oz/½ stick) unsalted butter
30ml (2 tbsp) Calvados

You will also need:
two 18cm (7inch) diameter,
  2.2cm (1 inch) deep tart tins

First, prepare & bake the pastry:

- Make the Pâte Brisée as instructed, then chill for 2–3 hours.

- Take the dough out of the fridge and divide into 2 equal parts. Roll each one out to 3mm (⅛ inch) thick and a minimum of 22cm (8½ inch) diameter and use to line each tart tin *(see pages 44–45)*.

- Put the tins on a baking tray (sheet) lined with a non-stick baking mat and chill for 30 minutes. Preheat the oven to 180°C (350°F/Gas 4).

- Take the lined tarts out of the fridge. Prepare the tarts for blind baking *(see pages 44–45)*, then bake for 12–15 minutes until the edges are lightly golden in colour. Remove the baking beans and cook for a further 10 minutes until the base of the tart is a light golden colour.

Next, make the filling:

- Put the milk and cream in a saucepan, add the split vanilla pod and scraped seeds, then bring to the boil. Take the pan off the heat, cover with cling film (plastic wrap) and leave to infuse for 30 minutes. Put the eggs into a mixing bowl, add the sugar and whisk together until light in colour. Pour the infused mixture over the eggs and whisk until smooth. Pass through a fine sieve (strainer).

Meanwhile, make the caramelized apples:

- Peel and core the apples. Cut in half, then each half into quarters. Make an amber dry caramel with the sugar *(see page 33)*, then add the butter and mix together. Toss in the prepared apples and mix again. *(1)*

- Once the juice begins to come out of the apples, add the Calvados. Cook over a low heat for 4–5 minutes, then set aside. *(2)*

To assemble & finish:

- Increase the oven temperature to 200°C (400°F/Gas 6). Strain the apples of any excess juice, then place them in the base of each tart, lining them in a spiral pattern (reserving a few to use as decoration). *(3)*

- Pour the filling into each tart very gently until each tart case is full. *(4–5)*

- Return the tarts to the oven and bake for 12–15 minutes until deep golden in colour.

- Take out of the oven and leave to cool. Decorate with the remaining caramelized apples and a crystallized vanilla stick.

Best served the same day.

1

2

3

4

5

This well-known and very popular English tart was created by chance by a female cook working in a hotel in the town of Bakewell, Derbyshire. The cook was making a flan using leftover pastry trimmings, which she then covered with jam. There were also extra eggs, sugar, almonds and butter. The cook mixed these all together, filled the flan and baked it – and the Bakewell Tart was born.

Bakewell Tarts   *Makes 18 small tarts*

1 quantity of **Raspberry Confiture** *(see page 108)*
1 quantity of **Pâte Sucrée** *(see page 47)*
1 quantity of **Crème d'Amande** *(see page 88)*
200g (7oz/2 cups) flaked almonds
100g (3½oz) **Apricot Nappage** *(see page 104)*

You will also need:
a 7.5cm (3 inch) pastry (cookie) cutter
eighteen 6.5cm (2½ inch) diameter, 2cm (¾ inch) deep tart moulds
a 10mm (½ inch) plain piping nozzle (tip)

First, make the confiture & the pastry:

- Prepare the confiture and leave to cool. Make the Pâte Sucrée and rest and chill as instructed. Place the rested dough on a lightly floured surface. Roll out to 3mm (⅛ inch) thick and cut out 18 pastry discs with the pastry (cookie) cutter. Line the tart moulds with the pastry *(see pages 44–45)*. Transfer to the fridge to rest.

Next, make the Crème d'Amande & finish:

- Take the lined tartlet cases from the fridge; spoon the raspberry confiture into a piping (pastry) bag pipe and pipe about 10g (¼oz/2 tsp) into the base of each tart. *(1)* Preheat the oven to 180°C (350°F/Gas 4).

- Make the Crème d'Amande and spoon it into a piping (pastry) bag fitted with a 10mm (½ inch) plain nozzle (tip). Pipe a bulb of cream into the base of each tart on top of the confiture. *(2)* Decorate the tops of each tart with the flaked almonds. *(3)*

- Place the tarts on a baking tray (sheet) and bake for 20–25 minutes until golden brown. Remove the tarts from their cases and place on a wire rack to cool. Reheat the Apricot Nappage and once the tarts have cooled, use a pastry brush to glaze each one. *(4)*

Best served the same day, or store in an airtight container for up to 2 days.

1

2

3

4

½ quantity of **Pâte Sucrée** *(see page 47)*
1 quantity of **Genoise** *(see page 66)*
½ quantity of **Lemon Curd** *(see pages 96–97)*
1 quantity of **Swiss Meringue** *(see page 75)*
icing (powdered) sugar *for dusting*

For the lemon syrup:
250ml (8½fl oz/1 cup) lemon juice
100ml (3½fl oz/½ cup) water
125g (4½oz/⅔ cup) caster (superfine) sugar

You will also need:
twelve 7cm (2 inch) diameter tart rings
10mm (½ inch) plain piping nozzle (tip)

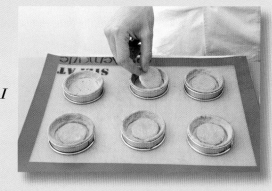

Lemon Meringue Pie *Makes 12 pies*

First, prepare some of the foundation recipes:

- Prepare the Pâte Sucrée as instructed and chill for 2–3 hours. Prepare the Genoise sponge sheet, then once baked and cooled, cut into eight 5cm (2 inch) discs. Prepare the Lemon Curd, then leave to set in the fridge.

Next, bake the tart cases:

- Preheat the oven to 180°C (350°F/Gas 4). Roll the rested pastry out to 3mm (⅛ inch) thick and cut 8 discs with a 9cm (3½ inch) cutter. Carefully line the tartlet rings *(see pages 44–45)*, then chill for at least 30 minutes. Blind bake *(see pages 44–45)* for 10–15 minutes, then remove the beans and return the tarts to the oven for a further 8 minutes.

Then, make the lemon syrup while the tarts are cooling:

- Put all the ingredients in a saucepan and bring to the boil.

To begin assembly:

- Increase the oven temperature to 200°C (400°F/Gas 6). Place the cut discs of sponge in the base of the tarts. Lightly soak with the lemon syrup. Spoon the prepared lemon curd into a piping (pastry) bag fitted with the 10mm (½ inch) plain nozzle (tip) and pipe it into the base of the baked tart cases on top of the sponge. *(1–2)*

Now, prepare the Swiss Meringue & finish:

- Make the meringue, then spoon into a piping (pastry) bag fitted with a clean 10mm (½ inch) plain nozzle (tip) and pipe bulbs on the top of each tart. *(3)*

- Dust generously with icing (powdered) sugar. *(4)*

- Bake for 4–5 minutes until the meringue has caramelized. *(5)*

Best stored in the fridge until prior to serving and then eaten the same day.

Lemon flavoured custards, puddings and pies have been enjoyed since medieval times but lemon meringue pie was perfected in the late 18th century. One of the first known recipes for lemon meringue pie appeared in an edition of Isabella Beeton's cookery book Household Management, *first published in 1893.*

Chocolate & Cherry Linzer Tarts

Makes 10 tarts

1 quantity of **Crystallized Pistachios** *(see pages 122–123)*

300g (10½oz) tempered dark (bittersweet) chocolate *(see page 34) used to make* **Copeaux** *(see pages 132–133)*

½ quantity of **Fruit Confiture** *(see page 108) made with whole cherries and cherry purée*

For the spiced chocolate pâte sucrée:

1 quantity of **Pâte Sucrée** *(see page 47) but replace 75g (2¾oz) of the flour with cocoa powder and also add 2g (a good pinch) cinnamon powder, 1g (a pinch) each of ground nutmeg and ground ginger*

For the spiced ganache:

1 quantity of **Dark Chocolate Ganache** *(see pages 90–91)*

1 cinnamon stick

1g (a pinch) of ground nutmeg

For the confit cherries:

90g (3oz/scant 1 cup) caster (superfine) sugar

15g (1 tbsp) pectin

750g (1lb 10oz) cherries *stoned*

120ml (4fl oz/½ cup) water

25ml (1fl oz/1½ tbsp) raspberry vinegar

You will also need:

a 9cm (3½ inch) round cutter

ten 7cm (2¾ inch) diameter, 1.5cm (¾ inch) deep tartlet rings

First, prepare the decorations & Pâte Sucrée:

- Prepare the pistachios, leave to cool, then store in an airtight container until needed. Temper the chocolate and make the decorations as instructed, then leave in a cool, dry place to set for 2 hours.

- To make the spiced pastry, sift together the flour, cocoa powder and spices together, then continue to prepare the pastry, as instructed, then chill for 2–3 hours. Take the spiced chocolate pastry from the fridge and roll out to 3mm (⅛ inch) thick. Cut out 10 discs with a 9cm (3½ inch) cutter and carefully line the tartlet rings *(see pages 44–45)*, then chill for at least 30 minutes. Preheat the oven to 180°C (350°F/Gas 4).

- Remove the rested tartlet cases from the fridge and blind bake *(see pages 44–45)* for 10–12 minutes. Remove the baking beans and continue to cook for a further 5 minutes. Remove from the oven and leave to cool. *(1)*

Next, prepare the ganache & confiture:

- Prepare the ganache, by making an infusion with the cream and spices first *(see pages 90–91)*. Cover and leave to infuse for 30 minutes before continuing with the rest of the ganache recipe.

- Prepare the cherry confiture, then spoon it into the base of each tartlet case. *(2)* Top with the ganache and leave to set at room temperature for 1 hour. *(3)*

Finally, make the confit cherries & finish:

- To make the confit cherries: put 20g (¾oz) of the sugar and the pectin in a small bowl and mix well. Put the cherries in a saucepan with the water and remaining sugar and bring to a simmer. *(4)*

- Simmer for 5 minutes until the cherries have softened. Add the pectin and sugar and the vinegar and mix well. *(5)*

- Turn up the heat, bring to the boil, then cook for 2–3 minutes until the juice has thickened. Spread out on a shallow tray to cool. *(6)*

- Drain the excess liquid from the confit cherries. Place about 10 cherries on top of each tart. *(7)* Decorate with the chocolate copeaux and Crystallized Pistachios.

Best stored in the fridge until prior to serving and then eaten the same day.

1

2

3

4

5

6

7

The Linzer torte originates from Austria and is named after the city of Linz. The torte is made with a spiced dough, traditionally has a lattice design on top and is usually filled with raspberry or redcurrant confiture. The Linzer torte is thought to be one of the oldest known cakes, after a Veronese recipe from 1653 was discovered in the archives of the Admond Abbey, Austria.

1 quantity of **Pâte Sucrée** (see page 47)
1 quantity of **Frangipane** (see page 89)
100g (3½oz) flaked almonds to decorate
icing (powdered) sugar for dusting
1 quantity of **Apricot Nappage** (see page 104)

For the poached pears:
1 quantity of **Light Syrup** (see page 103)
1 cinnamon stick
1 vanilla pod (bean) split lengthways
6 ripe, but not too soft Williams pears peeled, cored and halved

You will also need:
two 12 x 34cm (4¾ x 13¾ inch), 2cm (¾ inch) deep tart cases
a 14mm (⅝ inch) plain piping nozzle (tip)

Tarte Bourdeloue
Makes 2 large tarts
(each serves 6–8)

First, prepare the Pâte Sucrée:

- Prepare the Pâte Sucrée as instructed and chill for 2–3 hours.

Next, make the poached pears:

- Prepare the syrup with the cinnamon stick. Scrape the seeds from the split vanilla pod (bean) and drop in the empty pod (bean) too. Add the pears. Cover with a silicone paper cartouche (see page 32) and place a plate on top. Leave to gently cook over a low heat for 20–25 minutes. Remove from the heat and leave the pears to cool in the syrup. (1)

To assemble & bake:

- Place the rested dough on a lightly floured surface and roll out to 3mm (⅛ inch) thick. Line the tart cases (see pages 44–45) with the pastry, then chill for at least 30 minutes.

- Preheat the oven to 180°C (350°F/Gas 4). Take the tart cases from the fridge. Spoon the prepared frangipane into a piping (pastry) bag fitted with a 14mm (⅝ inch) plain nozzle (tip) and pipe the frangipane in lines into the base of each tart. (2)

- Remove the poached pears from the syrup, drain and slice each half into 3mm (⅛ inch) thin slices. (3)

- Push the pears down gently so that they sit at a slight angle, then place them in the tart cases, positioning each half in alternate directions – each tart should contain 6 halves. (4)

- Top with the flaked almonds (5), then dust with icing (powdered) sugar. (6)

- Bake the tarts for 30–35 minutes until golden. Leave to cool before demoulding from the tart cases. Gently heat the nappage, then use it to glaze the tarts to finish. Lightly dust the edge of the tarts with icing (powdered) sugar to finish.

Best served the same day.

This traditional tart originated from a pâtisserie that opened near Notre Dame Cathedral in 1824. In 1850 the first dessert made with baked crème d'amande was created and called Entremets Bourdeloue. *It was not filled with any fruits, nor did it have a pastry lining. A few years later poached pears were added to the recipe and by the 20th century the dessert was transformed into the dish we know today – a sweet pastry tart with a filling of frangipane and poached pears. It was first called* Poire Bourdeloue, *then renamed to* Tarte Bourdeloue.

Passion Fruit & Pink Grapefruit Tart

Makes 2 tarts (each serves 6)

1 quantity of **Pâte Sucrée** *(see page 47)*
300g (10½oz) tempered dark
(bittersweet) chocolate *(see page 34)
used to make* **Chocolate Curls**
(see page 130)
300g (10½oz) tempered white chocolate
(see page 34) used to make **Combed
Chocolate Sticks** *(see page 128)*
1 grapefruit *peeled and segmented
(use the flesh from the confit grapefruil)*
1 passion fruit *seeds removed*
edible gold leaf *to decorate*

For the passion fruit gimauve:
*(makes one 38 x 25 x 2.5cm (15 x 10 x
1 inch) block)*
10g (¼oz) leaf gelatine
100g (3½oz/⅔ cup) icing
(powdered) sugar
100g (3½oz/⅔ cup) cornflour
(cornstarch)
110g (3¾oz) **Fruit Purée** *(see page 110)
made with passion fruit*
225g (8oz/1 generous cup) caster
(superfine) sugar *plus 10g (¼oz) extra*
135ml (4¼ oz/scant ½ cup) water
38g (1½oz) egg whites *(about 1–2 eggs)*
10g (¼oz) caster (superfine) sugar
1g (a pinch) cream of tartar

For the confit grapefruit:
1 grapefruit
1 quantity of **Simple Syrup** *(see page
102)*

For the tart filling:
300ml (½ pint/1¼ cups) double
(heavy) cream
200g (7oz) whole eggs *(about 4 eggs)*
300g (10½oz/1½ cups) caster
(superfine) sugar
125g (4½oz) **Fruit Purée** *(see page 110)
made with passion fruit*
125ml (4¼fl oz/½ cup) freshly squeezed
pink grapefruit juice

You will also need:
a 38 x 25 x 2.5cm (15 x 10 x 1 inch)
frame for the gimauve
two 14cm (5¼ inch) tart rings

First, prepare the gimauve:

- Use the ingredients to make a passion
fruit gimauve following the instructions
on page 338. Once set, cut into 2cm
(¾ inch) cubes and roll in the leftover
dusting mixture. *(1–5)*

**Then, prepare the Pâte Sucrée &
decorations:**

- Prepare the pastry as instructed, then chill
for 2–3 hours. While it is resting, temper
the chocolate and make the decorations as
instructed, then leave in a cool, dry place
to set for 2 hours.

- Make the confit grapefruit following the
method for confit sudachi on page 216.

- Place the rested dough on a lightly floured
surface and roll out to 3mm (⅛ inch) thick.
Line the tart cases *(see pages 44–45)*, then
chill for at least 30 minutes. Preheat the
oven to 180°C (350°F/Gas 4).

- Prick the tart bases all over, then blind bake
(see pages 44–45) the tarts until lightly
golden brown, then leave to cool. Turn the
oven down to 140°C (275°F/Gas 1).

Now, prepare the tart filling:

- Put the cream in a saucepan, bring to the
boil, then leave to cool slightly. Whisk the
eggs and sugar together in a bowl. Add
the passion fruit purée and grapefruit
juice. Pour in the cream, mix well, then
pass through a fine sieve (strainer).

To assemble & finish:

- Fill the blind baked tart cases with the tart
filling, *(6)* then bake for 20–25 minutes
until the tart mixture has just set. Remove
from the oven and leave to cool. *(7)*

- Decorate with white chocolate sticks and
chocolate curls, grapefruit segments,
passion fruit seeds, passion fruit gimauve,
confit grapefruit strips and gold leaf.

*Best stored in the fridge until prior to
serving and then eaten the same day.*

A take on the classic lemon tart made famous by the The Roux Brothers during the 1980s. It is decorated with gimauve to add a different texture.

Classic Gâteau Basque *Makes 1 tart (serves 8–10)*

1 quantity of **Armagnac-marinated Prunes**
(see page 114)
egg wash *(see page 29) to glaze*

For the pastry:
250g (9oz/1¾ cups) plain (all-purpose)
   flour *sifted*
2.5g (½ tsp) baking powder
105g (3½oz/scant 1 cup) ground almonds
1.5g (a pinch) salt
200g (7oz/scant 1 cup) unsalted butter
¼ vanilla pod (bean) *split lengthways*
180g (6oz/¾ cup) caster (superfine) sugar
80g (3oz) whole eggs *(about 1–2 eggs)*

For the basque filling:
250ml (8½fl oz/generous 1 cup) full-fat milk
50ml (2fl oz/scant ¼ cup) double
   (heavy) cream
grated zest of ½ lemon
½ vanilla pod (bean) *split lengthways*
60g (2oz) egg yolks *(about 3 eggs)*
75g (2¾oz/⅓ cup) caster (superfine) sugar
60g (2oz/scant ½ cup) plain (all-purpose)
   flour *sifted*
20ml (¾fl oz/4 tsp) dark rum

You will also need:
a 20cm (8 inch) diameter,
   2.8cm (1 inch) deep ring
a 15mm (⅝ inch) plain piping nozzle (tip)

First, make the pastry:

- Use the ingredients to make the pastry following the creaming method on pages 42–43. Wrap the dough in cling film (plastic wrap) and chill for 2–3 hours.

Make the basque filling while the pastry is resting:

- Put the milk, cream and lemon zest in a saucepan. Scrape the seeds from the split vanilla pod (bean) into the pan and drop in the empty pod (bean) too. Bring to the boil. Meanwhile, whisk together the egg yolks and caster (superfine) sugar until they are light in colour. Add the flour and mix until smooth.

- Add one-third of the boiled milk to the base mixture and mix until smooth. Pass through a sieve (strainer) and return to the saucepan. Bring the custard back to the boil, stirring continuously, then reduce the heat to a simmer and cook for 5–7 minutes.

- Remove the pan from the heat and pour the thickened custard into a shallow tray and cool rapidly. When it is cold, spoon the filling into a mixing bowl and add the rum. Beat until smooth.

To assemble & finish:

- Split the rested pastry dough into two parts (one slightly bigger than the other). Roll out the larger piece of dough to a 5mm (¼ inch) thickness and use it to line the tart ring *(see pages 44–45)*. Roll out the smaller piece also to a 5mm (¼ inch) thickness – this will be the lid for the tart.

- Spoon the basque filling into a piping (pastry) bag fitted with a 15mm (⅝ inch) plain nozzle (tip) and pipe the mixture into the bottom of the lined tart in one complete spiral. *(1)*

- Drain the marinated prunes and place about 18 prunes into the filling of the tart in a circular pattern. *(2)* Lightly brush the edge of the pastry with the egg wash. Preheat the oven to 180°C (350°F/Gas 4).

- Use the rolling pin to lay the rolled out pastry lid on top of the tart. *(3)* Press down gently to seal, trim the edges and egg wash the top. Score the surface, then bake the tart for 40–45 minutes until golden on top. Leave to cool.

Store in an airtight container and eat within 1–2 days.

1　　　　　*2*　　　　　*3*

Gâteau Basque originates from the Basque region in France. I first came across this dish in the kitchens of La Tante Claire. Pierre favoured it filled with marinated prunes d'Agen from his region in southwest France. Other variations include using cherries or apricots. This really was one of Pierre's favourite dishes.

Mirliton d'Amiens

Makes 18 small tarts

Mirlitons originate from Rouen, in Normandy, France. The original recipe uses the same almond filling flavoured with vanilla and orange flower water. Each French region has their own speciality. Here we have used a Parisian variation, which has the addition of apricots or apricot confiture.

1 quantity of **Almond Pastry** *(see Variation, page 47)*

For the poached apricots:
360g (12½oz/1¾ cups) caster (superfine) sugar
700ml (1¼ pints/generous 3 cups) water
1 vanilla pod (bean) *split lengthways*
500g (1lb 2oz) fresh or frozen apricot halves

For the filling:
250g (9oz/generous 2 cups) ground almonds *sifted*
250g (9oz/1¾ cups) icing (powdered) sugar *sifted, plus extra for dusting*
300g (10½oz) whole eggs *(about 6 eggs)*
150g (5½oz/⅔ cup) unsalted butter, *melted*

You will also need:
a 10cm (4 inch) pastry (cookie) cutter
eighteen 7cm (2¾ inch) diameter, 3cm (1¼ inch) depth pomponette moulds

First, prepare the pastry:

- Prepare the pastry, then chill as instructed. Place the rested pastry on a lightly floured surface and roll out to 3mm (⅛ inch) thick. Use a 10cm (4 inch) pastry (cookie) cutter to cut out 18 discs. Line each pomponette mould with the pastry *(see pages 44–45)*, then place back in the fridge to rest for 30 minutes.

Next, make the poached apricots:

- Put the sugar, water and vanilla in a saucepan and bring to the boil. Add the apricot halves, cover with a silicone baking paper cartouche *(see page 32)* and cook over a low heat for 3–5 minutes until the apricots are cooked and soft. Leave to cool.

Then the filling:

- Mix the ground almonds and sugar together in the bowl of an electric mixer fitted with a whisk attachment. Add the whole eggs and mix on a medium speed until the mixture turns pale and thickens. Gently fold in the melted butter. Leave to thicken for 20 minutes.

To assemble & finish:

- Preheat the oven to 160°C (313°F/Gas 2–3). Place 2 cooked apricot halves into the base of each of the prepared tart cases. *(1)*

- Spoon the filling into a piping (pastry) bag and pipe it into each case until almost full. *(2)* Dust each tart generously with icing (powdered) sugar, then set aside for 5 minutes for the icing (powdered) sugar to melt. *(3)* Generously dust with sugar again, then use your finger to wipe the sugar from the edge of the tart. *(4)* Bake for 25–30 minutes, then leave to cool.

Best served fresh, but can be stored in an airtight container for up to 2 days.

I

2

3

4

300g (10½oz) tempered dark (bittersweet) chocolate *(see page 34)*, used to make twelve 6cm (2½ inch) **Chocolate Discs** and small **Chocolate Squares** *(see page 127 and 126)*
1 quantity of **Yuzu Marmalade** *(see Variation, pages 112–113)*
½ quantity of **Hazelnut & Almond Pastry** *(see page 47)*
1 quantity of **Genoise** *(see page 66)*
1 quantity of **Alcohol Syrup** *(see page 103), made with yuzu sake*
½ quantity of **Yuzu Bavaroise** *(see Variation, page 98)*
1 quantity of **Dark Chocolate Crémeux** *(see page 95) made with* 200g (7oz) dark (bittersweet) chocolate (70% cocoa solids) and 100g (3½oz) gianduja
1 quantity of **White Spray Chocolate** *(see page 35)*
1 quantity of **Fruit Glaze** *(see page 105) made with oranges*
edible gold leaf *to decorate*

You will also need:
twelve plastic tart top moulds (PCB, *see page 344*)
twelve 7cm (2¾ inch) pomponette moulds
a spray gun
an 10mm (½ inch) plain piping nozzle (tip)

Yuzu & Praline Tarts Makes 12 tarts

First, prepare the chocolate discs and decoration & the Yuzu Marmalade as instructed, then prepare the pastry, sponge, syrup, bavaroise & crémeux:

• Prepare the pastry and rest as instructed. Prepare and bake the Genoise. Once cooled, cut into twelve 4.5cm (1¾ inch) discs. Prepare the yuzu sake syrup as instructed and set aside. Prepare the Yuzu Bavaroise as instructed and once the mousse is prepared, spoon it into the tart top moulds. Freeze for at least 4 hours. Make the dark chocolate and gianduja crémeux.

• Place the rested pastry on a lightly floured surface and roll out to 3mm (⅛ inch) thick. Line 12 pomponette moulds *(see pages 44–45)* and chill for at least 30 minutes. Preheat the oven to 180°C (350°F/Gas 4). Trim the excess pastry and blind bake *(see pages 44–45)* for 12–15 minutes. Remove the baking beans, then bake for a further 8 minutes until golden.

Next, make the chocolate spray, assemble & finish:

• Now, prepare the white chocolate spray. Demould the mousse from the freezer, place on a wire rack and spray the mousse *(see page 35)*. Return the sprayed mousse to the freezer until ready to assemble.

• Spoon the crémeux into a piping (pastry) bag fitted with an 10mm (½ inch) plain nozzle (tip). Pipe a spiral around the inside of each tartlet *(1)* followed by a spoonful of the marmalade. *(2)* Soak the sponge circles with yuzu sake syrup and place one circle on top of the marmalade in each tartlet. *(3)*

• Top each with a chocolate disc. *(4)* Pipe a small bulb of the crémeux in the centre of each chocolate disc, then place the frozen sprayed bavaroise on top. *(5)* Gently melt some of the Fruit Glaze and half-fill a paper piping cornet *(see page 30)*. Pipe 3 bulbs on top of each tart. *(6)* Place on a serving dish, then leave to defrost for 1 hour in the fridge. When ready to serve, decorate with a chocolate square and some edible gold leaf. *Best served the same day.*

*The fragrant citrus notes of
the yuzu zest balance well
with the chocolate and
praline, cutting the richness
and adding a fresh flavour
to the tart. This pâtisserie
incorporates classic French
techniques with the influence
of Japanese ingredients.*

Rhubarb & Ginger Sablé *Makes 8 tarts*

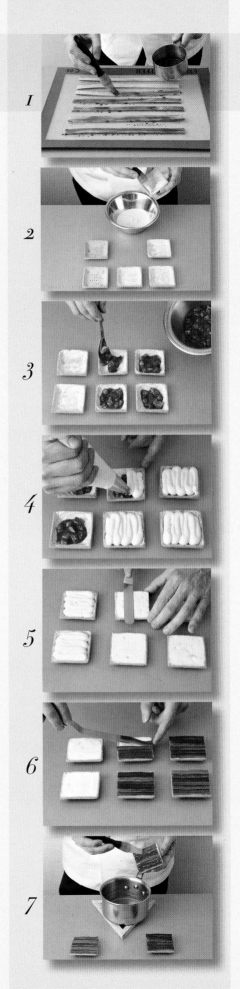

300g (10½oz) tempered dark (bittersweet) chocolate *(see page 34)*
  used to make **Triangle Flicks** *(see page 134)*
½ quantity of **Pâte Sablée** *(see page 46)*
1 quantity of **Fruit Compote** *(see page 111) made with chopped fraises des bois
  (wild strawberries) and wild strawberry purée, plus some extra berries to decorate*
300g (10½oz) tempered white chocolate *(see page 34) for brushing*
½ quantity of **Ginger Diplomat** *(see Variation, page 83)*
100g (3½oz) **Light Fruit Nappage** *(see page 105)*
½ quantity of **Crème Chantilly** *(see pages 84–85)*

For the roasted rhubarb:
500g (1lb 2oz) fresh rhubarb batons *thin stalks cut into 5mm (¼ inch) thick batons*
100ml (3½fl oz/scant 1 cup) grenadine syrup

You will also need:
eight 6.5cm (2½ inch) square tart tins
a 10mm (½ inch) plan piping nozzle (tip)

First, prepare the decorations & Pâte Sablée:

- Temper the chocolate and make the triangle flicks as instructed, then leave in a cool, dry place to set for 2 hours. Prepare the pastry as instructed, then place in the fridge to rest for 2–3 hours.

While the pastry is resting, prepare the fraise de bois compote & roasted rhubarb:

- Prepare the compote, cool, then leave in the fridge until needed. Make the roasted rhubarb: preheat the oven to 170°C (325°F/Gas 3). Lay the rhubarb batons out on a baking tray (sheet) lined with a non-stick baking mat. Brush the rhubarb with the grenadine syrup *(1)*, then turn over and repeat on the other side. Roast for 5–8 minutes until soft, then leave to cool.

To bake, assemble & finish the tart:

- Place the rested pastry on a lightly floured surface and roll out to 3mm (⅛ inch) thick and use to line the tart tins *(see pages 44–45)*. Prick the bases all over, then chill for at least 30 minutes.

- Preheat the oven to 180°C (350°F/Gas 4). Blind bake the tarts *(see pages 44–45)* until golden brown, then leave to cool.

- Use a pastry brush to cover the base of each tart with the tempered white chocolate *(2)*, then leave to set for 10 minutes. Place a teaspoon of compote in the bottom of each tart case. *(3)*

- Prepare the Ginger Diplomat cream, spoon it into a piping (pastry) bag fitted with a 10mm (½ inch) plain nozzle (tip) and pipe it into the tart until full. *(4)* Level off with a small step palette knife *(5)*, then chill for 10 minutes.

- Cut the roasted rhubarb batons into 6.5cm (2½ inch) lengths, then layer them over the top of the tart. *(6)* Gently warm the Light Fruit Nappage in a saucepan and use it to glaze the top of the tarts. *(7)*

- Prepare the Crème Chantilly. Using a teaspoon and warm water, make quenelles from the cream and place them onto the corner of each tart. Decorate with the glazed fraises des bois (wild strawberries) and the chocolate flicks.

Best stored in the fridge until prior to serving and then eaten the same day.

Rhubarb and ginger is a classic combination. Rhubarb is one of the most underrated and underused fruits that grows abundantly in Britain – and Yorkshire is known to produce some of the best. I wanted to create a pâtisserie based on classical French style and methods, using the best of this typically British ingredient.

Suzue and I first starting using sable Breton as a base for tarts during our time at The Savoy as it has a wonderful crisp, crumbly texture. The Breton base is easier to make than lining tarts – this was especially useful during the weekends at The Savoy when Suzue had to create hundreds of smaller versions of these beautiful tarts.

Strawberry & Pistachio Breton Tart

Makes 2 tarts (each serves 6–8)

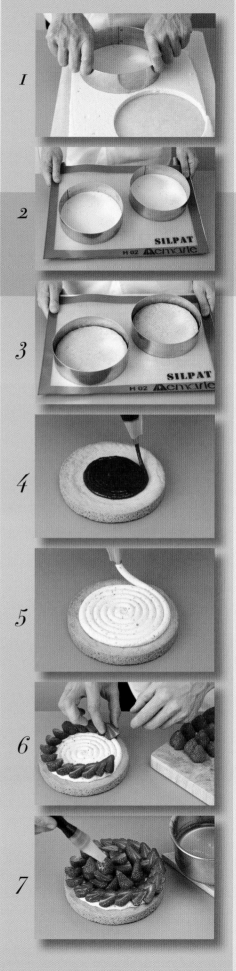

1

2

3

4

5

6

7

1 quantity of **Fruit Confiture** *(see page 108) made with strawberries and strawberry purée*

½ quantity of **Sable Breton** *(see pages 48–49)*

300g (10½oz) tempered dark (bittersweet) chocolate *(see page 34) used to make* **Chocolate Curls** *(see page 130)*

1 quantity of **Crème Mousseline** *(see pages 84–85)*

75g (2¾oz) **Pistachio Paste** *(see pages 116–117)*

40 fresh strawberries *hulled and halved*

100g (3½oz) **Light Fruit Nappage** *(see page 105)*

1 quantity of **Crystallized Pistachios** *(see pages 122–123)*

12 fresh blueberries

12 fresh raspberries

edible gold leaf *to decorate*

You will also need:

two 16cm (6¼ inch) entremet rings

a 7mm (⅓ inch) plain piping nozzle (tip)

a 10mm (½ inch) plain piping nozzle (tip)

Prepare the confiture & pastry:

- Prepare the confiture as instructed. Prepare the Sable Breton and rest as instructed. Roll the pastry out to 8mm (⅓ inch) thick. Chill for 1 hour.

- Temper the chocolate and make the decorations as instructed. Leave in a cool, dry place to set for 2 hours. Preheat the oven to 180°C (350°F/Gas 4).

To assemble & bake:

- Take the rolled out pastry from the fridge and use the 2 entremet rings to cut out 2 discs of pastry. *(1)* Place the pastry, still in the ring, on a baking tray (sheet) lined with a non-stick baking mat *(2)* and bake for 20–25 minutes until golden brown. Leave to cool. *(3)*

- Place the strawberry confiture into a piping (pastry) bag fitted with a 7mm (¼ inch) piping nozzle (tip) and pipe in the centre of the cooked Bretons. *(4)*

- Prepare the Crème Mousseline, then add the Pistachio Paste. Stir until combined. Spoon the pistachio mousseline into a piping (pastry) bag fitted with a 10mm (½ inch) nozzle (tip). Pipe a spiral on top of the confiture, piping to the edge of the tarts. *(5)*

- Position the strawberries in a spiral on the Crème Mousseline. *(6)* Melt the nappage and glaze the tarts. *(7)* Decorate with the chocolate curls, pistachios and berries.

Best stored in the fridge until prior to serving and then eaten the same day.

1 quantity of **Fruit Confiture** *(see page 108) made with blackcurrants and blackcurrant purée*

½ quantity of **Sable Breton** *(see pages 48–49)*

1 quantity of **Chocolate Tuile** *(see page 121)*

1 quantity of **Dark Chocolate Crémeux** *(see page 95)*

20–24 fresh blackcurrants

edible gold leaf *to decorate*

For the caramelized pears:

250g (9oz/1¼ cups) caster (superfine) sugar

2 pears *peeled, cored, quartered and cut into chunks*

50ml (2fl oz/scant 1 cup) water

You will also need:

two 16cm (6¼ inch) entremet rings

two 14cm (5¼ inch) entremet rings

a blow torch

Caramelized Pear, Blackcurrant & Chocolate Breton
Makes 2 large tarts (each serves 6–8)

First, prepare the confiture, pastry & tuiles:

- Make the blackcurrant confiture, cool, then chill until needed. Prepare the Sable Breton as instructed, then roll it 8mm (⅓ inch) thick. Chill for 1 hour.

- Make the tuiles and store in an airtight container until needed.

Next, bake the pastry:

- Preheat the oven to 180°C (350°F/Gas 4). Take the rolled out pastry from the fridge and use the 2 larger entremet rings to cut out two discs of pastry. Place the pastry, still in the rings, on a baking tray (sheet) lined with a non-stick baking mat and bake for 20–25 minutes until golden brown. Remove from the oven and leave to cool.

- Once cooled, remove the entremet rings and spoon the confiture into the dip in the centre. *(1)* Place the smaller entremet rings on top of the cooked Breton and leave on the side until needed again.

Now, prepare the crémeux:

- Prepare the Dark Chocolate Crémeux, cool for 15 minutes to thicken slightly, then place about two-thirds (about 300g/10½oz) on top of the confiture. *(2)* Chill for 1 hour.

Finally, prepare the caramelized pears:

- Make a dry caramel with the sugar *(see page 33)*. Add the pear chunks *(3)*, and cook over a low heat for 2–3 minutes. Add the water *(4)* and continue to cook over a low heat until the pears become soft. Pour the pears into a shallow tray and leave to cool in the caramel.

To finish:

- Run the blow torch carefully around the metal ring and slowly remove it. *(5)*

- Decorate the Breton with the caramelized pears *(6)*, pieces of chocolate tuile, blackcurrants and edible gold leaf.

Best stored in the fridge until prior to serving and then eaten the same day.

I

2

3

4

5

6

Chocolate is the star of this dish. When creating pâtisserie with chocolate it is important to make sure that you have the best. To balance well with the acidity of the blackcurrants, I like to use Amedei's Toscano 66%. This chocolate has a complex aroma containing forest fruits and notes of sweet honey, which complements the caramelized pear on top of the tart. The chocolate has a wonderful length with a fruity balsamic finish, marrying well with the cassis confiture.

Chausson aux Pommes

Makes 12

Translated into English this delicacy means 'slipper filled with apples' because of the resemblance in the shape to a type of shoe that was extremely fashionable at the time of the pastries creation. The English name, 'apple turnover', refers to the fact that the pastry is turned over and the apples encased inside. Apple turnovers were first made in Britain in the 15th century and at that time were known as 'apple pasties'.

1 quantity of **Pâte Feuilletée** *(see pages 50–51)*
egg wash *(see page 29) to glaze*

For the apple compote:
500g (1lb 2oz) Cox apples
  peeled, cored and diced into 1cm (½ inch) cubes
50g (1¾oz/scant ½ stick) softened unsalted butter
50g (1¾oz/¼ cup) caster (superfine) sugar
2g (a pinch) ground cinnamon
25ml (1fl oz/5 tsp) Calvados

You will also need:
a 17 x 12cm (6½ x 4½ inch) chausson aux pommes
  cutter *(see page 27)*

First, make the compote:

- Put the apples, butter, sugar and cinnamon in a saucepan. Cook over a low heat for about 15 minutes until softened. Add the Calvados and leave to cool. Transfer to the fridge until needed.

Then, prepare the pastries:

- Prepare the pastry as instructed and roll out to 5mm (¼ inch) thick on a lightly floured surface, then chill for 30 minutes.

- Cut the chilled pastry into 12 ovals, measuring 10 x 15cm (4 x 6 inches) and place them on a non-stick baking mat. Place a generous tablespoonful of the compote just to one side of the centre of each oval and brush the edges with egg wash. *(1)*

- Fold over the pastry to encase the compote inside and make a semi-circle shape. Press gently to seal each parcel. Use a pastry brush to egg wash the top of each chausson, then transfer them to the fridge to chill for 30 minutes. *(2)* Preheat the oven to 210°C (413°F/Gas 6–7).

- Score the tops of each chausson; place one score down the centre diagonally, then score lines close together coming out from the centre line. *(3)*

- Bake for 15 minutes, turn down the heat to 180°C (350°F/Gas 4) and bake for a further 15 minutes until golden.

Best served the same day.

1

2

3

4

The St Honoré cake is named for the French patron saint of bakers and pastry chefs, Saint Honore or Honoratus (600 AD), the Bishop of Amiens. His Saints Day on the 16th May is still celebrated today. According to accounts in 19th-century pastry books, the Gâteau St. Honore was invented around 1846 by a pâtissier named Chiboust, who ran a shop on the Rue Saint Honoré in Paris. Chiboust paid homage to both the saint and the name of the street with his cake but gave his own filling, made by folding beaten egg whites into a classic crème pâtissière.

Gâteau St Honoré

Makes 2 (each serves 6)

1 quantity of **Pâte Feuilletée** *(see pages 50–51)*
Icing (powdered) sugar *for dusting*
1 quantity of **Praline Paste** *(see pages 116–117)*
300g (10½oz) tempered dark chocolate *(see page 34)* used to make **Chocolate Curls** and **Squares** *(see page 130 and 126)*
1 quantity of **Crème Pâtissière** *(see page 80),* with the addition of 75g (2¾oz) Praline Paste
1 quantity of **Pâte à Choux** *(see pages 58–59)*
Egg wash *(see page 29)* for brushing
2 quantities of **Crème Chiboust** *(see page 82)*
100g (3½oz) **Fruit Glaze** *(see page 105)*
20g (¾oz) flaked almonds, *lightly roasted*

For the apricot jelly:
600g (1lb 4oz) apricots *halved and stoned*
200g (7oz/1 cup) caster (superfine) sugar
24g (1oz) pectin

For the poached apricots:
½ quantity of **Light Syrup** *(see page 103)*
4 apricots *halved and stoned*

For the caramel:
200g (7oz/1 cup) caster (superfine) sugar
50ml (2fl oz/¼ cup) water

You will also need:
an 8mm (⅓ inch) plain piping nozzle (tip)
a 6mm (¼ inch) plain piping nozzle (tip)
a 14mm (⅝ inch) plain piping nozzle (tip)
a St Honore piping nozzle (tip)

First, prepare the apricot jelly & the Pâte Feuilletée:

- Prepare the apricot jelly: chop the apricots and place in a pan with 75g (2¾oz) of the sugar, bring to the boil and gently simmer for 3–4 minutes. Put the pectin and the remaining sugar in a bowl and mix well. Add this to the simmering apricots and continue to cook for a further 3–4 minutes. Remove from the heat and spread out on 2 baking trays (sheets) lined with silicone paper, between two 37cm (14¾ inch) bar guides, set 8cm (3¼ inches) wide and 1cm (½ inch) high. *(1)* Level off *(2)*, then place in the freezer to set.

- Prepare the pastry (this can be done the day before if needed) as instructed and leave in the fridge to rest until needed.

- Cut the block of rested pastry in half and roll out each half to 2mm (just under ⅛ inch) thick. Dock with a pastry docker or prick with a fork, then chill for at least 30 minutes.

- Prepare the Praline Paste as instructed. Temper the chocolate and make the decorations as instructed, then leave in a cool, dry place to set for 2 hours.

Gâteau St Honoré *continued*

- Preheat the oven to 200°C (400°F/Gas 6). Cut the rolled out pastry into two 11 x 37cm (4¼ x 14¾ inch) rectangles. Place on a non-stick baking mat, dock with a pastry docker and dust with icing (powdered) sugar. *(3)* Place a sheet of silicone paper on top, followed by a wire rack. Bake for 20–25 minutes until golden and caramelized. *(4)* Remove from the oven, then leave to cool.

Prepare the praline crème pâtissière & the choux pastry:

- Prepare the crème pâtissière and once cool, mix in the praline paste. Pour into a shallow tray, cover with cling film (plastic wrap) and chill.

- Make the Pâte à Choux, then spoon it into a piping (pastry) bag fitted with an 8mm (⅓ inch) piping nozzle (tip). Pipe twenty-eight 2cm (¾ inch) bulbs on a baking tray (sheet) lined with a non-stick baking mat. Glaze the tops with egg wash, then bake for 8–10 minutes. Reduce the temperature to 180°C (350°F/Gas 4) and continue to cook for 5–8 minutes. Remove from the oven and leave to cool.

Then, the poached apricots & caramel:

- Prepare the Light Syrup in a pan. Add the apricots to the hot syrup. Cover with a cartouche and cook over a low heat for 6–8 minutes. Remove from the heat and leave the apricots to cool in the syrup.

- With a piping tube make a hole in the bottom of the choux buns, spoon the praline crème pâtissière into a piping (pastry) bag with a 6mm (¼ inch) piping nozzle (tip) and fill the choux buns.

- Prepare a wet caramel following the instructions on page 33. Carefully, dip the tops of the cooked choux buns into the caramel, place on a tray and leave to set. *(5)* Reserve any excess caramel.

To assemble & finish:

- Demould the frozen apricot jelly and place in the centre of the cooked puff pastry rectangles. *(6)*

- Prepare the Crème Chiboust and spoon it into a piping (pastry) bag fitted with a 14mm (⅝ inch) piping nozzle (tip). Pipe 4 lines down the centre of the puff pastry. *(7)* Use the reserved caramel (you may need to warm it up first) to stick the caramel choux buns at intervals down the edge of the pastry – you should have 6–7 on each side. *(8)*

- Spoon the remaining Chiboust cream into a piping (pastry) bag fitted with a St Honore piping tube (tip) and pipe the Chiboust in quenelles in the gaps between the choux buns. *(9)* Pipe a line of quenelles at an angle on the left-hand side of the puff pastry. Pipe a line of quenelles down the centre and finish with a line of quenelles running down the right-hand side. *(10)* Transfer to the fridge to set for 10–15 minutes.

- Cut the poached apricots into cubes and glaze lightly with the Fruit Glaze. Take the St Honoré from the fridge and decorate with the poached apricots, chocolate curls, squares and roasted flaked almonds. *Best stored in the fridge until prior to serving and then eaten the same day.*

Note: *the pointed shape that is created when using a St Honoré piping tube (tip) is referred to as a quenelle.*

5

6

7

8

9

10

This gâteau was created in the early 1500s by a French pâtissier who worked in the city of Pithivier, south of Paris. During the reign of Louise XIV, the gâteau reached its height of popularity and was exported all over the country. This take on the French classic incorporates confit chestnuts into the crème d'amande, adding another dimension.

Chestnut Pithivier

Makes 1 large tart (serves 6–8)

1 quantity of **Feuilletage Inverse** *(see pages 54–55)*
½ quantity of **Crème d'Amande** *(see page 88)*
100g (3½oz) shop-bought confit chestnut
egg wash *(see page 29) to glaze*
20g (¾oz) icing (powdered) sugar *for dusting*

You will also need:
a 14mm (⅝ inch) plain piping nozzle (tip)
a 12cm (4½ inch) diameter dome mould
a 20cm (8 inch) entremet ring (cutter)

The day before:

- Prepare the Feuilletage Inverse the day before it is needed and leave it to rest in the fridge overnight.

The next day, prepare the Crème d'Amande:

- Prepare the Crème d'Amande, spoon into a piping (pastry) bag fitted with a 14mm (⅝ inch) plain nozzle (tip) and pipe 120g (4½oz) of it into a dome mould until it is half full. *(1)* Gently push the pieces of confit chestnut into the cream. *(2)* Freeze for at least 2 hours.

Then, assemble the pithivier:

- Take the Feuilletage Inverse from the fridge and divide in half. Place the dough on a lightly floured surface and roll out each half to 5mm (¼ inch) thick. Chill for 30 minutes. Take the pastry from the fridge and cut out a 20cm (8 inch) circle. *(3)* Place on a baking tray (sheet) lined with a non-stick baking mat.

- Take the frozen dome out of the freezer, demould it and place in the centre of the pastry circle. *(4)*

- Use a pastry brush to dampen the edge of the pastry with a little water *(5)*, then place the other pastry sheet on top, covering the dome. *(6)* Use your hands to press the pastry down in a circle around the dome to eliminate any air bubbles. *(7)*

1

2

3

4

5

6

7

Chestnut Pithivier *continued*

- Use the entremet ring to trim the edge of the pastry to neaten. *(8)*

- Use the back of a small knife to score an indent around the dome centre *(9)*, then place in the fridge for 20 minutes.

To bake & finish:

- Preheat the oven to 200°C (400°F/Gas 6). Take the pithivier from the fridge and use a small knife to cut 10 petals around the edge of the pastry. *(10)*

- Brush the top with egg wash. *(11)* Score the top of the pithiver in curved lines across the top. *(12)* Lastly score the petals with a criss-cross pattern. *(13)*

- Bake for 15 minutes, then turn the temperature down to 180°C (350°F/Gas 4) and cook for a further 20 minutes.

- Remove from the oven, increase the temperature to 200°C (400°F/Gas 6) again, dust the top of the pithivier with the icing (powdered) sugar and return to the oven for a further 20 minutes until golden brown. Remove from the oven and leave to cool on a wire rack.

Best served the same day, but can be stored in an airtight container for up to 2 days.

8

9

10

11

12

13

1 quantity of **Feuilletage Inverse** (*see pages 54–55*)
1 quantity of **Crème Pâtissière** (*see page 80*)
300g (10½oz) tempered dark (bittersweet) chocolate (*see page 34*)
  used to make **Piped Copeaux** (*see page 131*)
icing (powdered) sugar *for dusting*
50ml (2fl oz) dark rum
20 strawberries, plus extra glazed with **Fruit Glaze** (*see page 105*)
40 raspberries, plus extra glazed with **Fruit Glaze** (*see page 105*)
1 quantity of **Crème Chantilly** (*see pages 84–85*)
edible gold leaf *to decorate*

You will also need:
a buche piping nozzle (tip)
a St Honoré piping nozzle (tip)

Gâteau Mille-feuille   *Makes 8*

The day before:

- Prepare the Feuilletage Inverse the day before it is needed and leave to rest in the fridge overnight.

The next day, prepare the Crème Pâtissière, decorations & bake the pastry:

- Make the Crème Pâtissière and leave in the fridge until needed. Temper the chocolate and make the decorations as instructed, then leave in a cool, dry place to set for 2 hours. Divide the rested puff pastry in half and roll out one half to 3mm (⅛ inch) thick (wrap and reserve the other half for another use). Place on a baking tray (sheet) lined with a non-stick baking mat. Chill for 30 minutes.

- Preheat the oven to 200°C (400°F/Gas 6). Take the puff pastry from the fridge, dock with a pastry docker and dust with icing (powdered) sugar. Place a sheet of silicone paper on top and a baking tray (sheet) on top of that to weigh it down. Bake for about 20–25 minutes until golden and caramelized, then leave to cool.

To assemble:

- Cut the cooked puff pastry into 3 rectangles, each measuring 10 x 28cm (4 x 11¼ inches). *(1)* Beat the Crème Pâtissière and the dark rum together and then spoon into a piping (pastry) bag fitted with a buche piping nozzle (tip) and pipe lines on top of 2 of the rectangles. *(2)*

- Slice the strawberries and place them on top of the crème on one of the rectangles. Halve the raspberries and lay them on top of the crème on the other rectangle. *(3)*

- Pipe a second layer of Crème Pâtissière over the top of the strawberries. Carefully lift the raspberry layer on top of the strawberry layer using a wide spatula. *(4)* Pipe another layer of Crème Pâtissière on top of the raspberries *(5)* and top with the remaining pastry rectangle. *(6)* Carefully cut the whole pastry into eight 3.5cm (1½ inch) wide pieces. *(7)*

- Prepare the Crème Chantilly, spoon it into a piping (pastry) bag fitted with a St Honoré nozzle (tip) and pipe a wave on top of the mille-feuille. Decorate with strawberries and raspberries glazed with Fruit Glaze, a piped chocolate copeaux and edible gold leaf.

Best stored in the fridge until prior to serving and then eaten the same day.

1

2

3

4

5

6

7

Mille feuille means 'a thousand layers or leaves' in English. The name is a perfect description of this gateau. Classically it consists of layers of puff pastry and rum-flavoured creme patisserie. The origin is uncertain, and there are known variations of it dating back to the 17th century. The first adaptation of what we know today was created by French pâtissier Rouget, in his recipe book in 1806. However, it was further evolved by Marie-Antonin Carême and re-christened 'mille feuille' by him in Patissier Parisien in 1815. During the 1860s, a pâtissier called Sergent began selling them from his pâtisserie on the Rue du Bac. They became so popular that he would sell hundreds every day.

This pâtisserie was created in the late 18th century, by a pâtissier called Boinin in Lyon, southwest France. We use feuillitage rapide, but it can also be made with pastry trimmings.

1 quantity of **Feuilletage Rapide** *(see pages 56–57)*
1 quantity of **Fruit Confiture** *(see page 108)*
  made with whole cherries and cherry purée
½ quantity of **Crème d'Amande** *(see page 88)*

For the royal icing:
120g (4oz/scant 1 cup) icing (powdered) sugar *sifted*
20g (¾oz) egg white *(about 1 egg)*
5ml (1 tsp) lemon juice

You will also need:
eight 6cm (2½ inch) pomponette moulds
a 7cm (2¾ inch) cutter
an 10mm (½ inch) plain piping nozzle (tip)

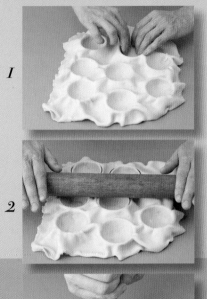

Gâteau Conversation
Makes 8 tarts

First, prepare the Feuilletage Rapide, confiture & Royal Icing:

- Prepare the pastry as instructed, then leave in the fridge to rest for 2–3 hours. Prepare the cherry confiture, cool, then leave in the fridge until needed.

- Now, make the Royal Icing. Put the sugar in a mixing bowl. Add the egg white and beat until well combined. Add the lemon juice and mix again until well combined. Keep covered with cling film (plastic wrap) until required.

- Place the rested puff pastry on a lightly floured surface and roll out to 2.5mm (⅛ inch) thick. Dock with a pastry docker, then chill for at least 30 minutes.

Then, prepare the tart cases:

- Take the pastry from the fridge, drape it over a rolling pin and carefully lay it on top of the pomponette moulds. *(1)* Gently press into each mould to line them with the pastry. Use the rolling pin to roll over the top of the moulds and cut off the excess pastry. *(2)* Use the small cutter to cut out an additional 8 discs and place on a non-stick baking mat. Transfer the lined moulds and the cut-out circles to the fridge for 30 minutes. Re-form the remaining pastry, roll it out to 1.5mm (just under ⅛ inch) thick and place in the fridge to rest.

Prepare the Creme d'Amande:

- Pipe a small bulb of the confiture in the base of each tart. *(3)* Spoon the Crème d'Amande into a piping (pastry) bag fitted with a 10mm (½ inch) nozzle (tip) and pipe it into the tartlets until three-quarters full. *(4)* Brush the edge of the tartlets with water, then place the smaller pastry discs on top. *(5)* Press down gently, then chill for 20 minutes.

To bake & finish:

- Trim any excess pastry from the edge of the tarts with a sharp knife. Place a teaspoon of icing on top of each tart and spread it evenly across the top. *(6)*

- Preheat the oven to 190°C (375°C/Gas 5). Take the rolled puff pastry from the fridge and cut out 32 batons measuring 0.3 x 7cm (⅛ x 2¾ inch). Place 4 batons on top of each tart in a lattice pattern *(7)*, then trim any excess pastry from the edge. Bake for 20–25 minutes. Leave to cool before removing from the moulds.

Best served fresh, but can be stored in an airtight container for up to 2 days.

1 quantity of **Feuilletage Rapide** *(see pages 56–57)*
½ quantity of **Crème Pâtissière** *(see page 80)*
1 quantity of **Raspberry Confiture** *(see page 108)*
icing (powdered) sugar *for caramelizing and dusting*

You will also need:
a 9cm (3½ inch) cutter
eight 6cm (2½ inch) pomponette moulds
a 6mm (¼ inch) and a 10mm (½ inch) plain piping nozzle (tip)
a caramelizer *(see page 26)* or blow torch

Puits d'Amour

Makes 8 tarts

The day before:

- Prepare the Feuilletage Rapide the day before it is needed and leave to rest in the fridge overnight.

The next day, bake the pastry:

- Place the rested pastry on a lightly floured surface and roll out to 2.5mm (⅛ inch) thick, then dock with a pastry docker. Place in the fridge to rest for at least 30 minutes.

- Prepare the Crème Pâtissière and the Raspberry Confiture and leave in the fridge until needed.

- Take the pastry from the fridge and use a 9cm (3½ inch) cutter to cut out 8 discs. Line the pomponette moulds with the pastry discs and return to the fridge for 20 minutes. Preheat the oven to 190°C (375°F/Gas 5).

- Blind bake the tarts *(see pages 44–45)* until golden brown. Remove from the oven and leave to cool.

To assemble & finish:

- Spoon the Raspberry Confiture into a piping (pastry) bag fitted with a 6mm (¼ inch) plain nozzle (tip) and pipe a large bulb on the base of each tart case. *(1)*

- Spoon the Crème Pâtissière into a piping (pastry) bag fitted with an 10mm (½ inch) nozzle (tip) and pipe it into each tartlet to the top. *(2)*

- Dust the tarts generously with icing (powdered) sugar *(3)* and caramelize with a caramelizer or by using a blow torch. *(4)*

- Repeat this process 1–2 times on each tart to get a deep caramel top. Dust the edges with icing (powdered) sugar.

Serve immediately.

Puits d'amour is a French expression carrying erotic connotations; it literally translates as 'well of love'. The first mention of the recipe appeared in Vincent De La Chapelle's 1735 recipe book, Le Cuisinier Moderne (The Modern Cook). La Chapelle presented two recipes for a gâteaux de puits d'amour (puits d'amour cake) consisting of a large puff pastry vol-au-vent topped with a pastry handle and filled with redcurrant jelly; the ensemble was meant to resemble the bucket of a well. The other recipe is for the petits puits d'amour *(mini puits d'amour) – a 'bouchée' sized variant of the cake. Nicolas Stohrer, a pâtissier for the exiled Polish King Stanislas, preferred to fill the dessert with vanilla pastry cream and glazed the top with a thick layer of caramel.*

1 quantity of **Crystallized Pistachios** *(see pages 122–123)*
1 quantity of **Feuilletage Rapide** *(see pages 56–57)*
6 mangoes *ripe, but not soft*
clarified butter *(see page 32)*
60g (2oz/generous ¼ cup) caster (superfine) sugar
30ml (1fl oz/2 tbsp) Grand Marnier
100g (3½oz) **Apricot Nappage** *(see page 104) melted*

You will also need:
a 12cm (4½ inch) round cutter

Thin Mango Tart *Makes 6 tarts (each serves 2)*

First, make the Crystallized Pistachios:

- Prepare the pistachios as instructed, leave to cool, then store in an airtight container until needed.

Next, prepare the Feuilletage Rapide:

- Make the pastry and rest as instructed. Place the rested pastry on a lightly floured surface and roll out to 2.5mm (⅛ inch) thick, dock the surface, then chill for 30 minutes.

- Take the pastry out of the fridge, cut out 6 discs using a 12cm (4½ inch) cutter and place them on a baking tray (sheet) lined with a non-stick baking mat. Push up the edges of the pastry discs against your thumb to create an edge and prick the bases. *(1)*

To bake & finish:

- Peel the mangoes and cut off the cheeks, then slice into very thin 1.5mm slices. *(2)* Preheat the oven to 200°C (400°F/Gas 6).

- Push the mangoes out, gently pressing into a long curve, and place on each pastry base, curving around the edge, then gradually twisting into the centre. *(3–5)*

- Brush with clarified butter and sprinkle with the sugar. Bake for 20 minutes, then remove from the oven and drizzle with the Grand Marnier.

- Using a large, wide palette knife, flip the tart over and return it to the oven to cook for a further 15 minutes. *(6–7)* Remove from the oven and leave to cool.

- Flip back over gently before glazing with some melted Apricot Nappage and decorating with the Crystallized Pistachios.

Best served the same day.

1

2

3

4

5

6

7

I first learnt how to make this simple yet delicious dish in the kitchen of the The Restaurant with Marco Pierre White. It is a take on a classic thin apple tart. This is lovely on its own, but you can also serve it as a dessert with the addition of Crème Anglaise (see page 92) or vanilla ice cream.

Pineapple Tarte Tatin *Makes 2 tarts (each serves 4)*

1 quantit*y of* **Feulletage Rapide**
(see pages 56–57)
icing (powdered) sugar *for*
dusting
100g (3½oz) **Fruit Glaze**
(see page 105) warmed

For the streusel decoration:
100g (3½oz/scant ¾ cup) icing
(powdered) sugar
100g (3½oz/scant 1 stick)
unsalted butter *cubed*
100g (3½oz/scant 1 cup)
ground hazelnuts
100g (3½oz/scant ¾ cup) plain
(all-purpose) flour *sifted*

For the caramelized pineapple:
300g (10½oz/1½ cups) caster
(superfine) sugar
27g (1oz/2 tbsp) pectin
30g (1oz/2½ tbsp)
unsalted butter
1 vanilla pod (bean)
split lengthways
2g (⅛ oz) red chilli
deseeded and finely chopped
9g (¼oz) fresh ginger
peeled and finely grated
1g (a pinch) freshly ground
black pepper
45ml (2fl oz/3 tbsp) dark rum
2 medium pineapples
peeled and trimmed

You will also need:
a 28 x 22cm (11 x 8¾ inch)
baking mat with raised sides

The day before it is needed, prepare the pastry:

- Prepare the pastry and rest as instructed.

The next day, bake the pastry:

- Preheat the oven to 200°C (400°F/ Gas 6). Place the rested pastry on a lightly floured surface and roll out to 4mm (¼ inch) thick. Put the sheet of pastry on a non-stick baking mat or baking tray (sheet) and roll over it with a pastry docker. *(1)*

- Dust generously with icing (powdered) sugar. *(2)*

- Place a sheet of silicone paper on top of the dusted pastry, then top with a wire rack. *(3)*

- Bake in the preheated oven for 15–20 minutes until golden. Take the pastry out of the oven, remove the silicone paper and wire rack and generously dust again with icing (powdered) sugar. *(4)*

- Return the pastry to the oven and continue to cook for 10 minutes, ensuring that the puff pastry is golden and the top is well caramelized. *(5)* Leave to cool.

- Once cooled, cut the pastry into 2 rectangles, each measuring 9 x 21cm (3½ x 8¼ inches).

Next, make the streusel decoration:

- Put the sugar, butter, ground hazelnuts and flour in a mixing bowl. Mix gently until it comes together, then place in the fridge to chill for 15 minutes. Preheat the oven to 170°C (325°F/Gas 3). Press the chilled streusel through a large grater to create threads of streusel and spread out on a baking tray (sheet). Bake for 10–12 minutes until golden.

Two sisters called Stephanie and Caroline Tatin created this tarte in 1850. It is said that it was the result of an accident that occurred in the kitchen of the small hotel they ran together. When Caroline was taking an apple tart out of the oven, she dropped the dish and it landed upside down on the table. In an attempt to salvage it, the tart was rebuilt upside down. The sisters thought the tart looked attractive and after serving it to their customers, it became an instant success. This is a modern take on the tarte, where the fruit and pastry have been cooked separately.

Pineapple Tarte Tatin *continued*

6

7

8

9

Then, the caramelized pineapple:

- Reduce the oven temperature to 160°C (313°F/Gas 2–3). Mix 2 tablespoons of the sugar with the pectin in a bowl.

- Make a dry caramel *(see page 33)* with the remaining sugar *(6–7)*, turn off the heat, then mix in the butter.

- Add the vanilla seeds and pod (bean), chilli and ginger and stir together. *(8–9)*

- Grind in the black pepper and stir. Pour in the dark rum. *(10)*

- Lastly, add the sugar and pectin mixture. *(11)* Bring the caramel back to the boil, then pour into the base of a silicone baking mat. *(12)*

To assemble:

- Cut the pineapple into quarters, remove the core and finely slice into 2.5mm (⅛ inch) slices. *(13)*

- Lay the pineapple in rows on top of the caramel. *(14)* Bake for 35–40 minutes. Leave to cool completely in the mould, then place in the freezer.

After at least 4 hours:

- Remove the cooked pineapple from the freezer and demould from the silicone baking mat. Cut into two 8 x 20cm (3¼ x 8 inch) rectangles.

- Glaze the pineapple with the warmed Fruit Glaze, then place on top of the puff pastry rectangles. Decorate the edges of the pastry with the cooked streusel.

Best served the same day.

10

11

12

13

14

This is a regional speciality of Gers, Toulouse and Couserans from the Gascony region of France. Pierre Koffmann grew up in Gascony so it comes as no surprise that I learnt this delicacy in the kitchen at La Tante Claire; it was one of their most famous desserts. I had never seen filo being made before – it was amazing to see someone go to such lengths to create pastry. It was worth it though, as the flavour difference was unimaginable. Handmade filo is light, crisp and buttery – a stark contrast to what I knew at the time as filo pastry. Perfect served with a Crème Anglaise (see page 92).

Croustade aux Pommes *Makes 6*

1 quantity of **Pâte Filo** *(see pages 60–61)*
150g (5½oz) clarified butter *(see page 32) melted*
flour *for dusting*
100g (3½oz/½ cup) caster (superfine) sugar
1 quantity of **Frangipane** *(see page 89)*
icing (powdered) sugar *for dusting*

For the apple filling:
6 braeburn apples
75g (2¾oz/¾ stick) unsalted butter
75g (2¾oz/generous ¼ cup) caster (superfine) sugar
30ml (1fl oz/2 tbsp) dark rum

You will also need:
twelve 7cm (2¾ inch) tart tins
a 12mm (½ inch) plain piping nozzle (tip)

First, prepare the pastry:

- Prepare the Pâte Filo and leave to rest as instructed. Lightly grease the tart tins with a little of the clarified butter.

- Line the table with a tablecloth and lightly dust it with flour. Put one piece of rested filo dough (wrap and reserve the other half for another use) in the centre of the tablecloth. Place your hands under the filo dough and gently begin to pull it out from underneath, going around the dough and pulling from every corner. Allow the dough to rest at intervals to let it relax. Continue to pull until it has reached a square measuring about 1m (40 inches). *(1–6)*

- Trim the thick edges and leave the dough to dry slightly for 5–10 minutes (how long will depend on the temperature and humidity in the room). Spray or brush the melted clarified butter over the pastry *(7)*, then sprinkle with the caster (superfine) sugar. *(8)* Leave to dry slightly.

1

2

3

4

5

6

7

8

185

Croustade aux Pommes *continued*

9

10

11

12

13

14

15

16

17

18

To assemble & bake:

- Cut the stretched filo into 30 rough pieces *(9)* and line 6 tart tins with 3 layers of filo. *(10)*

- For the lids, use 2 pieces of the filo and shape them into a crumpled crown. Put these in the remaining tart tins. *(11)* Leave the pastry to dry in the tart tins for at least 4–5 hours (or ideally overnight).

- Prepare the apple filling. Peel, core and cut the apples into eighths. Put the butter in a saucepan and melt over a medium heat for 4–5 minutes. Add the apples *(12)*, then the sugar and mix well. *(13)* Remove from the heat and add the rum. *(14)*

- Preheat the oven to 180°C (350°F/Gas 4). Prepare the Frangipane and put it in a piping (pastry) bag fitted with a 12mm (½ inch) piping nozzle (tip). Pipe it into the dried filo tart cases until they are half full. *(15)* Top each tart with the apple filling. *(16)* Brush the apples with clarified butter *(17)* and dust with icing (powdered) sugar.

- Bake for 20–25 minutes until golden brown. *(18)* Take out of the oven and demould from the tin. Place on a wire rack and leave to cool slightly while the crowns cook.

- Place the crown lids in the oven and bake for 7–8 minutes until golden, then remove from the oven.

- Place each croustade base on a serving dish and top with the cooked crown.

Best served the same day and can also be warmed up prior to serving if necessary.

Choux à la crème is the pâtisserie shop version of the popular dessert, profiteroles. The idea for this pâtisserie came from the larger and more elaborately decorated sweet croquembouche, creating an individual version available to enjoy not only at celebrations, but every day. Choux à la crème is traditionally filled with crème pâtissière and crème Chantilly. The recipes for these basic components can be adapted to create a variety of different flavour combinations.

Choux à la Crème *Makes 33*

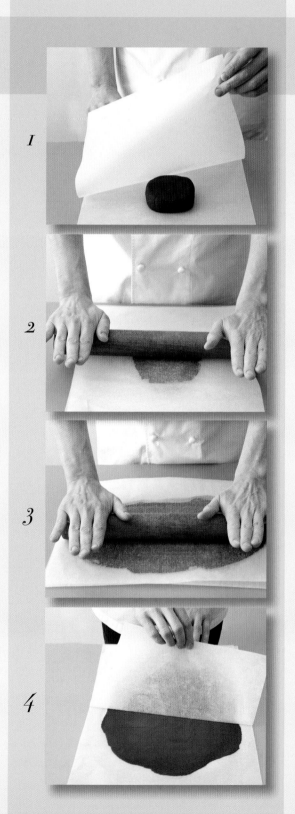

1

2

3

4

1 quantity of **Crème Pâtissière** *(see page 80)*
½ quantity of **Crème Pâtissière Chocolat** *(see page 81)*
1 quantity of **Fruit Compote** *(see page 111)*
  made with cherry purée and fresh cherries
1 quantity of **Fruit Compote** *(see page 111)*
  made with fresh apricots and apricot purée
1 quantity of **Pâte à Choux** *(see pages 58–59)*
1 quantity of **Crème Chantilly** *(see pages 84–85)*
1 quantity of **Chocolate Crème Chantilly** *(see pages 84–85)*
11 griottine cherries *marinated in kirsch (available to buy)*
100g (3½oz) red bean paste

For the chocolate craquelin:
80g (3oz/½ cup) plain (all-purpose) flour
10g (¼oz/2 tsp) cocoa powder
90g (3¼oz/scant ½ cup) caster (superfine) sugar
75g (2¾oz/¾ stick) unsalted butter

For the vanilla craquelin:
90g (3¼oz/generous ½ cup) plain (all-purpose) flour
90g (3¼oz/scant ½ cup) caster (superfine) sugar
75g (2¾oz/¾ stick) unsalted butter

For the red craquelin:
90g (3¼oz/generous ½ cup) plain (all-purpose) flour
10g (¼oz/2 tsp) freeze-dried raspberry powder
90g (3¼oz/scant ½ cup) caster (superfine) sugar
75g (2¾oz/¾ stick) unsalted butter

You will also need:
an 8mm (⅓ inch) plain piping nozzle (tip)
a 2cm (¾ inch) cutter
a 6mm (¼ inch) plain and a small star C6 piping nozzle (tip)

First, prepare the three craquelins:

· Sift the dry ingredients into a mixing bowl, add the sugar and butter and rub together until the mixture forms a dough. Roll out between 2 sheets of silicone paper *(1–4)* and leave to rest in the fridge for 30 minutes.

Next, prepare some of the fillings:

· Make the Crème Pâtissière, Crème Pâtissière Chocolat and the cherry and apricot compotes and set all aside in the fridge until needed.

Choux à la Crème *continued*

Prepare & bake the choux buns:

- Preheat the oven to 200°C (400°F/Gas 6). Prepare the Pâte à Choux as instructed and spoon it into a piping (pastry) bag fitted with an 8mm (⅓ inch) plain nozzle (tip). Pipe thirty-three 2cm (¾ inch) bulbs onto a baking tray (sheet) lined with a non-stick baking mat, leaving gaps in between. *(5)*

- Use a 2cm (¾ inch) cutter to cut each craquelin colour into discs. Top the piped choux with the craquelin discs (11 of each flavour) *(6)*, then bake for 14–15 minutes. Turn the oven temperature down to 180°C (350°F/Gas 4) and continue to cook for a further 6–8 minutes. Remove from the oven and leave to cool.

- Prepare the Crème Chantilly and the Chocolate Crème Chantilly, and use immediately.

- Once the choux buns are cooled, cut them in half lengthways. *(7)*

To finish the chocolate & cherry choux à la crème:

- Put a generous spoonful of the cherry compote in the bottom of the choux bun. *(8)* Put the Crème Pâtissière Chocolat in a piping (pastry) bag fitted with a 6mm (¼ inch) nozzle (tip) and pipe a bulb on top of the compote. *(9)* Place a griottine cherry into the crème. *(10)* Put the Chocolate Crème Chantilly in a piping (pastry) bag fitted with a small star C6 nozzle (tip) and pipe on top of the cherry *(11)*, then top with the chocolate lid of the choux bun. *(12)*

To finish the vanilla & apricot choux à la crème:

- Put a generous spoonful of the apricot compote in the bottom of the choux bun, place the Crème Pâtissière in a piping (pastry) bag and pipe a bulb on top of the compote. Put the Crème Chantilly in a piping (pastry) bag fitted with a small star C6 nozzle (tip) and pipe on top of the Crème Pâtissière, then top with the vanilla lid of the choux bun.

To finish the red bean & vanilla choux à la crème:

- Put a generous spoonful of the red bean paste in the bottom of the choux bun, pipe a bulb of the Crème Pâtissière on top and pipe the Crème Chantilly on top of this, then top with the red lid of the choux bun.

Best served the same day.

The French word éclair translated into English means 'lightening'. The pastries were given the name by the French because they could be eaten in a flash, hence the name. The small pastry was created by Marie-Antonin Carême (see page 10). Although choux pastry had first been created in the 16th century, it had always been piped in the shape of a bun. The first éclairs were smaller and glazed with caramel; the traditional fondant glaze came at a later date.

Matcha Eclairs *Makes 10*

300g (10½oz) tempered dark (bittersweet) chocolate *(see page 34) used to make* **Chocolate Slivers** *(see page 127)*
1 quantity of **Crème Pâtissière** *(see page 80)*
5g (1 tsp) matcha powder
1 quantity of **Pâte à Choux** *(see pages 58–59)*

For the matcha craquelin:
80g (3oz/½ cup) plain (all-purpose) flour
4g (1 tsp) matcha powder
90g (3¼oz/scant ½ cup) caster (superfine) sugar
75g (2¾/¾ stick) unsalted butter

For the matcha fondant:
8g (¼oz) matcha powder
40g (1½oz) **Simple Syrup** *(see page 102)*
600g (1lb 5oz) Fondant *(see page 31)*

You will also need:
a 15mm (⅝ inch) plain piping nozzle (tip)
a 6mm (¼ inch) plain piping nozzle (tip)

First, make the chocolate decorations & matcha craquelin:

- Temper the chocolate and make the decorations as instructed, then leave in a cool, dry place to set for 2 hours.

- To make the craquelin, sift the flour and matcha powder together in a mixing bowl. Add the sugar and butter and rub together until the mixture forms a dough. Roll the dough between 2 sheets of silicone baking paper, then chill for 30 minutes.

Next, prepare the matcha Crème Pâtissière:

- Begin to prepare the Crème Pâtissière: mix the matcha powder with 30ml (2 tbsp) of the milk in a small bowl, then add to the remaining milk and continue to prepare the Crème Pâtissière as instructed. Pour into a shallow tray, cover with cling film (plastic wrap) and leave in the fridge until needed.

Then, prepare & bake the pastry:

- Preheat the oven to 200°C (400°F/Gas 6). Prepare the Pâte à Choux as instructed and spoon it into a piping (pastry) bag fitted with a 15mm (⅝ inch) piping nozzle (tip). Pipe the choux pastry into 10 lines, each 10cm (4 inches) long, onto a baking tray (sheet) lined with a non-stick baking mat.

- Cut the craquelin into ten 1.2cm (½ inch) strips and place them on top of the piped eclairs. *(1)* Bake for 18–20 minutes. Turn the oven temperature down to 180°C (350°F/Gas 4) and continue to cook for a further 8–10 minutes. Remove from the oven and leave to cool. *(2)*

- Use a piping nozzle (tip) to pierce 3 holes in the base of each éclair, *(3)* then transfer to a wire cooling rack.

I

2

3

Matcha Eclairs *continued*

- Place the prepared Matcha Crème Pâtissière into a piping (pastry) bag fitted with a 6mm (¼ inch) nozzle (tip) and pipe it into the éclairs ensuring that they are well filled. *(4)*

Next, make the matcha fondant & finish:

- Mix the matcha powder and the Simple Syrup together with a matcha whisk. *(5)*

- Put the fondant and the matcha syrup in a bowl and place over a bain-marie (water bath). Gently heat until it reaches 35–37°C (95–98.6°F). *(6–7)*

- Dip each éclair into the fondant. *(8)*

- Remove any excess fondant with a clean finger. *(9)* Leave to set for 5 minutes, then decorate with the chocolate decorations.

Best served the same day.

Chocolate Eclair

Make as above, but use Crème Pâtissière Chocolat *(see page 81)* instead of the Crème Pâtissière and the following craquelin and fondant:

Chocolate craquelin: make as above, but replace the matcha powder with 10g (¼oz/2 tsp) cocoa powder.

Chocolate fondant: make as above, but replace the matcha powder with 60g (2oz) dark (bittersweet) chocolate (70% cocoa solids), finely chopped.

Gâteau Religieuse *Makes 8*

I

300g (10½oz) tempered dark (bittersweet) chocolate *(see page 34) used to make 5cm (2 inch)* **Chocolate Squares** *and small* **Triangle Flicks** *(see pages 126 and 134)*

300g (10½oz) tempered milk chocolate *(see page 34) used to make 5cm (2 inch)* **Chocolate Squares** *(see page 126)*

1 quantity of **Crème Pâtissière Caramel** *(see Variation, page 81)*

½ quantity of **Orange Curd** *(see Variation, page 96)*

1 quantity of **Craquelin** *(see page 191), made without the matcha powder*

1 quantity of **Pâte à Choux** *(see pages 58–59)*

½ quantity of **Creme au Beurre** *(see page 86) with the seeds from ½ vanilla pod (bean) beaten into the butter*

1 quantity of **Fondant** (see page 191), but use 8g (1½ tsp) freeze-dried orange powder instead of the matcha powder

1 quantity of **Confit Orange** *(see page 113) cut into 8 small triangles*

You will also need:

a 10mm (½ inch) plain piping nozzle (tip)

a 4.5cm (1¾ inch) round cutter

a 2cm (¾ inch) round cutter

a 6mm (¼ inch) plain piping nozzle (tip)

a small star nozzle (tip)

Prepare the chocolate decorations, Crème Pâtissière Caramel, Orange Curd & Craquelin:

- Temper the chocolate, make the decorations, then leave in a cool, dry place for 2 hours. Prepare the crème pâtissière, curd and craquelin. Chill.

Prepare the pastry:

- Preheat the oven to 200°C (400°F/Gas 6) and line 2 baking trays (sheets) with non-stick baking mats. Prepare the Pâte à Choux and spoon it into a piping (pastry) bag fitted with a 10mm (½ inch) nozzle (tip). Cut the chilled craquelin dough into eight 4.5cm (1¾ inch) discs and eight 2cm (¾ inch) discs. Pipe eight 5cm (2 inch) bulbs on one tray and top with the larger craquelin discs. Pipe eight 2.5cm (1 inch) bulbs on the other tray; top with the smaller discs. *(1)*

- Bake for 18–20 minutes. Turn the oven down to 180°C (350°F/Gas 4) and cook for 6–8 minutes. Remove the small choux buns, then continue to cook the large buns for 8–10 minutes. Place on a wire rack to cool.

Prepare the Crème au Beurre & fill the buns:

- Prepare the Crème au Beurre and set aside. Pierce a hole in the base of the larger buns. Place the Crème Pâtissière Caramel in a piping (pastry) bag fitted with a 6mm (¼ inch) piping nozzle (tip), then pipe the crème into the buns. *(2)*

2

- Place the curd in a piping (pastry) bag fitted with a 6mm (¼ inch) piping nozzle (tip). Pierce a hole in the base of the small buns and fill with curd.

Now, make the fondant & finish:

- Prepare the fondant as instructed. Dip all the buns in the fondant *(3)* and take off any excess fondant. Place the prepared Crème au Beurre in a piping (pastry) bag fitted with a small star nozzle (tip). Place one of each chocolate squares on top of the larger choux bun and stick them together with a little of the Crème au Beurre. *(4)* Place a small bulb of the Crème au Beurre on top of the chocolate disc in the centre and position the small choux bun on top. *(5)*

3

- Pipe around the bun with the Crème au Beurre *(6)* and pipe a rosette on top. Top with the Confit Orange and chocolate flick. *Best served the same day.*

4

5

6

Gâteau Religeuse is a French classic created in 1856 by a Parisian pâtissier called Frascati. Religieuse is an old French word dating back to 1165, meaning 'nun' in English. As with many of the classics, the original was quite different. It consisted of a pâte sucrée flan filled with choux pastry buns containing flavoured whipped cream and glazed with fondant. In 1890, Stohrer transformed the shape of the Religeuse; he wanted it to resemble a nun dressed in her habit. He made a medium- and small-sized choux bun, filled them with chocolate crème pâtissière and glazed with chocolate fondant to represent the nun's body and head. He then piped buttercream rosettes between the buns to represent the starched white collar and lastly a small rosette on top to represent the nun's white hat.

*Originating from Brittany in France, this is a round crusty pastry, made with yeast dough containing layers of butter and sugar folded in, similar in fashion to feuilletage (puff pastry) albeit with fewer layers. The resulting pastry is baked until the butter puffs up the dough and the sugar caramelizes. The name derives from the language of the region Breton; the words for cake (*kouign*) and butter (*amann*). Kouign-amann is a speciality of the town Douarenez in Finistère, in the west of France, where it originated in around 1860.*

Kouign-amann *Makes 12*

275g (9¾oz/2 cups) plain (all-purpose) flour *sifted*
5g (1 tsp) salt
235g (8¼oz/generous 1 cup) unsalted butter *plus extra for greasing*
5g (1 tsp) fresh yeast
165ml (6fl oz/¾ cup) tepid water
225g (8oz/generous 1 cup) caster (superfine) sugar *plus extra for folding*

You will also need:
pastry wheels
twelve 7cm (2¾ inch) rings

- Put the flour and salt in a bowl and rub in 10g (¼oz) of the butter. Mix the yeast with the water, then add to the flour and mix to form a dough. Knead for 6–8 minutes until it becomes elastic, then chill for 1 hour. Take the remaining butter out of the fridge and shape it into a rectangle measuring 10 x 6cm (5 x 2½ inches).

- Roll the dough into a rectangle on a lightly floured surface. Place the butter in the centre and fold over the sides of dough to encase it. Make 2 turns *(see pages 52–53)* and rest in the fridge for 1 hour. Preheat the oven to 180°C (350°F/Gas 4).

- Sprinkle the sugar on the work surface and make another turn. Sprinkle sugar on top as well – the dough should take all of the sugar. *(1)* Roll out the dough to 4mm (⅛ inch) thick and cut into 9cm (3½ inch) squares using a pastry wheel or sharp knife. *(2–3)*

- Make a sugar mound on the work surface and place a square of the dough on top. Fold in all 4 corners and press them into the centre. *(4)* Press the 4 corners into the centre again. *(5)*

- Use a pastry brush to brush the insides of the rings with butter. Place each piece of sugared dough into a tart ring and bake for 25–30 minutes until golden. *(6)* Leave to cool slightly, then run a spatula round the edge of the rings to release and leave to cool on a wire rack. *Best served the same day.*

196

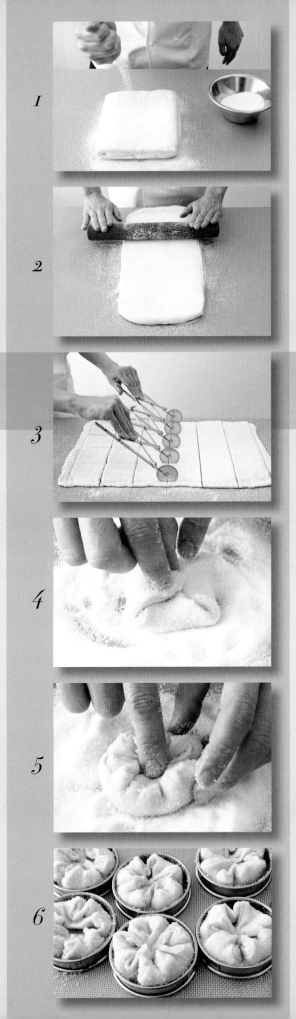

1

2

3

4

5

6

Baba au Rhum *Makes 12*

The Baba originated from Poland in the early 18th century, before being introduced to the French district of Alsace. The story of its invention claims that it was created by a fussy Polish king. He was served dry Kugelhopf that he dipped into his wine. After tasting the soaked cake, he was so pleased with the results that it became an instant favourite of his. Originally the dough was made with rye flour, and the babas were soaked in Hungarian wine after being cooked. In 1835, the famous Polish pâtissier Stohrer, brought the recipe to Paris. He opened a pâtisserie on rue Montorgeuil, where he specialized in making Baba au Rhum as it continues to do so to this day.

1 quantity of **Pâte à Savarin** (*see pages 62–63*)
1½ quantities of **Light Syrup** (*see page 103*)
  made with the addition of the grated zest of 1 orange
100ml (3½fl oz/scant ½ cup) dark rum
1 quantity of **Apricot Nappage** (*see page 104*)
½ quantity of **Crème Chantilly** (*see pages 84–85*)

You will also need:
a 10mm (½ inch) plain piping nozzle (tip)
twelve 5cm (2 inch) diameter non-stick baba (dariole) moulds

- Prepare the Pâte à Savarin and rest as instructed.

- Put the dough into a piping (pastry) bag fitted with a plain 10mm (½ inch) nozzle (tip) and pipe 45g (1½oz) into each baba mould. *(1)* Leave to prove for about 20–30 minutes until doubled in size. *(2)* Preheat the oven to 200°C (400°F/Gas 6).

- Bake for 20–25 minutes until golden brown in colour. *(3)* Remove from the moulds and leave to cool.

- Prepare the syrup in a saucepan, bring to the boil, then cool slightly to 90°C (194°F). Place the babas into the pan and turn them over so that they get soaked all over. *(4)*

- After about 3–4 minutes, when the babas have softened, remove them from the syrup with a slotted spoon and place into a tray. *(5)* Use a small ladle to cover the babas in more syrup to ensure they are fully soaked, then leave to cool. Pour the dark rum over the babas. *(6)*

- Warm the nappage and brush all over the babas. Prepare the Crème Chantilly and serve the babas with a large spoonful on the side.

Best served the same day.

198

1 quantity of **Pâte à Savarin** (*see pages 62–63*)
200ml (7fl oz/scant 1 cup) Sauternes
1 quantity **Apricot Nappage** (*see page 104*)
½ quantity of **Creme Chantilly** (*see pages 84–85*)

For the poached peaches & lemon thyme syrup:
1 quantity **Light Syrup** (*see page 103*)
8 lemon thyme sprigs, *leaves removed, plus extra to decorate*
4 peaches *washed, stoned and quartered*
150ml (¼ pint/generous ½ cup) Sauternes

You will also need:
a 10mm (½ inch) plain and a D6 star piping nozzle (tip)
twelve 8cm (3¼ inch) diameter non-stick savarin moulds

Savarin au Pêche *Makes 12*

The night before, make the peaches & syrup:

- Prepare the Light Syrup, bring to the boil and add the lemon thyme and peaches. Place a cartouche on top and cook for 8–10 minutes over a gentle heat until soft. Remove from the heat and leave to cool a little. Once cooled slightly, add the Sauternes, leave to cool completely, then store in an airtight container in the fridge overnight.

The next day:

- Prepare the Pâte à Savarin and rest as instructed. Put the proved and knocked back savarin dough into a piping (pastry) bag fitted with a 10mm (½ inch) plain nozzle (tip) and pipe about 40g (1½oz) into each savarin mould. *(1)* Leave to prove for about 30 minutes, until doubled in size. *(2)* Preheat the oven to 200°C (400°F/Gas 6).

- Bake for 20–25 minutes until golden in colour, remove from the tin and leave to cool on a wire cooling rack. *(3)*

- Drain the peaches, reserving the syrup in a saucepan. Bring the syrup to the boil, then cool slightly to 90°C (194°F). Immerse the savarins in the syrup for 2–3 minutes, then flip over so that both sides have been soaked. *(4)* Use a slotted spoon to remove the savarins from the syrup and place on a tray. *(5)*

- Use a spoon to pour some more syrup over the savarins so that they are completely soaked. Leave to cool. Once cooled, drizzle the savarins with the Sauternes. *(6)*

- Put the savarins onto a serving dish, warm the nappage and brush all over the savarins. Prepare the Crème Chantilly and spoon into a piping (pastry) bag fitted with a star nozzle (tip). Pipe a bulb into the centre of each savarin.

- Cut the poached peaches into slices, glaze with some Apricot Nappage and place them next to the bulb of Chantilly on the savarin. Sprinkle with a few lemon thyme leaves to finish.

Serve immediately.

1

2

3

4

5

6

1 quantity of **Brioche** (*see pages 64–65*)
egg wash (*see page 29*)
1 quantity of **Alcohol Syrup** (*see page 103*) *made
with Grand Marnier*
½ quantity of **Crème Pâtissière** (*see page 80*)
½ quantity of **Italian Meringue** (*see page 73*)

For the kumquat confit:
1 quantity of **Simple Syrup**
(*see page 102*)
10 kumquats
washed and finely sliced into 2mm thick slices

For the kumquat marmalade:
700g (1½lb) kumquats
250g (9oz/1¼ cups) caster
(superfine) sugar
200ml (7fl oz/scant 1 cup) water
15ml (1 tbsp) lemon juice
15ml (1 tbsp) Grand Marnier

You will also need:
twelve brioche à tête moulds
a 4mm (¼ inch) piping nozzle (tip)
a blow torch

Brioche Polonaise *Makes 12*

The day before, make the kumquat confit:

• Bring the Simple Syrup to the boil, add the sliced kumquats and cook over a low heat for 30 minutes. Lay each slice of kumquat out separately on a tray in a dehydrator and brush with a little of the cooking syrup. Dehydrate at 60°C (140°F) for 24 hours.

The next day, make the brioche:

• Brush the moulds with softened butter. Prepare the brioche and rest as instructed. Divide the dough into 50g (1¾oz) pieces using the edge of your hand, then gently roll into a shape resembling a squat bowling pin, creating a small ball (the head of the brioche) that is about one-quarter the size of the main body. Lift the brioche by the head and place in one of the buttered moulds. Press your fingers into the dough around the head to form an indentation, then gently push the small ball down into the centre. Repeat with the remaining brioche balls. Place on a tray and leave to prove for 1 hour until doubled in size. Preheat the oven to 200°C (400°F/Gas 6). Brush with egg wash. *(1)* Bake for 25–30 minutes until golden brown.

Then, the marmalade:

• Wash the kumquats, place them in a saucepan of boiling water and simmer for 2–3 minutes. Drain the kumquats and place them in cold water to cool. Once cooled, quarter the kumquats and remove the flesh from the pith. Deseed the flesh and put it in a saucepan. Roughly chop the pith and place in the pan with the flesh. Add the sugar and water to the kumquats and cook over a low heat for 45–50 minutes. Add the lemon juice and Grand Marnier and cook for a further 5–10 minutes.

To assemble & finish:

• Prepare the Grand Marnier Syrup, Crème Pâtissière and the Italian Meringue. Cut out the centre of each brioche. *(2)*

• Put the Grand Marnier Syrup in a saucepan and reheat over a low heat if necessary. Add the brioche to the warm syrup and leave to soak well. *(3)* Use a spoon to take the soaked brioche out of the syrup and onto a tray to cool.

• Put a good teaspoonful of the kumquat marmalade in the centre of each brioche.

• Put the Crème Pâtissière in a piping (pastry) bag and pipe it in the centre of each brioche up to the top. *(4)*

• Put the brioche on a serving dish or tray and use a step palette knife to cover each brioche with the Italian Meringue. *(5)*

• Put some of the meringue in a piping (pastry) bag fitted with a 4mm (¼ inch) plain nozzle (tip) and pipe decorative loops around the top of each brioche. *(6)*

• Toast the meringue gently with a blow torch. *(7)* Decorate with a piece of kumquat confit.

Best served the same day.

1

2

3

4

5

6

7

The origins are not clear for this pâtisserie, although like the Bostock (see pages 204–205) it comes from the boulanger wanting to utilize the day-old stale brioche à tête. The stale brioche is soaked in syrup to moisten it and filled with Crème Pâtissière. Suzue wanted to create a fusion of Europe and Asia with the incorporation of the citrus kumquat to balance with the sweetness of the syrup and the meringue. Over time I am sure the look of Polonaise has evolved to become this dish of beauty and elegance.

This is a popular almond brioche originating from Normandy. Bostock was created out of the need to use day-old stale brioche. It is brushed with syrup, covered with crème d'amande and baked.

1 quantity of **Brioche** *(see pages 64–65)*
½ quantity of **Creme d'Amande** *(see page 88)*
1 quantity of **Alcohol Syrup** *(see page 103) made with dark rum*

To decorate:
240g (8¾oz) shop-bought confit chestnuts *chopped*
flaked almonds
black sesame seeds *lightly toasted*
white sesame seeds *lightly toasted*

You will also need:
three baking tins or tin cans, measuring 10cm (4 inches)
  in diameter and 15cm (6 inches) in height

Bostock *Makes 12–15*

1

2

3

4

5

- Divide the proved and knocked back brioche dough into 3 pieces, about 300g (10½ oz) each. Shape each portion into a ball and place in the baking tins.

- Leave to prove for about 1 hour until doubled in size. Preheat the oven to 200°C (400°F/Gas 6).

- Cut a cross on the top of each proved brioche and bake in the preheated oven for 40–45 minutes until golden. Remove from the tin and leave to cool.

- Prepare the Crème d'Amande while the brioche is cooling. Reduce the oven temperature to 180°C (350°F/Gas 4).

- Slice the cooked brioche into 2cm (¾ inch) thick slices – you should get about 4 or 5 per brioche. *(1)*

- Put the slices on a non-stick baking mat and use a pastry brush to soak each slice of brioche generously with the rum syrup. *(2)*

- Top with the chopped confit chestnuts. *(3)*

- Use a step palette knife to spread the Crème d'Amande on top of the chestnuts. *(4)*

- Lastly, sprinkle the tops with flaked almonds and the black and white sesame seeds. *(5)*

- Bake for 16–18 minutes, then leave to cool.

Best served fresh, but can be stored in an airtight container for up to 2 days.

Beignet Alsacienne *Makes 30*

1 quantity of **Raspberry
   Confiture** (*see page 108*)
sunflower or vegetable oil
   for deep-frying

For the beignet dough:
500g (1lb 2oz/3½ cups)
   strong flour *sifted*
55g (2oz/¼ cup) caster
   (superfine) sugar
10g (¼oz/2 tsp) salt
125ml (4fl oz/½ cup)
   full-fat milk
40g (1½oz) fresh yeast
50g (1¾oz) whole egg
   (*about 1 egg*)
100g (3½oz) egg yolks
   (*about 5 eggs*)
10ml (2 tsp) dark rum
100g (3½oz/scant 1 stick)
   softened unsalted butter
   cubed

For the vanilla sugar:
300g (10½oz/1½ cups) caster
   (superfine) sugar
1 vanilla pod (bean)
   split lengthways

You will also need:
a deep-fat fryer
a garnishing piping nozzle (tip)

Make the vanilla sugar & the confiture:

- Put the sugar in a bowl. Scrape in the seeds from the vanilla pod (bean) and mix until the seeds are evenly dispersed. Prepare the Raspberry Confiture as instructed.

Next, make the dough:

- Put the flour, sugar and salt in the bowl of an electric mixer.

- Put the milk and fresh yeast in a small bowl and mix together.

- Add the milk and yeast mixture to the whole egg and egg yolks in another bowl, mix together, then add the rum.

- Add all of the wet ingredients to the dry ingredients and begin to mix with a dough hook.

- Continue mixing until the dough is smooth and elastic and comes away from the side of the bowl. Add the butter and continue to beat until the mixture comes away from the side again. Put the dough in a bowl, cover with cling film (plastic wrap) and place in the fridge for 1–2 hours.

To finish:

- Cut and weigh the chilled dough into 30g (1¼oz) pieces. Roll each piece into a ball, put on a sheet of silicone baking paper and leave to prove for 1½ hours or until doubled in size. *(1–3)*

- Once the dough is fully proved, turn on the deep-fat fryer and heat the oil to 170°C (325°F). Carefully lower each one into the oil and cook for about 3 minutes on each side. You may need to cook in batches. *(4)*

- Remove the beignets from the fryer and drain on kitchen paper to remove excess oil. Toss each beignet in the vanilla sugar, then leave to cool. *(5)*

- Spoon the Raspberry Confiture into a piping (pastry) bag fitted with a garnishing piping nozzle (tip). Press the nozzle (tip) into the centre of the beignet and fill with about 12–15g (¼–½ oz) of confiture per beignet. *(6)*

Best served the same day.

1

2

3

4

5

6

A beignet can be made with either choux pastry or yeast dough that is then deep-fried. Alsacienne doughnuts are spherical in shape and filled with either fruit compote or confiture. Alsacienne refers to the Alsace region of France.

125ml (4fl oz/½ cup) full-fat milk

85ml (3fl oz/⅓ cup) water

20g (¾oz) fresh yeast

500g (1lb 2oz/3½ cups) strong flour *sifted*

60g (2oz/generous ¼ cup) caster (superfine) sugar
   plus extra to finish

10g (¼oz/2 tsp) salt

110g (3½oz) whole eggs *(about 2–3 eggs)*

200g (7oz/scant 1 cup) room temperature butter
   cubed, plus extra for greasing

250g (9oz) **Rum-marinated Sultanas** *(see page 115)*

25ml (1fl oz/1¾ tbsp) kirsch

50g (1 ¾oz/generous ⅓ cup) roasted whole almonds

clarified butter *(see page 32) to finish*

You will also need:

three kugelhopf (bundt) moulds, measuring 16cm
   (6¼ inch) in diameter and 7cm (2¾ inch) deep

Kugelhopf *Makes 3*

- Warm the milk and water in a pan until it reaches
  30–34°C (86–93°F). Crumb the yeast and mix with
  the milk and water until dissolved. Add 30g (1oz) of
  the sifted flour and leave in a warm place for about
  20 minutes to prove until doubled in size (this is the
  sponge ferment).

- Sift the remaining flour, the sugar and salt into the
  bowl of an electric mixer fitted with the dough hook.
  Add the eggs and the sponge ferment and beat for
  10–12 minutes until the mixture is elastic and comes
  away from the sides.

- Add the butter to the mixture and continue to beat
  until the mixture comes away from the sides again.
  Add in the soaked sultanas and kirsch and mix until
  dispersed within the dough. Leave the mixture to prove
  for about 1½ hours or until doubled in size. Grease the
  kugelhopf moulds with softened butter and place the
  roasted whole almonds into the base. *(1)*

- Knock back the dough and divide into 3 portions, about
  400g (14oz) each. Roll each portion into a sausage
  shape and place it into the kugelhopf tin around the
  hole in the middle. *(2)*

- Put the moulds on a tray and leave to prove for about
  30–35 minutes or until it has doubled in size. *(3)*
  Preheat the oven to 200°C (400°F/Gas 6).

- Bake for 30–35 minutes. Leave to cool for 5 minutes,
  then demould from the tin and brush with clarified
  butter. *(4)* Sprinkle with sugar to finish. *(5)*

Keep in an airtight container and eat within 1–2 days.

The Kugelhopf was created in the city of Lemberg in 1609, which was under Polish rule at the time. The cake was brought to France by King Stanislas II of Poland; when he lost his kingdom his son-in-law gave him the Duchy of Alsace–Lorraine, a Provence in the northwest of France. He brought with him his entire Royal household, including his executive chef Chevriot. The Polish King's favourite sweet was the Kugelhopf. Chevriot always served it for him with Malaga wine or rum. However, it was not until later that Marie Antoinette made the cake fashionable in France – she particularly enjoyed it with her morning coffee. Pierre Lacam states in his book, Mémorial de la Pâtisserie *that the Kugelhopf was brought to Paris from Strasbourg in Alsace in 1840 by a French confectioner, who opened a Pâtisserie on the rue de Coq. The cake became so popular that the shop was producing hundreds each day. The small establishment had to employ 25 bakers and confectioners to meet the demands.*

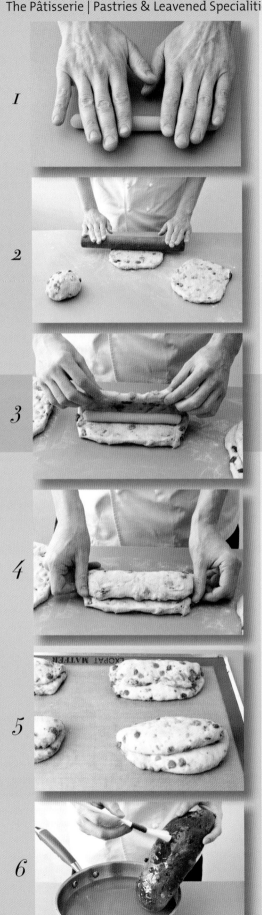

200g (7oz) marzipan
500g (1lb 2oz/3½ cups) strong flour *sifted*
60g (2oz/generous ¼ cup) caster (superfine) sugar *plus extra to finish*
10g (¼oz/2 tsp) salt
125ml (4fl oz/generous ½ cup) full-fat milk
25g (1oz) fresh yeast
165g (6oz) whole eggs *(about 3–4 eggs)*
250g (9oz/generous 1 cup) softened unsalted butter
40g (1½oz/⅓ cup) walnuts *chopped*
40g (1½oz/scant ½ cup) almonds *roasted and chopped*
200g (7oz) **Rum-marinated Sultanas** *(see page 115)*
1g (a pinch) grated lemon zest
40g (1½oz) **Confit Orange** *(see page 113) diced*
20ml (1½ tbsp) dark rum
2g (a pinch) ground cinnamon

To finish:
400g (14oz) clarified butter *(see page 32)*
icing (powdered) sugar *for dusting*

Stöllen *Makes 4*

- Divide the marzipan into 4 equal portions, shape into balls and roll each one out into a 15cm (6 inch) log on a lightly floured surface. Place on a baking tray (sheet). *(1)*

- Sift together the flour, sugar and salt into the bowl of an electric mixer fitted with a dough hook. Warm the milk in a saucepan until it reaches 30–34°C (86–93°F), then mix in the yeast.

- Add the eggs, yeast and milk to the flour mixture. Beat together for 10–12 minutes until the mixture is elastic and comes away from the sides of the bowl. Add the butter to the mixture and continue to beat until the mixture comes away from the sides again.

- Add the nuts, fruits, rum and cinnamon and mix until dispersed within the dough. Leave the mixture to prove for about 1½ hours.

- Knock back the dough, then divide into 4 equal pieces. Knock back each piece, shape into a ball and roll out into a 17 x 10cm (6½ x 4 inch) rectangle on a lightly floured surface. *(2)*

- Place the roll of marzipan inside each rectangle of dough and fold over the dough to enclose it. Press gently to seal. *(3–4)*

- Place each rectangle of dough on a tray and leave to prove for about 35–40 minutes, or until it has doubled in size. *(5)* Preheat the oven to 200°C (400°F/Gas 6).

- Bake for 35–40 minutes, then leave to cool for 10 minutes. Use a pastry brush to generously coat each stollen with clarified butter. *(6)* Leave to set, then dust with icing (powdered) sugar.

Keep in an airtight container and eat within 1 week. The stöllen can also be sliced and reheated or toasted.

The stöllen originates from Germany, where for centuries it has been eaten during the Christmas season. The spiced loaf, originally round in shape, is thought to originate from the 14th century, and is often referred to as Christoleen or Streizel. It was introduced to Britain by Prince Albert from the German royal family who married Queen Victoria in 1840.

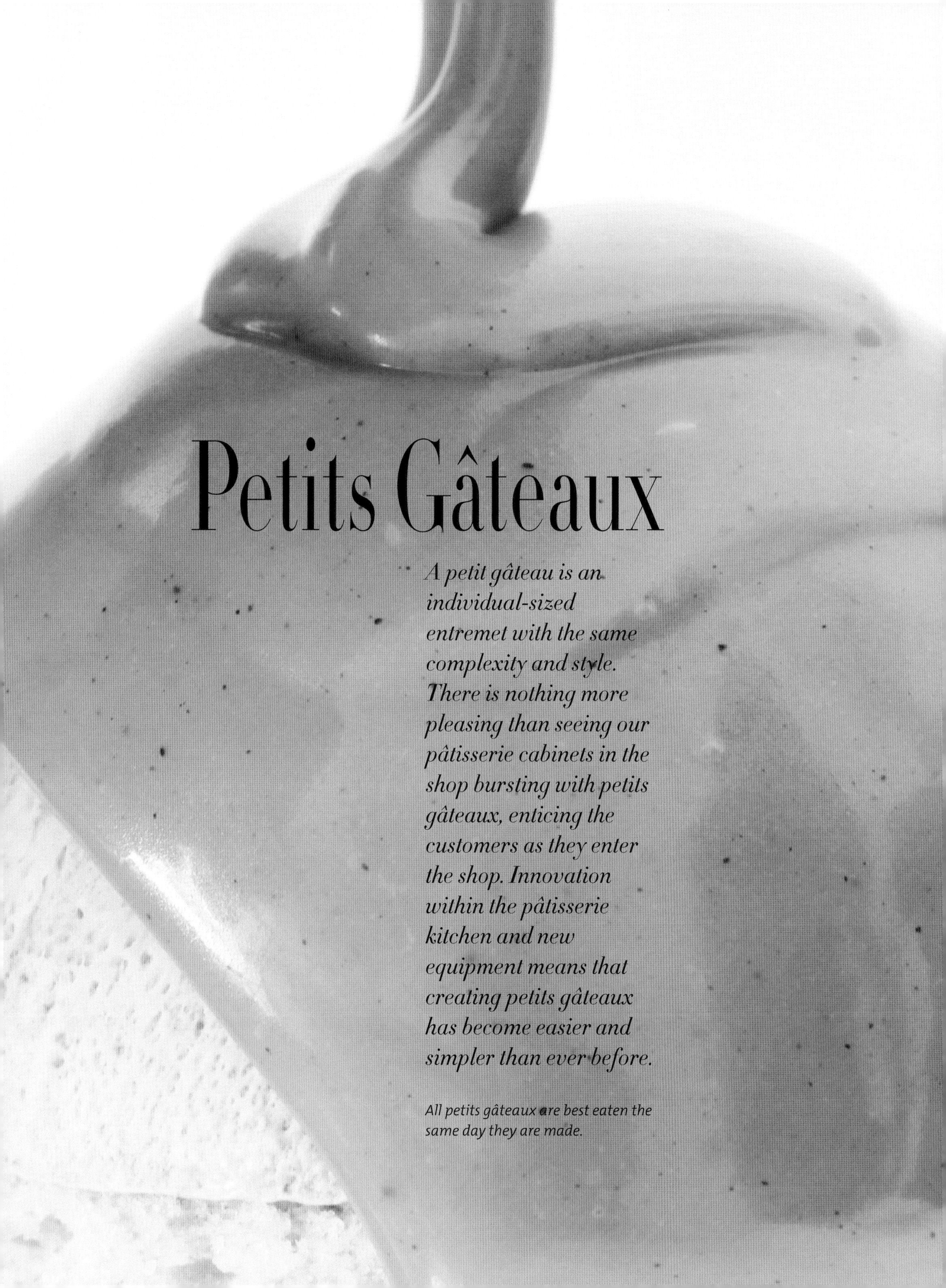

Petits Gâteaux

A petit gâteau is an individual-sized entremet with the same complexity and style. There is nothing more pleasing than seeing our pâtisserie cabinets in the shop bursting with petits gâteaux, enticing the customers as they enter the shop. Innovation within the pâtisserie kitchen and new equipment means that creating petits gâteaux has become easier and simpler than ever before.

All petits gâteaux are best eaten the same day they are made.

This pâtisserie encapsulates very much what we do; east meets west with its flavour combination and intricacy. The acidity of the sudachi brings out the subtle flavours of the fraises des bois (wild strawberries).

Fraise de Bois & Sudachi Teardrop   *Makes 8*

300g (10½oz) tempered dark (bittersweet) chocolate *(see page 34)*, used to make **Patterned Squares** *and* **Chocolate Curls** *(see pages 126 and 130)*
100g (3½oz) sugar paste
1 quantity of **Royal Icing** *(see box, page 217) light yellow in colour*
1 quantity of **Biscuit Joconde** *(see page 69)*
1 quantity of **Alcohol Syrup** *(see page 103) made with sudachi shochu*
½ quantity of **Sudachi Curd** *(see Variation, page 96)*
1 quantity of **Fruit Mousse** *(see page 99) made with fraise de bois (wild strawberry) purée*
1 quantity of **Fruit Glaze** *(see page 105), but replace the purée with water and add an extra ½ split and scraped vanilla pod (bean)*
1 quantity of **Fruit Glaze** *(see page 105) made with fraise de bois (wild strawberry) purée*
fraises des bois (wild strawberries) *to decorate*

For the strawberry decorative paste:
40g (1½oz) unsalted butter
40g (1½oz/¼ cup) icing (powdered) sugar
40g (1½oz) egg white *(about 1–2 eggs)*
45g (1⅔oz/¼ cup) plain (all-purpose) flour *sifted*
10g (¼oz/2 tsp) freeze-dried strawberry powder

For the fraise de bois compote:
1 quantity of **Fruit Compote** *(see page 111) made with fraise de bois (wild strawberry) purée and fraises des bois (wild strawberries)*
75g (2¾oz) fraises des bois (wild strawberries)

For the confit sudachi:
1 sudachi
1 quantity of **Simple Syrup** *(see page 102)*

You will also need:
a small daisy flower cutter
a fleximat dome mould with 4cm (1½ inch) diameter holes
a paper piping cornet *(see page 30)*
a No. 1 piping tube (tip)
a 10mm (½ inch) plain piping nozzle (tip)
a 4cm (1½ inch) dome mould tray
eight 4 x 8cm (1½ x 3¼ inch) teardrop moulds
8 strips of flexible 4 x 21cm (1½ x 8¼ inch) acetate
a 12mm (⅝ inch) plain piping nozzle (tip)

First, prepare the decorations:

- Temper the chocolate and make the decorations as instructed, then leave in a cool, dry place to set for 2 hours.

- Prepare the flowers. Roll out the sugar paste very thinly (to about 5mm/¼ inch), then use a small daisy flower cutter to cut out 8 flowers. *(1)* Place the flowers in small dome moulds so that the petals gently curve up. *(2)* Prepare the royal icing and spoon it into a paper cornet fitted with a No. 1 piping tube (tip). Pipe 7 small bulbs into the centre of each flower *(3)* then leave in a cool, dry place to set for at least 4 hours.

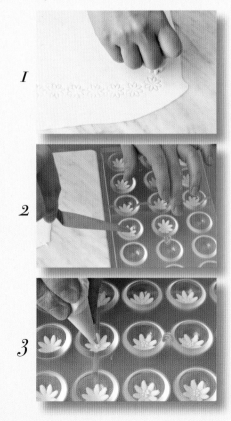

1

2

3

Fraise de Bois & Sudachi Teardrop *continued*

Prepare the strawberry decorative paste, sponge & sudachi syrup:

- First, make the paste. Put the butter in a mixing bowl and beat well. Add the icing (powdered) sugar and mix until light in colour. Mix in the egg white until well emulsified and lastly beat in the dry ingredients. Put a spoonful on a baking tray (sheet) lined with a non-stick baking mat and use a step palette knife to spread out evenly. *(4)* Use a comb scraper to scrape the mat in diagonal lines to create a striped pattern. *(5)* Transfer to the freezer to set for 30 minutes.

- Preheat the oven to 200°C (300°F/Gas 6). Prepare the Biscuit Joconde sponge, take the pattern-lined tray from the freezer, then spread the sponge mixture evenly on top. *(6–7)* Bake in the oven for 12–15 minutes until light and golden. Remove from the oven and leave to cool.

- Prepare the sudachi syrup, cool, then store in an airtight container in the fridge.

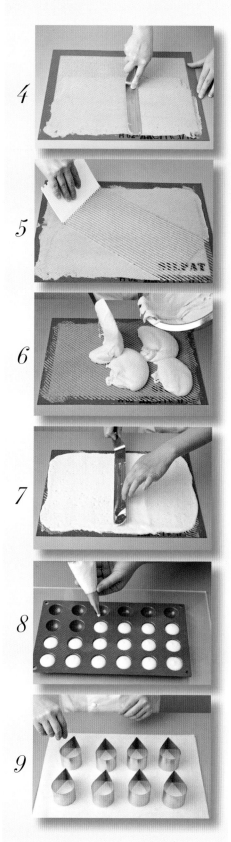

Prepare the curd, compote & confit:

- Make the curd as instructed. Spoon it into a piping (pastry) bag fitted with a 10mm (½ inch) plain nozzle (tip) and fill a 4cm (1½ inch) diameter dome mould tray. *(8)* Level off with a small palette knife, then place in the freezer to set for at least 2 hours.

- Prepare the fraise de bois (wild strawberry) compote and once cooled, add the extra fraises des bois. Store in an airtight container in the fridge until needed.

- To make the sudachi confit: peel the sudachi and cut the peel into thin strips. Place a pan of water on to boil, put the cut sudachi peel in the water for 20 seconds, strain and repeat the process. Put the Simple Syrup in a pan, add the blanched sudachi peel and cook over a gentle simmer for 12–15 minutes. Leave to cool in the syrup.

To begin the assembly:

- Place the teardrop moulds on a baking tray (sheet) lined with silicone baking paper and line the moulds with acetate. *(9)* Cut the baked sponge into 8 strips, measuring 18 x 3cm (7 x 1¼ inch) *(10)* and use the strips to line the teardrop moulds. *(11)* Cut out 8 smaller teardrop shapes from the remaining sponge to fit the base of the moulds. *(12)*

- Prepare the fraise de bois (wild strawberry) mousse, spoon into a piping (pastry) bag fitted with a 12mm (⅝ inch) plain nozzle (tip) and pipe a small amount into the base of the mould. *(13)*

- Place a teaspoon of the fraise de bois compote on top of the mousse and spread out across the base. *(14)*

- Remove the frozen curd from the freezer and place them in the moulds. *(15)* Top up the moulds with the remaining fraise de bois mousse and level off with a small step palette knife. *(16)* Transfer to the fridge to set for at least 1 hour.

To finish:

- Prepare the vanilla and fraise de bois (wild strawberry) glazes and leave them both to cool to room temperature.

- Take the frozen teardrops from the freezer, glaze the tops with the vanilla glaze, *(17)* then place them in the fridge to set for 20 minutes.

- Prepare a paper piping cornet *(see page 30)* and fill with the fraise de bois (wild strawberry) glaze. Remove the teardrops from the fridge and pipe 3 bulbs of the glaze on top of each teardrop. *(18–19)* Return to the fridge to set for a further 10 minutes.

- Take the teardrops from the fridge, demould from the teardrop rings and place on a serving dish. Glaze the fresh fraises des bois for the decoration.

- When ready to serve, decorate with the chocolate squares and curls, place the confit sudachi and fraises des bois (wild strawberries) on top and lastly add the daisy flowers.

Royal Icing

Place 25g (1oz) egg whites in a mixing bowl, beat at a low speed and graually add 250g (9oz/1¾ cups) icing (powdered) sugar. Once fully incorporated, beat at a high speed for 2 minutes. Add 10ml (½fl oz/2 tsp) lemon juice and beat for a further 1 minute. When ready, the icing will fall in a fine straight point whichever way you turn the beater. If the icing is too thick and does not form, add a touch more egg white. If it is too liquid and the point flops over when you hold it upwards, add a little more icing (powdered) sugar. Store in an airtight container to avoid a crust forming.

Jasmine & Mandarin Pyramid *Makes 12*

1 quantity of **Jasmine Crème Brûlée** (*see Variation, page 94*)
1 quantity of **Alhambra Chocolate Sponge** (*see Variation, page 67*)
1 quantity of **Dark Chocolate Glaze** (*see page 106*)
1 quantity of **Alcohol Syrup** (*see page 103*) *made with Grand Marnier*
1 quantity of **Dark Chocolate Mousse (sabayon method)** (*see page 100*)
300g (10½oz) tempered dark (bittersweet) chocolate (*see page 34*) *used to make* **Chocolate Sheets** *and* **Patterned Squares** (*see page 126*)
edible gold leaf *to decorate*

For the caramelized mandarin:

125g (4½oz/⅔ cup) caster (superfine) sugar
50ml (2fl oz/scant ¼ cup) mandarin juice *squeezed from the leftover flesh of the mandarin*
25ml (1fl oz/1½ tbsp) Grand Marnier
6 mandarins *peeled and segmented*

You will also need:

a 30 x 40 cm (12 x 16 inch) deep-sided silicone baking mat
two 6-hole, 7 x 7cm (2¼ x 2¼ inch) pyramid silicone mould

First, make the Jasmine Crème Brûlée:

• Preheat the oven to 140°C (275°F/Gas 1). Pour the prepared Jasmine Crème Brûlée into the baking mat and bake for 15–20 minutes or until set. Cool, then transfer to the freezer for 2 hours.

Then, make the chocolate sponge, caramelized mandarin, glaze & syrup:

• Preheat the oven to 190°C (375°F/Gas 5). Make the sponge mixture as instructed, then pour it into 2 non-stick baking mats and bake for 15 minutes. Leave to cool, then cut into twelve 5cm (2 inch) squares and twelve 7cm (3 inch) squares.

• To make the caramelized mandarins: make a dry amber caramel with the sugar (*see page 33*). Remove from the heat and carefully add the mandarin juice. Cool slightly, then mix in the Grand Marnier. Pour this over the mandarin segments, then leave for 1 hour. (*1*)

• Prepare the Dark Chocolate Glaze and the Grand Marnier Syrup, cool, then store both in airtight containers in the fridge.

To assemble:

• Once the Jasmine Crème Brûlee has frozen, demould from the baking mats and cut into twelve 5cm (2 inch) squares. Put the squares on a baking tray (sheet) lined with silicone baking paper and return to the freezer until needed.

• Drain the caramelized mandarins from the excess caramel. Put the pyramid moulds on a baking tray (sheet). Prepare the Dark Chocolate Mousse and use a palette knife to line the side of the mould with mousse. (*2*)

• Place 4 mandarin segments in the centre of each mould. (*3*) Top with a small sponge square and soak with syrup. (*4*) Top with the frozen Jasmine Crème Brûlée squares, then top up with mousse and level off. (*5–6*)

• Transfer to the freezer for at least 4 hours. Reserve the remaining chocolate mousse in the fridge to be used for finishing.

To finish:

• Demould the pyramids and return them to the freezer on a baking tray (sheet) lined with silicone baking paper.

• Soak the larger sponge squares with syrup, then stick the pyramids to the sponge with the reserved chocolate mousse. Place on a wire rack set over a tray. Gently melt the glaze in a saucepan, pour it into a jug, then leave to cool to about 30°C (86°F). Glaze the pyramids (*see page 35*), making sure the whole pyramid is covered. Transfer to the fridge to set for 10 minutes. Transfer the pyramid to a serving dish, then leave to defrost for at least 2 hours in the fridge. When ready to serve, arrange chocolate sheets around the pyramid and decorate with a chocolate square and gold leaf.

*I always use Amedei's
Toscano 63 for this pâtisserie;
the light nutty and floral notes
in the chocolate complement
the flavours and aromas of the
jasmine and mandarin. The
innovation behind this dish
comes from working with a
perfumier and engaging with
the senses in a different way.*

This is a very simple pâtisserie – the texture of the crunchy meringue combined with the creamy crème Chantilly is quite wonderful.

Caramel Chantilly *Makes 12*

40g (1½oz) flaked almonds *lightly toasted*
icing (powdered) sugar *for dusting*

For the meringue:
140g (5oz) egg white *(about 4–5 eggs)*
85g (3oz/scant ½ cup) granulated (white) sugar
40g (1½oz/⅓ cup) ground almonds
150g (5½oz/generous 1 cup) icing (powdered) sugar

For the caramel Chantilly:
200ml (7fl oz/scant 1 cup) double (heavy) cream
½ vanilla pod (bean) *split lengthways*
50g (1¾ oz) **Sea Salt Caramel** *(see pages 118–119)*

You will also need:
a 12mm (½ inch) plain piping nozzle (tip)
a C8 star piping nozzle (tip)

First, make the meringue:

- Preheat the oven to 120°C (250°F/Gas ½). Prepare the meringue using the French method on page 74, folding the ground almonds in with the icing (powdered) sugar. Spoon the mixture into a piping (pastry) bag fitted with a 12mm (½ inch) nozzle (tip) and pipe twelve 5 x 3cm (2 x 1¼ inch) ovals onto a baking tray lined with a non-stick baking mat. *(1)*

- Decorate with the flaked almonds *(2)* and dust with some icing (powdered) sugar. *(3)* Leave to sit for 2–3 minutes, then dust again with icing (powdered) sugar. Bake for about 40 minutes until crisp.

Meanwhile, make the caramel Chantilly & assemble:

- Put the cream in a mixing bowl. Scrape the seeds from the split vanilla pod (bean) into the bowl and whip until semi-whipped. Beat one-third of the cream into the Sea Salt Caramel, then fold in the remaining cream being careful not to over whip. Leave in the fridge until needed.

- Match up the meringues into pairs. Spoon the chilled caramel Chantilly into a piping (pastry) bag fitted with a C8 star piping nozzle (tip) and pipe a swirl of cream onto the base of half of the meringues. *(4)* Sandwich with the remaining meringues. Pipe a swirl of cream along the top of each sandwiched meringue pair to finish. *(5)* *Serve immediately.*

1

2

3

4

5

½ quantity of **Pâte Sablée** *(see page 46)*
½ quantity of **Alhambra Chocolate Sponge** *(see Variation, page 67)*
1 quantity of **Alcohol Syrup** *(see page 103)* made with dark rum
1 quantity of **Dark Chocolate Mousse (anglaise method)** *(see page 101)*
1 quantity of **Peanut Tuile** *(see page 121)*
1 quantity of **Sea Salt Caramel** *(see page 118–119)* made with the addition
   of 30g (1¼oz) **Peanut Paste** *(see Variation, page 116)*
1 quantity of **Dark Spraying Chocolate** *(see page 35)*
edible gold leaf *to decorate*

For the peanut praline feuillantine:
100g (3½oz) milk chocolate *chopped*
10g (¼oz/2 tsp) cocoa butter
75g (2¾oz) **Peanut Paste** *(see Variation, page 116)*
90g (3¼oz) feuillantine wafer

For the caramelized banana:
100g (3oz/⅔ cup) caster (superfine) sugar
350g (9oz) banana *peeled and roughly chopped*
30ml (1fl oz) dark rum

You will also need:
a 12mm (½ inch) and an 8mm (⅓ inch) plain piping nozzle (tip)
a 10-hole, 10 x 4cm (4 x 2½ inch) deep ingot silicone mould

Chocolate, Banana & Peanut Caramel Bar   *Makes 10*

First, prepare the pastry, sponge & rum syrup:

- Prepare the Pâte Sablée and rest and chill as instructed. Roll half of the pastry out to a 2.5mm (⅛ inch) thickness and place in the fridge to rest for at least 30 minutes. Preheat the oven to 190°C (375°F/Gas 5). Prepare the chocolate sponge and bake for 12–15 minutes. Meanwhile, prepare the rum syrup, cool and store in an airtight container in the fridge.

Next, make the peanut praline feuillantine:

- Prepare a baking tray (sheet) lined with silicone baking paper. To make the peanut praline feuillantine, put the chopped milk chocolate and cocoa butter in a bowl and melt it over a bain-marie (water bath) *(see page 31)*. Mix the Peanut Paste into the chocolate mixture and lastly mix in the feuillantine wafer. Spoon into the prepared tray and spread out thinly. Leave to set for at least 30 minutes. Once semi-set, cut into ten 10 x 4cm (4 x 1½ inches) rectangles, then leave to fully set for 1 hour.

Then, prepare the caramelized bananas:

- Make a dry amber caramel with the sugar *(see page 33)*. Add the chopped banana and cook for 2–3 minutes over a gentle heat. *(1)* Lastly add the dark rum. Pour into a shallow tray and leave to cool in the caramel. *(2)*

Prepare the chocolate mousse & begin to assemble:

- Prepare the mousse as instructed, then spoon into a piping (pastry) bag fitted with a 12mm (½ inch) piping nozzle (tip) and pipe into the base of the ingot mould. *(3)* Use a small palette knife to push the mousse up the sides. *(4)*

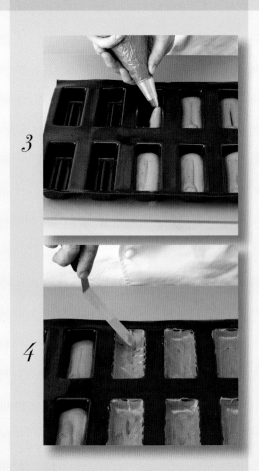

The combination of chocolate, peanut and caramel takes me back to my childhood, with nostalgic memories. I wanted to create a more sophisticated version, adding another dimension with the caramelized banana and bringing all the elements together.

Chocolate, Banana & Peanut Caramel Bar *continued*

- Spoon the caramelized banana into the middle of each of the ingot moulds. *(5)* Place a rectangle of chocolate sponge on top of the caramelized banana *(6)* and soak the sponge with the rum syrup. *(7)* Top up the moulds with the remaining mousse (reserving any leftover mousse in the fridge), leaving a 2mm (just under ⅛ inch) gap at the top, *(8)* then level off. *(9)*

- Top with the peanut praline feuillantine and press down gently. *(10)* Transfer to the freezer to set for at least 4 hours.

To finish:

- Preheat the oven to 190°C (375°F/Gas 5). Prepare and bake the Peanut Tuile, then turn the oven down to 180°C (350°F/ Gas 4). Take the rested Pâte Sablée from the fridge and cut out eight 11 x 5cm (4¼ x 2 inch) rectangles. Place them on a baking tray (sheet) lined with a non-stick baking mat and bake for 10–12 minutes until light golden in colour. Remove from the oven and leave to cool.

- Prepare the Sea Salt Caramel with Peanut Paste as instructed.

- Demould the set ingots, place them on a wire rack, then return to the freezer. Prepare the Dark Spraying Chocolate. Take the ingots from the freezer and spray with the spraying chocolate *(see page 35). (11)*

- Place the cooked Pâte Sablée on a serving dish, put a small dot of leftover chocolate mousse in the centre and place the sprayed ingots on top. *(12)* Spoon the prepared Peanut Caramel into a piping (pastry) bag fitted with an 8mm (⅓ inch) piping nozzle (tip) and pipe a line into the dent of the bar. *(13)* Leave to defrost in the fridge for at least 2 hours.

- When ready to serve, decorate with Peanut Tuile and gold leaf and serve immediately.

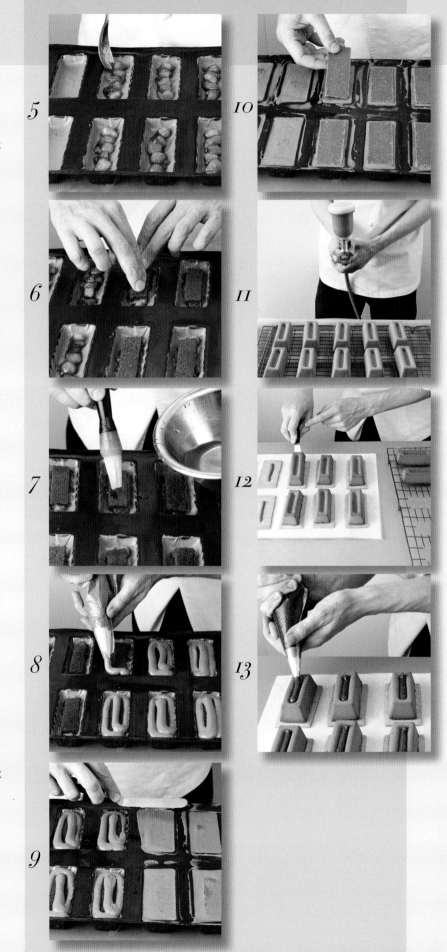

5

6

7

8

9

10

11

12

13

300g (10½oz) tempered dark
(bittersweet) chocolate
(see page 34) used to make sixteen
3 x 9cm (1½ x 3½ inches) **Chocolate
Rectangles** *and eight* **7-line Joined
Hoops** *(see pages 126 and 130–131)*
1 quantity of **Pistachio Biscuit
Macaron** *(see Variation, page 71)*
1 quantity of **Alhambra Chocolate
Sponge** *(see Variation, page 67)*
½ quantity of **Fruit Mousse** *(see page
99) made with apricot purée*
1 quantity of **Dark Chocolate
Crémeux** *(see page 95)*
1 quantity of **Alcohol Syrup** *(see page
103) made with Grand Marnier*
edible silver leaf *to decorate*

For the apricot jelly:
100ml (3½fl oz/scant ½ cup) **Simple
Syrup** *(see page 102)*
175g (6oz) **Fruit Purée** *(see page 110)
made with apricots*
½ vanilla pod (bean) *split lengthways*
6g (1 tsp) Sosa elastic powder *(see
page 344)*

You will also need:
thick 30 x 10cm (12 x 4 inch) flexible
acetate sheets
a 30 x 40cm (12 x 16 inch)
perspex tray
an 8mm (⅓ inch) plain piping
nozzle (tip)

*This pâtisserie is visually
stunning, the combination
of apricot and chocolate is
a winner; add the texture
of pistachio macaron and
it's sublime.*

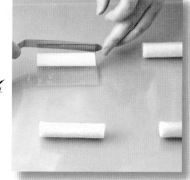

Apricot & Pistachio Delice *Makes 9*

First, prepare the chocolate decorations & sponges:

- Temper the chocolate and make the decorations as instructed, then leave in a cool, dry place to set for 2 hours.

- Preheat the oven to 190°C (375°F/Gas 5). Prepare the Pistachio Biscuit Macaron and bake as instructed. Prepare the Alhambra Chocolate Sponge and bake as instructed. Leave both sponges to cool.

- Cut the Alhambra Sponge and Pistachio Biscuit Macaron into 8 rectangles measuring 3 x 9cm (1½ x 3½ inches).

Next, prepare the mousse & crémeux:

- Make 2 acetate tubes that are 1.5cm (½ inch) in diameter and 30cm (12 inches) long, by curling the flexible acetate into cylinders and securing with sellotape. Secure the base of the cylinder with cling film (plastic wrap).

- Prepare the apricot mousse and spoon into a piping (pastry) bag. Gently fill the prepared acetate tubes, ensuring that there are no air pockets. *(1)* Transfer the tubes of mousse to the freezer to set for at least 2 hours.

- Prepare the Dark Chocolate Crémeux, spread into a shallow tray, cover with cling film (plastic wrap), cool and place in the fridge to set.

Next, prepare the mousse batons:

- Remove the apricot mousse from the freezer and demould from the acetate tube. Cut the mousse into 7cm (2¾ inch) lengths, then return to the freezer until required.

- Prepare the apricot jelly. Put the Simple Syrup, apricot purée and vanilla in a saucepan and bring to the boil. Whisk in the sosa elastic powder and remove from the heat. Line the perspex tray with an acetate sheet, spread the warm jelly out thinly on the tray so that you have a 7 x 25cm (2¾ x 10 inch) rectangle. Repeat twice more so that you have 3 rectangles of jelly. *(2)* Cut each jelly rectangle into 3 squares measuring 7cm (2¾ inches). *(3)* Take the cut apricot mousse from the freezer and roll the apricot jelly around the mousse. *(4)* Place the wrapped apricot mousses in the fridge until needed.

Apricot & Pistachio Delice *continued*

Training and development of our young chefs is one of our passions. We do this through training in the kitchen but also with competitions, helping the chefs to gain skills in organization and working under different pressures with times and working in a different kitchen. Sarah Frankland created a version of this pâtisserie while competing in the European final of the Wines of Roussillon Dessert Trophy 2013 with Robert Giorgione where subsequently the dessert and wine match won overall.

To assemble & finish:

- Place the cut Pistachio Biscuit Macaron onto a tray. Spoon the the prepared Dark Chocolate Crémeux into a piping (pastry) bag fitted with an 8mm (⅓ inch) piping nozzle (tip). Pipe 2 small bulbs of crémeux on top of the Pistachio Biscuit Macaron. *(5)*

- Place the piece of cut Alhambra Sponge on top, *(6)* then soak the Alhambra with the Grand Marnier syrup. *(7)*

- Pipe 2 small bulbs of crémeux on top of the Alhambra Sponge *(8)* and top with one of the prepared chocolate rectangles. *(9)*

- Pipe 2 rows of 6 large bulbs of crémeux along the top of the delice, *(10)* then transfer to the fridge to set for 30 minutes.

- Top with another chocolate rectangle, *(11)* then place a small line of cremeux in the centre of each rectangle. *(12)*

- Remove the prepared chocolate hoops from the acetate and place on top of each chocolate rectangle. *(13)* Remove the apricot mousse from the fridge and use a small step palette knife to carefully place them into the centre of the chocolate hoops. *(14)*

- Decorate with silver leaf to finish.

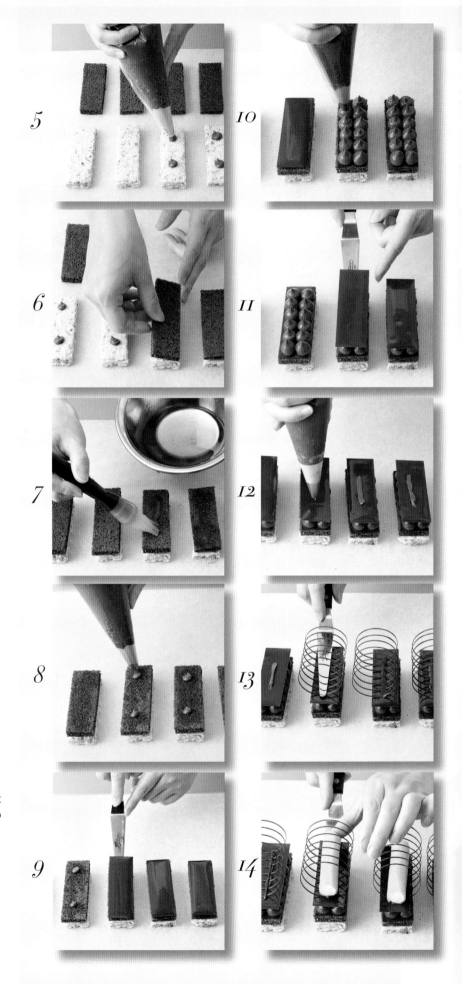

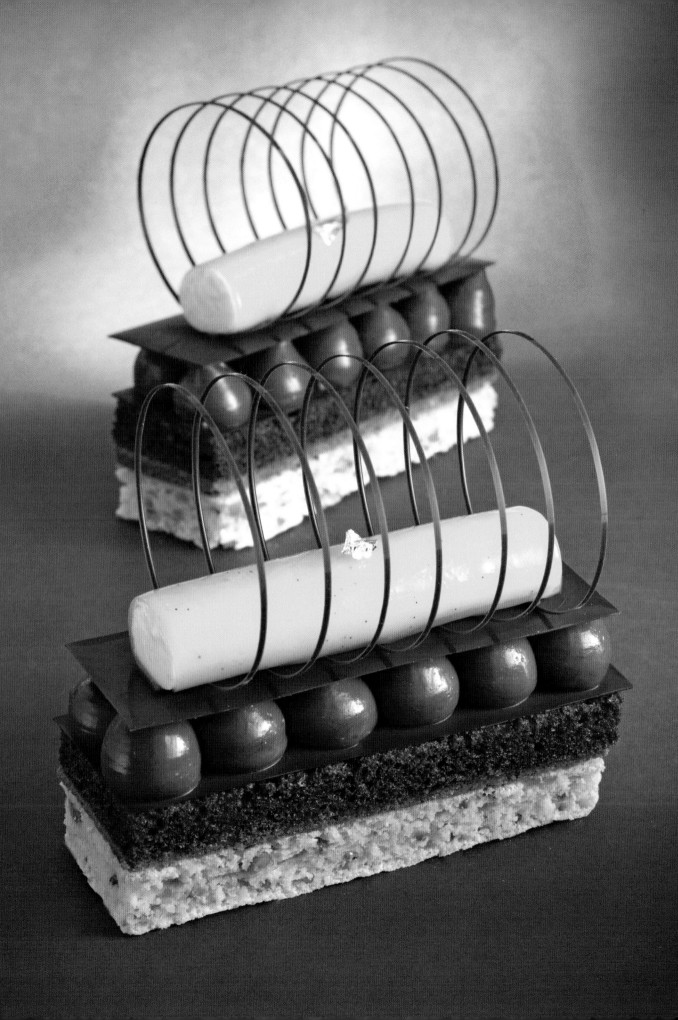

The origins of this dish are unknown, however I have seen it in many pâtisserie shops throughout France. The beauty is its simplicity, and the execution, but the Lenôtre version is my favourite.

Saint Marc *Makes 10*

300g (10½oz) tempered dark (bittersweet) chocolate *(see page 34) used to make 10* **Saint Marc Triangles** *(see page 127)*
1 quantity of **Crystallized Almonds** *(see pages 122–123)*
1 quantity of **Biscuit Joconde** *(see page 69) prepared and baked in one 30 x 40cm (12 x 16 inch) tray to make a thicker sponge*
1 quantity of **Chocolate Crème Chantilly** *(see pages 84–85)*
1 quantity of **Crème au Beurre** *(see page 86)*
1 quantity **Alcohol Syrup** *(see page 103) made with kirsch*
100g (3½oz/scant ¾ cup) icing (powdered) sugar
edible gold leaf *to decorate*

You will also need:
four 1cm (½ inch) bar guides
a caramelizer *(see page 27)*

First, prepare the decorations & the Biscuit Joconde:

- Temper the chocolate, make the decorations, then leave in a cool, dry place to set for 2 hours. Make the Crystallized Almonds, cool, then store in an airtight container.

- Preheat the oven to 200°C (400°F/Gas 6). Prepare the Biscuit Joconde, spread into a 30 x 40cm (12 x 16 inch) tray (sheet) lined with a non-stick baking mat with sides and bake for 15–18 minutes. Remove from the oven and leave to cool.

- Cut the cooled sponge into two 11 x 40cm (4¼ x 16 inch) strips the length of the tray. Place one of the strips on a tray lined with silicone baking paper. Place two 1cm (½ inch) bar guides stacked on top of each other either side of the sponge. *(1)*

Next, prepare the Chocolate Crème Chantilly:

- Make the Chocolate Crème Chantilly, spoon onto the sponge between the bar guides and level off with a step palette knife. *(2)* Place in the fridge to set for 15 minutes.

Prepare the Crème au Beurre & finish:

- Make the Crème au Beurre and take the part-assembled Saint Marc from the fridge. Stack another 1cm (½ inch) bar guide on each side of the sponge. Spread out the Crème au Beurre between the bars *(3)* and level off with a step palette knife. *(4)* Return to the fridge to set for at least 30 minutes.

- Soak the remaining strip of sponge with kirsch syrup. *(5)* Remove the Saint Marc from the fridge, remove the bar guides and top with the soaked sponge strip. *(6)* Use a warm serrated knife to cut the Saint Marc into 3cm (1½ inch) portions *(7)* and space out on another tray lined with silicone baking paper.

- Plug in the caramelizer and allow to heat up. Dust the tops of each Saint Marc with icing (powdered) sugar, *(8)* then transfer to a metal tray (sheet). Gently press each Saint Marc with the hot caramelizer to caramelize the sugar. *(9)* Place on a serving dish or plate and decorate with chocolate Saint Marc Triangles, Crystallized Almonds and gold leaf.

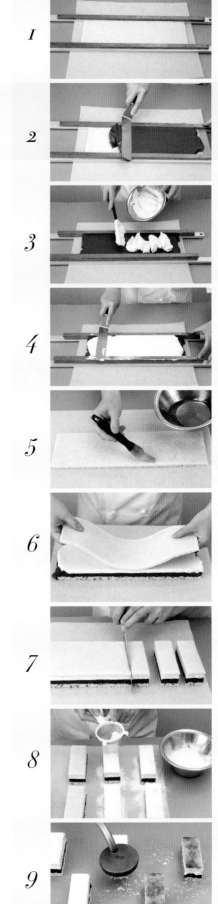

1
2
3
4
5
6
7
8
9

Coffee & Walnut Dacquoise *Makes 8*

I first made a variation of this pâtisserie when creating a dessert for Pierre Koffmann's La Réunion des Chefs, celebrating 35 years since he opened La Tante Claire. Pierre invited nine of his former protégés and over two nights, they each cooked a course. It was fabulous to work alongside Pierre and my former colleagues again.

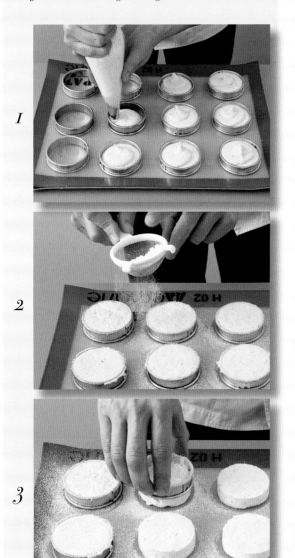

300g (10½oz) tempered dark (bittersweet) chocolate *(see page 34)* used to make 8 each of **Chocolate Squares, Triangle Flicks** and **Small Patterned Squares** *(see pages 126 and 134)*
½ quantity of **Sea Salt Caramel** *(see pages 118–119)*, made with an addition of 30g (1¼oz) **Walnut Paste** *(see Variation, page 116)*
½ quantity of **Dark Chocolate Mousse (anglaise method)** *(see page 101)*
1 quantity of **Dark Chocolate Glaze** *(see page 106)*
edible gold leaf *to decorate*

For the walnut dacquoise:
50g (1¾oz/scant ½ cup) ground almonds
50g (1¾oz/scant½ cup) ground walnuts
100g (3½oz/¾ cup) icing (powdered) sugar *sifted, plus extra for dusting*
32g (1¼oz/¼ cup) plain (all-purpose) flour *sifted*
150g (5½oz) egg whites *(about 5 eggs)*
65g (2¼oz) caster (superfine) sugar

For the coffee crémeux:
½ quantity **Dark Chocolate Crémeux** *(see page 95)*
15g (1 tbsp) ground coffee

For the walnut praline feuillantine:
100g (3½oz) milk chocolate
10g (¼oz/2 tsp) cocoa butter
75g (2¾oz) **Walnut Paste** *(see Variation, page 116)*
90g (3¼oz) feuillantine wafer

You will also need:
a 15mm (⅝ inch) and an 8mm (⅓ inch) plain piping nozzle (tip)
eight 6cm (2½ inch) tart rings
a 5.5cm (2¼ inch) cutter

First, prepare the decorations & caramel:

• Temper the chocolate and make the decorations as instructed, then leave in a cool, dry place to set for 2 hours.

• Prepare the caramel and mix in the Walnut Paste, then pour into a shallow tray to cool. Line a baking tray (sheet) with a non-stick baking mat, grease the tart rings and place them on the tray.

Next, prepare the walnut dacquoise:

• Preheat the oven to 170°C (325°F/Gas 3). Put the ground almonds, ground walnuts, icing (powdered) sugar and flour in a mixing bowl and mix well. Whisk the egg whites and half the caster (superfine) sugar in the clean bowl of an electric mixer fitted with a whisk attachment to a stiff meringue. Alternatively, use an electric hand-held whisk. Fold the dry ingredients into the meringue.

• Spoon the dacquoise into a piping (pastry) bag fitted with a 15mm (⅝ inch) plain nozzle (tip) and pipe into the tart rings. *(1)* Dust with icing (powdered) sugar *(2)*, then gently lift off the tart rings. *(3)* Bake for 16–18 minutes until light golden in colour, then leave to cool.

Then, prepare the coffee infusion for the crémeux:

- Begin to follow the recipe for the Dark Chocolate Crémeux as instructed. Put the cream and milk in a saucepan and bring to the boil. Add the ground coffee, cover with cling film (plastic wrap) and leave to infuse for 1 hour.

Meanwhile, prepare the feuillantine:

- Line a 30 x 40cm (12 x 16 inch) baking tray (sheet) with silicone baking paper. Put the milk chocolate and cocoa butter in a bowl and melt over a bain-marie *(see page 31)*. Mix the Walnut Paste into the chocolate mixture and lastly mix in the feuillantine wafer. Spoon onto the prepared tray and spread out thinly. Once semi-set, use a 5.5cm (2¼ inch) cutter to cut out 8 discs and leave to fully set for 1 hour.

Finish making the crémeux:

- Strain the coffee cream infusion into another saucepan. Continue to make the crémeux following the method as instructed, then pour into a shallow tray, cover with cling film (plastic wrap), cool, then leave to set in an airtight container in the fridge.

To assemble & finish:

- Line a baking tray (sheet) with silicone baking paper and place the tart rings on the tray. Prepare the Dark Chocolate Mousse. Place a walnut praline feuillantine disc in the base of each tart ring, then pipe a ring of the sea salt and walnut caramel on top. *(4)* Pipe the chocolate mousse into each ring and smooth off with a small step palette knife. *(5)* Transfer to the freezer to set for at least 2 hours.

- Prepare the chocolate glaze and leave to cool to about 30°C (86°F). Meanwhile, demould the chocolate mousse from the rings and place them on a wire rack. Glaze with the chocolate glaze *(see page 35)*, ensuring that all the sides are covered. Place in the fridge to set for 10 minutes. *(6)*

- Put the cooked dacquoise on a tray. Spoon the prepared coffee crémeux into a piping (pastry) bag fitted with an 8mm (⅓ inch) piping nozzle (tip) and pipe a spiral on top of the dacquoise. Transfer to the fridge to set for 10 minutes. *(7)*

- Top with the prepared chocolate square. *(8)* Take the bases and the glazed mousse from the fridge. Place the mousse on top of the chocolate square, *(9)* then leave to defrost for 1 hour in the fridge before serving. When ready to serve, decorate with chocolate triangle flicks, small patterned squares and gold leaf.

This combination of Japanese flavours was inspired by our many visits to Tokyo where there are some of the most wonderful pâtisserie shops. Our favourite is Hidemi Sugino, who has created his own unique style of pâtisserie with incredible precision.

Green Tea & Azuki Bean Dome

Makes 6

1 quantity of **Caramelized Almond Batons** *(see pages 122–123)*

½ quantity of **Pain de Gène** *(see page 68)*

1 quantity of **Simple Syrup** *(see page 102)* with 15g (1 tbsp) *matcha powder added*

1 quantity of **White Chocolate & Matcha Glaze** *(see Variation, page 107)*

100g (3½oz) azuki bean paste

300g (10½oz) tempered dark (bittersweet) chocolate *(see page 34)* used to make six **3-line Joined Hoops** *(see page 130)*

edible silver leaf *to decorate*

6 azuki beans

For the azuki bean crème:

175g (6oz) azuki bean paste

3g (⅒oz) leaf gelatine

125ml (4½fl oz/½ cup) whipping (pouring) cream

For the green tea mousse:

290ml (9fl oz/1¼ cups) whipping (pouring) cream

10g (½oz/2 tsp) green tea leaves

155g (5½oz) white chocolate *finely chopped*

3g (½ tsp) matcha powder *sifted*

5ml (1 tsp) water

3g (½ tsp) leaf gelatine

35g (1½oz) egg yolks *(about 1–2 eggs)*

10g (¼oz/2 tsp) caster (superfine) sugar

You will also need:

a 7cm (2¾ inch) round cutter

a 5cm (2 inch) round cutter

a 12-hole, 4cm (1½ inch) diameter fleximat dome mould

a 6-hole, 7cm (2¾ inch) diameter fleximat dome mould

First, prepare the foundation recipes:

- Prepare the Caramelized Almond Batons, cool, then store in an airtight container. Preheat the oven to 190°C (375°F/Gas 5). Prepare and bake the Pain de Gène, then once cool, cut into six 7cm (2¾ inch) discs and six 5cm (2 inch) discs. Prepare the matcha syrup and set aside and lastly, the White Chocolate and Matcha Glaze. Cool, then leave in the fridge until needed.

To prepare the centres:

- Prepare the azuki bean crème following the Fruit Mousse instructions on page 99 and pipe it into the fleximat dome mould. Freeze to set for at least 2 hours. *(1–2)*

Prepare the green tea mousse:

- Put 150ml (¼ pint/⅔ cup) of the cream in a pan and bring to the boil. Add the green tea, mix, then cover with cling film (plastic wrap), cool and leave to infuse for 1 hour. Put the white chocolate in a mixing bowl. Mix the matcha powder and water together and whisk until smooth. Put the remaining cream in a mixing bowl and whip until soft peaks form.

- Soak the gelatine in a bowl of ice-cold water for a few minutes until soft. Squeeze the gelatine to remove excess water *(see page 31)*.

- Strain the cream into another pan, add the matcha mixture and bring to the boil. Whisk the egg yolks and sugar together in a bowl until light in colour. Pour half of the infused cream onto the egg yolks and sugar mixture, whisk well, then pour all back into the pan and cook to 82–84°C (180–183°F) until the mixture coats the back of the spoon. Take off the heat and add the soaked gelatine. *(3)*

- Strain the custard onto the chocolate and mix until smooth and emulsified. Leave to cool, then fold in the semi-whipped cream. Use immediately. *(4–6)*

1

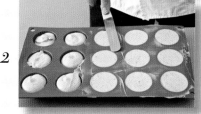

2

3

4

5

6

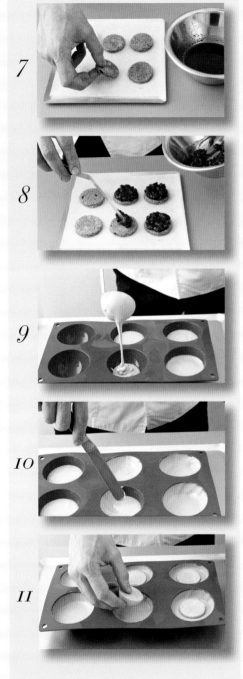

To assemble:

- Lay out the smaller discs of Pain de Gène and soak them with the matcha syrup, *(7)* then top with azuki bean paste. *(8)*

- Put a tablespoon of mousse into the base of each larger dome mould and use a small palette knife to spread the mousse up the side of the mould. *(9–10)* Put a frozen azuki bean crème dome inside each mould and top with the soaked sponge spread with azuki bean paste. *(11–12)* Top up the moulds with more green tea mousse, smooth the tops with a palette knife, then transfer to the freezer to set for at least 4 hours. *(13–14)*

To finish:

- Temper the chocolate and make the decorations as instructed, then leave in a cool, dry place to set for 2 hours.

- Put the larger discs of Pain de Gène on a glazing rack and soak with matcha syrup. Demould the green tea domes, then place them on top of the prepared Pain de Gène.

- Gently re-heat the White Chocolate and Matcha Glaze, leave to cool to 30°C (86°F) and pour it over the domes. *(15)* Transfer to the fridge to set for 10 minutes.

- Remove the domes from the glazing rack, place on a serving dish, then leave to defrost for at least 2 hours in the fridge.

- When ready to serve, decorate with the Caramelized Almond Batons, 3-line Joined Chocolate Hoops and silver leaf. Lastly place an azuki bean on the base of the hoops.

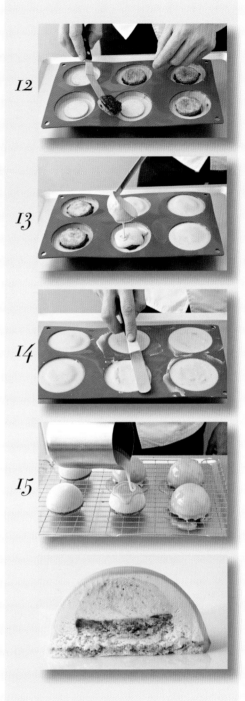

300g (10½oz) tempered
  dark (bittersweet)
  chocolate *(see page 34)*
½ quantity of **Alhambra
  Chocolate Sponge**
  (see Variation, page 67)
1 quantity of **Fruit Compote**
  *(see page 111) made
  with raspberries and
  raspberry purée*
1 quantity of **Alcohol Syrup**
  *(see page 103)
  made with kirsch*

**For the jasmine tea
panna cotta:**
4g (⅛oz) leaf gelatine
250ml (8½fl oz/1 cup) milk
250ml (8½fl oz/1 cup)
  whipping (pouring) cream
½ vanilla pod (bean)
  split lengthways
10g (¼oz/2 tsp) jasmine tea
25g (1oz) caster
  (superfine) sugar

To decorate:
blackberries
raspberries
strawberries
fraises des bois
redcurrants
Light Fruit Nappage
  (see page 105)
jasmine flowers
edible gold leaf

You will also need:
two chocolate moulds with six 7cm (2¾ inch) semi-spheres
a 5.5cm (2¼ inch) round metal cutter

Chocolate & Jasmine Sphere *Makes 6*

- Warm the base of a flat pan and gently melt the base of size of the semi-spheres. Fill the semi-sphere moulds with the tempered chocolate *(see pages 132–133)* and tap well to minimize any air pockets. Turn the moulds over and tap out as much excess chocolate as possible. Place in a cool dry area and leave to set for at least 2 hours.

- Prepare the jasmine tea pannacotta: put the cream and milk in a saucepan. Scrape the seeds from the split vanilla pod (bean) into the pan and drop in the empty pod (bean) too. Bring to the boil, add the jasmine tea leaves and cover with cling film. Leave to infuse for 1 hour.

- Prepare and bake the chocolate sponge as instructed. Leave to cool, then cut out 6 discs measuring 5.5cm (2¼ inches) in diameter.

- Prepare the raspberry compote and place in a shallow tray to cool. Prepare the kirsch syrup, cool, then store both in airtight containers in the fridge.

- Continue to prepare the jasmine panna cotta. Soak the gelatine in a bowl of ice-cold water for a few minutes until soft. Squeeze the gelatine to remove excess water *(see page 31)*. Strain the milk and cream into another pan, add the sugar and bring back to the boil. Take off the heat and dissolve the soaked gelatine into the mix. Pour through a sieve (strainer) into a jug and leave to cool to room temperature.

- Demould the chocolate semi-spheres from the moulds. *(1)* Place 6 semi-spheres into 5cm (2 inch) moulds to keep them sitting flat. Place the remaining 6 on a tray. Gently warm a 5.5cm (2¼ inch) metal cutter and cut out a hole at an angle in each of the semi-spheres for the top. *(2)*

- Place a tablespoon of the prepared compote into the base of the chocolate semi-sphere. *(3)* Top with a disc of chocolate sponge *(4)* and soak with the kirsch syrup. *(5)*

- Pour the jasmine panna cotta on top so that the semi-sphere is almost full, then transfer to the fridge to set for 30 minutes. *(6)*

- Remove the base semi-spheres from the fridge and place on a serving tray. Decorate with the fresh fruits. *(7–8)* Glaze the fruits with the nappage. *(9)*

- Warm the base of a flat pan and gently melt the top of the semi-spheres and place them on top. *(10)* Decorate with jasmine flowers and gold leaf to finish.

236

A great summer pâtisserie using seasonal red fruits and jasmine. The inspiration for this dish came from my time spent at Le Manoir Aux Quat'Saisons, where Raymond Blanc taught me the importance of using the freshest, most natural ingredients.

This was one of the first slice-style pâtisserie Suzue and I made in Richmond; simple to construct and delicious. I particularly like the texture that the roasted nuts through the dacquoise adds to this petit gâteau.

Citrus Slice *Makes 14*

1 quantity of **Alhambra Chocolate Sponge**
  (see Variation, page 67)
1 quantity of **Hazelnut & Almond Dacquoise**
  *(see pages 76–77) made with the addition of
  130g (4¾oz) each of chopped roasted almonds
  and hazelnuts*
1 quantity of **Basic Macaron** *(see page 296)
  but replace the raspberry powder with 18g (¾oz)
  freeze-dried lemon powder*
½ quantity of **Lemon Curd** *(see pages 96–97)
  made with 3g (⅒oz) leaf gelatine*
1 quantity of **Dark Chocolate Mousse
  (anglaise method)** *(see page 101)*
300g (10½oz) tempered white chocolate
  (see page 34) used to make 14 **Combed Waves**
  (see page 128)
1 quantity of **Dark Chocolate Ganache Glaze**
  (see page 107)
edible gold leaf *to decorate*

For the lemon syrup:
250ml (8½fl oz/1 cup) lemon juice
100ml (3½fl oz/scant ½ cup) water
125g (4½oz/generous ½ cup) caster
  (superfine) sugar
½ vanilla pod (bean) *split lengthways*

For the lemon ganache:
100g (3½oz) milk chocolate (35% cocoa solids)
  finely chopped
100g (3½oz) dark (bittersweet) chocolate
  (70% cocoa solids) *finely chopped*
60ml (2¼fl oz/¼ cup) lemon juice
100ml (3½fl oz/scant ½ cup) whipping
  (pouring) cream
12g (⅓oz) unsalted butter *softened*

You will also need:
one 54 x 9cm (21½ x 3½ inch) entremet mould

First, prepare the lemon syrup:

- Put the lemon juice, water, sugar and vanilla seeds and pod (bean) into a saucepan and bring to the boil. Leave to cool.

Next, prepare the sponge & dacquoise:

- Preheat the oven to 190°C (375°F/Gas 5). Prepare and bake the Alhambra Chocolate Sponge, then lower the oven temperature to 170°C (325°F/Gas 3).

- Prepare the dacquoise, spreading the chopped roasted nuts onto the baking tray (sheet) before topping with the dacquoise mixture. Bake as instructed.

Prepare the lemon macaron, ganache & curd:

- Prepare and bake the macarons using the freeze-dried lemon powder instead of raspberry powder.

- To make the ganache, put the chopped chocolates in a mixing bowl. Put the lemon juice in a pan and bring to the boil. Put the cream in a separate pan and bring to the boil. Pour the cream over the chopped chocolate and mix until a smooth consistency is formed. Mix in the lemon juice and lastly the softened butter until smooth. Leave on the side until required.

- To make the curd, soak the gelatine in a bowl of ice-cold water for a few minutes until soft. Squeeze the gelatine to remove excess water *(see page 31)*. Prepare the Lemon Curd as instructed, but add the soaked gelatine just prior to adding the butter. Reserve 100g (3½oz) of the curd to sandwich the macarons and place in an airtight container in the fridge to set until required.

Citrus Slice *continued*

**Begin assembly
& make the chocolate mousse:**

- Cut the cooked dacquoise to fit the base of the 54 x 9cm (21½ x 3½ inch) entremet mould and place it on a tray lined with silicone (baking) paper. Cut the chocolate sponge into two 54 x 9cm (21½ x 3½ inch) rectangles to fit the base of the entremet mould. Place these on another tray lined with silicone baking paper.

- Place the entremet mould over the dacquoise ensuring the mould sits flat on the tray. Spoon in the prepared lemon ganache *(1)* and spread out evenly. *(2)* Top with one layer of the chocolate sponge *(3)* and soak with the lemon syrup. *(4)*

- Spoon the remaining prepared lemon curd into the entremet mould *(5)* and spread out evenly *(6)*. Top with the remaining layer of chocolate sponge *(7)* and soak well with the lemon syrup. *(8)* Transfer to the fridge while you make the mousse.

- Prepare the chocolate mousse. Remove the citrus slice from the fridge and top up with the mousse *(9)* and level off. *(10)* Transfer to the freezer to set for at least 4 hours.

To finish:

- Temper the chocolate and make the decorations as instructed, then leave in a cool, dry place to set for 2 hours.

- Prepare the Dark Chocolate Ganache Glaze and cool to about 30°C (86°F). Take the citrus slice from the freezer and demould. Place on a chopping board, pour the glaze on top and spread out evenly. *(11)* Return to the fridge to set for 10 minutes. Meanwhile, sandwich the lemon macarons with the reserved lemon curd.

- Remove the citrus slice from the fridge and cut into 3.5cm (1¼ inch) portions and trim the top and bottom edges. *(12)* Place on a serving dish, then leave to defrost for at least 2 hours in the fridge before serving.

- When ready to serve, decorate with the lemon macarons, white chocolate Combed Waves and edible gold leaf.

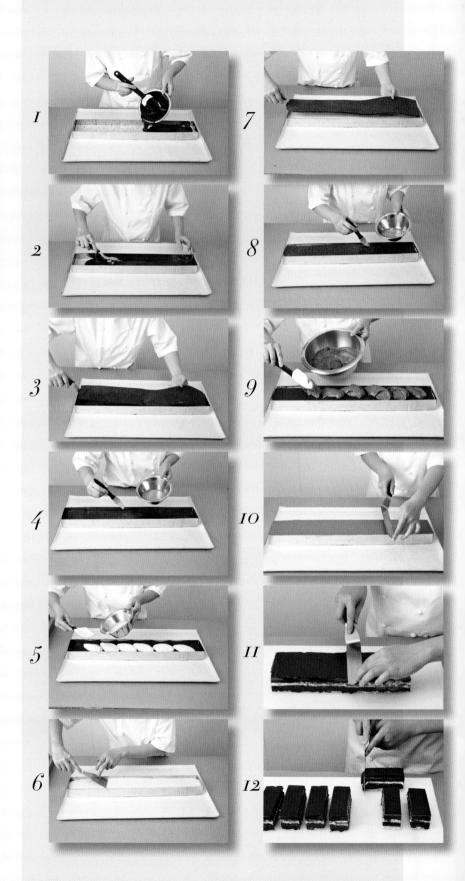

1 *2* *3* *4* *5* *6* *7* *8* *9* *10* *11* *12*

I first came across this pâtisserie when I worked for Pierre Romeyer at Maison du Bouche, just outside Brussels; it was often served in his restaurant in the traditional manner using almond sponge and buttercream. The dish is a classic Belgian pâtisserie; originally it was a dessert for the peasants as it was made using very basic ingredients.

Les Misérables *Makes 6*

1 quantity of **Biscuit Joconde** *(see page 69) made with 10g (¼oz/2 tsp) matcha powder added with the flour and prepared and baked in one 30 x 40cm (12 x 16 inch) sheet to make a thicker sponge*

1 quantity of **Almond Dacquoise** *(see Variation, page 77) prepared and baked in one 30 x 40cm (12 x 16 inch) sheet to make a thicker sponge*

1 quantity of **Alcohol Syrup** *(see page 103) made with yuzu sake*

300g (10½oz) tempered dark (bittersweet) chocolate *(see page 34) used to make 6* **Combed Wiggles** *(see page 128)*

20g (¾oz/4 tsp) matcha powder *for dusting*

edible silver leaf *to decorate*

Japanese muscovado sugar

For the Japanese muscovado caramel buttercream:
100g (3½oz) **Japanese Muscovado Caramel** *(see Variation, page 118)*

1 quantity of **Italian Buttercream** *(see page 87)*

You will need:
six 1cm (½ inch) bar guides
six 5mm (¼ inch) bar guides
a buche piping nozzle (tip)

Prepare the joconde sponge & the Almond Dacquoise:

• Preheat the oven to 200°C (350°F/Gas 4) and line 2 baking trays (sheets) with non-stick baking mats. Prepare the matcha joconde sponge: sift the matcha powder with the plain flour and prepare the joconde sponge as instructed. Spoon into one of the non-stick baking mat with sides and spread out evenly. Bake for 15–18 minutes. Remove from the oven and leave to cool.

• Reduce the oven temperature to 170°C (325°F/Gas 3). Make the dacquoise, spoon into the other non-stick baking mats with sides and spread out evenly. Bake for 15–18 minutes until light golden in colour. Remove from the oven and leave to cool.

Prepare the buttercream & syrup:

• Prepare the Japanese Muscovado Caramel as instructed. Continue to cook to an amber caramel.

• Prepare the Italian buttercream, and once finished, mix in the cooled Japanese Muscovado Caramel. Prepare the yuzu sake syrup and set aside.

Start the assembly:

• Cut the cooled dacquoise into two 6cm (2½ inch) strips the length of the tray, repeat for the matcha jaconde. Place one of the strips of dacquoise onto a tray lined with silicone baking paper. Place one 1cm (½ inch) bar guide and one 5mm (¼ inch) bar guide either side of the sponge. *(1)* Spoon some of the buttercream on top of the sponge and spread out evenly with a step palette knife. *(2)*

• Place a layer of the matcha joconde on top, *(3)* and add another 1cm (½ inch) and 5mm (¼ inch) bar guide on top of the others. Soak the sponge with the yuzu sake syrup. *(4)*

1

2

3

4

Continue the assembly:

- Spoon more of the buttercream on top of the sponge and spread out evenly. *(5)* Top with the second piece of matcha joconde *(6)* and soak with the yuzu sake syrup.

- Place another set of 5mm (¼ inch) bar guide on top of the others. Place a spoonful of the buttercream on top of the sponge and spread out evenly. *(7)* Place the final piece of almond dacquoise on top *(8)* and place into the fridge to set for 10 minutes.

- Remove the Les Misérables from the fridge and place on a chopping board. Remove the bar guides. *(9)* Cut into 6cm (2½ inch) square portions. *(10)* Place a ruler or palette knife over the centre of the cut portion, corner to corner, and dust one half with the matcha powder *(11)* Spoon the remaining buttercream into a piping (pastry) bag fitted with a buche piping nozzle (tip) and pipe a wiggle along the top of each of the Les Misérables. *(12)* When ready to serve, decorate with the chocolate wiggle, silver leaf and small pieces of the Japanese muscovado sugar.

8

9

5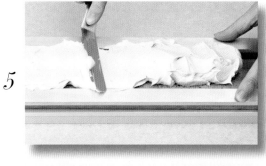

10

6

11

7

12

We created this pâtisserie in 2012 to celebrate the exhibition 'Balllgowns: British glamour since 1950' at the V & A museum in London. It was part of four pâtisseries inspired by the ballgowns featured in the exhibition. This dramatic striped pâtisserie reflects a gown made by British designer Victor Edelstein and was first presented as an exclusive afternoon tea at Harrods.

Raspberry Casket *Makes 8*

500g (1lb 2oz) dark (bittersweet) chocolate (65% cocoa solids)

1 quantity of **Flourless Chocolate Sponge** *(see Variation, page 71)*

I quantity of **Alcohol Syrup** *(see page 103) made with kirsch*

1 quantity of **Fruit Compote** *(see page 111) made with raspberries and raspberry purée*

1 quantity **Fruit Mousse** *(see page 99) made with 350g (10½oz) raspberry purée*

freeze-dried raspberries *and* **Chocolate Copeaux** *(see pages 132–133) to finish*

For the kirsch-marinated raspberries:
250g (9oz) raspberries
75ml (3fl oz/5 tbsp) kirsch
20g (¾oz/1½ tbsp) caster (superfine) sugar

For the raspberry white chocolate:
100g (3½oz) white chocolate *finely chopped*
50g (1¾oz) cocoa butter *finely chopped*
10g (¼oz) freeze-dried raspberry powder

For the white chocolate & kirsch diplomat cream:
250ml (8fl oz/1 cup) whipping (pouring) cream
½ quantity **Crème Pâtissière** *(see page 80)*
250g (9oz) white chocolate *chopped*
50ml (2fl oz/3½ tbsp) kirsch

You will also need:
eight thick 12 x 8.5cm (4½ x 3¼ inch) acetate sheets
a 3.5cm (1½ inch) round cutter
an 8mm (⅓ inch) plain and a C6 piping nozzle (tip)

I

2

The day before, make the kirsch-marinated raspberries:

- Lay the raspberries out in a shallow tray or dish. Drizzle with the kirsch *(1)* and sprinkle with sugar. *(2)* Cover with cling film (plastic wrap) and leave to marinate in the fridge overnight.

The next day, make the raspberry white chocolate:

- Put the white chocolate and cocoa butter in a bowl and melt gently over a bain-marie to 45°C (113°F). Once melted, add the freeze-dried raspberry powder and leave to cool to 32°C (90°F). Use immediately.

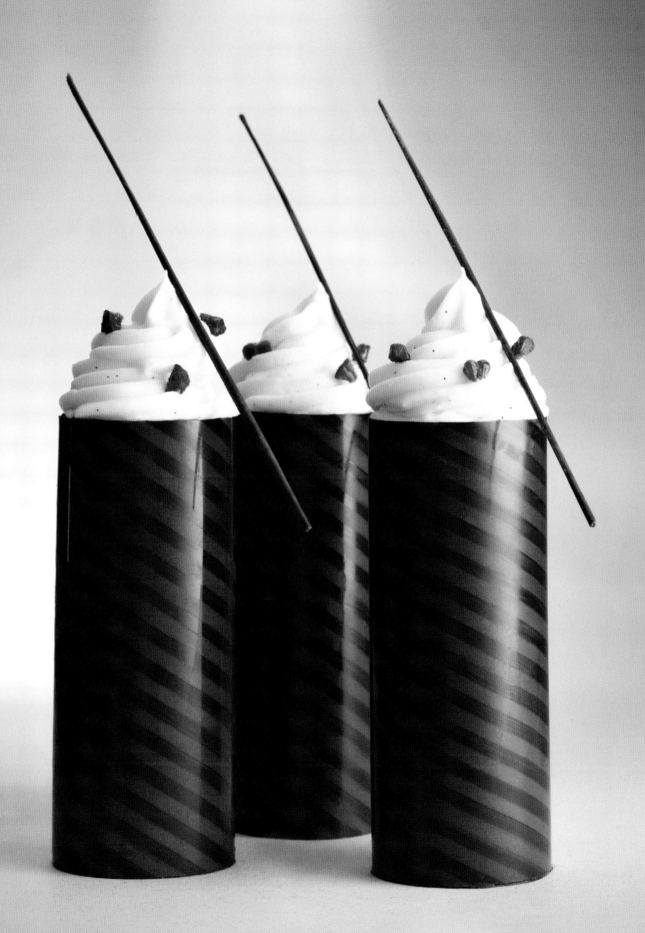

3

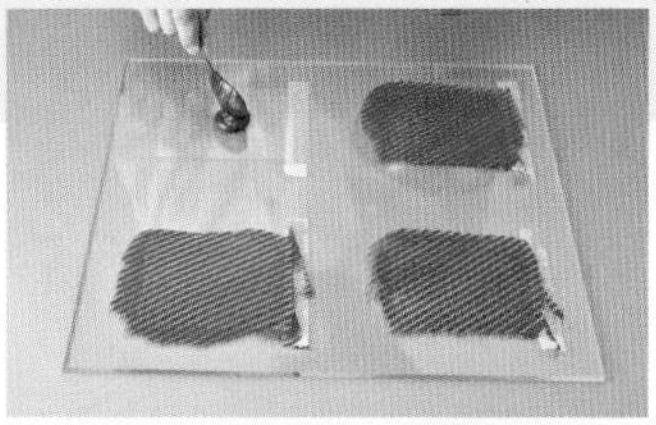

4

5

6

7

8

9

10

Now, make the chocolate caskets:

- Temper the dark (bittersweet) chocolate as instructed on page 34.

- Place the 8 acetate rectangles on a flat tray and secure with tape along one of the shorter sides. Polish the surfaces with cotton wool.

- Using a small palette knife, spread a thin layer of the raspberry white chocolate onto each acetate rectangle *(3)* Scrape across the chocolate with a comb scraper positioned at an angle. *(4)* Remove the layer of tape securing the acetate to the tray. *(5)*

- Individually spread the dark tempered chocolate on top of the set raspberry chocolate. *(6)* When almost set, carefully lift each sheet from the tray. *(7)*

- Position a small piece of tape on the acetate side of each rectangle *(8)* and roll up gently (chocolate on the inside) to form a tube. *(9)* Secure with the tape to keep the tube together. *(10)* Place tape at the top and base of the seal. Store the caskets in a cool, dry place to fully set.

Make the chocolate sponge, compote & begin assembly:

- Preheat the oven to 190°C (375°F/Gas 5). Prepare and bake the Flourless Chocolate Sponge and once cooled, cut out 24 discs measuring 3.5cm (1½ inches) in diameter. Make the kirsch syrup and raspberry compote.

- Put 8 of the sponge discs on a baking tray (sheet) lined with silicone baking paper. Soak the discs with the kirsch syrup. *(11)* Top 8 of the sponge discs with a spoonful of raspberry compote *(12)* and position a set chocolate casket on top of each of these discs. *(13)*

11

12

13

Then, make the raspberry mousse & white chocolate diplomat cream:

- Make the raspberry mousse following the instructions on page 99.

- To make the white chocolate diplomat cream, put the cream in a mixing bowl and whip to ribbon stage *(see page 32)*. Make the Crème Pâtissière as instructed. Stir the white chocolate into the hot Crème Pâtissière and mix until smooth. Stir through the kirsch and then fold in the whipped cream. Transfer to a sealed container and place in the fridge to set for about 30 minutes.

To finish:

- Soak the remaining sponge discs with kirsch syrup.

- Put the raspberry mousse in a piping (pastry) bag fitted with an 8mm (⅓ inch) plain nozzle (tip). Pipe a small amount of mousse into the base of each casket. *(14)* Put 3 kirsch-marinated raspberries in each casket *(15)* and top with a sponge disc. *(16)* Pipe in the raspberry mousse until three-quarters full. *(17)* Add another 2 marinated raspberries to each casket. *(18)* Pipe more raspberry mousse into each casket to about 2mm (just under ⅛ inch) below the rim. Add another sponge disc, then transfer to the fridge to set for 30 minutes.

- Put the white chocolate cream in a piping (pastry) bag fitted with a C6 fluted nozzle (tip) and pipe a rosette of cream on top of each casket. *(19)* Leave to set in the fridge for at least 30 minutes.

- Use a scalpel to gently cut the tape securing the acetate to the chocolate *(20)* and gently peel the acetate away. *(21)* Decorate the top of each casket with freeze-fried raspberries and chocolate copeaux.

14

15

16

17

18

19

20

21

Classic Opéra *Makes 16*

300g (10½oz) tempered dark (bittersweet) chocolate *(see page 34), used to make* **Patterned Squares** *and* **Curls** *(see pages 126 and 130)*

2 quantities of **Biscuit Joconde** *(see Variation, page 69)* to make 4 sheets of sponge

1½ quantities of **Coffee Crème au Beurre** *(see Variation, page 86)*

1½ quantities of **Dark Chocolate Ganache** *(see pages 90–91)*

1 quantity of **Dark Chocolate Ganache Glaze** *(see page 107)*

edible gold leaf *to decorate*

For the coffee syrup:
150ml (¼ pint/⅔ cup) filtered coffee *cooled*

150g (5½oz) **Simple Syrup** (see page 102)

25ml (1fl oz) cognac

You will also need:
a 60 x 40cm (24 x 16 inch) tray lined with silicone baking paper

a 54 x 9cm (21½ x 3½ inch) rectangle entremet ring

First, prepare the decorations, sponge, syrup, Crème au Beurre & ganache:

- Temper the chocolate, make the decorations as instructed, then leave in a cool, dry place for 2 hours.

- Preheat the oven to 200°C (400°F/Gas 6). Prepare the joconde sponge, spread into a a 60 x 40cm (24 x 16 inch) tray lined with silicone baking paper and bake for 12–15 minutes until light golden in colour. Remove from the oven and leave to cool.

- To prepare the coffee syrup, mix all the ingredients together in a bowl. Prepare the Coffee Crème au Beurre and the ganache.

- Cut the cooled joconde sponge into 3 rectangles, measuring 54 x 9cm (21½ x 3½ inches) to fit the rectangle mould.

Prepare the opéra:

- Put the rectangle mould on the prepared tray, put one of the sponge rectangles in the base and soak with the coffee syrup. *(1)* Spoon 300g (10½oz) of the prepared ganache into the mould *(2)* and spread out evenly. *(3)* Transfer to the fridge to rest for 20 minutes.

- Weigh 250g (9oz) of the Coffee Crème au Beurre into the mould *(4)* and spread out evenly. *(5)* Place a second sponge rectangle on top *(6)* and soak with the coffee syrup. *(7)* Spoon another 300g (10½oz) of the ganache on top and spread out evenly. Return to the fridge to set for 20 minutes.

- Weigh another 250g (9oz) of the Coffee Crème au Beurre into the mould and spread out evenly. Finally top with the remaining sponge and soak well with the coffee syrup. Place the built opéra in the fridge to set for at least 1 hour.

To assemble & finish:

- Prepare the Dark Chocolate Ganache Glaze and cool to about 30°C (86°F). Take the opéra from the fridge. Pour the cooled glaze on top of the opéra *(8)* and use a step palette knife to spread a thin, even layer across the top. *(9)* Place in the fridge to set for 10 minutes.

- Take the glazed opéra from the fridge and demould. Use a warm, sharp knife to cut into sixteen 3cm (1½ inch) portions; trim the short edges so that they are neat. *(10)* Place on a serving dish and decorate with the chocolate patterned squares, curls and gold leaf.

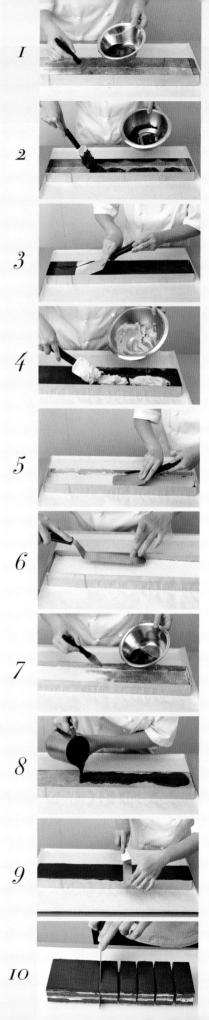

1

2

3

4

5

6

7

8

9

10

There are many conflicting stories as to who originally created this French classic. The best known version is that it was created by Cyriaque Gavillon who was chef pâtissier at Dalloyau in Paris in 1955. The cake was called 'Opéra' by his wife Andreé in honour of a prima ballerina at the Paris Opéra.

Matcha Mont Blanc *Makes 8*

300g (10½oz) tempered dark (bittersweet) chocolate *(see page 34) used for dipping and to make* **Copeaux** *(see pages 132–133)*
1 quantity of **Alcohol Syrup** *(see page 103) made with dark rum*
4 shop-bought confit chestnuts *cut in half and glazed with* **Fruit Glaze** *(see page 105)*
matcha powder *for dusting*

For the chestnut meringue:
½ quantity of **French Meringue** *(see page 74)*
15g (½oz) chestnut flour *sifted*

For the dacquoise:
110g (3½oz/1 cup) ground almonds
110g (3½oz/¾ cup) icing (powdered) sugar
18g (¾oz/1¼ tbsp) plain (all-purpose) flour
170g (6oz) egg whites *(about 5–6 eggs)*
55g (2oz/¼ cup) caster (superfine) sugar

For the chestnut mousse:
5g (⅛oz) leaf gelatine
40g (1½oz/scant ½ cup) caster (superfine) sugar
40ml (1½fl oz/2½ tbsp) water
110g (3½oz) unsweetened chestnut purée
200ml (7fl oz/scant 1 cup) double (heavy) cream
20ml (½fl oz/4 tsp) dark rum

For the chestnut cream:
175g (6oz) unsweetened chestnut purée
0.5g (a pinch) salt
150g (5½oz) sweetened chestnut purée
10ml (2 tsp) dark rum
50ml (2fl oz/¼ cup) double (heavy) cream

For the matcha cream:
2g (⅛oz) leaf gelatine
200ml (7fl oz/scant 1 cup) double (heavy) cream
20g (¾oz) **Simple Syrup** *(see page 102)*
4g (1 tsp) matcha powder

You will also need:
a 10mm (½ inch), 12mm (⅝ inch), 6mm (¼ inch) and a mont blanc piping nozzle (tip)
a 4cm (1½ inch) round cutter
eight 5cm (2 inch) mousse rings
eight 18 x 4.5cm (7 x 1¾ inch) flexible acetate sheets

The day before, make the meringues:

- Preheat the oven to 110°C (225°F/Gas ¼). Prepare the meringue as instructed. Fold in the chestnut flour at the end. Spoon the meringue into a piping (pastry) bag fitted with a 10mm (⅓ inch) plain piping nozzle (tip) and pipe the meringue into 2cm (¾ inch) diameter bulbs on a baking tray (sheet).

- Bake in the preheated oven for about 1½ hours until the meringue is cooked and dry, then leave to cool. Store the meringues in an airtight container until needed.

The next day, make the dacquoise:

- Preheat the oven to 170°C (325°F/Gas 3). Sift together the ground almonds, icing (powdered) sugar and flour into a mixing bowl.

- Whisk the egg whites and half the sugar in the clean bowl of an electric mixer fitted with a whisk attachment to a stiff meringue *(see page 29)*. Alternatively, use an electric hand-held whisk or by hand.

- Fold the dry ingredients into the meringue. Mix with the spatula until you have a smooth, homogeneous mixture.

- Spread onto a 30 x 40cm (12 x 16 inch) non-stick baking mat or a baking tray (sheet) lined with silicone paper and bake in the preheated oven for 18–20 minutes until light golden brown.

Next, coat the meringues & make the decoration:

- Temper the chocolate as instructed. Dip the meringues into the chocolate, then leave to set in a cool dry area.

- Prepare the chocolate Copeaux as instructed, then leave to set in a cool, dry place for 1 hour.

Then, the chestnut mousse:

- Soak the gelatine in a bowl of ice-cold water for a few minutes until soft. Squeeze the gelatine to remove excess water *(see page 31)*.

- Put the sugar and water in a saucepan and bring to the boil. Add the soaked gelatine, stir to dissolve, then add the chestnut purée. Blend together with a hand-held blender. Pass the mixture through a fine sieve (strainer) into a mixing bowl and leave to cool.

- Put the cream in another mixing bowl and whip until soft peaks form, then transfer to the fridge.

- Once the chestnut base has cooled, add the dark rum and mix together. Fold in the whipped cream. Ideally use immediately or cover with cling film (plastic wrap) and keep in the fridge until assembly.

And the chestnut cream:

- Put the unsweetened chestnut purée and salt in a mixing bowl and beat until smooth. Add the sweetened chestnut purée and beat again until smooth. Fold in the rum and cream, cover, then place in the fridge until ready to use.

Mont blanc was originally made with
puréed chestnuts that had been sweetened
through a pickling process and were yellow
in colour. The shape represents the famous
Mont Blanc snow-capped mountain.
First written down and described in an
Italian cookbook from 1475, this recipe
did not become popular in France
until the 17th century. Nowadays
the Classic Mont Blanc has
evolved with many pâtissiers
incorporating other
flavour elements as
we have with our
creation.

Matcha Mont Blanc *continued*

To begin the assembly:

- Cut 8 strips of the cooked dacquoise, measuring 14 x 4cm (5½ x 1½ inches), then use a 4cm (1½ inch) pastry (cookie) cutter to cut out 8 discs.

- Line the mousse rings with acetate strips, then line with the dacquoise strips. Dip the dacquoise discs into the rum syrup, then place these in the base of each ring. *(1)*

- Use a pastry brush to brush the dacquoise strips with rum syrup.

- Spoon the chestnut mousse into a piping (pastry) bag fitted with a plain 12mm (⅝ inch) nozzle (tip) and pipe into the base of each ring until one-third full. *(2)*

- Place one half of a confit chestnut on top of the mousse in each ring. *(3)*

- Then top up with more chestnut mousse until it is just below the top of the dacquoise. *(4)* Place in the fridge to set for 30 minutes.

- Place a dipped chestnut meringue on top of each mont blanc. *(5)*

- Spoon the chestnut cream into a piping (pastry) bag fitted with a 6mm (¼ inch) plain nozzle (tip) and pipe a spiral around, and over the top of, the chestnut meringue. *(6)* Place in the fridge for 20 minutes.

Lastly, prepare the matcha cream:

- Soak the gelatine in a bowl of ice-cold water for a few minutes until soft. Squeeze the gelatine to remove excess water *(see page 31)*.

- Put the cream in a mixing bowl and whip until soft peaks form, then transfer to the fridge.

- Put the Simple Syrup in a small saucepan and warm gently. Sift in the matcha powder, whisk until smooth, then add the soaked gelatine.

- Mix a little of the whipped cream into the matcha base, then fold all the mixture into the remaining whipped cream. Use immediately.

To finish:

- Demould the mousse from the mousse rings, then remove the acetate. *(7)* Spoon the matcha cream into a piping (pastry) bag fitted with a mont blanc nozzle (tip) and pipe around the top of each mont blanc in a spiral. *(8)* Place in the fridge to set for 1 hour.

- Dust gently with the extra matcha powder and decorate with the remaining confit chestnut halves and the chocolate copeaux decoration. *(9)*

This means 'chocolate gift' in French. Delicate vanilla crème brûlée, chocolate mousse and rum-soaked sultanas are encased inside a chocolate wrapping. Perfect to intrigue and delight guests at any dinner party.

Cadeaux au Chocolat *Makes 12*

½ quantity of **Crème Brûlée**
   (see page 94)
1 quantity of **Flourless Chocolate Sponge** *(see Variation, page 71)*
500g (1lb 2oz) tempered dark (bittersweet) chocolate *(see page 34) used for spreading and also to make 12* **Chocolate Squares** *and 12* **Swiped Flicks** *(see pages 126 and 135)*
1 quantity of **Dark Chocolate Mousse (sabayon method)** *(see page 100)*
1 quantity of **Rum-marinated Sultanas** *(see page 115)*
cocoa powder *for dusting*
edible gold leaf *to decorate*

You will also need:
a 12-hole 5cm (2 inch) silicone muffin mould
a 6cm (2½ inch) cookie cutter
a 4.5cm (1¾ inch) cookie cutter
twelve 18 x 6cm (7 x 2½ inch) curved acetate strips (PCB, see page 344)
three 4-hole cone moulds

First, prepare the Crème Brûlée:

- Preheat the oven to 140°C (275°F/ Gas 1). Fill the holes of the muffin mould with the prepared Crème Brûlée mixture until three-quarters full. *(1)* Bake for 18–20 minutes until the custard has just set. Leave to cool, then transfer to the freezer for about 2 hours.

Next, make the chocolate sponge:

- Preheat the oven to 190°C (375°F/ Gas 5). Pour the prepared sponge mixture into a non-stick baking mat with sides and spread evenly. Bake in the preheated oven for 12–14 minutes. Take out of the oven and place on a wire cooling rack. Once cooled, use a 6cm (2½ inch) cookie cutter to cut out 12 discs and a 4.5cm (1¾ inch) cookie cutter to cut out another 12 discs.

Then, make the chocolate cones & decorations:

- Prepare the tempered chocolate as instructed and place a generous spoonful on the curved acetate sheets. *(2)* Spread evenly with a small step palette knife. *(3)*

- Lift up the plastic acetate and place into the cone mould. *(4–5)* Repeat until all 12 are lined with chocolate.

- Use a small palette knife to seal the edge with tempered chocolate. *(6)*

- Prepare the chocolate decorations as instructed and leave in a cool, dry place for 2 hours.

Cadeaux au Chocolat
continued

To assemble & finish:

- Prepare the Dark Chocolate Mousse as instructed. Place a tablespoon of mousse in the bottom of each cone. *(7)*

- Use a small step palette knife to spread the mousse up the side of each cone. *(8)*

- Demould the frozen Crème Brûlée and place one in each cone on top of the mousse and push down gently. *(9)*

- Place a small chocolate sponge disc on top of the Crème Brûlée, then soak the sponge with some of the rum from the marinated sultanas. *(10)*

- Place a tablespoon of the marinated sultanas on top of the sponge. *(11)*

- Place a tablespoon of mousse on top of the sultanas and spread out evenly with a small step palette knife. *(12)*

- Place another disc of the sponge on top and soak with the rum from the marinated sultanas. *(13)*

- Transfer the cone moulds to the fridge to set for at least 2–3 hours.

- Remove the cadeaux from the fridge, turn each cone out onto silicone paper *(14)* and smooth off the top of the cone. *(15)*

- Dust the tops gently with cocoa powder, then remove the acetate sheet *(16)* and place on a serving dish.

- Decorate with chocolate squares, swiped flicks and edible gold leaf.

7

8

9

10

11

12

13

14

15

16

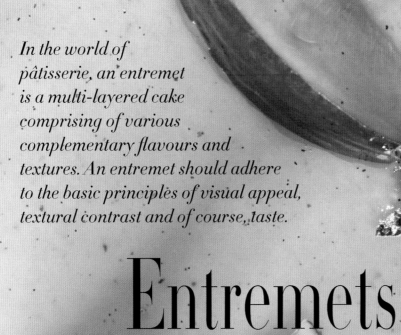

*In the world of
pâtisserie, an entremet
is a multi-layered cake
comprising of various
complementary flavours and
textures. An entremet should adhere
to the basic principles of visual appeal,
textural contrast and of course, taste.*

Entremets

*Its beauty comes from the variety
of shapes and colours that can be
used and its stunning appearance
makes it the perfect centrepiece
for any special occasion.*

*All entremets should be stored in the fridge until
prior to being served and should be eaten the
same day.*

Nectarine & Cassis Entremet

Makes 2 (each serves 4)

1 quantity of **Fruit Compote** *(see Variation, page 111) made with blackcurrant purée and blackcurrants*

1 quantity of **Biscuit à la Cullière** *(see page 70)* red fruit powder *for dusting*

1 quantity of **Alcohol Syrup** *(see page 103) made using kirsch*

1 quantity of **Fruit Glaze** *(see page 105)*

300g (10½oz) tempered dark (bittersweet) chocolate *(see page 34) used to make* **Chocolate Squares** *and* **Triangle Flicks** *(see pages 126 and 134)*

½ quantity of **Fruit Mousse** *(see page 99) made with nectarine purée*

1 nectarine *stoned, cut into segments and glazed with* **Fruit Glaze**

8 blackcurrant berries
edible gold leaf *to decorate*

For the poached nectarine:
2 nectarines *stoned and cut in half*
½ quantity of **Light Syrup** *(see page 103)*

You will also need:
two oval entremet rings, measuring 14 x 10cm (14½ x 4 inches)
two 42 x 4.5cm (16¾ x 1¼ inch) strips of flexible acetate
a 10mm (½ inch) piping nozzle (tip)

First, make the compote, sponge, syrup & glaze:

- Prepare the compote, place in a container, cool, then place in the fridge. Preheat the oven to 190°C (375°F/Gas 5). Prepare and bake the Biscuit à la Cullière sponge; split the mix in half and pipe one half in diagonal strips onto a baking mat and spread the remaining half into another baking mat. Bake as instructed. Cut the spread sponge into 12 x 8cm (4½ x 3¼ inch) ovals. Dust the piped sponge with red fruit powder once cooked. Prepare the Alcohol Syrup using kirsch and set aside. Prepare the Fruit Glaze, then place in a container in the fridge until needed.

- Temper the chocolate and make the decorations as instructed, then leave in a cool, dry place to set for 2 hours.

Then, the poached nectarines:

- Put the nectarine halves and syrup in a saucepan, cover with a cartouche and poach over a low heat for about 10 minutes until slightly soft. Leave to cool, then set aside until needed.

Next, prepare and line the entremets rings:

- Put the entremet rings on a baking tray (sheet) lined with silicone paper and line them with clear acetate strips. Cut the piped sponge into 3cm x 32cm (1¼ x 13 inch) strips. *(1)* Put the strips in the ring, lining it around the inside of the mould. Put the sponge ovals in the base, then use a pastry brush to soak it with the kirsch syrup. *(2)* Set aside while you make the fruit mousse.

Now, prepare the nectarine mousse & assemble:

- Prepare the mousse, using nectarine purée. Put a spoonful of the compote on top of the sponge. *(3)* Place a spoonful of mousse on top of the compote *(4)* and spread out. *(5)* Drain the nectarines, peel off the skins, then lay them on top of the mousse. *(6)* Top up with the remaining mousse *(7)* and level off. *(8)* Place in the fridge for 2–3 hours to set.

- Heat the nectarine glaze in a small saucepan over a low heat until the glaze has just melted, then leave to cool to room temperature. Take the entremets from the freezer and glaze the tops with the cooled nectarine glaze. *(9)* Return the entremets to the fridge to set for 20 minutes.

- Demould and place on a serving dish. When ready to serve, decorate with the glazed nectarine segments and blackcurrants, a chocolate square and triangle flick and gold leaf.

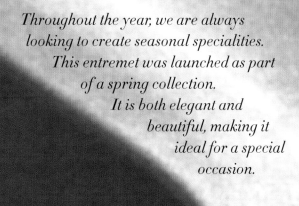

*Throughout the year, we are always
looking to create seasonal specialities.
This entremet was launched as part
of a spring collection.
It is both elegant and
beautiful, making it
ideal for a special
occasion.*

Raspberry & Pistachio Macaron *Makes 2 (each serves 6)*

300g (10½oz) tempered dark (bittersweet) chocolate *(see page 34) used to make* **Chocolate Squares** *and* **Curls** *(see pages 126 and 130)*
1 quantity of **Fruit Compote** *(see page 111) made with raspberries and raspberry purée*
1 quantity of **Raspberry Macaron** *(see page 296)*
1 quantity of **Crème Mousseline** *(see pages 84–85)*
100g (3½oz) **Pistachio Paste** *(see page 116)*
freeze-dried raspberry powder *for dusting*
60 fresh raspberries *plus 3 extra to decorate that have been halved and glazed with* **Fruit Glaze** *(see page 105)*
edible gold leaf *to decorate*

For the raspberry crémeux:
150g (5½oz) dark (bittersweet) chocolate (66% cocoa solids) *finely chopped*
190g (6½oz) **Fruit Purée** *(see page 110) made with raspberries*
75g (2¾oz) egg yolks *(about 3–4 eggs)*
22g (¾oz/1½ tbsp) caster (superfine) sugar
45g (1½oz/3½ tbsp) soft unsalted butter

You will also need:
two 12mm (½ inch) piping nozzles (tips)

First, make the decorations, compote & crémeux:

- Temper the chocolate and make the decorations as instructed, then leave in a cool, dry place to set for 2 hours. Make the raspberry compote, then cool. Store in an airtight container in the fridge.

- To make the crémeux, put the chocolate in a mixing bowl. Put the raspberry purée in a pan and bring to the boil. In another bowl, whisk together the egg yolks and sugar until light in colour. Add half of the boiling purée to the egg mixture, whisk until smooth, then return to the pan. Stir the mixture over a low heat and cook until it coats the back of a spoon and reaches 82–84°C (180–183°F) on a thermometer.

- Take the pan off the heat and pass through a fine sieve (strainer) over the bowl of chocolate. Mix until the chocolate has melted, then mix in the butter until smooth. Put in a container, cover, cool, then chill for at least 2 hours.

Meanwhile, prepare & bake the macaron:

- Prepare the Macaron following the instructions on page 296. Place the prepared Macaron mixture into a piping (pastry) bag fitted with a 12mm (½ inch) nozzle (tip) and pipe 4 spirals that are 16cm (6¼ inches) in diameter on a sheet of silicone paper. *(1)* Leave to dry for 30 minutes. Preheat the oven to 150°C (300°F/Gas 2). Bake for 25–30 minutes. Leave to cool.

Make the chocolate decorations & Crème Mousseline:

- Make the mousseline as instructed, add the Pistachio Paste, then beat until smooth.

To assemble & finish:

- Match the macarons so that you have two lids and bases. *(2)* Spoon the raspberry crémeux into a piping (pastry) bag fitted with a 12mm (½ inch) nozzle (tip) and pipe bulbs around the edge of the base macarons, leaving space in between for bulbs of the pistachio crème mousseline. *(3)*

- Spoon the prepared pistachio crème mousseline into a piping (pastry) bag fitted with a 12mm (½ inch) nozzle (tip) and pipe bulbs in the spaces between the crémeux. *(4)*

- Pipe a spiral of pistachio mousseline on each base, inside the ring of piped bulbs. *(5)* Position the fresh raspberries in circles on top of the mousseline. *(6)*

- Spoon the prepared compote into a paper piping cornet *(see page 30)* and pipe the compote on top of the raspberries. *(7)* Top with the macaron lids, dust with raspberry powder *(8)* and decorate with the raspberry halves, chocolate curls, squares and gold leaf.

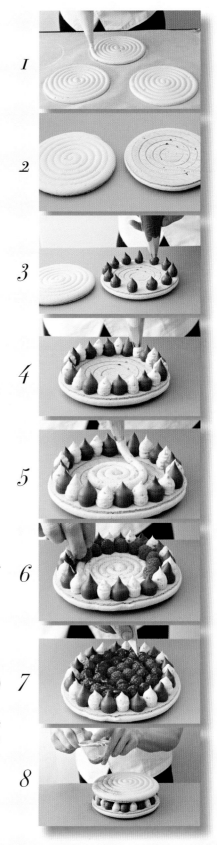

1

2

3

4

5

6

7

8

Macarons have become increasingly popular in London; with this in mind it seemed natural to create our own pâtisserie. Raspberry and pistachio is a classic flavour combination, which I felt was appropriate given the wonderful history of macarons.

This is inspired by a visit I made to Hamburg while researching German pâtisserie shops for an article I was writing at the time. This flavour combination stood out and inspired me to develop my own version.

Redcurrant & Fromage Frais Entremet *Makes 2 (each serves 6–8)*

300g (10½oz) tempered white chocolate *(see page 34) used to make* **Red & White Rectangles** *(see page 126)*

300g (10½oz) tempered dark (bittersweet) chocolate *(see page 34) used to make* **Chocolate Squares** *and* **Curls** *(see pages 126 and 130)*

1 quantity of **Pain de Gène** *(see page 68)*

1 quantity of **Alcohol Syrup** *(see page 103) made with kirsch*

1 quantity of **Fruit Compote** *(see page 111) made with redcurrant purée and redcurrants*

1 quantity of **Fruit Glaze** *(see page 105) made with redcurrant purée*

3g (⅒oz) leaf gelatine

½ quantity of **Redcurrant Curd** *(see Variation, page 96)*

about 200 fresh redcurrants

10 fresh redcurrants *glazed with* **Fruit Glaze** *(see page 105)*

edible gold leaf *to decorate*

For the fromage frais mousse:
180ml (6fl oz/¾ cup) whipping (pouring) cream

380g (13oz) fromage frais

12ml (1 tbsp) kirsch

12g (¼oz) leaf gelatine

60g (2oz) egg yolk *(about 3 eggs)*

50g (1¾oz) whole eggs *(about 1 egg)*

115g (4oz/generous ½ cup) caster (superfine) sugar

36ml (1¼fl oz/2½ tbsp) water

You will also need:
two 14cm (5½ inch) rings

two 16cm (6¼ inch) rings

a 12mm (½ inch) plain piping nozzle (tip)

First, prepare the decorations, Pain de Gène sponge, syrup, compote & glaze:

- Temper the white chocolate and make the red and white rectangles as instructed, then leave in a cool, dry place to set for 2 hours. Temper the dark (bittersweet) chocolate and make the chocolate squares and curls as instructed, then leave in a cool, dry place to set for 2 hours.

- Preheat the oven to 190°C (375°F/Gas 5). Prepare and bake the sponge, then once cooked and cooled, cut out 2 discs measuring 14cm (5½ inches) and 2 discs measuring 16cm (6¼ inches), then set aside until needed. Also prepare the kirsch syrup, redcurrant compote and redcurrant glaze as instructed. Place all in airtight containers and leave in the fridge until needed.

Then, begin to build the centre:

- Put the two 14cm (5½ inch) rings onto a baking tray (sheet) lined with silicone paper and place a 14cm (5½ inch) cut disc of Pain de Gène in the base of each. Use a pastry brush to soak the sponge with the kirsch syrup. *(1)* Brush a layer of the prepared redcurrant compote onto the soaked sponge. *(2)*

- Soak the gelatine in a bowl of ice-cold water for a few minutes until soft. Squeeze the gelatine to remove excess water *(see page 31)*. Prepare the Redcurrant Curd as instructed, but add the soaked gelatine just prior to adding the butter. Cool slightly, then spoon into a piping (pastry) bag fitted with a 12mm (½ inch) nozzle (tip). Pipe the curd on top of the compote, filling the mould one-third full. *(3)* Place the redcurrants on top, *(4)* then freeze for at least 4 hours.

To begin assembly:

- Put the 16cm (6½ inch) rings onto a baking tray (sheet) lined with silicone paper and place the 16cm (6½ inch) cut discs of Pain de Gène into the base of each. Use a pastry brush to soak with the kirsch syrup.

Now make the fromage frais mousse:

- Put the cream in a mixing bowl and whip until soft peaks form. Put the fromage frais and kirsch in a mixing bowl and beat until smooth. Mix in the semi-whipped cream. *(5–6)*

- Soak the gelatine in a bowl of ice-cold water for a few minutes until soft. Squeeze the gelatine to remove excess water *(see page 31)*. Whisk together the egg yolks and whole eggs.

- Meanwhile, put the sugar and water in a saucepan and boil until it reaches 121°C (250°F) on a thermometer. Add the soaked gelatine to the syrup and pour into the eggs. Whisk until it becomes a sabayon. Fold the sabayon into the whipped cream and fromage frais and use immediately. *(7)*

To finish:

- Spoon the prepared fromage frais mousse on top of the Pain de Gène in each ring. *(8)* Demould the frozen redcurrant centre and place in the middle. *(9)* Top up with extra mousse. *(10)* Level off with a palette knife, *(11)* then transfer to the freezer to set for at least 4 hours.

- Melt the redcurrant glaze, then leave to cool. Glaze the top of the set entremets with the redcurrant glaze, making sure that it is evenly covered. Transfer to the fridge to set for 10 minutes.

- Take the entremets out of the fridge and demould from the rings. Place on serving dishes and leave to defrost for at least 4 hours in the fridge. When ready to serve, decorate with the red and white chocolate rectangles, chocolate squares and curls, glazed redcurrants and gold leaf.

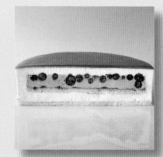

While at The Savoy we made a smaller version of this entremet for our Afternoon Teas – it was always popular. The balanced sweetness of the milk chocolate and the coconut work well with the sharpness of the caramelized oranges and the elegant notes from the Earl Grey tea.

Earl Grey & Coconut Entremet   *Makes 2 (each serves 6)*

½ quantity of **Flourless Chocolate Sponge** *(see Variation, page 71)*
½ quantity of **Hazelnut & Almond Dacquoise** *(see pages 76–77), replacing the ground hazelnuts with desiccated coconut*
½ quantity of **Fruit Mousse** *(see page 99), made with shop-bought coconut purée*
300g (10½oz) tempered dark (bittersweet) chocolate *(see page 34) used to make* 2 **Triangle Wiggles** *(see page 134)*
1 quantity of **Milk Chocolate Glaze** *(see page 106)*
100g (3½oz) toasted coconut strips *to decorate*
edible gold leaf *to decorate*

For the caramelized oranges:
125g (4½oz/⅔ cup) caster (superfine) sugar
50ml (2fl oz/scant ¼ cup) orange juice *squeezed from the leftover flesh of the oranges*
6 oranges *peeled and segmented*

For the milk chocolate mousse (anglaise method):
110ml (4fl oz/scant ½ cup) full-fat milk
470ml (17fl oz/scant 2 cups) whipping (pouring) cream
5g (1 tsp) Earl Grey tea leaves
2g (⅛oz) leaf gelatine
40g (1½oz) egg yolks *(about 2 eggs)*
24g (1oz/1½ tbsp) caster (superfine) sugar
400g (14 oz) milk chocolate (35% cocoa solids) *finely chopped*

You will also need:
two triangle entremet moulds 19cm (7½ inches) long, 8cm (3¼ inches) high
one 11 x 37cm (4¼ x 14¾ inch) rectangle mousse ring

First, make the caramelized oranges:

- Make a dry amber caramel with the caster (superfine) sugar *(see page 33)*. Remove from the heat and add the orange juice, mix well. Add the orange segments, then leave to marinate for at least 1 hour. *(1)* Drain, reserving any excess liquid as it will be used to soak the sponge.

I

Next, bake the Flourless Chocolate Sponge:

- Preheat the oven to 190°C (375°F/Gas 5). Spoon the prepared sponge mixture into a non-stick baking mat and spread evenly using a palette knife. Bake for 12–14 minutes, then leave to cool on the mat on a wire cooling rack. Once cooled, cut out a rectangle measuring 11 x 37cm (4¼ x 14¾ inches).

2

Prepare the dacquoise:

- Lower the oven temperature to 170°C (325°F/Gas 3). Prepare and bake the dacquoise, then once cooled, cut into two 8 x 19cm (3¼ x 7½ inch) rectangles to fit the base of the moulds.

3

Then, prepare the entremet centre:

- Put the rectangle mousse ring on a baking tray (sheet) lined with silicone baking paper. Place the cut rectangle of sponge into the base and soak it with the reserved caramel syrup from the oranges. Lay the caramelized oranges on the top. *(2)*

Prepare the coconut mousse:

- Prepare the mousse, then spoon the mousse into the frame until full, *(3)* using a palette knife to level off if necessary. *(4)* Transfer to the freezer to set for at least 4 hours.

4

**While the centre is setting,
prepare the decorations & milk chocolate glaze:**

- Temper the chocolate and make the decorations as instructed, then leave in a cool, dry place to set for 2 hours.

- Prepare the glaze as instructed. Take the centre from the freezer and demould from the entremet ring. Place it back on the baking tray (sheet) and return it to the freezer.

Then, make the chocolate mousse:

- Put the milk and 110ml (4fl oz/scant ½ cup) of the cream in a saucepan and bring to the boil. Add the Earl Grey tea, cover with cling film (plastic wrap), then leave to infuse for 30 minutes.

- Soak the gelatine in a bowl of ice-cold water for a few minutes until soft. Squeeze the gelatine to remove excess water *(see page 31)*. Strain the tea/cream infusion, return to the pan and bring back to the boil. Continue to make the mousse following the anglaise method on page 101 and add the soaked gelatine to the custard before pouring over the chocolate. Leave to cool and then fold in the semi-whipped cream. Use immediately.

- Put the triangle entremet moulds on a tray. Place a spoonful of the chocolate mousse in the base of each mould *(5)* and push the mousse up the sides.

- Take the centre from the freezer, cut into two 5 x 16cm (2 x 6¼ inch) rectangles, *(6)* and place them in the triangle moulds mousse-side facing down. *(7)* Top with extra chocolate mousse, *(8)* then top with the rectangle of coconut dacquoise. *(9)* Freeze for at least 4 hours.

To finish:

- Gently melt the Milk Chocolate Glaze in a pan, then leave to cool to 32°C (89°F). Take the entremets from the freezer and demould by pouring warm water on the mould. Place on a wire rack set over a tray. Pour over the melted glaze, making sure each entremet is evenly covered. *(10)* Transfer to the fridge to set for 10 minutes.

- Remove the entremets from the wire rack and place on a serving dish. Leave to defrost in the fridge for 4 hours. When ready to serve, decorate with the toasted coconut strips, chocolate triangle wiggles and gold leaf.

5

6

7

8

9

10

The Pâtisserie | Entremets

300g (10½oz) tempered dark (bittersweet) chocolate *(see page 34)*
  used to make **Chocolate Curls** *(see page 130)*
1 quantity of **Genoise** *(see page 66)*
1 quantity of **Fruit Compote** *(see page 111) made with strawberries*
  and strawberry purée
1 quantity of **Fruit Glaze** *(see page 105) made with raspberry purée*
1 quantity of **Alcohol Syrup** *(see page 103) made with Grand Marnier*
20 medium-sized strawberries
1 quantity of **Crème Diplomat** *(see page 83)*
4 raspberries
1 quantity of **Light Fruit Nappage** *(see page 105)*
edible gold leaf *to decorate*

You will also need:
11 x 4.5cm (4¼ x 1¾ inch) square entremet mould

Fraisier   *Makes 1 (serves 4)*

1

2

3

4

5

6

7

8

9

10

- Temper the chocolate and make the decorations as instructed, then leave in a cool, dry place to set for 2 hours. Preheat the oven to 190°C (375°F/Gas 5). Prepare and bake the genoise sponge as instructed and leave to cool. Prepare the strawberry compote, raspberry glaze and Grand Marnier syrup as instructed and set aside.

- Once cooled, cut the sponge into one 12cm (4½inch) square and one 10cm (4 inch) square. Place the larger sponge square on a baking tray (sheet) lined with silicone baking paper and place the entremet ring on top. Soak the sponge with the Grand Marnier syrup. *(1)*

- Place 2 tablespoons of the strawberry compote on the sponge and spread out evenly. Cut 1 strawberry into quarters and place in the corners of the entremet mould. *(2)*

- Cut 4 strawberries in half and line them around the side of the entremet mould (you may need more if the strawberries are small). *(3)* Cut 10 strawberries into small dice and mix together with a tablespoon of strawberry compote.

- Prepare the Crème Diplomat. Place a generous spoonful of the Crème Diplomat into the mould and spread up the sides. *(4)* Place half of the cut strawberries mixed with compote into the mould and top with the smaller sponge square. *(5–6)*

- Soak the sponge with the Grand Marnier syrup, then spoon the remaining cut strawberries on top. Top up with the remaining Crème Diplomat, and smooth with a palette knife. Place in the fridge to set for 1–2 hours. *(7–9)*

- Heat the raspberry glaze in a small saucepan over a low heat until the glaze has just melted, then leave to cool to room temperature. Take the frasier from the fridge and glaze the top with the cooled glaze. *(10)* Return the frasier to the fridge to set for another 20 minutes.

- Cut 2 strawberries into quarters, 2 in half and 4 raspberries in half. Glaze the fruit the Light Fruit Nappage. Take the frasier from the fridge, demould gently and place on a serving dish. Place the glazed fruit on top, then decorate with chocolate curls and gold leaf.

The fraisier has become a modern-day classic, which you will find in many pâtisserie shops. It goes without saying that to get the best out of this dish you should use flavoursome strawberries at the height of their season. Making a fraisier is a great starting recipe, because it is eye-catching yet simple to create.

White Chocolate & Tropical Entremet

Makes 2 (each serves 4)

½ quantity of **Coconut Dacquoise**
(*see Variation, page 77*)
icing (powdered) sugar *for dusting*
½ quantity of **Genoise** (*see page 66*)
1 quantity of **Sesame Tuile**
(*see page 121*)
1 quantity of **White Spraying
Chocolate** (*see page 35*)
mango cubes *to decorate*
½ quantity of **Fruit Glaze** (*see page
105*) made with passion fruit

**For the passion fruit
crème brûlée:**
500g (1lb 2oz) **Fruit Purée**
(*see page 110*) *made with
passion fruit*
120g (4½oz) egg yolks *(6 eggs)*
50g (1¾oz) whole egg *(1 egg)*
100g (3½oz/½ cup) caster
(superfine) sugar

For the marinated mango:
1 quantity of **Simple Syrup**
(*see page 102*)
20g (¾oz) fresh ginger
peeled and finely grated
20g (¾oz) lime juice
1 lime, zested
4 mangoes *peeled*

**For the white chocolate
bavaroise:**
3g (⅛oz) leaf gelatine
125g (4½oz) white chocolate (29%
cocoa solids) *chopped*
125ml (4½fl oz/½ cup)
full-fat milk
30g (1¼oz) egg yolks
(about 1–2 eggs)
15g (½oz/1 tbsp) caster
(superfine) sugar
190ml (6½fl oz/¾ cup)
whipping (pouring) cream

You will also need:
one 34 x 24cm (13½ x 9½ inch)
silicone baking mat with sides
a 12mm (½ inch) plain nozzle (tip)
two 14 x 10cm (5½ x 4 inch)
oval entremet rings
an 8mm (⅓ inch) plain nozzle (tip)

First, prepare the crème brûlée:

- Preheat the oven to 140°C (275°F/Gas 1) and place a non-stick baking mat with sides on a baking tray (sheet). Put the passion fruit purée in a saucepan, bring to the boil, then take off the heat. In a mixing bowl, whisk together the egg yolks, whole egg and sugar until light in colour. Mix the passion fruit purée into the egg and sugar mixture, pass through a fine sieve (strainer), then pour into the prepared baking mat. Bake for 20–25 minutes until the passion fruit crème brûlée has just set. Leave to cool, then place in the freezer for at least 4 hours.

Next, prepare the marinated mango:

- Make the Simple Syrup, add the grated ginger and the lime juice and zest and leave to infuse for 20 minutes. Meanwhile, dice the fresh mango into 1cm (½ inch) cubes, then place into a shallow tray. Strain the infused syrup and place into a another pan, bring back to the boil, then add the mango. *(1)* Cover with cling film (plastic wrap) and leave to cool in the syrup.

I

Then, the Coconut Dacquoise & Genoise:

- Make the dacquoise and spoon into a piping (pastry) bag fitted with a 12mm (½ inch) nozzle (tip). Pipe two oval discs, measuring 14 x 10cm (5½ x 4 inches), then dust with icing (powdered) sugar. *(2)* Cook in the preheated oven as instructed.

2

- Prepare the genoise sponge, and once cool, cut into 2 oval discs measuring 12 x 8cm (4½ x 3¼ inches).

**To begin assembly
& prepare the bavaroise:**

- Place the oval entremet rings onto a tray lined with silicone baking paper and place the oval coconut dacquoise discs into the base, trimming if necessary. *(3)*

3

- Take the passion fruit crème brûlée from the freezer and demould from the baking mat. Cut out 2 oval discs measuring 12 x 8cm (4½ x 3¼ inches), then place them back in the freezer.

- Prepare the white chocolate bavaroise. Soak the gelatine in a bowl of ice-cold water for a few minutes until soft. Squeeze the gelatine to remove excess water *(see page 31)*. Put the white chocolate in a bowl. Put the milk in a saucepan and bring to the boil. Put the egg yolks and sugar in a mixing bowl and whisk until light in colour. Pour half the milk over the egg yolks and sugar and whisk well. Pour all back into the pan and cook gently to 82–84°C (180–183°F). Add the soaked gelatine, then strain over the chopped chocolate. Mix well until emulsified, leave to cool to room temperature. Semi-whip the cream, then fold into the bavaroise.

I'm not the biggest fan of white chocolate but this entremet is one of my exceptions. The acidity and flavour intensity of tropical fruit cuts through the sweetness of the white chocolate.

To finish assembly:

- Place a generous spoonful of the white chocolate bavaroise into the base of the entremet mould. *(4)* With a small palette knife push the mousse up the sides.*(5)*

- Strain the marinated mango, reserve the syrup, then place the mango on top of the bavaroise, leaving a gap of 1cm (½ inch) around the edge. *(6)* Place the genoise sponge on top and press gently so that it is level. *(7)* Soak with the reserved syrup from marinated mango. *(8)* Place the passion fruit crème brûlée on top of the soaked genoise sponge. *(9)*

- Top up with the white chocolate bavaroise *(10)* and level off. *(11)* Make sure you keep the remaining white chocolate bavaroise in the fridge. Place the entremet in the freezer to set for 4 hours.

- Prepare the Sesame Tuile and store in an airtight container.

To finish:

- Take out of the freezer. Place the white chocolate mousse from the fridge into a piping (pastry) bag fitted with an 8mm (⅓ inch) nozzle (tip). Pipe 2 lines diagonally on top of the entremets. *(12)* Place back in the freezer to set for 1 hour.

- Prepare the white spraying chocolate. Demould the entremets from their rings and place on a glazing rack. Spray with the white chocolate spray. *(13)*

- Place on a serving dish, then leave to defrost for at least 4 hours in the fridge. Glaze the mango cubes with a little passion fruit glaze. When ready to serve, decorate with mango and the sesame tuile and a chocolate square.

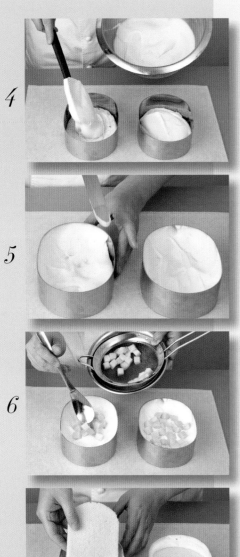

4

5

6

7

8

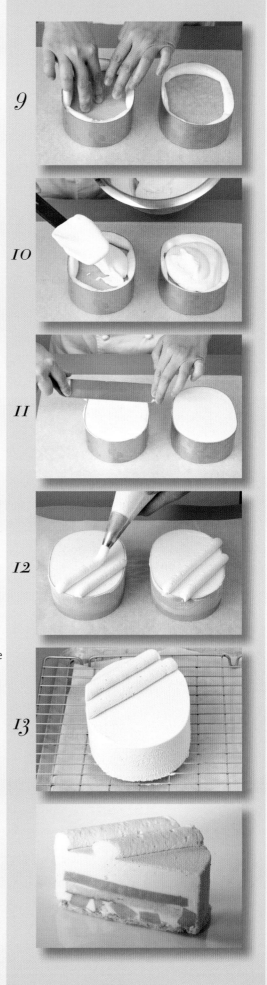

9

10

11

12

13

Originally created by the Julien brothers or 'Trois Frères' in the 18th century, it was initially a baked cake made of rice flour, eggs and maraschino. Once cooked, it was glazed with apricot nappage and decorated with angelica. Although this particular cake is rarely seen nowadays, the mould is called trois frères and many pâtissiers still use it to create modern pâtisserie.

Trois Frères *Makes 2 (each serves 6)*

300g (10½oz) tempered dark (bittersweet) chocolate *(see page 34)* used to make **Chocolate Curls** *(see page 130)*

½ quantity of **Rhubarb Bavaroise** *(see Variation, page 98)*

1 quantity of **Pain de Gène** *(see page 68)*

1 quantity of **Alcohol Syrup** *(see page 103) made with Grand Marnier*

1 quantity of **Fruit Compote** *(see page 111) made with rhubarb and rhubarb purée*

1 quantity of **Classic Bavaroise** *(see page 98)*

½ quantity of **Crème Chantilly** *(see pages 84–85)*

2 oranges *segmented*

6 fraises des bois (wild strawberries)

edible gold leaf *to decorate*

For the poached rhubarb:
1 quantity of **Light Syrup** *(see page 103)*
100g (3½oz) rhubarb *washed and chopped into chunks*

For the orange jelly:
peeled rind of 1 orange *pith removed*
200g (7oz) orange flesh *outer pith removed and chopped*
60ml (2fl oz/¼ cup) orange juice
165g (5¾oz/generous ¾ cup) caster (superfine) sugar
5g (1 tsp) pectin

You will also need:
four 14cm (5½ inch) entremet rings
acetate sheets
four 6cm (3¼ inch) entremet rings
a 16cm (6½ inch) ring cutter
a 6cm (2½ inch) ring cutter
two trois frères moulds
a 6mm (¼ inch) plain piping nozzle (tip)

First, prepare the decorations, poached rhubarb & rhubarb bavaroise:

- Temper the chocolate and make the decorations as instructed, then leave in a cool, dry place to set for 2 hours. To make the poached rhubarb: prepare the Light Syrup in a small pan, add the rhubarb, cover with a cartouche and cook over a gentle heat for about 5 minutes. Leave to cool.

I

- Line the four larger rings with acetate and secure with a rubber band. Place two each on separate trays lined with silicone baking paper. Place the smaller rings in the centres of each larger ring.

2

- Prepare the Rhubarb Bavaroise, spoon into a piping (pastry) bag and and pipe into two of the prepared rings until one-third full. *(1)* Freeze for 2 hours.

3

Next, prepare the orange jelly:

- Put the orange peel, chopped flesh, orange juice and 115g (4oz) of the sugar in a pan and bring to the boil. Reduce the heat and gently simmer for 4–5 minutes. *(2)* Meanwhile, place the remaining sugar and pectin in a bowl and mix well. Remove the orange mixture from the heat and leave to cool slightly. Place in a food processor and blend until smooth. *(3)* Return the orange mixture back to the pan, bring back to the boil, whisk in the sugar and pectin and continue to cook for 4–5 minutes. *(4)*

4

- Pour the jelly into the other 2 prepared ring moulds and smooth out with a small palette knife. *(5)* Place in the freezer to set for at least 2 hours.

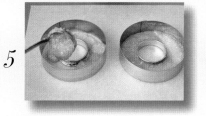

5

Then, prepare the sponge:

- Preheat the oven to 190°C (375°F/Gas 5), prepare the Pain de Gène mixture and bake for 12–15 minutes until light golden in colour. Remove from the oven and leave to cool. Use a 14cm (5½ inch) ring to cut 2 circles from the cooled sponge. Use a 6cm (2½ inch) ring to cut a circle from the centres. Use a 16cm (6½ inch) ring to cut out another 2 circles and use a 6cm (2½ inch) ring to cut a circle out from the centres.

To assemble:

- Prepare the Grand Marnier syrup and the rhubarb compote. Place the smaller rings of sponge on a tray lined with silicone baking paper and soak with the Grand Marnier syrup, then brush with the rhubarb compote. *(6)*

- Demould the orange jelly and place on the 2 sponges. *(7)*

- Take the Rhubarb Bavaroise from the freezer and demould from the ring. Place on top of the jelly *(8)* and transfer the finished centre back to the freezer until required.

- Prepare the Classic Bavaroise and spoon it into the base of the trois frères moulds. Use a small palette knife to push the bavaroise up the sides of the moulds. *(9)* Leave to semi-set in the fridge for 10–15 minutes.

- Remove the prepared centre from the freezer and place it in the centre of the trois frères mould with the rhubarb bavaroise facing down into the mousse. *(10)*

- Top up with additional Classic Bavaroise until there is only 5mm (¼ inch) left at the top of the mould. *(11)*

- Brush the remaining sponge rings with Grand Marnier syrup, then place on top of the bavaroise. *(12)* Transfer to the fridge to set for at least 4 hours.

To finish:

- Prepare the Crème Chantilly and place in the fridge. Take the set trois frères from the fridge and place the mould in a bowl of warm water. Gently demould and place on a serving dish.

- When ready to serve, spoon the Crème Chantilly into a piping (pastry) bag fitted with a 6mm (¼ inch) piping nozzle (tip) and pipe a bulb in the centre of each trois frères. Place the orange segments, poached rhubarb and fraises des bois (wild strawberries) into the centre of the bavaroise. Lastly, place on the chocolate curls and gold leaf and serve immediately.

6

7

8

9

10

11

12

Jaffa Cake   Makes 2 (each serves 8)

1 quantity of
Marmalade
(see pages 112–113)
300g (10½oz) tempered
dark (bittersweet)
chocolate *(see page
34) used to make*
**Combed Hoops, Small
Spheres** *and* **Triangle
Flicks** *(see pages 128,
132–133 and 134)*
1 quantity of
**Caramelized Almond
Batons** *(see pages
122–123)*
1 quantity of **Alcohol
Syrup** *(see page 103),
made with Grand
Marnier*
1 quantity of **Genoise**
(see page 66)
1 quantity of **Dark
Chocolate Mousse
(anglaise method)**
(see page 101)
1 quantity of **Dark
Chocolate Ganache
Glaze** *(see page 107)*
50g (1¾oz) **Confit
Orange** *(see page 113)*
edible gold leaf
to decorate

**For the praline
feuillantine wafer:**
100g (3½oz) milk
chocolate (35% cocoa
solids)
10g (½oz) cocoa butter
75g (2¾oz) **Praline
Paste** *(see page 116)*
90g (3¼oz)
feuillantine wafer

You will also need:
two 14cm (5¼ inch)
entremet rings
two 16cm (6¼ inch)
entremet rings
a 14cm (5½ inch) and
a 16cm (6½ inch)
round cutter

The day before:

• Prepare the marmalade. Line a tray with silicone baking paper
and place the smaller entremets rings on top. Pour 100g
(3½oz) of the prepared marmalade into each of the smaller
rings and level off. *(1)* Transfer to the freezer to set.

The next day:

• Temper the chocolate and make the decorations as instructed,
then leave in a cool, dry place to set for 2 hours. Prepare the
Caramelized Almond Batons. Store all in an airtight container
in a cool, dry place.

Next, prepare the praline feuillantine wafer:

• Put the chocolate and cocoa butter in a bowl and melt over a
bain-marie *(see page 31)* to 45°C (113°F). Take off the heat and
mix in the Praline Paste. Gently mix in the feuillantine wafer.
Spread out onto a baking tray (sheet) lined with silicone baking
paper and flatten to 2mm (just under ⅛ inch) thick. Leave to
set for 30 minutes, then cut out 2 discs measuring 16cm
(6¼ inches). Leave to fully set for 1 hour in a cool dry area.

Then, the syrup & the genoise:

• Prepare the syrup, cool, then store in an airtight container.
Preheat the oven to 190°C (375°F/Gas 5) and prepare the
bake the sponge. Once cooled, cut 2 discs measuring 14cm
(5¼ inches) and 2 discs measuring 16cm (6½ inches). Line a
baking tray with silicone baking paper and place the 2 larger
entremet rings on the tray. Place the set praline feuillantine
wafer into the base of each mould.

Next, prepare the mousse & begin assembly:

• Prepare the chocolate mousse and spread a thin layer on top of
the praline feuillantine wafer. *(2)* Put the larger disc of sponge
on top, then soak well with the Grand Marnier syrup. *(3)* Put a
generous spoonful of mousse on top of the sponge and use a
small palette knife to push the mousse up the sides. *(4)*

• Place the smaller disc of sponge on top of the chocolate
mousse and soak the sponge well with the syrup. *(5)* Demould
the frozen marmalade centres from their moulds and position
them on top of the sponge. *(6)* Top up the mould with the
remaining chocolate mousse *(7)* and level off with a palette
knife. *(8)* Transfer to the freezer to set for at least 4 hours.

To finish

• Prepare the Dark Chocolate Ganache Glaze and cool to 30°C
(86°F). Demould the frozen entremet, then place on a glazing
rack. Place the prepared glaze in a jug and pour gently over
the entremets ensuring that it is covered evenly. *(9)* Transfer
to a serving dish and leave to defrost for at least 4 hours in the
fridge. When ready to serve, decorate the bottom edge with
the caramelized almonds, then place the chocolate decorations
on top and finish with the confit orange and gold leaf.

I am always craving the confectionery items of my youth, which I would spend my pocket money on as a child. The jaffa cake bouchée was my first 'posh' nostalgic creation, and features as Orange Teacakes in my book Couture Chocolate. It has become a firm favourite with our customers.

Chocolate & Chestnut Buche

Makes 1 log (serves 8)

100g (3½oz) shop-bought confit chestnuts *plus extra to decorate*

300g (10½oz) tempered dark (bittersweet) chocolate *(see page 34) used to make* **Copeaux** *and* **Patterned Squares** *(see pages 132–133 and 126)*

1 bar or block of chocolate *to make* **Chocolate Shavings** *(see page 135)*

½ quantity of **Alhambra Chocolate Sponge** *(see Variation, page 67)*

½ quantity of **Hazelnut & Almond Dacquoise** *(see pages 76–77)*

1 quantity of **Dark Chocolate Mousse (sabayon method)** *(see page 100)*

1 quantity of **Alcohol Syrup** *(see page 103) made with dark rum*

1 quantity of **Dark Chocolate Glaze** *(see page 106)*

edible gold leaf *to decorate*

For the chestnut mousse:

5g (⅛oz) leaf gelatine

120g (4½oz) unsweetened chestnut purée

85g (3oz) **Simple Syrup** *(see page 102)*

20ml (¾fl oz) dark rum

200ml (7fl oz/generous ¾ cup) double (heavy) cream *semi-whipped*

You will need:

two 13.5 x 4cm (5¼ x 1½ inch) small buche moulds

a 25 x 9cm (10 x 3½ inch) buche mould

First, prepare the chestnut mousse:

- Soak the gelatine in a bowl of ice-cold water for a few minutes until soft. Squeeze the gelatine to remove excess water *(see page 31)*. Place the unsweetened chestnut purée in a pan with the syrup and bring to the boil. Take off the heat and add the soaked gelatine. Mix well and pass through a fine sieve (strainer), then leave to cool to room temperature. Mix in the dark rum, then fold in the cream. Spoon into a piping (pastry) bag and fill the small buche moulds to 5mm (¼ inch) from the top. *(1)*

- Cut the confit chestnut into small pieces and place them on top of the mousse. *(2)* Freeze for at least 2 hours.

Prepare the decorations, sponge & dacquoise:

- Temper the chocolate and make the decorations as instructed, then leave in a cool, dry place to set for 2 hours.

- Preheat the oven to 190°C (375°F/Gas 5). Prepare and bake the Alhambra Sponge and once cooled, cut one long strip, measuring 5 x 25cm (2 x 10 inches).

- Reduce the oven temperature to 170°C (325°F/Gas 3). Prepare the Hazelnut and Almond Dacquoise and spread it out on a baking tray (sheet) lined with a non-stick baking mat, bake, then leave to cool. Cut out one long strip, measuring 8 x 25cm (3¼ x 10 inches).

To assemble & finish:

- Demould the chestnut mousse centres from the moulds and return to the freezer until required.

- Prepare the chocolate mousse, place 2 large spoonfuls in the base of the larger buche mould and use a palette knife to push the mousse up the sides. *(3)* Take the chestnut centres from the freezer and place into the buche mould. *(4)* Add enough chocolate mousse to cover the chestnut mousse and level. *(5)* Place the strip of chocolate sponge on top of the mousse *(6)* and soak well with rum syrup. *(7)* Add the remaining chocolate mousse, leaving a 5mm (¼ inch) space at the top, and level off. *(8)* Place the strip of dacquoise on top, *(9)* then place in the freezer to set for at least 4 hours.

- Prepare the chocolate glaze and leave to cool to about 30°C (86°F). Demould the buche and place on a wire rack. Place the cooled glaze in a jug and pour gently over the buche ensuring that both sides are evenly covered. *(10)* Place in the fridge to set for 10 minutes.

- Place the buche on a chopping board and trim both sides to neaten. Place on a serving dish, then leave to defrost for at least 4 hours in the fridge. When ready to serve, decorate the sides with the chocolate shavings, then finish with the chocolate decorations, confit chestnuts and gold leaf.

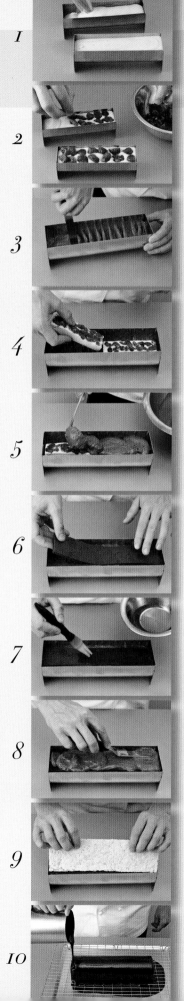

1

2

3

4

5

6

7

8

9

10

Traditionally Buche de Noel was made with genoise sponge, rolled and decorated with buttercream to resemble a log. In more recent years, with the adaption of moulds for pâtisserie, the buche has evolved to become a modern patisserie-style entremet. Originally it was an actual log of wood that was burned as a celebration of winter solstice. During the 1700s the Buche de Noel was invented in Paris.

I created this entremet for the Master of Culinary Arts award in 2013. It was well received, using classic techniques to create a contemporary design. The flavours were influenced by Pierre Hermé's famous combination of rose, raspberry and lychee. Since the days of Pierre Hermé at Fauchon in Paris, I have always been inspired by his creations.

Raspberry & Rose Entremet
Makes 1
(serves 8–10)

300g (10½oz) tempered white chocolate *(see page 34) to make* **Red and White Discs** *(see page 127)*

1 quantity of **Fruit Compote** *(see page 111) made with raspberries and raspberry purée*

1 quantity of **Pain de Gène** *(see page 68)*

½ quantity of **Fruit Mousse** *(see page 99) made with raspberry purée*

1 quantity of **White Chocolate Glaze** *(see page 107) but replace the water with raspberry purée that has been passed through a muslin (cheesecloth) cloth*

organic rose petals

45–50 raspberrries *halved*

edible silver leaf *to decorate*

For the rose infusion:

150g (5½oz/¾ cup) caster (superfine) sugar

250ml (8½fl oz/1 cup) water

2 vanilla pods (beans) split and scraped

50 dried rose buds

For the praline feuillantine:

75g (2¾oz) milk chocolate (35% cocoa solids) *chopped*

15g (¼oz/1 tbsp) cocoa butter

60g (2oz) **Praline Paste** *(see pages 116–117)*

65g (2½oz) feuillantine wafer

For the lychee curd:

2g (⅟₁₆oz) leaf gelatine

110g (3½oz) **Fruit Purée** *(see page 110) made with lychees*

35ml (1¼fl oz/2 tbsp) lime juice

200g (7oz) whole eggs *(about 4 eggs)*

80g (3oz/scant ½ cup) caster (superfine) sugar

85g (3¼oz/¾ stick) unsalted butter

For the champagne & rose jelly:

12 fresh raspberries *halved*

75ml (2fl oz/generous ¼ cup) rose infusion *(see above)*

5g (⅟₈oz) leaf gelatine

150ml (¼ pint/scant ½ cup) rosé champagne

For the champagne & rose syrup:

150ml (¼ pint/generous ⅔ cup) rose infusion *(see above)*

200ml (7fl oz/scant 1 cup) rosé champagne

For the sugar decoration:

a pinch of red sugar colour powder

20ml (4 tsp) cold water

200g (7oz) isomalt

You will also need:

a 6cm (2½ inch) and an 8cm (3¼ inch) round cutter

two 16cm (6¼ inch) rings

acetate sheets

two 8cm (3¼ inch) ramekins

one 18cm (7 inch) savarin entremet mould *(see silikomart, page 344)*

First, prepare the chocolate decoration & rose infusion:

- Temper the chocolate and make the decorations as instructed, then leave in a cool, dry place to set for 2 hours.

- To make the infusion: put the sugar, water and vanilla seeds and pod (bean) in a saucepan, bring to the boil and add the rose buds. *(1)* Cover with cling film (plastic wrap) and leave to infuse for 1 hour.

Next, prepare the praline feuillantine:

- Line a 30 x 40cm (12 x 16 inch) baking tray (sheet) with silicone (baking) paper. Put the chocolate and cocoa butter in a mixing bowl and melt over a bain-marie (water bath). Mix in the Praline Paste and lastly mix in the feuillantine wafer. Spoon the feuillantine mix onto the prepared tray and spread out thinly. Leave to set in a cool, dry place for at least 30 minutes. Once semi-set, cut out an 18cm (7 inch) disc, then use a 6cm (2½ inch) cutter to cut out the centre and create a ring. *(2)* Leave to fully set while you prepare the rest of the components.

Then, the compote & the Pain de Gène:

- Make the compote and set aside in the fridge until needed. Preheat the oven to 190°C (375°F/Gas 5). Make the Pain de Gène and once cooled, cut out an 18cm (7 inch) disc, then use a 6cm (2½ inch) cutter to cut out the centre and create a ring. Cut a 16cm (6¼ inch) disc, then use an 8cm (3¼ inch) cutter to cut out a centre and create another ring. *(3)*

Now, prepare the moulds:

- Line the two 16cm (6¼ inch) rings with acetate and secure with a rubber band. Place on a baking tray (sheet) and place the ramekins, upside down, in the centre of each ring.

Next, make the curd:

- Soak the gelatine in a bowl of ice-cold water for a few minutes until soft. Squeeze the gelatine to remove excess water *(see page 31)*. Use the rest of the ingredients to make the curd following the instructions on page 96, but add the soaked gelatine just prior to adding the butter. Spoon the curd into a jug and pour 150g (5½oz) of it into one of the rings around the ramekin. *(4–5)* Freeze for 2 hours.

Prepare the jelly & syrup:

- Line the base of the other ring mould with the halved raspberries. *(6)*

- Strain the rose infusion, then prepare the jelly. Soak the gelatine in a bowl of ice-cold water for a few minutes until soft. Squeeze the gelatine to remove excess water *(see page 31)*. Put 75ml (3fl oz) of the rose infusion in a pan and bring to the boil. Add the soaked gelatine, then mix in the champagne. Pour into a jug and pour over the raspberries, just covering them. *(7)* Freeze for at least 2–3 hours.

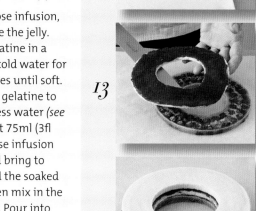

- To make the syrup, strain the remaining rose infusion and mix 150ml (¼ pint/²⁄₃ cup) of it with the champagne (any remaining rose infusion can be stored in an airtight container in the fridge for up to 1 week).

Begin to assemble:

- Demould the frozen jelly. *(8–10)*

- Soak the smaller ring of Pain de Gène with the rose syrup, *(11)* then spread the raspberry compote on top. *(12)*

- Place the sponge on top of the frozen jelly ring. *(13)*

- Take the lychee curd from the freezer, demould from the rings, then place on top of the Pain de Gène and jelly. *(14)* Return to the freezer until required.

Prepare the raspberry mousse & continue to assemble:

- Make the mousse, then spoon half into the base of the savarin entremet mould. *(15)* Use a small palette knife to spread the mousse up the sides. *(16)*

- Take the prepared curd and jelly centre from the freezer and place into the entremet mould with the lychee curd facing down into the mousse. Top up with extra raspberry mousse to 5mm (¼ inch) below the top of the mould and level off.

- Carefully place the larger ring of sponge on top of the mousse. *(17)* Soak the sponge with the rose and champagne syrup. *(18)*

- Spread a little more raspberry mousse over the top and level off. *(19)*

- Place the set feuillantine wafer ring on top. *(20)* Place the entremet into the freezer to set for about 4 hours.

Make the sugar decoration:

- Prepare a baking tray (sheet) lined with a non-stick baking mat. Dissolve the red colour powder with a little water in a small bowl. Put the cold water in a saucepan over a gentle heat, add one-third of the isomalt and gently stir to dissolve. Add another third of the isomalt and continue to stir again to dissolve. Add the final amount of isomalt, then stir once more. Leave the isomalt to begin to boil, then add the red colour. Leave the isomalt to continue to cook to 165–171°C (329–340°F), then pour out onto the non-stick baking mat. Leave to cool slightly. As it starts to cool around the edges, fold the cooled edges into the hotter isomalt in the centre. Continue to fold into the centre until the isomalt becomes a workable temperature and consistency. Pull the isomalt, folding it over so that it becomes shiny and glossy. Pinch a piece of the isomalt and pull gently to create a strand. Loop it over, then leave to cool. Place in an airtight container with a small sealed container of silica gel until required.

To finish:

- Prepare the white chocolate and raspberry glaze and leave to cool to 30°C (86°F).

- Demould the entremet from the savarin mould, then place on a glazing rack. Once the glaze has cooled, gently pour over the entremet to glaze, then place in the fridge to set for 10 minutes.

- Remove the entremet from the glazing rack and set on a serving dish. Leave to defrost for about 4 hours in the fridge before serving. When ready to serve, place the red and white chocolate discs around the edge of the entremet and decorate with the fresh rose petals, raspberry halves, sugar decoration and silver leaf.

Note: *Be aware that when making the sugar decoration, the cooked isomalt is very hot – it is advisable to wear protective gloves for working with the isomalt.*

300g (10½oz) tempered dark (bittersweet) chocolate *(see page 34)*
  used to make **Piped Copeaux** *(see page 131)*
½ quantity of **French Meringue** *(see page 74)*
10g (½oz/2 tsp) Japanese black vinegar *(see Note)*
½ quantity of **Crème Diplomat** *(see page 83)*
Light Fruit Nappage *(see page 105) for glazing the fruits*

A selection of seasonal fresh fruits:
apricots *stoned and halved*
kiwi *peeled and cut into chunks*
raspberries
blueberrie
blackberries
mango *peeled, stoned and cut into chunks*
redcurrants
strawberries *hulled and halved if large*
plums *stoned and cut into chunks*
peaches *stoned and cut into chunks*

You will also need:
a 10mm (½ inch) and a 12mm (⅝ inch) plain piping nozzle (tip)

Pavlova

Makes 1 (serves 6–8)

Prepare the decoration & meringue:

- Temper the chocolate and make the decorations as instructed, then leave in a cool, dry place to set for 2 hours.

- Preheat the oven to 140°C (275°F/Gas 1). Prepare the French Meringue and once the meringue is finished, mix in the Japanese black vinegar. Spoon the meringue into a piping (pastry) bag fitted with a 10mm (½ inch) piping nozzle (tip).

- Line a baking tray (sheet) with a non-stick baking mat, then pipe the meringue into a spiral, *(1)* 14cm (5¼ inches) in diameter. Bake for about 1 hour until lightly coloured. Take out the oven and leave to cool.

To assemble:

- Prepare the Crème Diplomat and spoon into a piping (pastry) bag fitted with a 12mm (⅝ inch) plain nozzle (tip). Pipe a spiral on top of the cooled meringue. *(2)* Place the cut fruits on top *(3–5)* and glaze with the Light Fruit Nappage. *(6)* Decorate with the Piped Copeaux and serve immediately.

Note: *we add the vinegar to the meringue to make it chewier and softer in the centre – the acid reacts with the proteins in the egg whites which breaks them down. I prefer to use Japanese black vinegar because it is less astringent than other vinegars and adds a light, malty note to the meringue.*

This popular dessert was created while the Russian ballet was touring in Australia and New Zealand in the 1920s. The dish was created in honour of the prima ballerina Anna Pavlova to commemorate her performance in the famous Swan Lake. The meringue for a pavlova has the addition of vinegar, which gives it a soft and chewy centre.

Apricot & Wasabi Entremet *Makes 2 (each serves 8)*

1 quantity of **Simple Syrup** *(see page 102)*
  infused with 12g (½oz) fresh wasabi
1 quantity of **Pain de Gène** *(see page 68)*
½ quantity of **Dark Chocolate Crémeux**
  (see page 95), made with addition of 45g
  (1½oz) freshly grated wasabi infused into
  the milk and cream for 30 minutes
300g (10½oz) tempered dark (bittersweet)
  chocolate *(see page 34) used to make*
  Palette, Square *and* **Copeaux** *(see pages*
  127, 126 and 132–133)
1 quantity of **Biscuit Macaron** *(see page 71)*
½ quantity of **Dark Chocolate Mousse**
  (sabayon method) *(see page 100)*
1 quantity of **Dark Chocolate Glaze**
  (see page 106)
1 quantity of **Light Fruit Nappage**
  (see page 105)
edible gold leaf to decorate

For the poached apricots:
400ml (14fl oz/1⅓ cups) plum wine
1 vanilla pod (bean) *split lengthways*
12 apricots *halved and stoned*

For the apricot curd:
2g (½ tsp) leaf gelatine
150g (5½oz) **Fruit Purée** *(see page 110)*
  made with apricots
50ml (2fl oz) lemon juice
300g (10½oz) whole eggs *(about 6 eggs)*
120g (4½oz/⅔ cup) caster (superfine) sugar
125g (4½oz/generous ½ cup) unsalted
  butter

For the decorative streusel:
100g (3½oz/scant 1 cup) ground hazelnuts
100g (3½oz/¾ cup) plain (all-purpose) flour
100g (3½oz/¾ cup) icing (powdered) sugar
100g (3½oz/1 scant stick) unsalted butter

You will also need:
two 14cm (5½ inch) entremet rings
a 12mm (½ inch) plain piping nozzle (tip)
two 16cm (6¼ inch) entremet rings

First, prepare the syrup, poached apricots & Pain de Gène:

- Prepare the wasabi syrup and set aside. To prepare the poached apricots, place the plum wine in a saucepan. Scrape the seeds from the split vanilla pod (bean) into the pan and drop in the empty pod (bean) too. Place in the apricots halves in the syrup and cover with a cartouche. Cook over a gentle heat for 6–8 minutes until the apricots are soft, then leave to cool in the wine. *(1)*

- Preheat the oven to 190°C (375°F/ Gas 5). Prepare the Pain de Gène and bake as instructed. Once cooled, cut into 2 discs measuring 14cm (5½ inch) in diameter.

- Line a baking tray (sheet) with silicone baking paper and place the smaller entremet rings on the tray.

Next, make the crémeux & the entremet centres:

- Prepare the chocolate and wasabi crémeux, then weigh 100g (3½oz) into the base of each entremets ring and spread out evenly. *(2)* Transfer to the fridge to set for 10 minutes. Remove the crémeux from the fridge, then place the Pain de Gène on top of the chocolate crémeux. *(3)* Soak with the wasabi syrup. *(4)*

- Drain the poached apricots from the plum wine, then cut each half into 2 pieces (reserve 1 piece, cut in half, for decoration that will need to be glazed with Light Fruit Nappage). Line the apricots around in a spiral and place in the fridge while you prepare the curd. *(5)*

- Soak the gelatine in a bowl of ice-cold water for a few minutes until soft. Squeeze the gelatine to remove excess water *(see page 31)*. Prepare the curd following the instructions on page 96, but add the soaked gelatine just prior to adding the butter. Place 120g (4½oz) of the curd on top of the poached apricots; spread out evenly. *(6)* Place in the freezer to set for at least 4 hours.

One of the highlights of my career was joining Relais Desserts International. After being nominated by Alain Roux and Pierre Hermé, I was then required to travel to the association's annual conference in Yssingeaux in France to present one of our house entremets to all the members. I chose our Apricot and Wasabi Entremet as I wanted to present our philosophy and inspiration as well as the combination of our cultural influences.

Apricot & Wasabi Entremet
continued

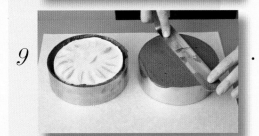

While the centres are freezing:

- Temper the chocolate and make the decorations as instructed, then leave in a cool, dry place to set for 2 hours.

- Preheat the oven to 170°C (325°F/Gas 3). Prepare the Biscuit Macaron, spoon into a piping (pastry) bag fitted with a 12mm (½ inch) piping nozzle (tip) and pipe 2 spirals that are 16cm (6¼ inches) in diameter onto a non-stick baking mat. Dust with icing (powdered) sugar, then bake for 18–20 minutes. Remove from the oven and leave to cool.

- Remove the apricot and wasabi centre from the freezer, demould from the ring and place back into the freezer until required.

- Place the cooked biscuit macarons on a tray lined with silicone baking paper. Place the 2 larger entremet rings around the dacquoise, trimming if necessary.

Finally, prepare the mousse, assemble & finish:

- Prepare the Dark Chocolate Mousse, place a generous spoonful into the base of the entremets moulds *(7)*, and use a palette knife to push the mousse up the side of the moulds. *(8)* Remove the apricot and wasabi centre from the freezer and place into the entremet ring. *(9)* Top up with the remaining mousse *(10)* and level off with a palette knife *(11)*. Place in the freezer to set for at least 4 hours.

- Preheat the oven to 180°C (350°F/Gas 4). To prepare the streusel decoration, place all the ingredients in a mixing bowl and rub together until a crumble texture forms. Line a tray with a non-stick baking mat, take a small amount of streusel and push together gently to form a small mound (you will need to make 32 pieces). Place on the prepared baking tray and bake for 10–12 minutes until light golden brown. *(12)* Remove from the oven and leave to cool. Meanwhile, prepare the Dark Chocolate Glaze and leave to cool to about 30°C (86°F).

- Remove the entremets from the freezer, demould and glaze *(see page 35)* with the Dark Chocolate Glaze. *(13–14)* Transfer to the fridge to set for 10 minutes.

- Remove the entremets from the glazing rack, place on a serving dish and leave to defrost in the fridge for 4 hours. When ready to serve, decorate each entremet with 16 pieces of the decorative streusel *(15)* and top with the chocolate decorations, glazed apricot pieces and edible gold leaf.

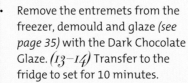

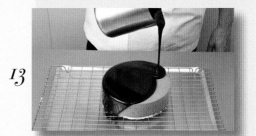

Ice cream gâteaux were popular in grand hotels until the evolution of plated desserts. It would have been a fitting finale to a grand banquet.

Nectarine & Sesame Gâteau   *Makes 2 (each serves 8)*

300g (10½oz) tempered
  white chocolate
  (see page 34)
300g (10½oz) tempered dark
  (bittersweet) chocolate
  (see page 34) used to make
  Patterned Squares *and*
  Triangle Flicks *(see pages
  126 and 134)*
1 quantity of **French
  Meringue** *(see page 74)*
1 quantity of **Crème
  Diplomat** *(see page 83)*
nectarine segments *glazed
  with* **Light Fruit Nappage**
  (see page 105)
toasted white sesame seeds
toasted black sesame seeds

For the sesame ice cream:
1 quantity of **Crème Anglaise**
  (see pages 92–93)
30g (1¼oz) toasted white
  sesame paste

For the nectarine sorbet:
500g (1lb 2oz) **Fruit Purée**
  *(see page 110) made with
  nectarines*
100g (3½oz) **Simple Syrup**
  (see page 102)

You will also need:
a Pacojet *(see page 27) or
  other ice cream churner*
two 14cm (5½ inch)
  entremet rings
a 10mm (½ inch) plain
  piping nozzle (tip)
a 14mm (⅝ inch) plain
  piping nozzle (tip)

The day before, make the ice cream & sorbet:

• Prepare the Crème Anglaise and once cooled, use a hand-held blender to blitz in the toasted sesame paste. Cover the custard and chill for at least 4 hours in the fridge to thicken.

• To make the sorbet, place the nectarine purée and Simple Syrup together in a bowl and mix well. Place in a Pacojet container and leave to freeze overnight. Alternatively, place in the fridge until it is ready to be churned.

• Put the sesame crème anglaise in a Pacojet container. Place in the freezer to freeze overnight. Alternatively, leave it in the fridge until it is ready to be churned.

The next day, prepare the white chocolate discs, chocolate decorations & meringue:

• Temper the white chocolate and prepare two 15cm (6 inch) chocolate discs and two 16cm (6¼ inch) chocolate discs. Temper the dark chocolate and prepare the chocolate squares and flicks for the decoration. Place the chocolate decorations in a cool, dry place to set for 2 hours.

• Preheat the oven to 120°C (235°F/Gas ½). Prepare the French Meringue and spoon it into a piping (pastry) bag fitted with a 10mm (½ inch) piping nozzle (tip). Line a baking tray with a non-stick baking mat, then pipe 4 spirals, measuring 14cm (5½ inches) in diameter onto it. *(1)* Bake the piped meringue for about 1½ hours until lightly coloured and dry. Take out of the oven and leave to cool. Use the entremets ring to trim the meringue discs to size. *(2)*

Then begin to assemble:

• Line a tray with silicone baking paper and place the entremet rings on the tray. Place one of the spirals of meringue into the base of the rings.

• Place the frozen sesame ice cream into the Pacojet (or other ice cream machine) and churn. Spoon the churned sesame ice cream into a piping (pastry) bag fitted with a 14mm (⅝ inch) nozzle (tip) and pipe in a spiral on top of the meringue in the entremet moulds. *(3)* Place the smaller discs of white chocolate on top of the sesame ice cream. *(4)* Transfer to the freezer.

5

6

7

8

- Place the frozen nectarine sorbet into the Pacojet (or other ice cream machine) and churn.

- Take the entremet rings from the freezer. Place the nectarine sorbet into a piping (pastry) bag fitted with a 14mm (⅝ inch) nozzle (tip) and pipe a spiral onto the top of the white chocolate discs. *(5)* Place the second spiral of meringue on top, ensuring that the flat side is at the top. Press gently to ensure that it is flat. *(6)* Transfer to the freezer to set for at least 2 hours.

To finish:

- Prepare the Crème Diplomat and leave to set in the fridge for 30 minutes. Take the frozen gâteau from the freezer and demould from the ring. Put a large spoonful of the cream on top of the gâteau *(7)* and spread and smooth over with a step palette knife.

- Use the palette knife to spread more cream around the sides of the gâteau. *(8)* Use a triangle comb scraper to scrape the side. *(9)*

- Level off the top again with a palette knife. *(10)* Top with the larger white chocolate disc. *(11)*

- Place the remaining Crème Diplomat in a piping (pastry) bag fitted with a 10mm (½ inch) piping nozzle (tip) and pipe a spiral of the cream on top of the entremet. *(12)*

- Serve immediately or return to the freezer. Prior to serving, leave the gâteau to stand for 20–25 minutes. When ready to serve, decorate with the prepared chocolate decorations, glazed nectarine segments and the white and black sesame seeds.

9

10

11

12

Pistachio & Cherry Arctic Roll
Makes 1 (serves 8)

300g (10½oz) tempered dark (bittersweet) chocolate *(see page 34)* used to make a thin **Red Rectangle** *(see page 126)*
1 quantity of **Fruit Compote** *(see page 111) made with only cherry purée and no fruit*
½ quantity of **Biscuit Joconde** *(see page 69) with the addition of 75g (2¾oz)* **Pistachio Paste** *(see page 116)*
edible gold leaf *to decorate*

For the pistachio ice cream:
1 quantity of **Crème Anglaise** *(see pages 92–93)*
40g (1½oz) **Pistachio Paste** *(see page 116)*

For the cherry sorbet:
250g (9oz) **Fruit Purée** *(see page 110) made with cherries*
40g (1½oz) **Simple Syrup** *(see page 102)*

You will also need:
a Pacojet *(see page 27)*
two firm acetate sheets

The day before, prepare the ice cream and sorbet:

- Make the ice cream: prepare the Crème Anglaise and once cooled, use a hand-held blender to blitz in the Pistachio Paste. Cover the pistachio crème anglaise and chill for at least 4 hours to thicken.

- Make the cherry sorbet: put the cherry purée and syrup in a bowl and mix together well. Transfer into a Pacojet container and place in the freezer overnight. Alternatively, place the mixture in the fridge until it is ready to be churned.

- Put the pistachio crème anglaise into a Pacojet container and place in the freezer overnight. Alternatively, place the mixture in the fridge until it is ready to be churned.

The next day, prepare the sorbet tube:

- Make an acetate tube 22cm (8½ inches) long and 3cm (1¼ inches) diameter, by curling the acetate into cylinders and securing with tape. Secure the base of the cylinder with cling film (plastic wrap).

- Place the frozen cherry sorbet in the Pacojet (or other ice cream machine) and churn. Place the churned cherry sorbet into a piping (pastry) bag and gently fill the prepared acetate tube, *(1)* tapping gently to ensure that there are no air pockets. Transfer to the freezer to set for at least 2 hours.

Next, make the decorations, compote & sponge:

- Temper the chocolate and make the decorations as instructed. Leave in a cool, dry place to set for 2 hours. Make the cherry compote, pour into a shallow tray; leave to cool. Preheat the oven to 200°C (400°F/Gas 6). Prepare the Biscuit Joconde, mixing the Pistachio Paste in with the dry ingredients and egg mixture. Spread onto a 30 x 40cm (12 x 16 inch) tray lined with a non-stick baking mat with sides and bake for 15–18 minutes. Leave to cool.

To assemble & finish:

- Make an acetate tube, 22cm (8½ inches) long and 8cm (3¼ inches) diameter, by curling the it into a cylinder and securing with tape. Secure the base with cling film (plastic wrap).

- Place the frozen pistachio anglaise into a Pacojet (or other ice cream machine) and churn. Take the frozen sorbet tube from the freezer and demould from the acetate. *(2)* Stand the larger acetate tube in a bowl, leaning against the side and position the frozen cherry tube along one side of the larger empty tube. *(3)* Fill the rest of the tube with the churned pistachio ice cream *(4)* and transfer to the freezer to set for at least 4 hours.

- Cut the sponge into a 20 x 30cm (8 x 12 inch) sheet and spread thinly with the cherry compote. *(5)* Take the ice cream tube from the freezer and demould from the acetate. Trim off any excess so that the ice cream is 20cm (8 inches) long. Place on the sponge and carefully roll the sponge around the ice cream. *(6–7)* Turn the roll on its side and trim the edge to neaten. *(8–9)* Decorate with the red chocolate stripe and gold leaf.

Either serve immediately or return it to the freezer and serve later.

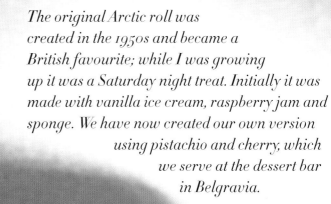

The original Arctic roll was created in the 1950s and became a British favourite; while I was growing up it was a Saturday night treat. Initially it was made with vanilla ice cream, raspberry jam and sponge. We have now created our own version using pistachio and cherry, which we serve at the dessert bar in Belgravia.

Macarons originated in Venice in the 13th century. The Venetians christened the small cakes macerone, which was the Venetian word meaning fine paste. Catherine de' Medici brought this Venetian delicacy to the French court; it quickly became fashionable within the court and then spread across France, with many cities eventually producing their own special recipe.

Macarons

The modern popular style of macaron are also known as Parisian Macarons, created by a young French pâtissier called Paul Desfontaines. While working at a small pâtisserie in Lausanne, he was greatly impressed by the speciality of the establishment, which was a biscuit-based gâteau filled with ganache. On his return to France, he started working for his uncle, Jean Ladurée who owned his own small pâtisserie. The young pâtissier adapted the recipe; instead of using the biscuit base, he used individual macarons which he sandwiched together with different flavours of ganache.

Basic Raspberry Macaron
with Raspberry Ganache

These small almond cakes are made with a mixture of sugar, ground almonds and egg whites. These have become increasingly popular in recent years, with endless imaginable flavour variations *(see pages 298–303)*. This is a basic recipe from start to finish, but the variations really are limitless. This section of the book gives some examples of the classic and contemporary flavour combinations that we use in our shops.

Makes 18 macarons

1 quantity of **Raspberry Ganache** *(see Variation, page 91)*

For the macaron:
240g (8¾oz) egg whites *(about 8 eggs)*
250g (9oz/generous 2 cups) ground almonds *sifted*
250g (9oz/1¼ cups) icing (powdered) sugar *sifted*
15g (½oz/1 tbsp) freeze-dried raspberry powder
 plus extra for dusting
250g (9oz/1¼ cups) caster (superfine) sugar

You will also need:
a 10mm (½ inch) plain piping nozzle (tip)

First, make the ganache:

- Make the ganache as instructed.

Next, prepare the macarons:

- Preheat the oven to 150°C (300°F/Gas 2). Put half the egg whites in a mixing bowl with the ground almonds, icing (powdered) sugar and raspberry powder. Beat to a paste. *(1)*

- Put the remaining egg whites and the caster (superfine) sugar in a separate mixing bowl and beat with a whisk until smooth. *(2)*

- Place the bowl over a bain-marie *(see page 31)* and whisk until the meringue is hot at around 65°C (149°F). *(3)* Transfer to the bowl of an electric mixer (or continue by hand) and whisk until a stiff meringue forms and the mixture returns to room temperature.

- Using a spatula, fold the meringue into the raspberry paste until it is smooth. *(4)* Spoon the mixture into a piping (pastry) bag fitted with a 10mm (½ inch) plain nozzle (tip) and pipe an even number of 5cm (2 inch) diameter bulbs (you will need a total of 36 to make 18 sandwiched macarons) on a baking tray (sheet) lined with a non-stick baking mat. Leave to dry out for 30 minutes. *(5)* Bake for 20–25 minutes. Dust half of the macarons with raspberry powder to finish (these will be the lids).

To assemble & finish:

- Spoon the firmed ganache into a piping (pastry) bag fitted with a 10mm (½ inch) plain nozzle (tip) and pipe a spiral of the raspberry ganache on half the macarons. Sandwich together with a macaron lid. *(6)* Leave to set for about 20 minutes. *Store in a cool, dry place and eat within 2–3 days.*

Basic Macaron Flavour Variations

Make the macarons following the recipe on the opposite page, but replace the freeze-dried raspberry powder with different flavours as listed below.

Chocolate Macaron: use 50g (1¾oz/⅓ cup) sifted cocoa powder. Sprinkle half the piped macarons with 40g (1½oz) cocoa nibs before drying, then baking.

Blueberry Macaron: use the same amount of freeze-dried blueberry powder. Dust half the the baked macarons with some extra blueberry powder.

Pistachio Macaron: use 50g (1¾oz) Pistachio Paste *(see page 116)*. Sprinkle chopped pistachios on top of half the piped macarons before drying, then baking.

Strawberry Macaron: use the same amount of freeze-dried strawberry powder. Dust half the baked macarons with some extra strawberry powder.

Vanilla Macaron: use the scraped seeds from a vanilla pod (bean).

Milk Chocolate & Piedmont Hazelnut Macaron: use half ground almonds and half ground hazelnuts and replace the raspberry powder with 25g (1oz) cocoa powder. Sprinkle half the piped macarons with 20g (¾oz) feuillantine wafer before drying, then baking.

Beetroot Macaron: use the same amount of freeze-dried beetroot powder. Sprinkle half the baked macarons with some extra beetroot powder.

Coconut Macaron: use 35g (1½oz) toasted desiccated coconut. Sprinkle half the piped macarons with desiccated coconut before drying, then baking.

Sesame Macaron: use 15g (½oz) each of white and black sesame seed paste. Mix 10g (¼oz) each of toasted white and black sesame seeds together in a bowl, then use to sprinkle over half of the piped macarons before drying, then baking.

Purple Sweet Potato Macaron: use the same amount of freeze-fried purple sweet potato powder. Dust half the baked macarons with some extra sweet potato powder.

Apple Macaron: use the same amount of freeze-dried green apple powder. You can also sprinkle some crumble mixture *(see page 302)* on one side of half then macarons before drying, then baking.

Matcha Macaron: use 10g (¼oz) matcha powder. Dust half the baked macarons with some extra matcha powder.

Red Pepper Macaron: use the same amount of red pepper paste instead of raspberry powder. Top half the piped macarons with a little dehydrated red pepper before drying, then baking.

RASPBERRY

CHOCOLATE

BLUEBERRY

PISTACHIO

STRAWBERRY

VANILLA

MILK CHOCOLATE & PIEDMONT HAZELNUT

BEETROOT

COCONUT

SESAME

PURPLE SWEET POTATO

APPLE

MATCHA

RED PEPPER

Classic Macarons

All recipes make 18 macarons. They should be stored in a cool, dry place and eaten within 2–3 days.

Chocolate Macaron
with beurre de sel ganache & sea salt caramel

1 quantity of **Beurre de Sel Ganache** *(see Variation, page 91)*
1 quantity of **Chocolate Macaron** *(see Variation, page 297)*
½ quantity of **Sea Salt Caramel** *(see pages 118–119)*

* Make the ganache and spoon into a piping (pastry) bag fitted with a 10mm (½ inch) plain nozzle (tip) ready for piping once firm. Preheat the oven to 150°C (300°F/Gas 2). Prepare and bake 36 macarons. Pipe a ring of ganache around the outside edge of half the chocolate macarons and a bulb of Sea Salt Caramel in the centre. Sandwich together with the macaron lids (the ones with cocoa nibs on top), then leave to set for about 20 minutes.

Blueberry Macarons
with lemon ganache & blueberry confiture

1 quantity of **Lemon Ganache** *(see Variation, page 91)*
1 quantity of **Blueberry Macaron** *(see Variation, page 297)*
½ quantity of **Fruit Confiture** *(see page 108) made with blueberries and blueberry purée*

* Make the ganache and spoon into a piping (pastry) bag fitted with a 10mm (½ inch) plain nozzle (tip) ready for piping once firm. Preheat the oven to 150°C (300°F/Gas 2). Prepare and bake 36 macarons. Pipe a ring of ganache around the outside edge of half the blueberry macarons and a bulb of confiture in the centre. Sandwich together with the macaron lids, then leave to set for about 20 minutes.

Pistachio Macaron
with pistachio ganache & cherry confiture

1 quantity of **Pistachio Ganache** *(see Variation, page 91)*
1 quantity of **Pistachio Macaron** *(see Variation, page 297)*
1 quantity of **Fruit Confiture** *(see page 108) made with 200g (7oz) whole, pitted cherries and 50g (2¾oz) cherry purée*

* Make the ganache and spoon into a piping (pastry) bag fitted with a 10mm (½ inch) plain nozzle (tip) ready for piping once firm. Preheat the oven to 150°C (300°F/Gas 2). Prepare and bake 36 Pistachio Macarons. Pipe a ring of ganache around the outside edge of half the pistachio macarons and a bulb of confiture in the centre. Sandwich together with the macaron lids, then leave to set for about 20 minutes.

STRAWBERRY MACARON WITH STRAWBERRY
MOUSSELINE & RHUBARB COMPOTE

VANILLA MACARON WITH
FROMAGE FRAIS BUTTERCREAM
& APRICOT COMPOTE

PISTACHIO
MACARON WITH
PISTACHIO
GANACHE
& CHERRY
CONFITURE

MILK CHOCOLATE
& PIEDMONT
HAZELNUT
MACARON WITH
MILK CHOCOLATE
GANACHE & PRALINE
FEUILLANTINE

RASPBERRY
MACARON
WITH RASPBERRY
GANACHE

BLUEBERRY MACARON
WITH LEMON GANACHE &
BLUEBERRY CONFITURE

CHOCOLATE MACARON
WITH BEURRE DE SEL
GANACHE & SEA SALT
CARAMEL

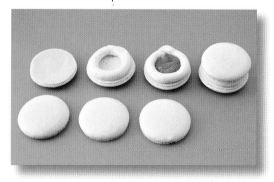

Vanilla Macaron *with fromage frais buttercream & apricot compote*

1 quantity of **Vanilla Macaron**
  (see Variation, page 297)

For the apricot compote:
15g (½oz/1 tbsp) caster (superfine) sugar
5g (1 tsp) pectin
150g (5½oz) **Fruit Purée** (see page 110)
  made with apricots and apricot purée
150g (5½oz) apricots *stoned and chopped*
½ vanilla pod (bean) *split lengthways*

For the fromage frais filling:
300g (10½oz) white chocolate *chopped*
150g (5½oz) fromage frais
1 vanilla pod (bean) *split lengthways*

- Preheat the oven to 150°C (300°F/Gas 2). Prepare and bake 36 macarons. Make the compote. Use the ingredients above to make the compote following the instructions on page 111, then spoon into a piping (pastry) bag ready for piping.

- Make the fromage frais filling. Put the chopped chocolate in a mixing bowl and place over a bain-marie (water bath) to melt to 45°C (113°F). Put the fromage frais in a bowl and scrape in the seeds from the split vanilla pod (bean). Beat together until smooth. Add one-third of the fromage frais mixture into the melted chocolate and mix well to form an emulsion. Mix in another one-third of the fromage frais. Lastly fold the remaining fromage frais into the chocolate mixture, leave to set for 10 minutes before spooning into a piping (pastry) bag fitted with a 10mm (½ inch) plain nozzle (tip) ready for piping.

- Pipe a ring of buttercream around the outside edge of half the vanilla macarons and pipe a bulb of apricot compote in the centre. Sandwich together with the lids, then leave to set for about 20 minutes.

Milk Chocolate & Piedmont Hazelnut Macaron *with milk chocolate ganache & praline feuillantine*

1 quantity of **Milk Chocolate Ganache** *(see Variation, page 91)*
1 quantity of **Milk Chocolate & Piedmont Hazelnut Macaron**
  (see Variation, page 297)
½ quantity of **Praline Feuillantine Wafer** *(see page 276) left to set for 1 hour, then cut into eighteen 3cm (1¼ inch) discs and left to fully set for 2–3 hours*

- Make the ganache and spoon into a piping (pastry) bag fitted with a 10mm (½ inch) plain nozzle (tip) ready for piping once firm. Preheat the oven to 150°C (300°F/Gas 2). Prepare and bake 36 macarons. Pipe a ring of the ganache around the outside edge of half the macarons and place a disc of feuillantine in the centre. Sandwich together with the macaron lids, then leave to set for about 20 minutes.

Strawberry Macaron *with strawberry mousseline & rhubarb compote*

1 quantity of **Strawberry Macaron** *(see Variation, page 297)*
1 quantity of **Crème Mousseline** *(see pages 84–85) made with 250g (9oz) strawberry purée (see page 110) instead of the milk*
1 quantity of **Fruit Compote** *(see page 111) made with 200g (7oz) chopped rhubarb*
freeze-dried strawberry powder *for dusting*

- Preheat the oven to 150°C (300°F/Gas 2). Prepare and bake 36 macarons. Spoon the strawberry crème mousselline into a piping (pastry) bag fitted with a 10mm (½ inch) plain nozzle (tip). Pipe a ring of mousseline around the outside edge of half the macarons. Fill the centre with a bulb of rhubarb compote. Sandwich together with the macaron lids, dust with the extra strawberry powder, then leave to set for about 20 minutes.

Contemporary Macarons

All recipes make 18 macarons. They should be stored in a cool, dry place and eaten within 2–3 days.

Beetroot Macarons
with orange balsamic ganache

1 quantity of **Orange & Balsamic Ganache** *(see Variation, page 91)*
1 quantity of **Beetroot Macaron** *(see Variation, page 297)*

- Make the ganache and spoon into a piping (pastry) bag fitted with a 10mm (½ inch) plain nozzle (tip) ready for piping once firm. Preheat the oven to 150°C (300°F/Gas 2). Prepare and bake 36 macarons. Pipe a spiral of ganache on the flat side of half the macarons, then sandwich together with the macaron lids. Leave to set for about 20 minutes.

Coconut Macarons
with passion fruit & mango ganache

1 quantity of **Passion Fruit & Mango Ganache** *(see Variation, page 91)*
1 quantity of **Coconut Macaron** *(see Variation, page 297)*

- Make the ganache and spoon into a piping (pastry) bag fitted with a 10mm (½ inch) plain nozzle (tip) ready for piping once firm. Preheat the oven to 150°C (300°F/Gas 2). Prepare and bake 36 macarons. Pipe a spiral of ganache on the flat side of half the macarons, then sandwich together with the macaron lids. Leave to set for about 20 minutes.

Sesame Macarons
with chestnut buttercream & confit chestnuts

1 quantity of **Sesame Macaron** *(see Variation, page 297)*
1 quantity of **Chestnut Crème au Beurre** *(see Variation, page 86)*
100g (3½oz) confit chestnut *chopped*

- Preheat the oven to 150°C (300°F/Gas 2). Prepare and bake 36 macarons and the Chestnut Creme au Beurre. Spoon the crème into a piping (pastry) bag fitted with a 10mm (½ inch) nozzle (tip) and pipe a ring around the outside edge of half the macarons. Fill the centre with chopped confit chestnut and sandwich together with the macaron lids. Leave to set for about 20 minutes.

Purple Sweet Potato Macaron *with roasted sweet potato ganache & blackcurrant pâte de fruit*

1 quantity of **Roasted Sweet Potato Ganache** *(see Variation, page 91)*
1 quantity of **Purple Sweet Potato Macaron** *(see Variation, page 297)*
1 quantity of **Blackcurrant Pâte de Fruit** *(see page 109)*
  set and cut into eighteen 2cm (¾ inch) discs

- Make the ganache and spoon into a piping (pastry) bag fitted with a 10mm (½ inch) nozzle (tip) ready for piping once firm. Preheat the oven to 150°C (300°F/Gas 2). Prepare and bake 36 macarons. Pipe a ring of ganache around the outside edge of half the macarons and place a disc of the pâte de fruit in the centres. Sandwich with the macaron lids. Leave to set for 20 minutes.

Green Apple Crumble Macarons *with jasmine crème mousseline & green apple pâte de fruit*

1 quantity of **Pâte de Fruit** *(see page 109) made with 290g (10oz) green apple purée instead of blackcurrant, set and cut into eighteen 2cm (¾ inch) discs*
1 quantity of **Apple Macarons** *(see Variation, page 297)*

For the jasmine crème mousseline:
250ml (8fl oz/generous 1 cup) full-fat milk
10g (¼oz/2 tsp) jasmine tea leaves
30g (1oz) egg yolks (about 1–2 eggs)
25g (1oz) caster (superfine) sugar
12g (⅓oz) plain (all-purpose) flour
125g (4½oz/½ cup) unsalted butter

For the crumble mixture:
100g (3½oz/scant 1 stick) unsalted butter
100g (3½oz/⅔ cup) icing (powdered) sugar *sifted*
100g (3½oz/scant 1 cup) ground almonds *sifted*
100g (3½oz/⅔ cup) plain (all-purpose) flour *sifted*

- Make the mousseline. Put the milk in a saucepan, bring to the boil and add the jasmine tea. Take off the heat, cover with cling film (plastic wrap) and leave to infuse for 1 hour. Strain into a clean pan and bring back to the boil. Continue to make the mousseline following the instructions on page 84. Store in an airtight container until needed. Make the pâte de fruit.

- Make the crumble mixture. Put all the ingredients into a mixing bowl and rub together until a crumble consistency is formed.

- Preheat the oven to 150°C (300°F/Gas 2). Prepare and bake 36 macarons. Sprinkle half the macarons with the crumble mixture before leaving to dry, then baking.

- Spoon the jasmine crème mousseline into a piping (pastry) bag fitted with a 10mm (½ inch) plain nozzle (tip) and pipe a ring around the outside edge of half the macarons. Place a disc of the apple pâte de fruit in the middle. Sandwich together with the macaron lids, then leave to set for about 20 minutes.

Matcha Macarons
with matcha ganache & yuzu marmalade

1 quantity of **Matcha Ganache** *(see Variation, page 91)*
1 quantity of **Matcha Macaron** *(see Variation, page 297)*
1 quantity of **Yuzu Marmalade** *(see Variation, pages 112–113)*
matcha powder *for dusting*

- Make the ganache and spoon into a piping (pastry) bag fitted with a 10mm (½ inch) plain nozzle (tip) ready for piping once firm. Preheat the oven to 150°C (300°F/Gas 2). Prepare and bake 36 macarons. Pipe a ring of ganache around the outside edge of half the macarons and pipe a bulb of the marmalade in the centre. Sandwich together with the macaron lids, dust with matcha powder, then leave to set for about 20 minutes.

Red Pepper Macaron
with shiso ganache

2 red peppers *deseeded and finely chopped*
1 quantity of **Shiso Ganache** *(see Variation, page 91)*
1 quantity of **Red Pepper Macaron** *(see Variation, page 297)*

- Make the dried red pepper pieces. Spread the chopped red pepper out onto a baking mat. Place in a dehydrator and dehydrate for 2–3 hours. Alternatively, bake in an oven preheated to its lowest setting and dry out until crisp.

- Make the ganache and spoon into a piping (pastry) bag fitted with a 10mm (½ inch) plain nozzle (tip) ready for piping. Preheat the oven to 150°C (300°F/Gas 2). Prepare and bake 36 macarons. Sprinkle half with dried red pepper pieces before drying, then baking. Pipe a spiral of ganache on half the macarons, sandwich with the lids, then leave to set for 20 minutes.

MATCHA MACARON WITH
MATCHA GANACHE & YUZU MARMALADE

PURPLE SWEET POTATO MACARON WITH
ROASTED SWEET POTATO GANACHE
& BLACKCURRANT PÂTE DE FRUIT

RED PEPPER MACARON
WITH SHISO GANACHE

SESAME MACARON WITH
CHESTNUT BUTTERCREAM
& CONFIT CHESTNUTS

BEETROOT MACARON
WITH ORANGE BALSAMIC GANACHE

COCONUT MACARON
WITH PASSION FRUIT & MANGO
GANACHE

GREEN APPLE CRUMBLE MACARON WITH
JASMINE CRÈME MOUSSELINE
& GREEN APPLE PÂTE DE FRUIT

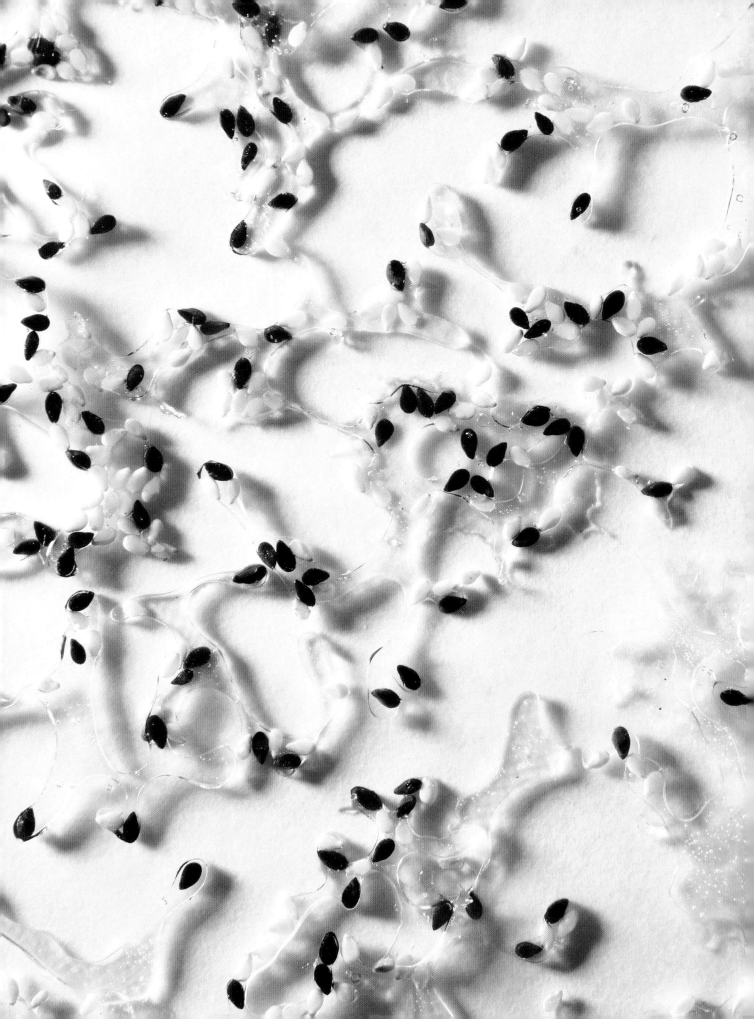

Verrines

The name 'verrine' comes from the French word for glass.
Verrines have become increasingly popular due to their simplicity and
modern style. They are based on the principle of building pâtisserie
or desserts in a glass and constructing them vertically rather than
horizontally on a plate. They create a different visual aesthetic for the
pâtisserie shop, one of brightly coloured layers of varying textures.

Crème caramel is a custard dessert traditionally with soft caramel on top and cooked in a bain-marie. It's another one of those dishes that brings back nostalgic memories. The key is to be able to cook the custard so it just sets. Here we have infused the cream with lemon thyme leaves, adding a light citrus flavour.

Lemon Thyme Crème Caramel *Makes 12*

Crystallized lemon thyme leaves *(see Note)* to decorate

For the caramel:
300g (10½oz/1½ cups) caster (superfine) sugar
100ml (3½fl oz/scant ½ cup) cold water
75ml (3fl oz/⅓ cup) hot water

For the crème caramel custard:
500ml (17fl oz/generous 2 cups) full-fat milk
6g (⅛oz) lemon thyme *leaves picked*
150g (5½oz) whole eggs *(about 3 eggs)*
10g (¼oz) egg yolks *(about 1 egg)*
100g (3½oz/½ cup) caster (superfine) sugar

You will also need:
twelve double-size shot glasses

Note: *To make the crystallized thyme leaves: soak some lemon thyme leaves in a bowl of Simple Syrup (see page 102) for 4–5 minutes. Strain, then place on a baking tray (sheet) lined with a silicone baking mat and dry out in a dehydrator (see page 27) or in an oven preheated to 100°C (225°F/Gas ¼) for about 1 hour.*

First, make the caramel:

• Preheat the oven to 150°C (300°F/Gas 2). Put the sugar and the cold water in a saucepan and cook to an amber caramel. Gradually add the hot water. When all the water is added, bring back to the boil. Pour about 1 tablespoon of the caramel into the base of each shot glass.

Next, make the custard:

• Put the milk in a saucepan. Bring to the boil, then take off the heat and add the lemon thyme leaves. Cover with cling film (plastic wrap) and leave to infuse for 30 minutes.

• Meanwhile, whisk the whole eggs, egg yolks and sugar together in a bowl until light in colour. Strain the infused milk into the egg and sugar mixture, mix until the mixture is smooth, then pass through a fine sieve (strainer). Pour about 50g (1¾oz) of the custard into each shot glass on top of the caramel.

To bake & finish:

• Bake in a bain-marie *(see page 31)* in the preheated oven for about 45 minutes until the custard has set. Remove from the oven and leave to cool in the bain-marie. Remove from the bain-marie, then transfer for the fridge for at least 2 hours. Decorate with a few leaves of crystallized lemon thyme leaves.

Store in the fridge and serve within 2 days.

Peach Melba is a classic dessert created by the great Auguste Escoffier in the early 1890s at The Savoy Hotel, London. This dish brings back happy memories for both of us from our time working at The Savoy. It is a dish that has lasted the test of time on the menu there and is still served to this very day. This is our modern take on the iconic dish, taking all the classic flavours and transforming it into this verrine.

Peach Melba *Makes 8*

½ quantity of **Crystallized Almonds**
   (see pages 122–123)
1 quantity of **Almond Tuile**
   (see Variation, page 121)
2 quantities of **Fruit Compote**
   (see page 111), made with raspberries and raspberry purée
16 raspberries, *halved and glazed with* **Fruit Glaze** *(see page 105)*
16 small fresh mint sprigs *to decorate*

For the vanilla panna cotta:
300ml (½ pint/1¼ cups) whipping (pouring) cream
300ml (½ pint/1¼ cups) milk
1 vanilla pod (bean), *split lengthways*
5g (⅛oz) leaf gelatine
30g (1¼oz/2 tbsp) caster (superfine) sugar

For the poached peaches:
1 quantity of **Light Syrup**
   (see page 103)
4 peaches, *cut in half and stoned*

You will also need:
eight Champagne coupe glasses

First, make the Crystallized Almonds & Almond Tuile:

- Prepare the Crystallized Almonds and tuiles. Store in an airtight container.

Next, make the panna cotta & the Fruit Compote:

- To start making the panna cotta, put the cream and milk in a saucepan. Scrape the seeds from the vanilla pod (bean) into the pan and drop in the empty pod (bean) too. Bring to the boil, then take off the heat. Cover with cling film (plastic wrap) and leave to infuse for 1 hour.

- Prepare the compote and set aside.

- Continue with the panna cotta: soak the gelatine in a bowl of ice-cold water for a few minutes until soft. Squeeze the gelatine to remove excess water *(see page 31)*.

- Add the sugar to the pan of cream and vanilla, return to the heat and bring to the boil. Take off the heat and add the soaked gelatine. Pour the mixture through a sieve (strainer) into a bowl or ice bain-marie *(see page 31)* and leave to cool for about 20 minutes. Once the panna cotta has semi-set, whisk so the vanilla seeds are evenly dispersed.

While the panna cotta is setting, make the poached peaches:

- Prepare the Light Syrup in a small saucepan, then add the peaches, cover with a cartouche and cook over a gentle heat for about 10 minutes until the peaches are slightly soft. Take off the heat and leave the peaches to cool in the syrup in the fridge.

To assemble & finish:

- Spoon 40g (1½oz) of the raspberry compote into the bottom of each glass. Carefully pour 75g (2¾oz) of the semi-set panna cotta on top of the compote, then place in the fridge for about 1½ hours to fully set.

- Take the poached peaches from the fridge and drain from the syrup. Cut the peaches into segments and lay on top of the set panna cotta. Spoon 3 small bulbs of the remaining raspberry compote on top of each panna cotta glass and decorate with raspberry halves, Crystallized Almonds, pieces of Almond Tuile and fresh mint sprigs.

This verrine can be made up to 1 day in advance before adding any decorations. Serve immediately once the decorations have been added.

A posset was originally a British hot drink of milk curdled with wine or ale, often spiced, which was popular during medieval times. Adding the layer of citrus jelly and the fresh segments adds another dimension to the dish.

Lemon & Basil Posset *with a citrus fruit jelly*   *Makes 8*

1 quantity of **Lemon Tuile**
  (see page 120)

For the lemon & basil posset:
300ml (½ pint/1¼ cups) double
  (heavy) cream
4g (⅛oz) fresh basil
75g (2¾oz/⅓ cup) caster
  (superfine) sugar
Finely grated zest and juice
  of 1 lemon *(about 45ml/
  2fl oz juice)*
½ vanilla pod (bean),
  split lengthways

For the citrus jelly:
3g (½ tsp) leaf gelatine
100g (3½oz/scant ½ cup) **Light
  Syrup** *(see page 103)*
50ml (2fl oz/scant ¼ cup)
  orange juice
50ml (2fl oz/scant ¼ cup)
  grapefruit juice
2 oranges *peeled and
  segmented*
2 pink grapefruits *peeled and
  segmented*

You will also need:
eight sherry glasses

First, make the tuiles:

• Make the tuiles and store in an airtight container.

Next, make the posset:

• Set the sherry glasses at an angle on a tray. Put the cream in a saucepan and bring to the boil. Add the basil, then cover with cling film (plastic wrap) and leave to infuse for 30 minutes.

• Strain the infused cream into another saucepan and add the sugar and lemon zest. Scrape the seeds from the vanilla pod (bean) into the pan and drop in the empty pod (bean) too. Bring to the boil, then simmer over a gentle heat for 2–3 minutes.

• Take off the heat and whisk in the lemon juice. Pass the mixture through a sieve (strainer) into a jug. Pour 40g (1½oz) of posset into each of the glasses. Carefully transfer the tray to the fridge and leave to set for about 2–3 hours.

While the posset is setting, make the jelly:

• Soak the gelatine in a bowl of ice-cold water for a few minutes until soft. Squeeze the gelatine to remove excess water *(see page 31)*.

• Put the Light Syrup, orange and grapefruit juices in a saucepan and bring to the boil. Add the softened gelatine, then strain into a jug and leave to semi-set for about 20 minutes.

To assemble & finish:

• Take the glasses from the fridge and place upright on a tray. Gently pour in the citrus jelly until each glass is half full. Carefully place 2–3 segments each of orange and grapefruit into the jelly, then cover with the remaining jelly. Transfer to the fridge to fully set for at least 1 hour. Take the glasses out of the fridge and decorate with pieces of lemon tuile.

This verrine can be made up to 1 day in advance before adding any decorations. Serve immediately once the decorations have been added.

Apple & Edamame Verrine *Makes 12*

In 2009, Suzue and I opened our Belgravia shop, incorporating London's first dessert bar concept, offering a five-course tasting menu of desserts created by one of our pâtissiers in front of your eyes. It was during a trip to Tokyo that Suzue and I first came across this; in Japan, many restaurants have open kitchens and this concept is becoming more popular here in the UK. This popular dish is one of our 'amuse' courses, creating fresh apple spaghetti using a Japanese vegetable turner.

1 quantity of **Sesame Tuile**
  (see page 121)
½ quantity of **Fruit Mousse** *(see page 99) made with the same weight of blanched, puréed edamame beans*
100g natural yogurt
8 blanched edamame beans *glazed with* **Light Fruit Nappage or Fruit Glaze** *(see page 105)*

For the apple & wasabi jelly:
750ml (25fl oz/3¼ cups) apple juice
¼ vanilla pod (bean) *split lengthways*
5g (1 tsp) fresh wasabi
10g (½oz) leaf gelatine
20g (¾oz/5 tsp) caster (superfine) sugar

For the apple spaghetti:
20ml (½fl oz/1½ tbsp) lime juice
50ml (1⅔ fl oz/scant ¼ cup) **Light Syrup** *(see page 103)*
2 Granny Smith apples

You will also need:
twelve double shot glasses

Note: *blanch edamame beans in a pan of simmering water for 15 minutes.*

312

First, make the Sesame Tuile:

- Make the tuiles and store in an airtight container.

Next, make the jelly:

- Put the apple juice and vanilla in a saucepan and bring to the boil. Continue to cook over a low simmer until the apple juice has reduced by one-third (to about 500ml/17fl oz/2 cups).

- Bring the juice back to the boil and add the wasabi, take off the heat and cover the pan with cling film (plastic wrap). Leave to infuse for at least 1 hour. Soak the gelatine in a bowl of ice-cold water for a few minutes until soft. Squeeze the gelatine to remove excess water *(see page 31)*.

- Add the sugar to the apple juice and wasabi infusion, bring back to the boil, take off the heat, then add the soaked gelatine. Pass through a sieve (strainer) and leave to cool.

- Put about 1 tablespoon into the bottom of each glass, then leave to set for 30 minutes.

Now, make the edamame mousse:

- Make the mousse, then spoon it into a piping (pastry) bag. Pipe a layer of mousse (about 1 tablespoon) on top of the set jelly in each glass, then leave to set for about 30 minutes.

And finally, the apple spaghetti:

- Mix the lime juice and Light Syrup together in a small bowl. Chop the top off the apples *(1)* and prepare the spaghetti using a vegetable turner. *(2–3)* Put the apple spaghetti in a bowl, pour over the lime and syrup mixture and toss through the spaghetti *(4)*. Create a nest of the spaghetti on top of the mousse in each glass.

To finish:

- Place a spoonful of natural yogurt in the centre of the spaghetti nest in each glass, then decorate with the blanched edamame beans and pieces of Sesame Tuile.

This verrine can be made up to 1 day in advance up to the point of layering the jelly and mousse. Serve immediately once the decorations have been added.

Rice Pudding, Rhubarb & Elderflower Verrine *Makes 8*

1 quantity of **Rhubarb Tuile**
 (see page 121)
200g (7oz) tempered dark (bittersweet)
 chocolate *(see page 34)* used to make
 Chocolate Curls *(see page 130)*
2 quantities of **Fruit Compote**
 *(see page 111) made with 400g (14oz)
 rhubarb purée*
½ quantity of **Pain de Gène** *(see page 68)*

For the granola:
75g (2¾oz) roasted almonds
 roughly chopped
75g (2¾oz) roasted hazelnuts
 roughly chopped
20g (¾oz) sunflower seeds
50g (1¾oz/½ cup) rolled oats
25g (1oz) clear (runny) honey
35g (1½oz/2 tbsp) caster
 (superfine) sugar
12g (½oz) golden (corn) syrup
25g (1oz/2 tbsp) unsalted butter

For the vanilla rice pudding:
40g (1½oz) pudding rice
 washed in cold water
400ml (14fl oz/1¾ cups) full-fat milk
32g (1¼oz/2 tbsp)
 caster (superfine) sugar
1 vanilla pod (bean) *split lengthways*
70ml (3fl oz/¼ cup) double
 (heavy) cream

For the poached rhubarb:
½ quantity of **Light Syrup** *(see page 103)*
100g (3½oz) rhubarb *washed and
 chopped into chunks*

For the elderflower jelly:
7g (⅛ oz) leaf gelatine
300ml (½ pint/1¼ cups) water
100ml (3½fl oz/scant ½ cup)
 elderflower cordial
1 vanilla pod (bean) *split lengthways*

You will also need:
a 6cm (2½ inch) round cutter
eight small martini glasses

First, make the Rhubarb Tuile & decorations:

- Prepare and make the tuile. Store in an airtight container and set aside. Temper the chocolate and make the decorations as instructed, then leave in a cool, dry place to set for 2 hours.

Next, make the granola:

- Preheat the oven to 160°C (313°F/Gas 2–3). Put the roasted nuts, sunflower seeds and oats in a bowl. Put the honey, sugar, golden (corn) syrup and butter in a saucepan and bring to the boil. Pour this over the nuts, seeds and oats and mix well. Spread the mixture out on a non-stick baking mat and bake for 12–15 minutes, turning over occasionally. Remove from the oven, leave to cool for 5 minutes, then separate the granola with a spoon. Leave to cool completely, then store in an airtight container.

Next, prepare the rice pudding:

- Preheat the oven to 150°C (300°F/Gas 2). Put the washed rice, milk and sugar in an ovenproof saucepan. Scrape the seeds from the split vanilla pod (bean) into the pan and drop in the empty pod (bean) too. Bring to the boil.

- Transfer the pan to the oven, cover with a cartouche and bake for about 1 hour, stirring occasionally, until the rice is soft and the milk has been absorbed. Take out of the oven, pour into a shallow tray and chill rapidly. Once cooled semi-whip the cream and fold into the chilled cooked rice. Return to the fridge until required.

Then, make the Rhubarb Compote & poached rhubarb:

- Prepare the compote using rhubarb. To make the poached rhubarb: prepare the Light Syrup in a small saucepan. Add the rhubarb, cover with a cartouche and cook over a gentle heat for 5 minutes until soft. Take off the heat and leave to cool in the syrup in the fridge.

Now, make the Pain de Gène & jelly:

- Preheat the oven to 190°C (375°F/Gas 5). Prepare and bake the Pain de Gène sponge. Once cooled, cut out 8 discs measuring 6cm (2½ inches) each.

- Make the jelly. Soak the gelatine in a bowl of ice-cold water for a few minutes until soft. Squeeze the gelatine to remove excess water *(see page 31)*. Put the water and cordial in a pan. Scrape the seeds from the split vanilla pod (bean) into the pan and drop in the empty pod (bean) too. Bring to the boil. Add the soaked gelatine, then strain. Leave to cool.

To assemble & finish:

- Put 1 tablespoon of the rhubarb compote into the base of each glass. Place 2 pieces of poached rhubarb on top of the compote, then spoon 2 tablespoons of the rice pudding on top. Place a disc of sponge on top and soak with the rhubarb poaching syrup. Spoon about 1–2 tablespoons of rhubarb compote on top of the sponge, then leave to set for 30 minutes in the fridge.

- Gently spoon about 1–2 tablespoons of the elderflower jelly on top, then place in the fridge to set for 1 hour. Remove from the fridge and decorate with the rhubarb tuile, granola and a chocolate curl.

This verrine can be made up to 1 day in advance before adding any decorations. Serve immediately once the decorations have been added.

Rice puddings are found in nearly every area of the world; different types of pudding vary in their method of preparation – the rice is either boiled or baked. The earliest British rice pudding was called whitepot and dated from the Tudor period. In 1615, Gervase Markham documented the first written recipe of rice pudding. To complement the creamy rice pudding, we have combined other British ingredients; rhubarb and elderflower. The granola topping adds wonderful flavour and texture.

Baked Cakes

The history of cake dates back to ancient times. The first cakes were more bread-like and sweetened with honey, and nuts and dried fruits were often added. Medieval European bakers often made fruit cakes and gingerbread; these foods could last for many months. It was not until the middle of the 19th century that cake as we know it today, made with extra refined white flour and baking powder, became available.

The town of Dundee on the east coast of Scotland is famous for two local specialities, Dundee cake and Dundee marmalade. The world-renowned Dundee marmalade was created by a local grocer in the town at the beginning of the 18th century. The commercial production of the marmalade resulted in a by-product of orange peel. This is where Scottish ingenuity came into force. Instead of wasting the surplus orange peel, the canny Scots created the recipe for Dundee cake using the orange peel, giving this speciality cake its distinctive flavour.

Dundee Cake *Makes 1 round cake*

170g (6oz/1¼ cups) plain (all-purpose) flour
4g (1 tsp) baking powder
115g (4oz/1 stick) unsalted butter
85g (3oz/scant ½ cup) demerara sugar
85g (3oz/scant ½ cup) granulated (white)
  sugar
115g (4oz) whole eggs *(about 2–3 eggs)*
225g (8oz) **Rum-marinated Sultanas**
  (see page 115)
115g (4oz) **Confit Orange** *(see page 113)*
  chopped
grated zest of 1 orange
1 quantity of **Alcohol Syrup** *(see page 103)*
  made with Grand Marnier

To decorate:
1 quantity of **Apricot Nappage** *(see page 104)*
4 dried prunes
4 dried apricots
10 dried cranberries
10 dried cherries
2 **Confit Orange** *(see page 113) cut
  into quarters*
1 quantity of **Crystallized Pistachios**
  (see pages 122–123)
1 quantity of **Crystallized Almonds**
  (see pages 122–123)

You will also need:
a 15cm (6 inch) round cake tin (pan) *greased
  with butter and lightly dusted with flour*

First, make the cake:

- Preheat the oven to 170°C (325°F/Gas 3). Sift together the flour and baking powder into a mixing bowl. Cream the butter and both sugars together in a separate bowl until light and a fluffy consistency. Slowly add the eggs, being careful not to split the mix (if the mixture does begins to split, add a little of the flour).

- Take one-quarter of flour and mix it with the Rum-marinated Sultanas, Confit Orange and orange zest in a separate bowl, making sure all the fruits are coated. Fold the remaining flour into the wet mixture, then fold in the fruits and zest.

- Spoon the mixture into the prepared baking tin (pan) and bake for 1¼–1½ hours. Leave to cool for 10 minutes, then turn out of the tin and soak generously with the Grand Marnier syrup. Leave to cool completely.

To finish:

- Melt the Apricot Nappage in a saucepan. Glaze the top of the cake with the nappage and decorate with the dried fruits, Confit Orange and crystallized nuts (any leftover nuts can be stored in an airtight container for future use).

Store in an airtight container and consume within 2 weeks.

Almond & Fruit Cakes   *Makes 22 small cakes*

These are a real favourite of mine. They are one of the first things we made in the Richmond shop and are still popular today.

100g (3½oz/1 scant stick) unsalted butter
200g (7oz/1¾ cups) ground almonds
200g (7oz/1 cup) caster (superfine) sugar
40g (1½oz) egg whites *(about 2 eggs)*
50g (1¾oz) **Fruit Purée** *(see page 110)*
   made with apricots
40g (1½oz) honey
200g (7oz) whole eggs *(about 4 eggs)* beaten

For the toppings:
16 cherries *cut in half and stoned*
20g (¾oz) pistachios
16 raspberries *cut in half*
20g (¾oz) almond batons *lightly roasted*
2 plums *cut in half, stoned and thinly sliced*
20g (¾oz) hazelnuts *lightly roasted and chopped*

You will also need:
a 12mm (½ inch) plain piping nozzle (tip)
two 11-hole, 4.5cm (3¾ inch) diameter mini-muffin
   silicone moulds

- Put the butter in a saucepan and melt over a gentle heat.

- Put the ground almonds, sugar and egg whites in a bowl and beat to a paste. This can also be mixed in the bowl of an electric mixer fitted with a paddle attachment.

- Gradually add in the apricot purée and honey and beat until you have a smooth paste. Gradually mix in the whole eggs and lastly the melted butter.

- Put in a container and place in the fridge to rest for at least 1 hour. Preheat the oven to 180°C (350°F/Gas 4).

- Take the mixture from the fridge and spoon into a piping (pastry) bag fitted with a 12mm (½ inch) plain nozzle (tip). Pipe into each hole of the mini-muffin mould until three-quarters full.

- Decorate the cakes with a variety of different toppings: cherries and chopped pistachios; raspberries and baton almonds; and plum and chopped hazelnuts.

- Bake for 12–15 minutes until golden on top.

Best eaten the same day, but can be stored in an airtight container and consumed within 1–2 days.

Kinako Madeleines

Makes 24 madeleines

235g (8½oz/1⅓ cup)
  plain (all-purpose) flour *sifted*
6g (1 tsp) baking powder
20g (¾oz) kinako powder
125g (4½oz/generous ½ cup)
  unsalted butter
150g (5½oz) whole eggs *(about 3 eggs)*
120g (4oz/⅔ cup) caster (superfine) sugar
75ml (3fl oz/⅓ cup) full-fat milk
75g (2¾oz/¼ cup) honey

You will also need:
a 12mm (½ inch) plain piping nozzle (tip)
two 12-hole large madeleine moulds

- Sift the flour, baking powder and kinako powder together twice (for even distribution of the baking powder) in a large bowl and mix well.

- Put the butter in a saucepan and melt over a gentle heat.

- Put the eggs and sugar in a bowl and beat together until light in colour.

- Fold the mixed dry ingredients into the egg and sugar mixture. Mix in the milk and honey. Add the melted butter and mix until fully incorporated.

- Put in a container and place in the fridge to rest for at least 1 hour. Preheat the oven to 180°C (350°F/Gas 4).

- Take the mixture from the fridge and spoon into a piping (pastry) bag fitted with a 12mm (½ inch) plain nozzle (tip). Pipe into each hole of the madeleine mould until almost full.

- Bake for 10–12 minutes until golden.

Best served immediately or eaten the same day.

Note: *if you are using a tin mould you will need to grease with a little extra softened butter and dust with flour. If you have a non-stick silicone mould this will not be necessary.*

These small sponge cakes, baked in traditional shell-shaped madeleine moulds, were created in the 17th century by a French cook called Madeleine Simonin. Madeleine created the recipe in 1661 in the kitchens of a cardinal's residency in the city of Commercy in the northeast of France. The cardinal was so delighted with the little cakes he christened them 'madeleine' after his cook.

The origin of these cakes dates back to the 1700s, where they were produced in a convent and named visitandines. During the 1890s they were brought into Parisian vogue by an enterprising pâtissier called Lasne. His small pâtisserie was located in Rue Saint-Denis, in the financial district of Paris. He noticed that the working environment of the stockbrokers was so pressurized, many of them would buy pâtisserie to eat on the floors of the stock exchange when there was no time for lunch.

225g (8oz/1 cup) unsalted butter
75g (2¾oz/½ cup) plain (all-purpose) flour
10g (¼oz/2 tsp) houji cha powder
125g (4½oz/generous 1 cup) ground almonds
25g (1oz) ground hazelnuts
225g (8oz) egg whites *(about 7–8 eggs)*
255g (9oz/1¼ cups) caster (superfine) sugar
20g (¾oz) roasted hazelnuts *chopped, to decorate*
icing (powdered) sugar *for dusting*

You will also need:
a no.12 piping nozzle (tip)
two 16-hole oval silicone financier moulds

Houji Cha & Hazelnut Financier *Makes 24 small cakes*

Lasne developed the cakes as an alternative to the elaborately decorated pâtisserie so the financiers could eat without getting their fingers sticky or needing cutlery. They were christened 'financiers' and produced in a rectangular shape to resemble a gold brick. This attracted wealthy clientele, and the popularity of these small cakes continued to grow.

- Put the butter in a saucepan and bring to the boil. Cook over a gentle heat until you have a beurre noisette *(see page 32)*. Take off the heat and leave to cool.

- Sift the flour and houji cha powder together into a bowl. Add the ground almonds and hazelnuts and mix well.

- Put the egg whites and sugar together in a mixing bowl. Mix gently until fully combined (do not aerate).

- Fold in the dry ingredients to the egg white and sugar mixture, then mix in the cooled beurre noisette. Mix until fully combined. Keep in an airtight container in the fridge to rest for 1 hour.

- Preheat the oven to 170°C (325°F/Gas 3). Take the financier mixture out of the fridge and spoon into a piping (pastry) bag fitted with a no.12 piping nozzle (tip). Pipe into each hole in the moulds until three-quarters full. Decorate with the chopped roasted hazelnuts and bake for 12–15 minutes until a light golden colour. Leave to cool, then remove from the moulds. Lightly dust with icing (powdered) sugar to finish.

Store in an airtight container and consume within 2–3 days.

145g (5oz/1 cup) plain (all-purpose) flour *sifted*
3g (a good pinch) baking powder
1g (a pinch) salt
50g (1¾oz) whole eggs *(about 1 egg)*
155g (5¾oz/¾ cup) caster (superfine) sugar
80ml (2¾oz/⅓ cup) olive oil
10g (⅓oz) grated lemon zest
5g (a good pinch) poppy seeds
110ml (3½fl oz/scant ½ cup) full-fat milk

For the water icing:
100g (3½oz) **Fondant** *(see page 31)*
30ml (1fl oz/2 tbsp) **Simple Syrup**
  (see page 102)

You will also need:
a 12mm (½ inch) piping nozzle (tip)
two 6-hole 7cm (2¾ inch) diameter
  kugelhopf (bundt) silicone moulds

Lemon Poppy Seed & Olive Oil Cake *Makes 12 small cakes*

- Sift the flour, baking powder and salt twice (for even distribution of the baking powder) into a bowl and mix well together. Place the eggs and sugar into another bowl and whisk together until light in colour and it reaches the ribbon stage consistency *(see page 29)*. Mix together the olive oil with the lemon zest, poppy seeds and milk in a separate bowl.

- Mix the oil mixture into the egg mixture, then gently fold in all the dry ingredients. Put in a container and place in the fridge to rest for at least 1 hour.

- Preheat the oven to 180°C (350°F/Gas 4). Meanwhile, make the water icing. Put the Fondant and the Simple Syrup in a saucepan and warm gently over a low heat to 35–37°C (95–99°F).

- Take the cake mixture out of the fridge and spoon it into a piping (pastry) bag fitted with a 12mm (½ inch) piping nozzle (tip). Pipe into each hole of the silicone mould until three-quarters full.

- Bake for 15–18 minutes until golden in colour. Remove from the oven and turn the oven temperature up to 220°C (425°F/Gas 7).

- Turn the cakes out of the moulds onto a baking tray (sheet) and brush with the water icing. Return the cakes to the hot oven for 30 seconds.

Store in an airtight container and consume within 2 days.

With the success of our rosemary and olive oil couture chocolate, I wanted to continue using the wonderful olive oil from the Port Noval olive groves in the Douro Valley in Portugal. Lemon works wonderfully here with the subtle olive notes and the texture of the poppy seeds.

Far Breton

Makes 12 small cakes

The recipe for Far Breton originated in Brittany, northwest France. It dates back to the 18th century and over the years it has evolved from a savoury flan into the sweet version we know today. Each district within the region has its own variation. Here, I have used marinated prunes, which are the speciality of the Quiberon region.

65g (2oz) whole eggs
   (about 1–2 eggs)
50g (1¾oz/¼ cup) caster
   (superfine) sugar
70g (2½oz/½ cup) plain (all-purpose)
   flour *sifted, plus extra for lining
   the mould*
2g (⅛oz) salt
155ml (¼ pint/⅔ cup) full fat milk
155ml (¼ pint/⅔ cup) double
   (heavy) cream
60g (2oz/½ stick) cold unsalted
   butter *cut into 5g (1 tsp) cubes, plus
   extra softened butter for greasing*
24 **Armagnac-marinated Prunes**
   (see page 114)

You will also need:
twelve 7cm (2¾ inch) diameter
   pomponette moulds

- Put the eggs and sugar in a mixing bowl and mix well together. Mix in the sifted flour and salt.

- Gradually add the milk and cream, mixing as you go. Transfer to the fridge to rest overnight.

- Preheat the oven to 180°C (350°F/ Gas 4) and take the mixture out of the fridge.

- Grease the pomponette moulds with some softened butter using a pastry brush and line with a dusting of flour *(see page 30)*. Place the moulds on a baking tray (sheet).

- Pour the cake mixture into each mould until they are two-thirds full.

- Put 2 marinated prunes into each mould, followed by 1 cube of cold butter.

- Bake for 25–30 minutes. Leave to cool slightly, then remove the cakes from the moulds while still warm.

Best served immediately.

Cannelés de Bordeaux au Rhum

Makes 12 small cakes

This French delicacy originates from the city of Bordeaux; a busy shipping port that received luxury goods from the French colonies like Tahiti – such as sugar, vanilla and rum – which only the wealthy were able to afford. Often, as the cargo was being unloaded, the crates would be damaged and local nuns would wait by the ships and beg for the damaged goods to give out to the poor. With these exotic ingredients the nuns added eggs, flour and milk and created a delicious gâteau.

375ml (13fl oz/1⅔ cups) full-fat milk
155g (5½oz/¾ cup) caster (superfine) sugar
30g (1¼oz/2 tbsp) unsalted butter *plus extra for greasing*
1 vanilla pod *split lengthways*
75g (2¾oz) whole eggs *(about 1–2 eggs)*
20g (¾oz) egg yolks *(about 1 egg)*
68g (2¼oz/½ cup) plain (all-purpose) flour
50ml (2fl oz/¼ cup) dark rum

You will also need:
twelve 4.5cm (2 inch) tin cannelé moulds or a 12-hole silicone cannelé tray

- Put the milk, 125g (4oz/⅔ cup) of the sugar and the butter in a saucepan. Scrape the seeds from the split vanilla pod (bean) into the pan and drop in the empty pod (bean) too. Warm gently over a low heat to 85°C (185°F).

- Beat the whole eggs, egg yolks and the remaining sugar in a mixing bowl. Mix in the flour, then gradually add the warm milk, sugar, butter and vanilla solution. Finally mix in the rum. Pass through a sieve (strainer), then place in the fridge to rest overnight. The vanilla pod will be in the strainer – I always add it back into the mix for it to infuse further.

- The next day, preheat the oven to 200°C (400°F/Gas 6). Grease the cannelé moulds with some softened butter. Fill each mould to the top.

- Bake in the oven for 20 minutes, then turn the oven temperature down to 180°C (350°F/Gas 4) and continue to cook for a further 30 minutes.

- Leave to cool for 5 minutes before removing the cannelés from the moulds. Leave to cool, then serve.

Best eaten the same day.

Yuzu Gâteau Weekend *Makes 8 small loaf cakes*

80g (3oz/¾ stick) unsalted butter *plus extra for greasing*
220g (8oz/1½ cups) plain (all-purpose) flour *plus extra for dusting*
4g (¾ tsp) baking powder
1g (a pinch) salt
200g (7oz) whole eggs *(about 4 eggs)*
280g (3oz/scant 1½ cups) caster (superfine) sugar
grated zest of 4 yuzu
120ml (4fl oz/generous ½ cup) whipping (pouring) cream
20ml (1½ tbsp) dark rum
1 quantity of **Light Syrup** *(see page 103) with the addition of*
   200ml (7fl oz/scant 1 cup) yuzu juice
1 quantity of **Apricot Nappage** *(see page 104)*

To decorate:
50g (1¾oz) **Fondant** *(see page 31)*
5ml (1 tsp) yuzu juice
20g (¾oz) crystallized **Confit Yuzu***(see Variation, page 113) cubed*

You will also need:
eight 4 x 4 x 7cm (1½ x 1½ x 2¾ inch) small loaf tins (pans)
a paper piping cornet *(see page 30)*

A Gâteau Weekend does not have a specific recipe, but refers to a style of baked cake eaten in France. This is our version – it is like a lemon cake but made with the wonderful addition of yuzu, giving it a distinct and more fragrant flavour.

- Preheat the oven to 170°C (325°F/Gas 3), grease the loaf tins (pans) with soft unsalted butter, dust with flour and line with silicone paper.

- Sift the flour, baking powder and salt together twice in a bowl. Melt the butter in a saucepan and leave to cool.

- Put the eggs, sugar and yuzu zest in a mixing bowl and beat together. Gradually add the cream and dark rum. Gradually add in the melted butter, then fold in the dry ingredients. Spoon the mixture into the prepared moulds.

- Bake for 25–30 minutes. Remove from the oven and place the cakes on a wire rack to cool in their tins slightly. Brush with the yuzu syrup while still warm and then glaze with Apricot Nappage.

- Put the Fondant and yuzu juice in a saucepan and warm gently over a low heat to 35–37°C (95–99°F). Spoon it into a paper piping cornet.

- Pipe lines of the Fondant across the top of the cakes and decorate with the crystallized Confit Yuzu.

Store in an airtight container and consume within 2–3 days.

Orange & Praline Cake

Makes 2 loaf cakes

This simple cake recipe uses praline paste and orange, giving it a good depth of flavour and taste profile. The decoration of confit orange, nuts and vanilla gives it a striking finish.

165g (5¾oz/1½ sticks) unsalted butter *softened, plus extra for greasing*

200g (7oz/scant 1½ cups) plain (all-purpose) flour *plus extra for dusting*

4g (¾ tsp) baking powder

80g (3oz/generous ½ cup) cornflour (cornstarch)

65g (2¼oz) **Confit Orange** *(see page 113) diced*

65ml (2¼fl oz/¼ cup) full-fat milk

Scraped seeds from ½ vanilla pod (bean)

265g (9½oz/1⅓ cups) caster (superfine) sugar

1g (a pinch) salt

65g (2¼oz) **Praline Paste** *(see pages 116–117)*

200g (7oz) whole eggs *(about 4 eggs)*

1 quantity of **Alcohol Syrup** *(see page 103) made with Grand Marnier*

To decorate:

1 quantity of **Apricot Nappage** *(see page 104) to glaze*

2 **Confit Oranges** *(see page 113) cut into quarters, then in half lengthways*

20g (1¾oz) chopped hazelnuts *roasted*

Crystallized Vanilla Stick *(see page 31)*

You will also need:

two 18 x 8cm (7 x 3½ inch) loaf tins (pans)

- Preheat the oven to 170°C (325°F/Gas 3), grease the loaf tins (pans) with soft unsalted butter, dust with flour and line with silicone paper.

- Sift the flour, baking powder and cornflour (cornstarch) twice into a bowl.

- Put the diced Confit Orange, milk and vanilla seeds in a saucepan and warm gently to a temperature of 37°C (99°F).

- Put the softened butter, sugar and salt together in the bowl of an electric mixer, beat until light and creamy in texture, then add the Praline Paste.

- Gradually add the eggs and continue mixing until fully incorporated. Add the milk and orange peel, then fold in the sifted flour, cornflour (cornstarch) and baking powder.

- Divide the mixture between the two prepared loaf tins (pans) and bake for 40–45 minutes.

- Brush the top of each cake with the Grand Marnier syrup once they are out of the oven, then remove from the tins and leave to cool completely.

- Once the cakes are cool, glaze with Apricot Nappage and decorate with the Confit Orange, hazelnuts and vanilla stick.

Store in an airtight container and consume within 2–3 days.

Chestnut & Rum Cake

Makes 3 loaf cakes

The Japanese adore chestnuts, so it was no surprise I came across this wonderful cake in a pâtisserie in Osaka. It's a great combination and I love the elegant look of the long tin.

180g (6oz/1½ sticks) unsalted butter *plus extra for greasing*
24g (1oz) plain (all-purpose) flour *plus extra for dusting*
54g (2oz/⅓ cup) cornflour (cornstarch)
3g (½ tsp) baking powder
260g (9½oz/2¼ cups) ground almonds
180g (6oz/scant 1 cup) caster (superfine) sugar
260g (9½oz) whole eggs *(about 5–6 eggs)*
220g (8oz) shop-bought confit chestnuts *chopped*
20ml (1½ tbsp) dark rum
1 quantity of **Alcohol Syrup** *(see page 103) made with dark rum*

To decorate:
1 quantity of **Apricot Nappage** *(see page 104) to glaze*
3 confit chestnuts *cut in half*
6 roasted almonds *cut in half*
1 vanilla pod (bean) *cut into 2 strips and rolled in caster (superfine) sugar*

You will also need:
three 23 x 3.5 x 6cm (9 x 1¼ x 2½ inch) loaf tins (pans)

- Preheat the oven to 170°C (325°F/Gas 3), grease the loaf tins (pans) with soft unsalted butter, dust with flour and line with silicone baking paper.

- Sift the flour, cornflour (cornstarch) and baking powder together twice in a bowl. Put the butter in a saucepan and melt gently over a low heat.

- Put the ground almonds, sugar and eggs in the bowl of an electric mixer fitted with the paddle attachment and beat for 5 minutes.

- Gradually fold in the dry ingredients until they are fully incorporated. Fold in the chopped confit chestnuts and the dark rum. Lastly mix in the melted butter.

- Divide the mixture between the two prepared cake tins (pans) and bake for 30–35 minutes.

- Brush the top of each cake with the rum syrup once the cake is out of the oven, then remove from the tins (pans) and leave to cool completely.

- Glaze with Apricot Nappage and decorate with confit chestnuts, almonds and vanilla strips.

Store in an airtight container and consume within 2–3 days.

Carrot & Chocolate Chip Cakes

Makes 24 small cakes

150g (5½oz/generous 1 cup)
  plain (all-purpose) flour
25g (1oz/scant ¼ cup)
  ground almonds
12g (½oz) baking powder
1g (a pinch) ground cinnamon
150g (5½oz/¾ cup)
  caster (superfine) sugar
150g (5½oz) carrots *grated*
100g (3½oz) whole eggs *(about 2 eggs)*
75g dark (bittersweet) chocolate
  (66% cocoa solids) *chopped*
150g (5½oz/1⅓ sticks) unsalted butter
  melted

You will also need:
a 12mm (½ inch) piping nozzle (tip)
a 3 x 5cm (1¼ x 2 inch) 8-hole
  dome-shaped silicone baking mat

- Sift the dry ingredients together twice in a bowl. Mix together the grated carrot and the eggs in a separate bowl. Fold the dry ingredients into the carrot and egg mixture.

- Mix in the chopped chocolate and lastly the melted butter. Put in a container and rest in the fridge for 1 hour. Preheat the oven to 180°C (350°F/Gas 4).

- Take the mixture out of the fridge and spoon it into a piping (pastry) bag fitted with 12mm (½ inch) plain nozzle (tip).Pipe the cake mixture into the holes on the dome-shaped baking mat until three-quarters full.

- Bake for 12–15 minutes until golden brown. Leave to cool, then remove from the moulds.

Store in an airtight container and consume within 1–2 days.

Suzue first made these in the kitchens of The Savoy. She created her own twist on the British tea cake classic with the addition of chocolate and a subtle cinnamon note. They were a part of the famous afternoon tea selection while we were working there.

Petits Fours

In 19th-century France, there were no gas ovens, only a single type of oven – a huge cabin made out of stone, underneath which a fire would be lit. These types of ovens took a long time to get going, became really hot for some time, then took a long time to cool. In addition, they did not have a setting to modify the heat. In fact, they only had two settings. The first setting was the grand four, *the big oven,* where the fire was at its strongest. This setting was used to bake the large cakes, sponges and fermented items. The second setting was the petit four, *the small oven,* when the fire started to die out and the heat began to dissipate. This setting was used for baking small biscuits and baked cakes, and is how such after dinner delicacies were named as 'petits fours', describing the way in which they were prepared. Originally, there were six distinct categories of petits fours – frais *(fresh),* fruits déguises *(glazed fruits),* glacés *(glazed with fondant),* amandes *(made with almonds),* secs *(dry),* and salés *(savoury).* Essentially they must all be bite-sized delights.

Petits Fours Sec

Jammy Dodger
Makes 25–30

½ quantity of **Pâte à Sablée**
  *(see page 46) but add 1g (a pinch)
  ground cinnamon and 1g (a pinch)
  ground nutmeg*
½ quantity of **Raspberry Confiture**
  (see page 108)
½ quantity of **Dark Chocolate
  Ganache** *(see page 90) with the
  addition of 15ml (1 tbsp) kirsch*
icing (powdered) sugar *for dusting*

You will also need:
a 4cm (1½ inch) fluted cutter
a 2cm (¾ inch) fluted cutter
a 5mm (¼ inch) piping nozzle (tip)

- Prepare the Pâte à Sablée and rest
  in the fridge as instructed. Prepare
  the confiture and leave to cool. Roll
  out to 3mm (⅛ inch) thick and rest
  in the fridge for at least 30 minutes.
  Prepare the kirsch ganache and
  leave to set. Preheat the oven to
  180°C (350°F/Gas 4).

- Take the Pâte à Sablée from the
  fridge and use the large fluted
  cutter to cut out 50–60 discs. Place
  them on a baking tray (sheet) lined
  with a non-stick baking mat. Use
  the small fluted cutter to cut out
  a hole from the centre of 25–30 of
  the discs. Bake for 10–12 minutes
  until light and golden in colour, then
  leave to cool.

- Once the ganache is semi-set, place it
  in a piping (pastry) bag fitted with a
  5mm (¼ inch) piping nozzle (tip) and
  pipe circles around the edge of the
  cooked discs with no hole. Spoon the
  confiture into a paper piping cornet
  (see page 30) and fill the centre of the
  ganache. Lightly dust the discs with
  the holes in the centre with the icing
  (powdered) sugar and place on top.

*Store in an airtight container.
Best consumed within 1–2 days.*

Sablés a la Poche
Makes 25–30

170g (6oz/1¼ cup) plain
  (all-purpose) flour
10g (¼oz/2 tsp) cocoa powder
160g (5¾oz/1½ sticks) unsalted
  butter *softened and cut into cubes*
65g (2¼ oz/½ cup) icing (powdered)
  sugar *sifted*
30ml (2 tbsp) full-fat milk
15 griottine cherries in kirsch
  cut into half

For the vanilla sugar:
200g (7oz/1 cup)
  caster (superfine) sugar
1 vanilla pod (bean) *split lengthways*

You will also need:
a 6mm (⅓ inch) star nozzle (tip)

- To make the vanilla sugar, put the
  sugar in a bowl, scrape in the seeds
  from the split vanilla pod (bean) and
  mix together.

- Sift the flour and cocoa powder
  together into a bowl. Put the
  softened butter in a mixing bowl.
  Add the sifted icing (powdered)
  sugar and beat until light in colour.
  Gradually add the milk until fully
  incorporated. Fold in the flour and
  cocoa powder and mix to a smooth
  homogeneous mass.

- Place into a piping (pastry) bag with
  a star 6mm (⅓ inch) nozzle (tip) and
  pipe rosettes onto a baking tray
  (sheet) lined with a non-stick baking
  mat. Place a cherry half on top and
  transfer to the fridge to rest for
  30 minutes.

- Preheat the oven to 180°C (350°F/
  Gas 4). Bake for 12–15 minutes.
  Remove from the oven, sprinkle with
  vanilla sugar, then leave to fully cool.

*Store in an airtight container.
Best consumed within 2–3 days.*

Miso & Walnut Biscuits
Makes 25–30

200g (7oz/scant 1 cup) unsalted
  butter *softened and cut into cubes*
100g (3½oz/¾ cups) icing
  (powdered) sugar *sifted*
60g (2oz) miso paste
40g (½oz) egg yolks *(about 2 eggs)*
240g (8½oz/1¾ cups) plain
  (all-purpose) flour *sifted*
60g (2oz/½ cup) walnuts *roughly
  chopped*
20g (¾oz) egg whites *(about 1 egg)*
100g (3½oz) white sesame seeds
  lightly toasted
40g (1½oz/scant ¼ cup) caster
  (superfine) sugar

- Put the butter in a mixing bowl. Add
  the icing (powdered) sugar and miso
  paste and beat until light in colour.
  Gradually add the egg yolks and
  mix until fully incorporated. Fold in
  the flour until you have a smooth
  homogeneous mass. Lastly, mix in
  the chopped walnuts.

- Divide the dough evenly into 2 and
  place on a baking tray (sheet) lined
  with silicone baking paper. Transfer
  to the fridge to rest for 30 minutes.

- Remove the dough from the fridge
  and roll out into 2 thick cylinders
  25–30cm (10–12 inches) long.
  Gently flatten with the heel of your
  hand to create an oval shape, then
  leave to rest for 30 minutes.

- Preheat the oven to 180°C (350°F/
  Gas 4). Brush the dough with egg
  white, roll in the white sesame
  seeds and sprinkle with the caster
  (superfine) sugar. Cut into 5mm
  (¼ inch) slices. Lay out on a baking
  tray (sheet) lined with a non-stick
  baking mat and bake for 12–15
  minutes until golden brown. Remove
  from the oven and leave to cool.

*Store in an airtight container.
Best consumed within 2–3 days.*

Petits Fours Amandes

Pistachio Evoras *Makes 25*

50g (1¾oz/½ stick) melted unsalted butter *plus a little extra softened butter for greasing*
25g (1oz) nibbed almonds *lightly roasted*
75g (2¾oz) pistachios *chopped*
100g (3½oz) whole eggs *(about 3 eggs)*
15g (1 tbsp) caster (superfine) sugar
75g (2¾oz/¾ cup) ground almonds
75g (2¾oz/½ cup) icing (powdered) sugar
100g (3½oz) **Apricot Nappage** *(see page 104)*

You will also need:
two 12-hole, 4cm (1½oz) non-stick dome moulds

- Preheat the oven to 180°C (350°F/ Gas 4). Brush the inside of the dome moulds with the softened butter. Mix together the almonds and pistachios. Tip them into the buttered dome moulds, then tip out the excess – the nuts should leave a layer lining the mould. Put the moulds on a baking tray (sheet).

- Put the whole eggs in a mixing bowl, add the caster (superfine) sugar and mix until light in colour. Mix in the ground almonds and icing (powdered) sugar. Mix in the melted butter.

- Spoon the mixture into a piping (pastry) bag and pipe into the prepared baking moulds until full. Bake for 12–15 minutes until golden. Leave to cool before removing from the moulds.

- Melt the Apricot Nappage in a small saucepan over a medium heat, then glaze the domes to finish.

Best eaten the same day.

Toscaner *Makes 40*

100g (3½oz/scant 1 stick) unsalted butter
190g (6½oz/scant 1 cup) caster (superfine) sugar
190g (6½oz/1⅔ cups) ground almonds
240g (8¾oz) whole eggs *(5 eggs)*
50g (1¾oz/⅓ cup) plain (all-purpose) flour *sifted*
300g (10½oz) dark (bittersweet) chocolate (70% cocoa solids),

For the topping:
100g (3½oz) unsalted butter
100g (3½oz/½ cup) caster (superfine) sugar
100g (3½oz) liquid glucose
50ml (2fl oz/scant ¼ cup) milk
150g (5½oz/1½ cups) flaked almonds *lightly roasted*

You will also need:
a 28 x 22cm (11 x 8¾ inch) non-stick baking mat with raised sides

- Preheat the oven to 190°C (375°F/ Gas 5). Place the baking mat on a tray. Beat the butter, sugar and almonds in a bowl. Add the eggs gradually, then fold in the flour. Pour the mixture into the baking mat and bake for 16–18 minutes until golden.

- For the topping, put the butter, sugar, glucose and milk in a pan, boil, then simmer for 1–2 minutes. Take off the heat and mix in the almonds.

- Turn the temperature up to 200°C (400°F/Gas 6). Spread the topping evenly over the sponge and return to the oven for 6–8 minutes until the topping is golden. Leave to cool slightly, then cut into 3cm (1¼ inch) squares. Leave to cool fully.

- Line a baking tray (sheet) with plastic acetate. Temper the chocolate *(see page 34)*. Dip in the bases of the squares and place on the tray. Leave in a cool dry area to set for 1 hour.

Best eaten within 1–2 days.

Apricot Frangipane *Makes 20*

½ quantity **Pâte Sucrée** *(see page 47)*
½ quantity **Frangipane** *(see page 89)*
100g (3½oz) flaked almonds *toasted*
50g (1¾oz/⅓ cup) icing (powdered) sugar

For the poached apricots:
½ quantity **Light Syrup** *(see page 103)*
2 apricots *halved and stoned*

You will also need:
a 4cm (1½ inch) round cutter
two 12-hole, 5cm (2 inch) non-stick mini-muffin moulds
a 10mm (½ inch) piping nozzle (tip)

- Prepare the Pâte Sucrée as instructed. Prepare the poached apricots: make the syrup in a pan. Put the apricot halves in the syrup, cover with a cartouche and cook over a low heat for 5 minutes. Leave the apricots to cool in the syrup.

- Roll the pastry out to 2mm (⅛ inch) thick on a lightly floured surface. Use a 4cm (1½ inch) cutter to cut out 20 pastry discs and place them in the base of the muffin moulds. Prick the bases with a fork, then rest in the fridge for at least 30 minutes.

- Preheat the oven to 180°C (350°F/ Gas 4). Prepare the Frangipane, then place it in a piping (pastry) bag fitted with a 10mm (½ inch) piping nozzle (tip). Take the muffin moulds from the fridge and pipe the Frangipane on top of the pastry discs until the moulds are two-thirds full.

- Drain the apricots from the syrup, dice them and place a spoonful on top of the Frangipane. Place a few flaked almonds on top of each frangipane, then dust with sugar. Bake for 12–15 minutes until golden brown. Leave to cool, before demoulding.

Best eaten the same day.

Petits Fours Frais

Fruit Tart *Makes 35–40*

½ quantity **Pâte Sucrée** *(see page 47)*
½ quantity **Crème Pâtissière**
  (see page 80)
50g (1¾oz) white chocolate *chopped*

To decorate:
a selection of fruit: 1 each of
  kiwi, mango and apricot, some
  strawberries, raspberries,
  blackberries, and blueberries
100g (3½ oz) **Fruit Glaze**
  (see page 105)

You will also need:
lots of 5 x 3.5cm (2 x 1½ inch) fluted
  petit four tart cases *(about
  40 will be needed, or cook in batches)*
a no.8 plain piping nozzle (tip)

- Prepare the pastry and rest twice in the fridge as instructed. Prepare the Crème Pâtissière, then put it in the fridge until required. Take the pastry from the fridge, roll out to 2mm thick and chill to rest for 30 minutes.

- Line the tartlet cases *(see pages 44–45)* with the Pâte Sucrée; chill for 30 minutes. Preheat the oven to 180°C (350°F/Gas 4). Blind bake *(see pages 44–45)* for 8–10 minutes, remove the beans and cook for a further 2–3 minutes. Leave the tart cases to cool.

- Melt the white chocolate over a bain-marie *(see page 31)*, brush the inside of the tart with the chocolate, then chill for 2–3 minutes.

- Cut the fruit into various sized pieces. Spoon the prepared Crème Pâtissière into a piping (pastry) bag fitted with a no. 8 plain piping nozzle (tip) and pipe a bulb into the base of each tartlet. Decorate the tartlets with the fruit. Gently melt the glaze in a pan over a low heat, then brush the tartlets with glaze to finish.

Best eaten the same day.

Lemon Tart *Makes 35–40*

½ quantity **Pâte Sucrée** *(see page 47)*
½ quantity **Lemon Curd**
  (see pages 96–97)
1 quantity **Fruit Compote**
  *(see page 111) made with
  raspberries and raspberry purée*
100g (3½oz) white chocolate *chopped*
200g (7oz) **Fruit Glaze** *(see page 105)*
½ vanilla pod (bean) *split lengthways*
4 raspberries *halved and glazed with*
  Fruit Glaze *(see page 105)*
1 quantity **Confit Lemon**
  (see Variation, page 113)

You will also need:
two 12-hole, 4cm (1¾ inch) diameter
  non-stick dome moulds
lots of 4cm (1½ inch) diameter petit
  four tart moulds *(about 40 will be
  needed, or cook in batches)*

- Prepare the pastry as instructed. Prepare the curd, spoon into a piping (pastry) bag and pipe into the moulds until each hole is two-thirds full. Place in the freezer for 2 hours.

- Prepare the raspberry compote, pour into a shallow tray, then chill.

- Prepare and bake the tartlet cases following the same method as the Fruit Tarts opposite, except use the petit four moulds instead of fluted tart cases. Leave to cool.

- Melt the white chocolate over a bain-marie *(see page 31)*, then brush into the inside of the tarts. Once set, place a small spoonful of compote in the base of each tart.

- Gently melt the fruit glaze and add the scraped seeds and vanilla pod (bean). Demould the curd domes and place on top of each tartlet. Use a brush to glaze the tarts, then leave to defrost in the fridge for 20 minutes. Decorate each tart with a glazed raspberry half and some Confit Lemon.

Best eaten the same day.

Marron Barquette *Makes 35–40*

½ quantity **Pâte Sucrée** *(see page 47)*
1 quantity **Chestnut Mousse**
  (see page 250)
½ quantity **Crème d'Amande**
  (see page 88)
100g (3½oz) shop-bought confit
  chestnuts *reserve 30–35 pieces to
  decorate and finely chop the rest*
½ quantity **Crème Chantilly**
  (see pages 84–85)
300g (10½oz) each of tempered dark
  chocolate and white chocolate *(see
  page 34) used to make* **Two-Tone
  Copeaux** *(see pages 132–133)*

You will also need:
a 2.5 x 6.5cm (1 x 2 ½inch) petit four
  barquette mould
a Mont blanc piping tube (tip)
a small b6 star piping nozzle (tip)

- Prepare the pastry as instructed and prepare the Chestnut Mousse. Line the tartlet cases following the same method as the Fruit Tarts opposite, using the petit four mould. Preheat the oven to 180°C (350°F/Gas 4).

- Prepare the Crème d'Amande and spoon into a piping (pastry) bag. Pipe into the cases until two-thirds full. Push 2–3 pieces of confit chestnut into the cream. Bake for 10–12 minutes until golden, then cool.

- Pipe a teaspoon of the Chestnut Mousse into the tarts, then smooth and shape it into a triangle of cream on top. Put the remaining mousse in a piping (pastry) bag fitted with a Mont blanc nozzle (tip) and pipe over the top of the tarts. Remove the excess mousse from the sides.

- Prepare the Crème Chantilly and place in a piping (pastry) bag fitted with a small B6 star nozzle (tip). Pipe a small rosette on top of each tart, then decorate with the confit chestnut and two-tone copeaux.

Best eaten the same day.

Petits Fours Confiserie

Passion Fruit & Mango Pâte de Fruit
Makes 35–40

230g (8oz) **Fruit Purée**
  (see page 110) made with passion fruit
230g (8oz) **Fruit Purée**
  (see page 110) made with mangoes
360g (12½oz/1¾ cups)
  caster (superfine) sugar
150g (5½oz) liquid glucose
15g (½oz) pectin
5g (1 tsp) lemon juice
75g (2¾oz/⅓ cup) caster (superfine)
  sugar *for coating*

You will also need:
a 28 x 22cm (11 x 8½ inch) non-stick
  baking mat with raised sides

- Place the baking mat on a baking tray (sheet). Use the ingredients to make Pâte de Fruit following the instructions on page 109.

- Leave the pâte de fruit to set for at least 4 hours in a cool, dry place. Cut into 2.5cm (1 inch) cubes, roll in the sugar and serve.

Store in an airtight container. Best consumed within 2–3 weeks.

Nougat Montélimar
Makes 35–40

oil *for greasing*
icing (powdered) sugar *for dusting*
75g (2¾oz) egg whites *(about 3 eggs)*
185g (6½oz) clear (runny) honey
335g (11oz/1⅔ cups) caster
  (superfine) sugar
110ml (4fl oz/scant ½ cup) water
105g (3½oz) liquid glucose
100g (3½oz/⅔ cup) pistachio nuts
40g (1½oz) flaked almonds *roasted*
65g (2¼oz) whole almonds *roasted*
85g (3oz) whole hazelnuts *roasted*

You will also need:
one 37 x 11 x 5cm (14¾ x 4¼ x
  2 inch) rectangle entremet frame

- Place the frame on a baking tray (sheet) lined with a non-stick baking mat. Brush the mould with oil and dust the mat and mould with icing (powdered) sugar to prevent sticking. Put the honey in one pan. Put the caster (superfine) sugar, water and glucose in another. Put the egg whites in the bowl of an electric mixer fitted with a whisk attachment and whisk on a slow speed.

- Bring the honey to the boil and cook to 121°C (250°F). Pour into the whisking egg whites and continue whisking on a medium speed.

- Place the sugar pan over a medium heat and cook to 145°C (293°F), then gently pour this into the egg white mixture. Continue to whisk on a medium speed for about 5 minutes until the meringue becomes firm.

- Remove the bowl from the machine. Mix in the nuts. Place the mixture in the prepared mould, dust with a little icing (powdered) sugar, then roll out to fit the mould using a rolling pin. Leave to set for overnight in a cool dry area. Cut into 2.5cm (1 inch) cubes.

Store in an airtight container. Best consumed within 1 week.

Blackcurrant Gimauve
Makes 35–40

10g (¼oz) leaf gelatine
100g (3½oz/¾ cup)
  icing (powdered) sugar
100g (3½oz/¾ cup) cornflour
  (cornstarch)
110g (3¾oz) **Fruit Purée** *(see page
  110) made with blackcurrants*
225g (8oz/1 generous cup) caster
  (superfine) sugar *plus 10g (¼oz)*
135ml (4¼fl oz/scant ½ cup) water
38g (1½oz) egg whites *(about 2 eggs)*
1g (a pinch) cream of tartar

You will also need:
one 37 x 11 x 2.5cm (14¾ x 4¼ x
  1 inch) rectangle entremet frame

- Soak the gelatine in a bowl of ice-cold water for a few minutes to soften. Squeeze the gelatine to remove the excess water *(see page 31)*. Sift the icing sugar and cornflour into a bowl.

- Put one-quarter of the blackcurrant purée in a pan over a medium heat. Heat to 50°C (122°F). Stir in the soaked gelatine until dissolved. Pour into the remaining purée.

- Put 225g (8oz/1 generous cup) of the caster (superfine) sugar and water in a saucepan over a medium heat and heat to 130°C (266°F). Whisk the egg whites with the cream of tartar and the additional 10g (¼oz) of sugar in a clean bowl to a soft peak.

- Mix the purée with the sugar syrup and pour into the whisking egg. Continue to whisk until cold. Prepare the frame as with the previous recipe and pour and spread the mixture into the frame. Cover the surface with the icing sugar and cornflour, reserving some for dusting, then leave to set. Once set, cut into 2.5cm (1 inch) cubes and roll in the leftover dusting mixture.

Store in an airtight container. Best consumed within 1 week.

INGREDIENTS

Pâtisserie & Chocolate Ingredients

Wild Harvest *www.wildharvestuk.com*
Fresh As *www.fresh-as.com*
Keylink *www.keylink.org*

Couverture Chocolate

Amedei

www.kingsfinefood.co.uk
www.amedei-us.com
www.lario.com.au

Other Couverture Chocolate

Valrhona *www.chocolatetradingco.com*
Worldwide Chocolate
www.worldwidechocolate.com
Amano Artisan Chocolate
www.amanochocolate.com
Guittard Chocolate Company
www.guittard.com
Michel Cluizel
www.tcfinefoods.co.uk
www.chocosphere.com
Scarffen Berger
www.scharffenberger.com
Simon Johnson
www.simonjohnson.com
Albert Uster Imports
www.auiswisscatalogue.com

Spices & Salts

India Tree *www.indiatree.com*
Steenbergs Organic
www.steenbergs.co.uk

Fine Teas & Quality Coffee

TeaSmith *www.teasmith.co.uk*
Square Mile Coffee Roasters
www.shop.squaremilecoffee.com/

Japanese Ingredients

Keisho Limited
www.keisholimited.co.uk
Atari-Ya Foods *www.atariya.co.uk*
Asian Food Grocer
www.asianfoodgrocer.com
Japan Centre *www.japancentre.com*

EQUIPMENT

Kitchen Equipment

Russums *www.russums-shop.co.uk*
Nisbets *www.nisbets.com*
Abbiamo *www.abbiamo.co.uk*
Mora *www.mora.fr*
Deco Relief *www.deco-relief.fr*
Silikomart *www.silikomart.com*
Silicone Moulds
www.siliconemoulds.com
Sur la Table *www.surlatable.com*
Williams-Sonoma
www.williams-sonoma.com
Culinary Cookware
www.culinarycookware.com

Chocolate Equipment & Moulds

DécoRelief *www.deco-relief.fr*
Home Chocolate Factory
www.homechocolatefactory.com
The Chocolate Mold Factory
www.thechocolatemoldfactory.com

Chef Rubber *www.chefrubber.com*
Chocoley *www.chocoley.com*
Savour Chocolate & Patisserie School
www.savourschool.com.au
Albert Uster Imports
www.auiswisscatalogue.com

Stencils & Decorations

PCB (France) *www.pcb-creation.fr*
Squires Kitchen *www.squires-shop.com*
Sugarcraft *www.sugarcraft.com*

Kitchenware & Glasses

David Mellor Design
www.davidmellordesign.com

Below William's chocolate sculpture from the final of the Master of Culinary Arts *(see page 15).*

Reference

Classic Patisserie: An A-Z Handbook by Claude Juillet (1998, Butterworth-Heinemann)

Our Shops

William Curley
10 Paved Court
Richmond upon Thames TW9 1LZ
William Curley
198 Ebury Street
Belgravia, London SW1W 8UN
William Curley at Harrods
87–135 Brompton Road
Knightsbridge
London SW1X 7XL
www.williamcurley.co.uk

This book has been a journey and it wouldn't have been possible without Jacqui Small and her team – many apologies for all of the delays!

A huge thanks to the incredibly talented Robin Rout for his stunning design work and to our friend Jose Lasheras for his brilliant and beautiful photography. You are both geniuses. Also to our editor Abi Waters for her endless patience, and to pâtissier Sarah Frankland for her incredible commitment on this project. And to Paola Francesi for help on translation.

A huge thank you also for their inspiration: Pierre Koffmann, Marco Pierre White, Anton Edelmann, Raymond Blanc, Marc Meneau, Scott Lyall, Willie Pike, Bruce Sangster, Mike Nadel, Yolande Stanley, Benoit Blin and Claire Clark. Also to all the pâtissiers who work so hard for the common good of our beautiful profession.

Special thanks to our team of dedicated Pâtissiers and Chocolatiers, especially Alistair Birt, Melissa Paul, Steven Sherry, Rhiann Mead, Sophie Bamford, Nicole Waefler, Anna Fiedler and Sarah Dean.

Our gratitude to Cecilia Tessieri of Amedei for supplying the best couverture chocolate in the world. Additionally to Sara Jayne Staines, the chocolate expert, and George Vaughan. Also the team at The Royal Academy of Culinary Arts, Relais Desserts International and The World Famous at Tannadice.

A special thanks to Pierre Hermé for his kind words but also for being an incredible inspiration.

Finally a thank you to my father, Big Bill, my sister Karen and the Aoyama family in Osaka, Japan who supply us with special local ingredients.

William & Suzue